Library of
Davidson College

SCAPEGOAT

PREJUDICE/POLITICS/PRISON

Boyd E. Payton

WHITMORE PUBLISHING CO.
Philadelphia

Copyright © 1970 by Boyd E. Payton
All Rights Reserved
Standard Book Number: 87426-022-1
Library of Congress Catalog Card Number: 70-94361
Printed in the United States of America

This book is dedicated to the men and women of Henderson, North Carolina, who kept the faith throughout one of organized labor's most dramatic and prolonged struggles.

Their loyalty and courage inspired all who were privileged to associate with them. Their humor, even in dark hours, lightened the burden and lifted the spirits of those responsible for their leadership. They kept the banners flying in the face of adversities that would have overwhelmed others.

Their devotion and trust sustained those who were imprisoned on their behalf, and the wives and children left behind. These heroic people should be honored by all who engage in any struggle for human rights. Their epic struggle to preserve their union is an inspiration for those who would fight for their freedom.

CONTENTS

Foreword	vii
Prologue	ix
Acknowledgements	xiii
CHAPTER I The Henderson Strike	1
What Caused The Henderson Strike?	2
What About The Union?	3
The Negotiations	4
Mediation By Governor Hodges	12
False Armistice	20
Strike Violence	30
Strike Publicity	34
The Biased Courts Of Henderson	50
The Conspiracy Arrests	52
Defense Attorneys	62
Cloak-And-Dagger Interlude	64
The Special Court	67
Guilty As Charged	82
Appeals	84
CHAPTER II Prisons Are Not Made For Men	91
Eight Innocent Men	92
On-The-State	97
Visiting Sunday	118
Classification Examination	121
Medical Examination	122
I Become A Run-boy	124
Sunday School In Prison	133
The Blue Goose	139
Prison Road Camp	144
On-The-Roads	152
Death of Escapee	182
Back To The "Wall"	186
The Parole Board	191
The Shipping Corridor	196

The Lie Detector Test	205
The Literacy School	220
The Mess-Hall	222
The Main Cell-Block	224
The Schoolroom Guard	224
The Prison Yard	226
The Prisons Director	228
Prison Mail-Call	230
Christmas Eve—1960	233
Christmas Day	234
Prison Payday	239
New Year's Day 1961	239
The Long Wait	242
"Hero" Of Henderson	272
"Payoff" For Visit To Doctor	275
Harry Golden's Letter	282
The *Christian Century* Article	284
Hope For Freedom	285
CHAPTER III Parole And Freedom	301
I Meet My Parole Officer	301
I Lose My Job	303
My Impressions of Prison Life	303
Petition For Pardon	308
Pardon At Last	319
Epilogue	324
Restoration Of Citizenship	324
Confession Of Harold Aaron	326

FOREWORD

In December, 1960, the famous Reverend Billy Graham and I tried to make an appointment with Governor Luther Hodges for the purpose of seeking a commutation of sentence for Boyd Payton. The Governor told us on the telephone that the time was not right for this plea and that we should withhold it for awhile.

Boyd Payton's conviction came out of the Harriett-Henderson Cotton Mills strike. The strike was a revolution, as desperate and violent and as real as any revolution in our history books.

Boyd Payton was director of the Textile Workers Union of America for North and South Carolina and a member of its International Executive Council. The local union in Henderson was asking only to renew its contract with the company, which had been in effect for 14 years.

The mills, however, wanted to say what would or would not go to arbitration before a neutral third party in the event of dispute between the company and the union. In addition, the company wanted the union to be denied the right to strike and to collect dues from employees' wages through the check-off system. Boyd Payton said, "If they break this strike they've broken this union, and if they break this union they can break any union in America."

So the power structure decided to frame Boyd Payton, and frame him they did. They got an unemployed ex-convict by the name of Aaron to testify in court that Payton was part of a conspiracy to blow up the power station of the Harriett-Henderson Mills. The state claimed that Payton was linked to the conspiracy through a telephone call which Aaron said he had made to Payton.

In a letter which I wrote to Governor Sanford pleading for a pardon for Payton I pointed out that Billy Graham and I had gone over the testimony and at our own expense engaged an attorney to advise us on some of the legal points. We have come to this conclusion—that the prosecution witness Aaron might have continued his testimony as follows:

"After I hung up on Boyd Payton I called one after the other, Billy Graham at Montreat; Harry Golden at Charlotte; and Governor Terry Sanford at Fayetteville, and each of them said, 'that's fine.'"

On the basis of Payton's conviction, the court would also have had to convict Billy Graham, Harry Golden and Governor Sanford. The Attorney General later admitted that the State Bureau of Investigation had paid Aaron more than $1,000 for this bit of dirty work.

Payton spent nine months in prison, but his punishment was for a much longer period—13 long months of frustration and discouragement during the appeal procedure before prison, and more than three years of humiliation and discrimination, because of the undeserved ex-con title, before pardon was granted.

Eventually Governor Sanford pardoned Payton and the book *Scapegoat* records a remarkable climax to this case. A call came from Aaron saying that he could not live with himself and that he meant to make a clean breast of the frame-up. He finally reneged on his promise and that's the end of the story.

This is the story of the attempt of the textile industry to smash the trade unions and the cooperation of the state of North Carolina in the frame-up. In all elections held after this frame-up, the textile mills handed out circulars to the workers with the headline: "Payton Goes to Jail for Conspiracy."

Payton writes a fine story of the history of the strike and of his prison life with many interesting anecdotes.

This is also the story of an innocent man in jail and the misery of his wife and daughters because of it.

Charlotte, North Carolina   Harry Golden

PROLOGUE

> I know not whether laws be right,
> Or whether laws be wrong,
> All that we know who lie in jail
> Is that the wall is strong;
> And that each day is like a year,
> A year whose days are long;
> That every prison that men build
> Is built with bricks of shame,
> And bound with bars, lest Christ should see
> How men their brothers maim.

The above words were found written on the wall of one of the cells which I occupied at Central Prison in Raleigh, North Carolina. When I first read these lines, I did not know whether or not they were original with a previous occupant; but they expressed much of what I was feeling at that time, and I copied them and reread them many times during the months which followed. Since being released from prison, I have learned that these lines were taken from a poem by Oscar Wilde. Apparently his feelings and reactions to prison were much like mine, and I doubt that he would have objected to their use here.

Scapegoat is the story of my nine months in prison. It is an attempt to set forth the actual happenings of those days in order to bring to the general public a little known phase of our society which should be of interest to every citizen who is concerned about men as human beings; to every taxpayer who is concerned about the high cost of maintaining penal systems; to every person who is alarmed about the increasing crime rate and the apparent failure of present rehabilitation programs.

It is the general opinion of the public, I believe, that men are sent to prison either to protect society from them, or to punish them for their crimes against society. The theory is, apparently, that men who are convicted of crimes must be given a dose of enforced discipline so that they may eventually become self-disciplined enough to be accepted back into society with the necessary character for orderly living. In theory, a man is not punished by the State for the sake of revenge. By sending a man to prison, the courts are supposed to be protecting society from the menace of the transgressor; and it is hoped that the transgressor will realize the error of his ways and resolve to live a good, clean, sin-free life forever after. It is hoped, too, that his fate will be a warning of sufficient strength to influence all other would-be transgressors away from criminal acts. This is the theory, but actual practice is something entirely different.

If we wanted to protect our children from a dread disease, would we crowd them into a home that was already filled with children who were dying of the dread disease?

If we wanted to rid our dog of fleas, would we lock him up in a kennel with other dogs who also had fleas?

The answer to these questions, of course, is negative. Yet, often a judge sentences a young first offender to prison, where he is forced into association with the most hardened criminals and where he is taught not only the "finer points" of the particular crime for which he was convicted, but is also schooled in ways to avoid getting caught the next time. In addition, he learns about a dozen other ways "to make an easy living."

Many of the men whom I met in prison told me of coming to prison before they were twenty years old for a comparatively minor offense, knowing nothing of criminal methods, and of being released a year later feeling that they were "expert" in a variety of criminal occupations. In addition, they were armed with a list of contacts in every known line of vice. Is it any wonder that so many of these men are soon back in court where they are denounced as "bad characters" and labeled "habitual criminals"?

The general public apparently gives little thought to the operations of the courts and/or the prisons in their states. All that we know about them is what we read in the newspapers, hear on the radio or see on television. These matters are of only passing interest unless a relative or a personal friend becomes involved.

Most people seem to believe that prisons are filled with

desperate criminals who do nothing but plan new crimes for the moment of their release. This is an entirely false picture. *The majority of the people in prison are exactly like those on the outside.* They have the same variety of interests that can be found among any group of similar size. They have the same hopes and dreams, the same aspirations, and the same desires as those of the average citizen. The great majority would much rather work and make an honest living than make a profession of crime; but economic and social problems, coupled with a little moral weakness, are obstacles which they cannot overcome. I am convinced that just a little kindness and understanding and a little help at the right time would save many of these men and make them worthwhile citizens of the State, instead of a constant drain on it.

Of course, there are incorrigible criminals, "bad" people; but, just as in any community, they are certainly in the minority. And, just as in any community, there are in prison some of the finest men that one could find anywhere.

Much good could be accomplished for society, and a great saving made for the taxpayer by intelligent and humanitarian treatment of these men by the courts, and by the use of social service workers and psychiatrists in conjunction with a humanized and *non-political* parole system. Crime will continue to be paid for by the taxypayer on an ever more costly installment plan system until steps are taken in this direction. *Criminals will continue to be produced and crime will continue to be promoted, rather than curbed, by our prisons.*

When a convict is released from prison, it is often said that "he has paid his debt to society." After serving nine months in prison, during which I tried to draw objective and constructive conclusions, I am forced to ask in all sincerity, "When and how will society ever pay its debt to the convict?"

It would be the height of conceit and arrogance for me to pose as an expert and expect my opinion to be given equal weight with the opinion of those who have spent a lifetime in this particular field. I would hope, however, that all men of good will and honest intent will accept this account as a contribution to the wealth of material accumulated through studies and research on crime and its punishment in an effort to find a solution to a problem that often pricks the conscience of democratic and freedom-loving people.

ACKNOWLEDGMENTS

The author wishes to thank the following publishers for permission to reprint material:

Editorial from the February 26, 1969 issue of *The Charlotte Observer*. Reprinted by permission of *The Charlotte Observer*.
"Textile Union 'On the Run,'" by Don Oberdorfer, from the January 17, 1959 issue of *The Charlotte Observer*. Reprinted by permission of *The Charlotte Observer*.
"Henderson Hit Hard and Hurt Badly By Strike," by Chester Davis from the March 18, 1959 issue of the *Winston-Salem Journal*. Reprinted by permission of the Piedmont Publishing Company.
"21-Week Walkout Hurts Mill Town," by Claude Sitton from the April 12, 1959 issue *The New York Times* © 1959 by the New York Times Company. Reprinted by permission.
"Incitement to Violence," from the April 25, 1959 issue of the *Greensboro Daily News*. Reprinted by permission of the Greensboro News Company.
"'We'll Stick It Out,' Textile Worker Says," by Joe Doster, from the May 2, 1959 issue of *The Charlotte Observer*. Reprinted by permission of *The Charlotte Observer*.
"Calling of the Guard Adds New Fuel to Flaming Strike at Henderson Mills," by Richard J. Whalen, from the May 13, 1959 issue of *The Richmond News Leader*. Reprinted by permission of *The Richmond News Leader*.
"Life Difficult At Times For Those Who Chose to Work At Harriet-Henderson Mills," by Joseph C. Koenenn, from the June 3, 1959 issue *The News and Observer*, Raleigh, North Carolina. Reprinted by permission of *The News and Observer*, Raleigh, North Carolina and United Press International.
"Textile Strike Has Far-Reaching Effect," by William T. Plunkett, from the June 4, 1959 issue of *The News and*

Observer, Raleigh, North Carolina. Reprinted by permission of *The News and Observer*, Raleigh, North Carolina and United Press International.

Article by William Duscha, from the June 16, 1959 issue of *The Washington Post*. Reprinted by permission of *The Washington Post*.

"Bitterness Evident, But Not Defeat," by Roy Thompson, from the November 22, 1960 issue of the *Winston-Salem Journal*. Reprinted by permission of the Piedmont Publishing Company.

"In A Second-Floor Office, Unionist Fought And Lost," by Victor K. McElheny, from the November 3, 1960 issue of *The Charlotte Observer*. Reprinted by permission of *The Charlotte Observer*.

"Executive Is Fined In Death," from the November 19, 1959 issue of *The Charlotte Observer*. Reprinted by permission of *The Charlotte Observer*.

"Payton And Seven Other Union Men Are Committed To Prison," from the November 3, 1960 issue of *The Charlotte Observer*. Reprinted by permission of *The Charlotte Observer*.

"Wentworth Your Street... You Hope Not... Not Today," from the November 3, 1960 issue of *The Charlotte Observer*. Reprinted by permission of *The Charlotte Observer*.

"New 'Sacco-Vanzetti' Case To Haunt JFK?" by Victor Riesel, from the November 23, 1960 issue of the New York *Mirror*. Reprinted by permission of the New York *Mirror* and the New York *News*.

"The Strange Case of Boyd Payton," from the December 21, 1960 issue of the *Greensboro Daily News*. Reprinted by permission of the Greensboro News Company.

"Strike 'Informer' Held In Shooting," from the April 9, 1961 issue of *The Charlotte Observer*. Reprinted by permission of *The Charlotte Observer*.

"Write Hero of Henderson Care of Martinsville Jail," by Kays Gary, from the April 15, 1961 issue of *The Charlotte Observer*. Reprinted by permission of *The Charlotte Observer*.

"Is Society In Debt to The Convict," by Boyd Payton, from the September 2, 1962 issue of the *Greensboro Daily News*. Reprinted by permission of the Greensboro News Company.

"Shouts of 'We've Got It' Greet Payton on Return From Last Try in Raleigh," by Kays Gary, from the January 1, 1965 issue of *The Charlotte Observer.*

"A State Pardon For Boyd Payton," from the January 3, 1965 issue of *The Charlotte Observer.* Reprinted by permission of *The Charlotte Observer.*

"Court Restores Citizenship to Boyd Payton," by Kays Gary, from the June 23, 1965 issue of *The Charlotte Observer.* Reprinted by permission of *The Charlotte Observer.*

Chapter 1
THE HENDERSON STRIKE

In 1929, in a textile strike at Marion, North Carolina, six workers were killed and twenty wounded by the sheriff and his deputies. At the funeral of the six, no regular minister would officiate, but Cicero Queens, an old mountain preacher, stepped out of the crowd and prayed:

> O Lord Jesus Christ, here are men in their coffins, blood of my blood, bone of my bone. I trust, O God, that these friends will go to a better place than this mill village or any other place in Carolina. Oh God, we know we are not in high society, but we know Jesus Christ loves us. The poor people have their rights, too. For the work we do in this world, is this what we get if we demand our rights? Jesus Christ, your son, O God, was a working man. If He were to pass under these trees today, He would see these cold bodies lying here before us.
>
> O God, mend the broken hearts of these loved ones left behind. Dear God, do feed their children. Drive selfishness and cruelty out of your world. May these weeping wives and little children have a strong arm to lean on. Dear God—what would Jesus do if He were to come to Carolina?

* * * * *

"Oh, but that was 1929," someone says. "Unions are strong and powerful today. The laws no longer favor the employer, and the courts will protect the worker's right to have a union. Nothing like the Marion or Gastonia situations of 1929 and 1930 could happen today."

Well, let's see. While it is true that the prayer of Cicero Queens is not applicable when it speaks of dead bodies of strikers, take out that reference, and the remainder was as appropriate in 1960 in Henderson, North Carolina, as it was in 1929 at Marion, North Carolina.

Just fifty miles north of the state capital, a textile strike began on November 16, 1958, which was not officially ended until June 1, 1961—a strike about which it was said, many times, that this is a perfect example of the age-old struggle of human rights versus property rights, with law and government squarely on the side of property rights.

This was a strike in which one-fifth of the state police force was used to support a stubborn mill management in its dogged determination to operate its mills with strike-breakers rather than continue to deal with the fourteen-year-old union of employees who had given twenty, thirty, and forty years of service to the company.

This was a strike in which a virtual police-state was established by injunction and enforced by highway patrolmen and National Guardsmen with fixed bayonets, and with authority to arrest civilians, given to them by a special act adopted by the state legislature.

This was a strike in which bail bonds of nearly $300,000 were exacted from nearly 200 union members, arrested on the flimsiest of pretexts.

This was a strike in which the State sent a special judge and a special prosecutor to hold special court in which union members and their sympathizers were, in most cases, given heavy fines and/or sentenced to terms "on-the-roads," while company sympathizers and strike-breakers were found "not-guilty" or given suspended sentences.

This was a strike in which the state's highest law enforcement officers engaged the services of an ex-convict "undercover agent" to entrap union members and build a false conspiracy case against three international representatives of the union and five local union members; a situation in which the trial of these eight men was likened to that of the Sacco-Vanzetti case; and in which the severity of sentence was determined on the basis of rank or position in the union, rather than on the testimony or evidence pertaining to the individual.

What caused the Henderson strike?

This is a question which was asked by every newspaper man or woman who came to write about the strike. It was a mystery which plagued every union official, every governmental agency, and every public-spirited individual who became involved in any way.

Was this a strike for union recognition? No, the union had been recognized by the company for fourteen years.

Was it a strike for higher wages, shorter hours or greater benefits? No, the union had voted to ask for no wage increase and no change in the contract.

Had relations between management and the union been strained, unpleasant, or antagonistic? No, the company president had, on several occasions, praised the union's leaders as being responsible and cooperative. Likewise, the union had spoken publicly of management as being forward-looking, enlightened and fair. On one occasion, the company president had appeared with a representative of the union to testify in favor of a higher federal minimum wage.

What, then, caused the strike? Why did the company insist upon turning the clock back to the discredited days of the 1930's?

Although many theories were advanced, this mystery remained for the three and one-half years of the strike; and, insofar as a plausible excuse is concerned which would justify the situation, the mystery still exists today.

What about the union?

The Textile Workers Union of America was established as the bargaining agent for employees of the Harriett-Henderson Cotton Mills in 1943 when the National Labor Relations Board conducted secret ballot elections in the two mills. The vote at Harriett was 409 for the union and 120 against. At Henderson, the vote was 352 to 124 in favor of the union. Contractual relations were continued year after year until November 10, 1958, either by negotiating new contracts or by joint agreement to extend the existing contract.

On August 31, 1958, both local unions met in joint session and voted to allow the contract to renew itself, without change. The company was so advised, but declared on September 6, 1958, that it was terminating the contract for the purpose of modification.

No one was disturbed by this action. The union recognized that the company had the same right as the union to seek modifications. However, the union did become concerned when the company failed to submit any proposal until October 28th (only 13 days before the termination deadline). Furthermore, union leaders were amazed to find that company proposals called for the contract to be completely rewritten. Every section was changed except the one which protected the seniority of returning servicemen.

In addition to a general weakening of each section, insofar as the union's effectiveness was concerned, the company was proposing a drastic change in the grievance and arbitration sections which would have eliminated the union's power to enforce any of the contract provisions. The local and international leaders of the union could not believe the company was serious.

The Negotiations

On November 6, international representative Julius Fry called the company president, Mr. John D. Cooper, and spoke of the great amount of study required by the company's wide and drastic proposals; he suggested that the contract be extended to allow time for full negotiations without being faced with an immediate deadline.

Mr. Cooper replied, "We will agree to extend the contract on a day-to-day basis provided we are satisfied that progress is being made toward agreement on our proposals; but in no event will we extend beyond November 15th." He confirmed this statement by telegram, and copies of same were posted on the bulletin boards in the mills.

Union and company negotiators met for the first negotiating session on November 10th. The contract was due to expire at 3 P.M. on that day. The company was represented by Mr. Cooper; Mr. Camp, textile engineer; attorneys Perry and Gholson; and plant superintendents Mr. Farmer and Mr. Proctor. Mr. Page of the company's payrolls and standards department was also present.

Local Union 578, from the Harriett mill, was represented by President Charles Ranes, Vice President Johnnie Martin, and by Roy Faulkner, David Pulley and Darrell Hedgepath. The Henderson mill local union 584 was represented by President

Luther Jackson, Melvin Renn, James Reardon, William Pegram, and Richard Parrott. International Representative Julius Fry was the union's chief spokesman. Mr. E. Gail Barker represented the North Carolina Conciliation Service.

Mr. Cooper read a prepared statement which said, in effect, that the company was willing to restore the checkoff provision if agreement was reached to the company's satisfaction on the remainder of the company proposals.

Mr. Fry stated that while the checkoff was important, the union was more concerned about other changes which had been proposed, especially the one which eliminated arbitration. He said, according to the transcript of the meeting, "Without arbitration, the remainder of the contract becomes meaningless because we would have no way to enforce compliance. It is like our laws and the police force. They don't just pass a law and expect it to enforce itself—they have policemen to make sure that the law is obeyed. We consider arbitration as the policeman of the contract."

Mr. Cooper voiced his disapproval of arbitration and stated that he would never agree again to the kind of arbitration which had been in effect over the years.

The remainder of the conference was devoted to a review of the changes proposed by the company. No progress was made and it was obvious to the union committee that no progress would be made until the issue of arbitration was settled.

After Mr. Fry had reported on the situation by phone, it was agreed that I should attend the next meeting, which was scheduled for November 12th, and that I should arrange to have a representative of the Federal Conciliation Service present.

At the November 12th conference, with Mr. George Roseberry of the Federal Conciliation Service present, I spoke at length about the good relationship which had existed and expressed bewilderment at the company's insistence on such wholesale revisions. I tried to explore the reasons behind the company's action, but was stopped in mid-sentence by Mr. Cooper who, with obvious irritation, said, "I don't see any point in continuing that kind of discussion. You don't seem to understand that we are serious about our proposals. We spent a lot of time on each section of the contract and we proposed exactly what we want in each section. There is no piecemeal solution—its all tied together.... Let me make it very plain. I am prepared to accept full responsibility for our actions in terminating the contract and for the kind of proposals which we have made. I went into this with my eyes wide open and with a definite plan. My plan is to operate these mills under my kind of contract, if that is possible. If that is not possible, I will operate them without a contract, if that is possible. *IF I CAN'T DO THAT, I WILL LIQUIDATE THE MILLS AND SELL THEM PIECE BY PIECE."*

The members of the committee, most of whom had worked for the company for many years and had thought of "John D." as a personal friend, were stunned by the strongly worded statement, but more so by the near-animosity which was reflected in Mr. Cooper's voice.

Mr. Roseberry, sensing the shock of the committee members and the potentially explosive situation, took command of the conference and directed both parties to list the points at issue in the order of their importance, in the opinion of each. When these statements had been given to him, he directed the parties to give careful study to the opposing point of view and make an honest effort to find a compromise route around the obstacle presented in each section.

The union committee worked most of the night in preparing a complete counter-proposal. In each section, an honest effort made to go as far as possible toward meeting the company's objective without nullifying the effectiveness of the union. However, when this proposal was presented to the company on November 14th, Mr. Cooper read from a quickly prepared statement to inform the union that none of its counter proposals were acceptable. The frustrations and disappointments of the union representatives turned to anger and some sharp words were exchanged before the Conciliator adjourned the conference.

On Saturday, November 15th, Mr. Roseberry arranged an "off-the-record" conference between Mr. Cooper and this writer. Numerous approaches were tried, but Mr. Cooper remained adamant. Finally, he became quite irritated, and said, "I'm a sick man. I should be home in bed. You still don't seem to understand our position. *I don't intend to change one comma in our proposal until I see some indication that the union is willing to accept our proposal on arbitration."*

Mr. Roseberry urged further extension of the contract to allow time for further efforts at settlement, but Mr. Cooper refused.

Both locals met in joint session on November 26th and, after hearing a report from the negotiating committee, voted to strike.

On Monday morning, November 17, 1958, no one reported to work except supervisors and office workers. The mills were then closed, and no effort was made to operate for the next three months.

During the remainder of November and throughout December, the conciliators kept in touch with both parties, but kept reporting that no change had occurred in the position of either party which would warrant further attempts to negotiate in joint conference.

On December 27, 1958, the company advised the union by letter that unless a satisfactory agreement was reached by January 2, 1959, the company would withdraw all of its proposals. No one was quite clear as to the significance of this action, and the conciliators asked the union committee to stand by for possible joint conference. The questions in the minds of committee members were: Does this mean that the company is abandoning its program for seeking the drastic changes? Or does it mean withdrawal of its tentative promise to restore the check-off and make other minor concessions which had been promised in return for agreement on the elimination of arbitration?

We didn't have to worry about it for many minutes. The conciliators soon returned from meeting with company representatives and reported that the company's letter was only meant to cut all ties to any kind of contractual relations with the union and to withdraw any concession which had been expressed or implied.

The next joint conference was held on January 30, 1959. The fact that the company representatives appeared somewhat less rigid in discussing some minor points encouraged the union to propose that while negotiations continued, the mills be reopened for a sixty-day period under the terms of the previous contract. The union was further encouraged when company representatives asked for time to study this proposal. But that evening the conciliators reported its complete rejection. However, on February 6th, the company proposed to open the mills for a sixty-day period during which negotiations would be continued, with the old contract in effect, *except for the sections on arbitration and checkoff.* The company also advised the union of its intention to reopen the mills, regardless of the position of the union, and set 5 P.M. of February 10th as the deadline for the union to have any voice in the matter.

The conciliators arranged a joint conference for February 10th. The company refused to discuss any of the issues until the union gave a reply to its letter of February 6th. Finally I said, "The union did not terminate the contract; we were perfectly willing to continue working under the old contract, without any change and without a wage increase. It was the company that terminated and made proposals under which the union could not live. We have been on strike for three months because of the company's arbitrary and unreasonable position. Now the company proposes that the strike be called off under conditions which maintain the company's position without doing anything to promote a mutually satisfactory settlement. To the union, the company's letter of February 6th was a proposal for our complete surrender. We still feel that the union cannot survive under the terms proposed by the company and must therefore reject it."

On February 9th and 10th, the company had attempted to have truckloads of cotton delivered to its mills across the union's picket lines, although it was a known fact that both mills had a plentiful supply of cotton on hand. It was also a known fact that the company had never ordered cotton from five different companies on the same day. Furthermore, identically worded telegrams of protest were received by the union from each of the cotton delivery companies whose drivers had been persuaded by union pickets not to cross the picket lines, and it was a known fact that at least one of these telegrams was prepared in the office of attorney Perry, chief counsel for Harriett-Henderson Cotton Mills.

All drivers of these trucks except one had been peaceably persuaded not to cross the picket lines. In this one instance, an official of the Rose Gin Company became engaged in an argument with pickets, and a brief scuffle ensued. He claimed that he was pulled from his truck. The pickets claimed that he fell from his truck while waving his arms and angrily denouncing the union.

Based upon this one instance, and despite the fact that picketing had been in progress for three months without the slightest sign of violence, the company sought and promptly obtained an injunction which restrained the union, its officers, and most of its active members from interfering in any manner with free ingress and egress of the company's property. Pickets were limited to eight per gate, and they were required to remain at least 75 feet away from the entrance. All others, *"excepting those having official business to transact with company representatives,"* were prohibited from approaching within 75 feet of any entrance to the company's property.

It was rumored that the entire injunction document had been prepared by company attorney Perry, but this was never verified. However, it was strange that Judge Bickett, who was ill at his home several miles away and hadn't been in Henderson for some time, was able to include in the injunction, by full name, all those who had been in any way connected with strike activity.

Any doubt about the company's purpose in ordering the delivery of the unneeded cotton was dispelled when the *Henderson Daily Dispatch* ran a company advertisement on February 12th, announcing that the mills would open on the following Monday morning, urging all former employees to return to work, and giving assurance that adequate police protection would be available to protect those who wanted to work. It was obvious that the company strategy had been to have the cotton delivered in the hope that an incident would be created which would provide an excuse for seeking an injunction that would be binding on the union if and when workers decided to return.

Large numbers of state police as well as the sheriff and his deputies were at each entrance on the morning of February

17th, but only 54 production and maintenance workers returned out of the 982 who had worked on the last full day of operations, on November 14, 1958. (The company had urged *all* employees to return at 7 A.M., regardless of their previous shift assignment.)

The conciliators were working night and day in an effort to find a solution. Numerous conferences were held with the parties in separate caucuses. Progress in these conferences led the conciliators to call another joint conference for March 3rd. Tentative agreement was reached on a number of points. The conciliators were encouraged to continue the conference on the following day. However, instead of continuing the calm and deliberate discussions of the previous day, the company representatives launched an attack on arbitration procedures and told stories of a derogatory nature about various arbitrators. After an hour of this, the committee walked out with angry mutterings. The conciliators promptly adjourned the conference with obvious frustration and disappointment. (Reports were rampant concerning the company's efforts to recruit strikebreakers. Numerous stories were relayed to us to the effect that recruiters had been hired in several towns within a radius of 100 miles of Henderson and cars bearing Virginia and South Carolina license plates began appearing in the lines of cars entering the mill gates along with cars carrying license plate tabs from neighboring North Carolina towns. Strangely enough, a state police car always seemed to precede or immediately follow these lines of foreign cars as they wended their way through the streets leading to mill entrances.)

At the next joint conference on March 9th, it quickly became obvious that the question of job rights for the strike-breakers was now the most important consideration to the company. The union committee, after a vote in caucus, proposed a "share-the-work-plan" under which all returning strikers and all newly hired workers would work only six hours per day until normal terminations had reduced the work force sufficiently to warrant a return to regular shift hours. The company held a five-minute caucus and announced rejection of the union proposal. The conciliators quickly adjourned the conference, after announcing that future conferences would be held "away from the antagonisms and pressures of the strike-bound mills."

Mr. John Chupka, the union's general secretary-treasurer, attended the next joint conference at the Vance Hotel on March 12th. As the highest ranking union officer present, he assumed the role of chief spokesman for the union. His masterful presentation of the union's argument made a good impression on the committee and seemed to command the respect of the company. However, before the conference was concluded, the company presented what was described as "a revised proposal designed to overcome the union's objection to the company's original proposal on arbitration," but a quick reading revealed that the company was still maintaining its position of having veto power over the union's right to carry a grievance to arbitration.

Meetings were held with the parties again on March 19th and 20th. While some progress was made in resolving minor points of dispute, the question of arbitration and the question of super-seniority for strike-breakers were obstacles which could not be overcome.

As we were about to adjourn on the 20th, Luther Jackson said, "Before we adjourn, I'd like to give the company something to think about overnight.... I believe we might accept the company proposal on arbitration if you will agree that we have unrestricted right to go to arbitration on six cases each year. That's only three cases in each mill. Surely, that can't hurt you too much."

Mr. Perry said, "Will you give that to us in writing?"

Luther said, "Oh, for God's sake—forget about it."

However, I quickly wrote the suggestion in longhand and handed it to Mr. Perry.

The next day, instead of replying to the suggestion on arbitration, the company presented a formal statement which advised of the intent to grant super-seniority to all employees who had been hired since the strike began and have them hold job rights over all returning strikers. This move cancelled any hope of further progress in a joint session. The conciliators separated the two groups and spent the remainder of the day shuttling back and forth between them in an effort to find a mutually acceptable compromise.

Finally, they called the parties together in joint session and announced that they were notifying the Governor that the negotiations were in a state of complete deadlock. That evening, the Governor wired both parties and asked them to meet in his office in Raleigh on Monday, March 23rd.

Mediation By Governor Hodges

When we arrived at the Governor's office on March 23rd, he advised that he only wanted two representatives from each side and wanted the sessions held at the Governor's Mansion—"away from public gaze."

The union committee voted to have Fry and me as the union's representatives while the remainder of the committee waited in a hotel room. Mr. Cooper said that he and Mr. Camp would speak for the company.

While having coffee at the Mansion, the Governor stressed the seriousness of the situation; urged careful consideration of the obligations, responsibilities, and rights of all parties, "including the State." Then he said, "The conciliators have reported that the question of job rights for those hired since the strike began is now the paramount issue. They say that settlement of the contract issues would not end the strike unless this question can be resolved."

Both sides indicated agreement with his statement.

He said, "As I understand it, you did not assure any newly-hired workers of permanent employment until after you advised all strikers that they would be replaced if they failed to return before February 23rd. Now, I'd like to know how many that involves. How many have been hired since February 23rd?"

Mr. Camp spoke at length about the various jobs involved in an apparent attempt to point up the difficulty of stating a definite figure.

Mr. Cooper interrupted, "We can't just talk about those hired since February 23rd. The others were also told they would be permanent."

The Governor expressed surprise and said, "Then how could you assure strikers on February 20th that they would get their old jobs if they returned by February 23 . . . what would you have done with the newly hired workers if all strikers had accepted your promise and returned before February 23rd?"

Mr. Cooper grinned and said, "But they didn't accept, and now another month has gone by."

The Governor said, "That doesn't answer my question."

When it was obvious that no reply to the Governor's question was to be given, he said, "Now look here, you must have a record of some kind on the newly hired workers. It doesn't have to be to the man, but I don't see how we can approach this problem until we have some idea of the number of people we are talking about. Is it one hundred, two hundred, or three hundred?"

Mr. Camp said, "You see, sir, we can't give an exact figure because it is changing every day. What is true today may be totally untrue next week, or even tomorrow."

The Governor said, "I can't understand why you can't give an approximation which would give us something to work on—but let's leave that for the moment and see if we can define the major points in dispute."

Mr. Cooper said, "I'd say job rights of the newly hired workers is number one, and arbitration is number two. Then, there is another big problem—we can't reinstate any striker who has been convicted of violence."

Mr. Fry pointed out that all convictions had been appealed, and final guilt or innocence would not be established until the appeals were heard. He asked, "What would you do about a man to whom you had denied reinstatement based on a conviction in Recorder's Court who was declared not guilty on appeal?"

Mr. Cooper said, "That's not my problem. I can only act on the basis of present circumstances. I didn't get him into trouble. I didn't even tell him to go on strike."

The Governor said, "Couldn't we forget about the convictions until we see where we stand on the other points?"

Mr. Cooper said, "We can talk about the other points, but we're not forgetting this question for a minute. These new people have to be told promptly whether they are permanent. We can't wait for months for decisions on appeal."

The Governor said, "I'm not sure that I agree with your reasoning. It seems to me that you also have considerable obligation to your old employees, but I don't want to argue now about which obligation is the greater. . . . Let's try to move on—what about this question of arbitration?"

Mr. Cooper launched into a denunciation of arbitration procedures. He concluded by saying, "We have decided that we are not going to continue having crackpot college professors telling us how to run our business."

"Let's get some facts," the Governor said. "How many arbitration cases have you had? And what is the score on wins and losses?"

Mr. Fry said, "I've done some recent checking on that, Governor. The record will show that only eleven cases have gone to arbitration in the past five years. That's one per year for each mill. In the fourteen years that contracts have been in existence in these mills, the record will show only twenty-five cases which have gone to arbitration out of nearly 200 grievances which came to top leadership of the company and the union. That is still about one per year, per mill, with nearly 1,000 workers involved."

Mr. Camp disputed this and argued that some arbitration cases had involved more than one issue. He and Fry became involved in a rather heated exchange of sarcastic opinions of each other until the Governor broke in with: "Let's see if we can't get a little more light and less heat. Can't we get down to brass tacks?"

Mr. Cooper said, "Well, on the points of dispute, I suppose the checkoff is of great importance to the union. It certainly is of great importance to us. We don't intend to agree to the checkoff again and keep on building up the union treasury to finance a strike against us every year."

The Governor said, "Now, wait a minute. We started out by listing two or three major points of dispute, but you keep adding new ones. We can't make much progress that way. I understood that the checkoff would be no problem if we found a solution for the job-rights question and the matter of arbitration."

I stated that, in my last off-the-record conference with Mr. Perry, he had stated that the checkoff would present no problem if we could settle the other points. I also took issue with

Mr. Cooper's statement about a strike every year. I said, "I believe the record will show only two strikes in fourteen years. I think it is unfair to imply that we are in the habit of striking every year."

Mr. Camp said, "We figure that strikes have cost us an average of two weeks' production, per year."

Fry took issue with this statement, recounted the strike history in detail, and concluded with a reference to the need for truth and honesty, which sparked a sarcastic and angry retort from Mr. Camp. The Governor's face was very red as he shook his head sadly.

Mr. Cooper said, "Mr. Payton, I don't know how you got the impression that the checkoff would be no problem. We deliberately eliminated it from our proposal. *We didn't want any more to do with collecting your dues, and we haven't changed our minds.*"

Fry said, "Mr. Cooper, didn't you say in our first conference that you would reinstate the checkoff if we reached agreement on other points?"

"I did not. What I said was, 'the company is willing to restore the checkoff provided agreement is reached, *to the company's satisfaction*, on the remainder of the company proposals'," he replied.

The Governor suggested that private conferences might produce better results. He asked the company representatives to wait in an adjoining room. Then he proceeded to lecture Fry and me about the need for avoiding sarcastic and antagonistic remarks.

After spending some time with company representatives, the Governor asked us to meet again in joint conference. He said, "Mr. Cooper, would you repeat the statement which you made to me a few minutes ago concerning arbitration?"

Mr. Cooper said, "Our main objection to arbitration is that the arbitrators are crackpot college professors who feel that they have a right to overstep the authority granted to them by the contract. If we can draw contract provisions so that their meaning is clear, and if the arbitrators are kept within that meaning, we would have no objection to arbitration of disputes involving interpretation and application of contract terms.

However, Governor, I haven't discussed this with my associates. I would want to do that before making a definite decision."

The Governor said, "What is your reaction to that, Mr. Payton?"

I said, "Well, I'm not sure what it means and would want to see some specific language, but it sounds like it has definite possibilities."

The Governor was quite pleased, and the conference adjourned on a note of optimism, with the parties being instructed to return the next day at 11 A.M.

When we met the next day, the company stated that a document on arbitration was being typed and would be delivered by special messenger. The representatives of the company asked the Governor to meet with them privately. Later, he returned and advised that the company was proposing that arbitration would be by mutual consent only for such period of time as John D. Cooper remained as president of the company. The Governor explained the company's reasoning: "Relations have always been good between Mr. Cooper and the employees, and they would have confidence that he would agree to arbitration in any case of importance."

Fry said, "It is true that the employees have always had a high regard for John D., but I'm not so sure that he hasn't destroyed that now. I'm sure the company would never agree that Mr. Payton should hold veto power over any action the company wanted to take, and I think the same should apply to Cooper. In my opinion, that suggestion doesn't have enough merit to warrant further discussion. We were on the right track when we adjourned yesterday. Let's get back to that."

The Governor returned to company representatives in the other room, but returned in a few minutes to announce a recess until 2 P.M.

When the joint conference was reconvened, the company presented a single typewritten page. (This, apparently, was the document which had taken so many hours to prepare.) It proposed arbitration for discharge and discipline cases, *only*.

The Governor was obviously irritated and discouraged. He tried to explore changes, but Mr. Cooper said, "What's on the paper is *it*."

The Governor suggested a recess until Friday, March 27th, and urged both parties to give serious consideration to changing their positions in an effort to meet the objective of the other party.

When the parties met again on the 27th, Mr. John Chupka sat in, replacing Fry. The company presented a new proposal on "Grievances and Arbitration" which was more in line with the Governor's proposal on the previous Monday. After some discussion, it was agreed that the grievance section was now acceptable to both parties. However, the new proposal on Arbitration failed completely to meet the union's basic objection. In fact, it further complicated the matter by providing that final determination of any dispute be through use of the "Declaratory Judgement Act of North Carolina" before the Superior Court of Vance County.

The "Work Assignment" section was discussed, and the company made a proposal which met the union's previous objection. So, Section 5 was marked as "tentatively agreed."

Section 9 (Strikes and Lockouts) was discussed and tentative agreement reached, subject to possible change in connection with arbitration.

The Governor was quite pleased with the day's accomplishments and praised the negotiators. He urged the parties to be in touch with each other over the weekend and try to have an agreed upon summary of differences when we met with him again on Tuesday, March 31st.

Through telephone conversations on Saturday, Sunday, and Monday, tentative agreement was reached on all points except Arbitration, Checkoff, and Job Rights of returning strikers.

The Governor was elated when he was advised of the progress made. However, his happiness was short-lived. The company had brought attorney Perry to discuss the Declaratory Judgement angle, and he and Fry became engaged in a heated exchange over the question of the closed shop which the bar association maintained. The argument had been precipitated when Mr. Perry had tried to make a bad joke about Fry not being permitted to handle arbitration cases if they were argued in Superior Court.

I said, "I think it is a waste of time to discuss this matter.

Aside from its merits or demerits, I understand that the resident judge who would hear such cases would be Judge Bickett. If you think the union members will ever agree to have their grievances decided by the same judge who issued that injunction against them and has been sending them to jail for alleged violations of it, I just don't believe you are being very realistic."

Attorney Perry was not to be denied. He had come to talk about the Declaratory Judgement Act of North Carolina and, by golly, he was going to talk about it. He did, too, until the Governor stopped him by suggesting that our time might be spent to a better advantage by reviewing all points agreed upon and attempting to "put them behind us, as settled."

Camp and Fry promptly became involved in an argument over the application of the newly agreed-upon rule concerning the right of an employee to run his own job if more than 50 per cent of it was in operation. The Governor became angry and charged both with wasting valuable time on technical and unimportant hypothetical questions. He suggested a recess until 3 P.M.

When we reconvened, Mr. Perry was armed with several books which he said concerned the Declaratory Judgement Act. He insisted upon reading from them until I said, "Just before the recess, the Governor spoke of wasting time. We consider any further discussion of this Act to be a total waste of time because we could not, under any circumstances, accept it as a substitute for arbitration. That is final."

The Governor again suggested separate conferences, and he spent the remainder of the afternoon shuttling between the two groups, but finally called the parties together to say, "You seem to be completely deadlocked, but I'm going to ask you to make one more try. I would urge both parties to reconsider their positions overnight and meet here again at 10:30 tomorrow morning. It is such a shame—I feel that we are so close to a possible settlement."

The next day, Mr. Camp read a statement which provided that no change would be made in present workloads until after a general wage increase was made effective, within fifty-six days after all three shifts were in operation, provided the union would agree to consider its last position on a point-by-point basis rather than as a package.

I said, "Our last proposal covered only the absolute minimum. There is no further room to compromise on any point. Therefore, the package must stand."

The company requested a recess until three o'clock. When they returned, they promptly requested a private conference with the Governor. He came back alone to advise that the company had indicated possible agreement on arbitration and checkoff if they could be assured of the union's agreement on job rights for those who had been hired since the strike began.

Fry pointed out that the company was asking the union to agree to discriminate against its most active members and leaders. I said, "You know as well as we do that the membership will never agree to discriminate against those who have been in the forefront of this struggle to preserve their union. It would be foolish for Fry and me to agree to any such proposal while knowing that the members would not approve our action. We would be misleading you, and we would be no closer to a settlement of the strike."

The Governor called the parties together in joint conference, and said, "I'm willing to spend just one more day on this. I'm asking both parties to search every nook and cranny for a solution and meet here again at eleven tomorrow. That will be the final effort. We will either agree or agree to disagree."

Company representatives, who were late in arriving the next morning, immediately requested a private conference with the Governor. He soon returned to Fry and me to advise us that the company had a new proposal, but was reluctant to present it without some assurance that it would receive favorable consideration. He explained that the company was willing to reinstate the checkoff provision and would modify its proposal on arbitration if the union would agree that newly hired workers would carry job rights over the strikers.

I said, "That's where we were yesterday. What is new about that proposal?"

The Governor said, "Well, I don't have the full details. Will you listen to their proposal all the way through before you reject it?"

We agreed that we would say nothing until the company had made its complete statement.

The company's statement retained the declaratory judgment proposal on arbitration. On the checkoff, they did propose to reinstate it, but with the provision that the company reserved the right to cancel it in the event of strike. The statement also proposed acceptance by the union of the company proposal on job rights of the newly hired workers. Finally, it raised a new angle in asking that the union agree to withdraw all charges pending before the National Labor Relations Board and promise not to file any new charges concerning matters involved in the strike situation.

The Governor asked to speak to Fry and me privately, before we gave our reply. In the private conference, he made a strong plea for our acceptance of the company proposal. When we indicated that it was impossible for us to accept it, he asked us to wait while he talked to company representatives. In just a few minutes, he called the parties together and said, "I've spent a lot of time on this and have done everything in my power to find a solution. It appears that my best efforts have not been enough. I see no purpose in further meetings at this time. If I see brighter prospects for settlement at some future date, I will call you together again."

False Armistice

During the period between April 2nd and April 16th, numerous conferences were held by the conciliators with representatives of both parties, and the Governor kept in close touch by telephone.

On April 17th, the conciliators delivered a new proposal from the company to the union which indicated a slight relaxing in the company's position. Within minutes after delivery of this new statement, the Governor called me and asked that I stand by for a possible conference call. A few minutes later, the Governor's secretary called me to advise that he was on his way to Henderson to seek a change in the company's latest proposal.

At four-thirty, Federal Conciliator Heafner called and asked me to come to the company's main office where the Governor was meeting with company officials. When I met the Governor, he advised that the company was willing to change its newest proposal so that *only* those strikers whose convictions for acts of violence had *not* been appealed would be denied immediate reinstatement.

I said, "Well, that's an improvement, but the entire proposal will have to be considered by the full committee before I give a definite answer, and before I meet with them I want to make sure that I understand everything. Am I correct in assuming that most of the jobs on the second shift and all of the jobs on the third shift are available for returning strikers? And does our agreement on this mean reinstatement of the checkoff provision?"

He said, "That's my understanding, but let me check to make sure."

I waited in the hallway for nearly an hour before he returned to announce that the company would not agree to reinstate the checkoff provision, but would agree to erect dues collection booths at each main entrance which could be manned by the union on paydays. He said, "They also agreed that the union would be permitted to use company bulletin boards to publish the names of delinquent members, but that's as far as they will go at this time."

"What about the number of job vacancies?" I asked.

The Governor said, "Let's not be too technical on that. I can't get an exact figure, but they indicate that your figure of 450 is not too far wrong. And it's my opinion that many of the new ones won't be coming back once a settlement is announced."

He asked to be allowed to speak to the committee. The members agreed, and he was successful in getting a unanimous vote in favor of recommending acceptance to the membership. He asked for a secretary, and dictated, "The company and the union have resolved their differences and have arrived at an agreement which is mutually satisfactory. The agreement is subject to ratification by memberships of locals 578 and 584 at a meeting on Sunday afternoon, April 19, 1959."

While the statement was being typed, I tried to question Mr. Cooper about the number hired during the strike. He said, "We don't have the exact figure, but you have been counting them—you know how many have been working."

The Governor motioned me aside, and said, "Be careful not

to upset what we've worked so hard to achieve. I wouldn't press for answers on that point. I feel sure that most of your old members will be back on their old jobs in a short time."

When the typed copies were ready, Mr. Cooper signed for the company, and I signed for the union. The Governor stood between us and raised our hands above his head for the benefit of the photographers.

As news of the conference had spread, several hundred people, including newspaper, radio and TV reporters, had gathered outside the wire fence which enclosed the company office. When the negotiators emerged with the Governor, a great cheer arose as dozens of flash bulbs exploded. The Governor and I spoke briefly about the settlement.

The whole town went wild. Church bells rang, prayer meetings were quickly arranged and continued throughout the night; parades and dancing in the streets went on until long after midnight.

The first indication that all was not well came with the Saturday edition of the *Henderson Dispatch* in which the company ran a quarter-page advertisement urging all newly hired workers to report for work on the following Monday "as previously instructed."

When union members began gathering for Sunday's mass meeting, disturbing reports were being circulated that strikers who had notified their supervisors that they would return to work on Monday were being told that their jobs had already been filled, *even on the second and third shifts.*

Despite the growing resentment and a general feeling of uneasiness, the new contract was overwhelmingly approved by an estimated vote of 800 to 30.

In accordance with the understanding reached with the company on Friday, in the Governor's presence, all strikers were instructed to report to their immediate supervisor of their availability for work. In addition, the union sent a telegram to the company advising that the strike was terminated and making a blanket application for reinstatement of all striking employees.

The committee had presented a resolution to the mass

meeting which was adopted by unanimous vote. It read as follows:
> WHEREAS ours has been a long and bitter strike, and
>
> WHEREAS the lately resolved dispute between our unions and mill management served to divide the people of Henderson and Vance County along pro-union and pro-management lines, and
>
> WHEREAS the men and women of locals 578 and 584 learned, under fire, who their good and faithful friends were, and
>
> WHEREAS these good and faithful friends gave generously of their moral and material support, with gifts of food, money and encouragement, and
>
> WHEREAS many merchants, hard-pressed themselves for the cash required to operate their businesses, nevertheless waived payments due on purchases made before the strike and even provided much-needed credit while our incomes were cut off, therefore
>
> BE IT RESOLVED by the members of locals 578 and 584 that we extend our heartfelt gratitude to those staunch friends who proved their worth in our time of need, and assure them of our continued patronage in the better days that lie ahead, and
>
> BE IT FURTHER RESOLVED that we forgive those who were misled into positions of opposition to us; that we pledge to our city and county officials, to the leaders of business, and to the whole citizenry of our community our fullest cooperation in restoring Henderson and Vance County to the path of peace, progress and prosperity, and
>
> BE IT FINALLY RESOLVED, most importantly, that we give thanks to God for the strength He gave us; for the faith which sustained us through 22 difficult weeks; and for the courage and fellowship that united us.

The next indication that the company was not acting in good faith began immediately after adjournment of the mass meeting when workers began reporting that they had called their supervisors and had been advised: "Your job has already been filled . . . you will have to be rehired."

Others reported that their supervisors had expressed complete ignorance of any plans for reinstatement of the strikers. The union's phones rang constantly, and each call brought new evidence that the company was either acting in bad faith or that its supervisors were deliberately trying to create confusion.

After hours of attempting to contact someone in authority from the company, I finally reached Camp and reported the confusion and ill-feeling which was being created. I asked,

"Didn't we have an agreement that we were to instruct all striking employees to call their immediate supervisor and state that they were available for work? And wasn't it agreed that the supervisor was only to say, "Thank you for calling—I have your name—you will be notified when to report'?"

He agreed that this had been the understanding, but admitted that the supervisors had not been notified of the procedure. He agreed to call a meeting of all supervisors and make sure that they understood.

By this time, many members were furious. Charges of "double-cross" and threats of reprisals were heard on all sides. The local union officers, my assistant Dave George, and I spent most of Sunday night trying to allay the fears of the members and urging them to remain calm and orderly.

The scene at the gates on Monday morning could only be described as bedlam. Some strikers were saying that they had been instructed to report at 7 A.M. Others, in identical circumstances, reported that they had been told that they were replaced and would have to be rehired. To add to the confusion, many new employees were crowding through the gates, insisting that they had been told to report at that time. Several hundred people were in the crowd—strikers who, according to them, had been told to report; strikers who had been told not to report, and wanted to know why; strike-breakers who had been working; workers who wanted to become strike-breakers (mostly from out-of-town); and a host of interested bystanders, including many reporters and photographers. With the loud talk, the arguments, the jostling, and the fears and doubts which were in evidence, it was amazing that the entire first shift of strike-breakers was successful in getting inside the mills without the slightest violence.

The union offices were a beehive of activity throughout the day. Large crowds milled about, the phones rang constantly. All other committee activity was suspended, and all committee members were pressed into service trying to keep the members as fully informed as possible.

The negotiating committee was scheduled to meet at the company's main office at 4 P.M. to sign the new contract. However, when less than thirty strikers were permitted to return to their jobs at three o'clock (at the same time nearly 200 strangers passed through the gates and into the mills), the committee quickly met and voted not to sign the contract until specific information had been given regarding the number of jobs available for returning strikers.

When we arrived at the company office, Mr. Camp ushered us into a side office. Mr. Cooper came in with copies of the new contract which had been prepared for signatures. I spoke of the concern of the committee members and advised of their action in voting not to sign the contract until they learned of the number of jobs available for returning strikers. I said, "It was my understanding and the understanding of the Governor that most of the jobs on the second shift and all of the jobs on the third shift would be available for returning strikers, but we have now learned that very few returning strikers were permitted to go to work at three o'clock, while a large number of newly hired workers were assigned to the jobs."

Mr. Cooper said, "The returning strikers were assigned to *all of the jobs which were available on the second shift*, just as we promised. We've had people hired for those jobs since March. They were all told to report today, and most of them did. Those who didn't report as instructed lost their places, and those places were given to returning strikers. That's why we couldn't give figures. We didn't know until today how many would report. The same thing is true of the third shift. We've had people hired for those jobs, too, for weeks, but we don't know how many of them will report. The ones who don't report will have their places taken by returning strikers—just like what happened at three o'clock."

I said, "I just can't understand that kind of dealing. If you had people hired for those jobs in March, why didn't you tell us that when we were here with the Governor on Friday?"

"Nobody asked me," Mr. Cooper replied with a grin.

I said, "But you knew that we were talking in terms of 450 newly hired workers who had actually been at work, leaving about 450 jobs available for returning strikers. You knew, too, that we would have no way of knowing about the ones you had hired for later reporting."

Mr. Cooper said, "I didn't know what you knew. You have

some real smart people. They've come up with all kinds of information during this strike—some of it concerned company matters that even I didn't know about."

I said, "Let's be fair, Mr. Cooper. You knew that we were talking about the 100 union members who had been working, plus about 350 newly hired workers. Do you think it was fair and honest to let the Governor lead us into an agreement based on information which you knew to be false?"

"I didn't know then that it was false. If none of the new people had shown up today, you would have been entirely correct," Mr. Cooper countered.

Several members of the committee tried to reason with him. Others tried to shame him by recalling incidents which demonstrated the mutual respect and confidence which had existed in the past, but he remained stone-faced. Finally, he said, "I'm sorry if you people were misled, but it wasn't me that did the misleading. All I ever said was that returning strikers would be assigned to all available jobs. This was done and will continue to be done. If vacancies occur among the newly hired workers, those jobs will go to the strikers. That's all I can say."

I said, "Can you tell us now how many jobs will be available for returning strikers?"

Cooper said, "No, I can't tell you that because I don't know how many strikers will return, and I don't know how many of the newly hired workers will show up."

Fry said, "Mr. Cooper, you're becoming a master at double-talk. Can't you tell us simply how many you have hired and how many jobs that leaves for returning strikers?"

"Not off the top of my head, but I suppose we can get it for you," Cooper replied.

Fry said, "When?"

Cooper turned to Camp, who said, "Sometime tomorrow."

When Fry asked if this information would be delivered or if he should stop by to pick it up, Camp said, "We'll deliver it to your motel."

I said, "I think we are heading for more trouble. I'd like to make an official request that the company cancel the second and third shift operations until we have the job status of the strikers clarified."

"No sir—not on your life. I'm not going to wait any longer. I had planned to start the second shift more than a week ago and I held off at the request of the Governor," Cooper almost shouted, "*I'm continuing the second shift and I'm going to start the third shift just as soon as possible.* As the old saying goes— *Come hell or high water*! That's it, gentlemen."

As the afternoon and evening wore on, reports continued of strikers being told that they had been replaced and would have to be rehired as new employees.

Then, many of the strikers who had gone to work at 3 o'clock began leaving the mills and reporting to union officers of their harrassment and mistreatment by supervisors and strike-breakers.

Just before eleven o'clock, a radio announcement advised that all those inside the mills were being held there until daylight "because of threats of violence from strikers."

It was the opinion of union leaders that threats, if any, were greatly exaggerated in order to provide an excuse to bring back the state police who had been removed when the settlement was announced.

The Governor issued a strongly worded press release in which he accused the company of misleading him, the conciliators, and the union. He called upon the company to cease operations on the second shift. The company curtly refused. The governor requested the four principle negotiators to meet him at his Raleigh office the next day at 3 P.M.

When Fry and I appeared as requested, the Governor informed us that Mr. Cooper had wired that he could not be there until the next day. The "false armistice" was discussed with the Governor. He expressed extreme indignation toward the company and sympathy for the position of the union. When told of the company promise to furnish specific job information, the Governor suggested that Fry call Camp at once. The call was made, but Camp advised that it would not be ready for another twenty-four hours. The usually mild and soft-spoken Governor gave vent to an angry tirade against the company. He asked us to return at eleven the next day.

Federal and state conciliators were present with the Governor when we met on April 22nd. Mr. Camp read from a prepared statement which said, in effect, that 920 jobs had been in operation prior to the strike (429 at Harriett and 491 at Henderson) and only 222 jobs were open in both mills on all three shifts.

I expressed keen disappointment. The Governor expressed amazement. Fry asked, "Is it the company's position that a learner is to be retained even if the qualified worker who held that job is available?"

"That paper shows 698 people whose performance is satisfactory to the company—all of them," Mr. Cooper snapped. "It is our position that they will continue to hold those jobs as long as their performance continues to be satisfactory. *And we intend to be the judge of that.*"

The Governor asked, "Do I understand that the replacement will be given job preference over a completely qualified worker, who has been on strike, as long as you feel that the replacement is making satisfactory progress toward becoming qualified?"

"That is our position, *exactly*, Governor," Mr. Cooper replied.

Fry said, "Well, that seems to make the company's position very clear. What you are really saying is that you intend to punish those employees who went on strike. Isn't that the purpose of your action?"

"You can call it anything you want to call it, Mr. Fry. I'm not interested in your opinion one way or the other," Mr. Cooper retorted. "I have been reliably informed that I am within my rights, and this is the way we intend to handle it."

Fry said, "I wasn't present when the Governor effected a settlement in Henderson but, from what I see now, it is obvious that the settlement was obtained through false pretences, misrepresentation, and bad-faith bargaining. The definition of *agreement* is *mutual understanding or meeting of minds.* It is certainly clear that there was no meeting of the minds in this case. You weren't even talking about the same set of facts. The Governor and the union were talking about one set of facts while the company was talking about a completely different set of facts. So—no meeting of the minds—no agreement."

I said, "Certainly, the union has gone more than half-way in an effort to find a solution to the problems with which we were presented. I emphasize the words 'with which we were presented' because none of our present difficulties were of our making. The company must accept full responsibility for all that has happened."

The Governor suggested that we recess for lunch. When we reconvened, he talked to me privately and urged that I make one last attempt to get the committee to authorize the signing of the contract. I said, "I don't mind talking to them again, but I doubt that they will agree to sign."

To my surprise, the committee instructed me to advise the Governor that they would sign if he could get the company to agree to have all jobs shared between the strikers and the non-strikers until such time as the work force was reduced by quits and release of unqualified workers to a point where available jobs and available qualified workers were equal.

The Governor relayed this to company representatives, but soon returned to advise that the proposal had been rejected. He asked to speak to the committee. When his request was granted, he made a great effort to "sell" the committee on having faith that the company would soon "weed-out" the strike-breakers and reinstate the old employees.

When the committee refused to accept his reasoning, he said, "All right, then, I'm finished. I'm washing my hands of the whole thing."

The conference simply disintegrated without formal adjournment; the Governor quickly assembled newsmen who had been waiting in the corridors. Although I wasn't invited, I managed to find a seat at the rear of the room.

The Governor explained the situation in detail and reviewed his mediation efforts. He scored the company again for misleading him, but returned to his attack on the union for its failure to control violence. He also blamed the attitude of one of the union negotiators for blocking a settlement in his earlier mediation effort which, he said, would have meant the retention of the checkoff for the union and would have saved more than 250 additional jobs for union members. He concluded by saying, "I am calling upon the union to give me written assurance that there will be no violence or encouragement of violence on the part of members of the union."

Newsmen asked me for a statement. I said, in part, "This is a perfect example of the age-old struggle between property rights and human rights, with law and government squarely on the side of property rights. It is also a perfect example of what many labor leaders said after the passage of the Taft-Hartly Act: 'Given unemployed workers and an Administration which is unfriendly to Organized Labor, this law can completely wreck the American Labor Movement. . . . '

"As to whether or not an agreement was signed last Friday— it was not. The only thing signed was a simple statement, prepared by the Governor, which said that the parties had resolved their differences. We thought then that we had done this, but it is now evident that the Governor, the conciliators, and the union were misled by company representatives . . . The position of the union now is that an end to the strike was voted at last Sunday's meeting . . . we are now engaged in a lock-out."

That evening, I discussed the situation with Mr. Jonathan Daniels, Editor of The Raleigh *News and Observer*. He asked, "Do you think the Governor really put forth his best effort and made a sincere attempt to find a mutually satisfactory solution?"

"Yes, I do," I replied. "I was much impressed with his ability as a mediator, his sincerity and patience and his fair-mindedness. The only fault I find with him is that he waited until March to do what he should have done last December. I honestly believe that if he had intervened at any time prior to the time the mills reopened in February, and had put forth the same effort, he could have secured a settlement which would have prevented all of the hardship of the past months, and we would never have been faced with our present difficulties."

Thus ended all negotiations between the parties except for off-the-record conferences arranged by the conciliators from time to time to keep the lines of communication open.

Strike Violence

Although no violence or disorder of any kind occurred between November 17th (the first day of the strike) and the incident of February 9th when a Rose Gin supervisor "was pulled or fell" from his truck, incidents of violence were reported almost daily from that point on. A review of some newspaper clippings will present that aspect of the strike:

The Raleigh *News & Observer* of February 17, 1959, carried a picture of many state police cars lined up in front of the Henderson state police headquarters. The story:

> Sunday night, after it became apparent that the patrol was in Henderson in some force, it was not known in Henderson who had requested the Governor to send the patrol. Sheriff Cottrell was called at the police station and asked if he had originated the request ... He replied, "No!—now wait a minute—I'm not going to be put on the spot on this. John D. Cooper was the man that wanted them here, and they've been got here.

The Raleigh *News & Observer* of February 24, 1959, carried a story:

> Boyd Payton of Charlotte, Carolinas director for the Textile Workers Union of America, was beaten last night at his motel room in Henderson. Mr. Payton, who only yesterday described the town as an "armed camp," was lured to the door of his motel shortly after midnight and struck on the head with a pop bottle. He apparently was not seriously injured and a hospital spokesman reported he had spent a satisfactory night. Mr. Payton, who had been broadcasting hourly appeals for calmness, was found unconscious on the stoop of the motel where he was registered. His companion, Robert Freeman, another union representative, said they heard a rap on the door and heard a voice outside call, "Mr. Payton, this is Charlie." Mr. Freeman said Payton went to the door and was beaten. When he (Payton) failed to return to the room within a few minutes, Mr. Freeman said he went to the door and found Mr. Payton lying on the motel porch. Mr. Freeman said he saw no one else and did not know who did it.

The Charlotte Observer of February 26, 1959, carried an editorial which said, in part:

> "A bitter, violent strike has disrupted fifteen years of peaceful working relationship between union and management at the Harriett-Henderson Cotton Mill. ... Pickets yell and jeer at a group of non-union workers manning a part of the machines; crowds of strikers tip over cars; unidentified trouble-makers have touched off three bombs; hoodlums have assaulted an official of ... the union; state highway troopers stand by to quell overt outbreaks. In such an atmosphere, Governor Luther Hodges has warned both union and management that they bear direct and personal responsibility to prevent further trouble. The warning is timely, but the governor may

go a step beyond this point. H. D. Lisk, a TWUA vice president, thinks the governor ought to call both sides together in an effort to end the stalemate. The suggestion is sound.... Perhaps Governor Hodges, with his vast executive experience and demonstrated talent for public relations, might bring the weight of his judgement to effect a meeting of the minds. It's worth a try."

The Raleigh *News & Observer* of March 4, 1959, carried an editorial which read, in part, as follows:

> "The industrial dispute at Henderson which has closed two cotton mills since last November and has been the scene of some violence since the mills attempted to reopen more than two weeks ago, definitely has two sides—as most disputes do. Recently, most of the news from the strike has centered on violence. For the violence, and threats of violence, union members are largely responsible—although the principal actual damage to persons resulted from a brutal, unprovoked assault upon a union official...."

The Raleigh Times of March 12, 1959, carried the headline "New York Labor Hits at Hodges." The New York dateline story:

> "North Carolina's industry-seeking governor... ran into some labor opposition here Wednesday.... While the Governor addressed a hosiery promotion meeting at the Savoy-Hilton Hotel, union pickets demonstrated outside. Two of the placards carried by the pickets read, "Governor Hodges—get your strike-breaking troops out of Henderson", and, "Governor Hodges—how about mediation instead of terror?" The pickets distributed leaflets charging that Hodges had come here to lure industry to his low-paid state.

The Governor, in an attempt to justify the use of National Guardsmen, summarized the violence as follows:

> There have been 40 reported instances of bombings or dynamiting in the area since the strike began. Homes of workers and others have been bombed or damaged by nearby blasts, and many dynamite blasts have been set off in open fields or lots for the apparent purpose of disturbing the peace and terrorizing the community. The Harriett Mill boiler and boiler building were extensively damaged by persons who entered the building at night and set off charges of dynamite there. During the same night, approximately 30 card machines were damaged extensively by having acid poured on them.

He then listed numerous acts of violence and lawlessness, including the highly questionable one of the "bombing of the nursery."

Certainly, no one could find fault with his listing the incidents or deny the seriousness of the situation. However, the Governor's statement would have carried more weight if it had not been so obviously designed to place blame for all violence on the union. For instance, an explanation that the "nursery" had housed no children for many months prior to the strike and that it was in a bad state of decay would have done much to avoid the implications of bias and prejudice.

It was the opinion of most union members, and of many neutral observers, that the "nursery bombing" as well as the reported damage to the boiler house and the card machines had been "arranged" to discredit the union and provide an excuse to call in the National Guard. A clear appraisal of these two incidents would have lead to the conclusion that the union and its supporters would have done everything possible to avoid their occurrence because of the potential damage to the union's public image, to say nothing of the certainty that any violence at that particular time would automatically bring the National Guard and Martial Law to Henderson.

It was significant, too, that the Governor's summary did not include the incident on the first day of the back-to-work movement in which assistant foreman Spain broke his leg when he plunged from a second-story window of the mill, and kept screaming, "They are after me," pointing to the mill where only supervisors and strike-breakers were.

Also, it was strange that the Governor did not mention the fact that a striker's son, James Manning, who was home on leave from the army and had been the first to reach Spain, was seriously wounded that night by a shotgun blast directed by a Supervisor.

Stranger still, perhaps, was the fact that the Governor omitted any mention of the two attacks on me—once (as previously mentioned) on February 23, 1959, when I was hit with a pop bottle at my motel door and again, on March 26, 1959, when rocks were thrown from a passing car through my car window. Newspapers gave widespread publicity to both these incidents.

Of course, the Governor's summary was in keeping with the apparent design of all those opposed to the union to blame it for all the violence and disorder. This, despite the fact that on the first day of the back-to-work campaign, I issued a statement in which I urged all members and sympathizers to exercise restraint and to keep all actions above reproach. I said, "Violence and disregard for law and order can only hurt the just cause of the union and turn public sentiment against us." This statement was carried in newspapers and was repeated in paid radio broadcasts several times each day.

In addition, the union's General President, William Pollock, issued a strongly worded statement in which he denounced violence and stated that the union would not condone or support any disregard for law and order. His statement was carried in newspapers and was posted on bulletin boards in both union halls. Furthermore, the union offered numerous rewards for information leading to the arrest and conviction of those responsibile for acts of violence. Finally, the union hired a private detective in an attempt to secure information concerning the real culprits.

Strike Publicity

It has been said that millions of words were written about the Henderson strike and that thousands of pictures were taken of strike activity. Until the back-to-work movement began on February 17, 1959, the publicity was limited to local and labor newspapers and was concerned mostly with the issues of the dispute, the efforts of the union and public-spirited citizens to induce intervention by Governor Hodges, and the merits or demerits of arbitration.

However, with the company's announcement of its back-to-work movement, the Governor's assignment of large numbers of state-police (before any violence had occurred), and the subsequent instances of violence, the strike became of national interest. Major news services, as well as leading area newspapers, assigned staff members on a full-time basis to Henderson. In addition, numerous state and out-of-state feature writers and photographers moved in.

The union's principle source of contact with its members and the general public was through regular morning and evening radio programs over station WHVH in Henderson. To cover specific points or to reach special audiences, the union sponsored many special broadcasts in a particular area or on a state-wide basis. The scripts of these broadcasts would, in themselves, present a word picture of the strike. Likewise, the stories and articles written about the strike would present a vivid documentation of all aspects of the strike of great interest to those who are students of labor history or to those who are making a study of southern unionism and/or labor-management relations.

While space does not permit a full review here, certain excerpts may serve a useful purpose to this story in presenting certain views by disinterested writers:

Don Oberdorfer, writing for *The Charlotte Observer* said:

> National leaders of the Textile Workers Union of America see the Harriett-Henderson strike as an important battle in a South-wide campaign to annihilate textile unionism.
>
> The union's Southern strength has ebbed in recent years. Its organizing efforts haven't been widely successful, and some unionized mills have been victims of a general mill-closing wave in the industry. "Now they're trying to eliminate us completely," said John Chupka, general secretary-treasurer of the TWUA.
>
> Chupka related that in the last few months, the union has been confronted with impossible demands each time one of its long-standing contracts has run out.
>
> "When we met in Charlotte with our Southern staff . . . and reviewed contracts, it became clear that an almost uniform south-wide pattern has developed." Chupka said.
>
> Chupka said the pattern was developed by Frank Constangy, an Atlanta attorney who often represents management in textile labor disputes.
>
> He said the "almost uniform" contract renewal demands include:
> 1. A clause allowing management to set work loads and change work assignments without the union having a regular procedure to file grievance objections which ultimately lead to arbitration by impartial outside parties.
> 2. Contractual responsibility on the part of the union for any authorized or unauthorized strike, including responsibility to repay the company for damages incurred.
> 3. An end to the system of dues "checkoff" whereby a company will make deductions for dues from union members' payrolls.
>
> "No union could in any way exist with that kind of contract. The workers would be at the mercy of the employers. They'd be better off without a union under those circumstances," Chupka declared.

Chester Davis, writing for the *Winston-Salem Journal*:

> The town of Henderson has been hit hard and hurt badly by the four months old strike. . . .

The national publicity picturing Henderson as a place of unrestrained violence has hurt. So has the loss of the town's largest single payroll. Most of all, the people of Henderson have been hurt by the bitterness which has split families and which, today, causes a gas station attendant in this pleasant, progressive small town to shrug his shoulders and say, "What do I think about the strike? I can't say. I've got friends on both sides."

"Who should be blamed for what has occurred in Henderson? Is this, as some say, the result of management's stubborn determination to "bust the union?" Or, as others claim, is the prolonged strike, with its overtones of hatred and violence, the result of a union contract which has undermined a company's ability to compete efficiently in the price-sensitive textile market?

The two mills involved, the Henderson Cotton Mill (founded in 1895) and the Harriet Cotton Mill (founded in 1900), are the second largest producers of corded knitting yarns in the United States. . . . They employ a total of just under 1,000 production workers and their payroll runs about $3 million a year or $60,000 a week.

The two mills were built by the Cooper family of Henderson, and down the years they have been managed by members of the Cooper family. John D. Cooper, Jr., a man roughly 70 years of age, is the president of both mills. His younger brother, Marshall Y. Cooper, is vice president and treasurer of both mills. . . .

Marshall Cooper . . . is also the president of the Citizens Bank and Trust Co., the largest bank in this section of North Carolina.

Like most prominent and influential families the Coopers are respected, and that respect is tinged with just the slightest touch of resentment. They are suspected of "running the town" of "discouraging new industry," etc.

The one clear fact about the strike . . . is that it involves good, decent people on both sides.

The picture of John D. Cooper as a flinty-hearted Southern mill operator who is "out to get the union" simply is not supported by the facts. Even today this small, white-haired, shy man is respected by the workers on the picket line. They are puzzled by "John D.'s" stubborn refusal to negotiate the arbitration issue. But they say that he is a good man and a man who feels a genuine concern for his workers.

The picture of the striking workers as hoodlums and vandals who spend most of their time tipping over cars, bombing homes, pitching rocks and bottles and cursing the police is equally distorted.

There is nothing duller than a photograph of pickets marching back and forth before a plant gate singing hymns or, perhaps, of pickets pitching horse shoes. Yet that's the typical picture on the Harriet-Henderson picket lines. The news reports and news photographs feature the top of each day's news. For the past three weeks, ever since the mill gates reopened, there have been incidents of violence each day. These incidents provided the bulk of the news. They created a national impression of Henderson as a place of unrestrained violence.

There has, of course, been a great deal of violence on the ... picket lines. ... But ... the intention, inexcusable though it is, seems to be to frighten rather than to hurt. ...

Despite the hatred and the terrible tension no one has been hurt on the picket line as yet. ... "

Claude Sitton, writing for *The New York Times*:

A costly, violence-ridden strike enters its twenty-second week ... and there is no indication that a settlement is in sight.

The 18,500 persons living in and around Henderson have been split into factions by bitterness and hate generated in the strike.

... The overriding issue [in the strike] was a demand that the union agree to drop an arbitration clause that had been in force since 1944. ...

Independent observers contended that the basis of the dispute lay in the work of Julius Fry, the union's area representative. ... These observers said that Mr. Fry's knowledge and ability had given the union a decided edge in pressing cases in arbitration. Union officials conceded the point but argued that the company should hire a specialist in labor relations to offset Mr. Fry.

Friends and relatives find themselves on both sides of the controversy. Almost half of the city policemen and sheriff's deputies have wives, brothers or sisters among the strikers.

Few of the strikers expressed any bitterness toward Mr. Cooper. Many said he was liked and respected. Three women who worked in the mills before the dispute recently baked a cake for the president. They then presented it to him in his office and spent an hour talking to him about the strike.

With further regard to strike publicity, two editorials seem to be appropriate. They were written just after the company had rejected the Governor's plea to "hold off" second and third shift operations. One in The Raleigh *News and Observer*, dated April 24, 1959, was headed "A Sad Spectacle"; it said:

I'm not going to mess with mill affairs tonight," said John D. Cooper, Jr., after leaving, with the Governor's condemnation, an all-day Wednesday meeting. "I'm tired."

Mr. Cooper might well be tired. ...

Mr. Cooper, his workers and the state have come a long tiresome and bitter and violent way since then [November 16, 1958]. And yesterday Mr. Cooper answered a telegram from the Governor of

North Carolina asking him to "hold off" operations of the second and third shifts "until matters are cleared up satisfactorily."

"No," said Mr. Cooper.

... Obviously Governor Hodges and the people of North Carolina behind him are just as much concerned about violence as John D. Cooper, Jr. In the same statement in which the Governor sharply criticized Mr. Cooper in connection with the breakdown of last week's settlement, the Governor sternly rebuked labor for the violence which has occurred. The Governor's rebuke concerning labor violence was well deserved, regardless of whether the responsible leaders of the strikers approved it or not. They have not stopped it. And violence has come from some of those they presume to lead.

In Mr. Cooper's case, however, there is now no question about his direct assumption of responsibility for the danger the Governor asked him to help avert. Repeatedly Mr. Cooper and associates have asked the Governor for State police. More than a hundred have been allotted to the protection of his property, taking time from other essential safety needs. Requests have come from him—or those associated with him—for the Governor to send troops to the mills for the first time in a quarter of a century in North Carolina. But when Governor Hodges asked his cooperation in helping reduce the danger of violence the answer was, "No."

John D. Cooper, Jr., is a tired, old man. And he must be a sad old man. Undoubtedly the world has much changed since his father helped establish the mills more than sixty years ago. Also undoubtedly Mr. Cooper feels a deep sense of resentment about his troubles in a town which his family helped build. Perhaps he has even reached the point where, as he has suggested, he is about ready to shut up the mills in the town of his family and traditions rather than reach a settlement on any terms save his own.

As a stubborn, tired man it is easy to feel sorry for John D. Cooper, Jr. But it is impossible to sympathize with him in his stubborn reply to the Governor's request. Governor Hodges has no patience with violence. Governor Hodges' own experience has been as a textile mill executive. He has recently been loudly and unjustly damned by some labor spokesmen. But he is Governor of North Carolina. His responsibility is the peace and safety of the State. And when Mr. Cooper rejected his request. Mr. Cooper also lost his right to public support.

At this point John D. Cooper, Jr., is not only tired and old—but also stubborn and alone.

The other editorial came from the *Greensboro Daily News*. It was headed "Incitement To Violence" and read as follows:

Further evidence that Harriet-Henderson Mills management is

determined to go ahead with expanded operations, despite warnings and appeals from both Governor Hodges and Henderson Mayor Carrol V. Singleton comes in an announcement by President John D. Cooper, Jr., that a third shift will begin operations at the strike-bound mills Tuesday night.

What happened after inauguration of the second shift apparently made no impression whatever upon President Cooper and his aides. They are not merely willing but apparently determined to go ahead with other night operations and thus to increase the likelihood of violence under cover of darkness.

No one questions the strictly legal right of the mills to do what its president has decided to do. But legality surely is not the only factor involved. What will be the effect of the third shift, following closely upon the second shift which saw violence flare to a new height at Henderson, upon the community, the good name of the state, the maintenance of peace and waning hope for a settlement which offers the only real hope of protection and security?

For the record, let it be remembered that Governor Hodges warned against opening of the second shift. His warning went unheeded and violence was sparked anew, especially when, in the Governor's own words, mill spokesmen were "misleading" regarding the number of jobs which would be open to workers on the added shifts.

... When Mr. Cooper's rights, as an individual, clash with the welfare and peace of the state and the community, and their exercise is officially deplored because of the increased bitterness and violence which are foreseen, reason and understanding dictate the course which should be followed.

Violence is to be condemned on anybody's part. But incitement to violence by a stubborn, heedless and self-centered individual elicits its own condemnation in the public mind and accountability.

Of course, all strike publicity was not sympathetic to the union. And, in order to present the factual story, in regard to strike publicity, we should refer the reader to the most uncomplimentary writings from the anti-union *America's Textile Reporter* which boasts that it is the "Most Powerful Influence in the Textile Industry." It devoted much space to the Henderson strike and then issued a special supplement which combined the various articles into one document under the title, "The Henderson Story" dated (April 30, 1959). As expected, the union was charged with full responsibility for the strike and all difficulties flowing therefrom while company representatives were pictured as innocent victims of this "all powerful union."

Joe Doster, writing for *The Charlotte Observer*:

Homer Price threw a final handful of dried beans into a brown paper bag and rolled the top down.

"We'll stick it out," he said. "That's all we can do."

Homer is one of about 1,000 Textile Workers Union of America members who are on strike against the Harriet-Henderson Cotton Mills.

He and six or seven other... members had been bagging beans for the union commissary. Later they would be passed out to striking workers.

In the evening Homer would report to a part-time job he had taken at a local fish market to supplement the money and food he had been getting from the union since the strike began 25 weeks ago.

Prior to the strike, he had earned... $59.80 a week as a slasher hand....

"It's tough," Homer said. "But we're sticking together."

... "I started work here when I was 14 years old," he said. "My daddy brought me here with him—he always followed textile work.... I'm 49 years old and this is all I know....

"It's mighty hard for a man that's been here that long to watch somebody come in from another state and take his job...."

Several times while he talked Homer raised his hand to the shirt pocket where he carried his cigarettes, but each time he pulled it away again.

Finally he took a cigarette out and lit it. He smoked it until less than a half-inch remained between his fingers.

Homer's 17-year-old son, Bruce, is a senior at Henderson High School where children of both strikers and non-strikers attend classes together.

"It's [the strike] divided them up," he said. "They have to take sides."

"You ought to see my little two-year-old grand-daughter. She'll stand up there when they're going in the mill and yell 'scab' big as any of 'em....

"We're all broke," he said. "But we're happy—I mean we're friendly and kind to each other.

"About 95 per cent have been out all the time, and I guess we'll stay out till its settled," Homer said.

"We didn't ask for a thing but to keep our old contract," he said. "Old Cooper just came in and threw down the list of what he wanted and said, 'Let me know when you're ready to agree to that.' He didn't even want a comma changed."

A striker drove up in his car and came over toward the union building.

"How's it going?" Homer asked.

"I'm still out," the striker said.

Richard J. Whalen, writing for *The Richmond Virginia News Leader*:

As they walked along the dusty blacktop, the two teenagers—one tall and gangly, the other freckled and chunky—were unaware that their words carried to the stranger a few paces behind them.

"I never thought he'd go back in, I never did," said the taller boy. The chunky one nodded.

"You know," the taller one added slowly, "there are people I've known all my life I'd like to see dead now."

The boys melted into the shifting throng of men, women and children beside the road a hundred yards from the strike-bound north plant of the Harriet-Henderson Cotton Mills. And the hate that spilled from the boy's lips swelled in the murmur of the crowd. Hate hangs heavy on Henderson today, a deep, foul cloud that has accumulated over 27 weeks, during one of the longest strikes in the history of the Southern textile industry.

Since November 17, 1958, two locals of ... [TWUA] have been out at the ... mills, located at either end of this city of 15,000, which straddles U.S. 1 ... Most of the 1,000 workers have stayed out; some have returned to work, and their adamant neighbors despise them. But the strikers' special wrath is reserved for several hundred new workers hired by the mill since February. . . .

At sundown yesterday, some 400 National Guardsmen arrived here, preceded by rumors, threats, and a tightening of tension. Monday night had been one of the wildest in the long strike: Dozens of rocks were thrown, cars were riddled with bullets (miraculously, no one was hurt), and a small building was dynamited. . . .

Five truckloads of Guardsmen drove up at the besieged south mill at 10:30 P.M., 30 minutes before the end of the second shift. . . .

Arrayed in single file along the street, facing the howling strikers, the Guardsmen grimly obeyed the order: "Fix bayonets!" Then, marching in close order to the edge of the street, they opened an escape route for the workers behind them.

An eerie yellow flare and glaring TV lights showed a nervous Guardsman, knuckles white around his unloaded M-1, while a teenaged girl, perched on the fender of a parked car, her pony tail twitching, never ceased for a moment her abuse of the new enemy in khaki. One of the most striking aspects of the scene was the brooding silence of the men and the unceasing clamor of the women.

... As the quitting whistle sounded, a roar went up from the mob. *There they are*! A row of automobiles, almost bumper to bumper, roared through the gates and down the troop-lined street. Now the men were shouting too; everyone was shouting. Something sailed through the air ... and clunked against a car hood. Farther up the line, rifle fire was heard. Then, suddenly, it was over; the cars were out. Despite their steel helmets and naked bayonets, the troops had not altered the nightly violence.

... Governor Hodges' use of the National Guard for strike duty—the first such use in more than a quarter of a century—reveals the desperate seriousness of the Henderson situation. The troops, reluctant, griping civilians who loathe their chore, are not yet backed by martial law, but that drastic step may be coming.

Law and order are fast being consumed here by the passions of mob rule. Either these fires will be checked by State authority, or they will burn out of control until nothing is left at the core of this small community but cold, bitter ashes.

Shirley Mudge, writing for *The Raleigh Times*:

The strike has become a way of life for union members who, prior to November 17, 1958, went to work every day at the Harriet-Henderson Mills.

A police officer, watching over the jeering lines of strikers at one mill gate yesterday observed, "They're hungry. They're just existing now. You couldn't call it living."

But a striking wife and mother, still faithful to the cause for which she fights, disagreed. "It's not as hard as you might think," she said. "The union helps... pays rent, lights, water, food." After five months, life along the tree-shaded streets, in the modest homes of the union mill workers, is pretty well set around the strike.

... While the workers waited for the Guard, the strikers waited for the workers. Hours passed and the crowd grew. And the people behind the mill fence and the people outside, just a few hundred yards from the gate, glared at each other.

The women came from all the houses along the street and sat on the porch of a striker's home near the gate. They moved chairs into the yard and sat and talked about the police, the Guard and the size of the crowd.

The babies played in the yard. Children came home from school, tossed their books on the porches and joined the crowd.

... Teenagers milling about autographed each other's annuals. ...

One asked, "Do you think this will be in history?" Another groaned when, at a word from a union leader, the crowd began to disperse. "Don't they know that when everybody leaves the workers will come out? They haven't got a grain of sense."

For five months it's been virtually the same. Union and non-union workers, separated literally by a few hundred yards, remain separate figuratively by a vast chasm. ...

On May 24, 1959 the North Carolina Catholic Edition of *Our Sunday Visitor* carried an editorial which gave cause for some provoking thought. It was headed "Tragedy At Henderson." It follows, in part:

The Henderson strike is logical. It is the logic of frustration, the inexorable grinding out, step by step, remorselessly of a Greek tragedy.

Mute, the spectators watch spellbound as the inevitable climax nears. To the straining audience the outcome is foreseen. Who challenges the gods must die.

The "gods" are the social forces of the South: the complex of traditions, attitudes, values, hallowed prejudices, fears.

... The true and real stage setting is the South. "Private Property" is the theme of the drama. Yet while the precise issue of the Affaire Henderson is Property, Property speaks and acts against a chorus of many voices.

... Numbered among the chorus of the now subdued and dying worker pawn are: Class Consciousness, Civil Rights, Equality at Law, Insecurity, Ambition, Class Conflict, Fear and Face Saving.

Behind all the symbols and dramatics of the Henderson tragedy is the issue of rights. Property rights versus job rights. In our emerging Southern industrial age, both property and workers' rights are ill defined.

Property concepts in the South are still closely knit with the traditional ideas of agricultural property. A man does with his property as he wishes. It is his own. A hundred years ago that very property concept extended to human beings as well. This was the legal, the institutional concept, even though caring for one's slaves frequently engendered close bonds of affection between master and slave.

... Property rights, the papal encyclicals of Leo XIII (1891) and Pius XI (1931) so simply explained, are clear-cut and strong. But they are also relative—relative to the welfare of the whole community. God gave the earth for the welfare of all mankind. Simply because a man or family or corporation owns a factory and tools gives him no prerogative to do with that property "whatever" he pleases.

Workers, the local town, the State and the Nation all have correlative rights. Why? One reason is because no industrialist, Henry Ford or John Cooper, for that matter, owns his industry purely and exclusively by right of his own brains and drive. The community also contributed. Every worker that gave years of his life and skill and company profit had a hand in the process. He had a vested interest.

Job rights are less tangible than a cotton mill. But they are just as real, and latterly the courts have begun the work of defining these rights. A man who puts in 25 years towards building a prospering company has done surely as much as the stockholder who invested a few thousand dollars some years back. The workers contributed human personality. Wages alone do not absolve the owner of his obligation to his workers. Severance pay, seniority rights, back pay for jobs unjustly lost—all indicate legal cognizance of workers' rights.

> Who must define and guarantee the mutual rights of owners and workers? The community must, through its law-makers and its courts and through its conscience.
>
> Violence at Henderson we condemn as we condemn all lawlessness, including public denunciation and flagrant disobedience to the law of the land in the matter of school integration. It is all one piece. Lawlessness is a social product of enraged frustration. One understands but does not condone.
>
> By sending in state troopers or state militia to nullify strikers' rights to protect their job rights is a travesty on justice and an open cause for worker violence. And by "worker" we do not mean the strike-breaking scabs.
>
> Pedestrian picketing against strike-breakers in cars is outmoded. Add court injunctions, including the latest Joe Doe mass injunctions (with contempt charges served at the discretion of youngsters in uniform and with mounted bayonets) is a complete farce.
>
> Disillusioned, Governor Hodges has publicly washed his hands of the whole affair... but only after guaranteeing that the mills will have their strike-breakers. No mention is made of the workers' rights to protect their right to legitimate organization and a decent contract.
>
> Governor Hodges at least made an honest try to conciliate... That's more than can be said of the "moderates" who should demand, by force of public opinion, that the Henderson affair be arbitrated. Can anyone give a healthy reason why the company refused to have the issues arbitrated? Right from the start the workers were more than willing to let the community decide the justice of their cause. Aha! Remember! Thou shalt not question the final and arbitrary right of property. That must come before the law of justice.
>
> ... Surely in so progressive a State as North Carolina there are still enough intelligent and moderate men, social-minded and just, who are courageous enough to demand publicly and insistently for arbitration by an informed panel of honest citizens. The time is already late.

United Press International, interested in exploring the effect of the strike on the textile industry as a whole; on union-management relations, generally; and, on Wall Street investors considering further financing of industry moves to the South, assigned staff writers to the Henderson situation.

Joseph C. Koenenn said, in part:

> Eighteen-year-old Jimmie Adams is a high school senior who next fall will be a Morehead scholar at the University of North Carolina.
>
> He dates dark-haired Barbara Procktor, whose father is a supervisor at the Harriet-Henderson Cotton Mills. ...

... Recording secretary of one of the Locals is Mrs. Edith Adams, Jimmy's mother. She had been a spinner ... for 27 years, until the strike started. Jimmy's father, Raymond Adams, has been a section man in the Spinning Department for the same number of years—twenty seven.

... Henderson's economy is at a standstill. Long-time friends are now enemies.

The reasons behind the strife that has torn this small town ... is in some respects more important to the rest of the South's textile industry than to Jimmie Adams and Barbara Procktor; to Mrs. Adams or to Barbara's father.

Mrs. Adams' paycheck is not at issue. Working conditions at the mills are not objected to.

The fight is over something not nearly so tangible, the union's voice in the operation of the mills.

The union has had this voice through the means of arbitration.

... But, as one Henderson resident put it, "Mr. John D. doesn't want a bunch of college professors telling him how to run his business." The State's Labor Arbitration Board has several professors as members.

... Out of this grew the disaster which, according to even Cooper, will leave its scars for generations, will affect the lives of a great many Jimmie Adamses.

The results of this strike may be a turning point in labor relations throughout Southern textile mills. In recent years management throughout the industry has been gradually stiffening toward TWUA.

... Henderson, however, is the first place management has taken on a really strong TWUA local. The Henderson locals are acknowledged to be two of the strongest in the TWUA.

The union maintains this strike is the test of its strength throughout the South. It comes, union leaders say, as part of a pattern to destroy the union. ...

Industry spokesmen in Wall Street are inclined to regard the Henderson strike as an isolated incident in a market currently enjoying the best activity in several years. Cotton textile mills generally, they say, are in an excellent position, riding along on a big backlog of orders and enjoying a broadening demand for their product. ...

Cotton mills currently are enjoying the most favorable profit margin since January, 1957, according to Agriculture Department reports. The spread between cloth selling prices and raw cotton costs widened in April to 27.18 cents a pound, compared with 22.75 cents a year ago. ... "

William T. Plunkett, UPI commodity editor, wrote, in part, as follows:

Is the South's pitch to industry to "move down and escape labor troubles" being hurt by the bitter textile strike at Henderson, N. C.?

Wall Street investors say no. Chamber of Commerce officials in Henderson say yes.

Wall Street sources point to two factors in saying they aren't worried.

First, the strike represents a move by management for more control—not a move by labor for more concessions. Secondly, cotton mills are in the best shape profit-wise they have been in for several years. . . .

Julius Duscha, writing for *The Washington Post* of June 16, 1959:

The shooting has stopped in Henderson, but National Guardsmen still patrol the town in jeeps and stand by with fixed bayonets when the shifts change at the . . . mills.

. . . No one walks to work any more, and mill hands keep their car windows rolled up even on a hot June afternoon. The fear and memory of violence hang heavy in the summer air. . . .

Arbitration is the issue which led to the strike last November, but the struggle has come to have industry-wide and perhaps even Nation-wide implications.

The . . . union . . . looks upon the strike as part of an effort by mill owners to destroy the union in the South . . . the president and principal owner of both mills, denies that he has been helped by other manufacturers. . . .

The TWUA also claims that the dispute shows how the Taft-Hartley Act can be used to destroy union locals. Mayor Carroll V. Singleton . . . and others in the state consider the strike to be a test of the right-to-work laws which prohibit the union shop and are in effect in North Carolina and 18 other states. . . .

On the one side is an individualistic mill executive, Mr. John D., as almost everyone in Henderson calls Cooper. Opposing him is a militant union with a generally good record.

The TWUA, a former CIO union . . . is not to be confused with the United Textile Workers of America, the old AFL union. . . .

Some of the signs carried by the pickets are familiar: "Solidarity Forever"; "Jesus Leads Us, The Union Feeds Us, John D. Needs Us"; "We Want None of Cooper's Lockout Conditions." But there are significant differences between Henderson in 1959 and the general textile strike of 1934 when flying squadrons of union leaders went from town to town calling out workers.

Twenty-five years ago the struggle was for union recognition. Today in Henderson, the TWUA is trying to hold what gains it has won at the two mills since they were organized 14 years ago. Less than 15 per cent of the Southern textile industry is organized.

The union has been providing the strikers with food since last winter. In recent weeks it has also been helping the strikers to pay their rent, to meet installments on stoves and refrigerators. . . .

"How am I doing?" asked Esther Robertson, the recording secretary of Local 578. "Look at me. I've gained 18 pounds since this thing started."

Another striker, Esther Johnson, said that many union members were eating better than they were before the strike.

The TWUA and other AFL-CIO unions are paying for the relief program, which . . . is now costing $25,000 a week. A well-balanced diet is provided, including some fresh vegetables and meat as well as such Southern staples as fatback and grits. One week toothpaste was distributed. . . .

Many other stories and articles were written about the strike during the Spring and Summer of 1959. Among them were: "You've Paid Plenty For Henderson Troops" by Jay Jenkins of *The Charlotte Observer*; "Textile Strike Could Be Test For Arbitration" by Roy Thompson of the *Winston-Salem Journal*.

On November 15, 1959, the *Durham Morning Herald* carried a headline: "Violence-Torn Henderson Strike Began Year Ago Tuesday"; and Charles Dunn wrote in part, as follows:

A year ago Tuesday . . . some 1,000 workers walked out of two textile mills.

Now—12 months later—most of the workers . . . have not returned to work in the mills . . . which have long since reopened.

The 12 months have had many ugly moments. Violence has flared on numerous occasions. Homes, automobiles, and even a nursery have been dynamited. North Carolina Highway Patrolmen have been called in to keep the peace, and National Guardsmen with bayonets have lined the streets. "But despite all its ugliness—the things one would never have believed could happen . . .—the year-old situation still exists.

. . . In the months that followed [the reopening of the mills], as all attempts to settle the strike failed, the names of many men were to be spread across newspapers in headlines, their pictures flashed on television screens, and their acts praised or condemned by thousands.

These characters in this labor-management drama included Gov. Luther H. Hodges who attempted to settle the strike and once appeared to have accomplished his goal, and who later called in the Highway Patrol and National Guard to protect people and property.

Then there was John D. Cooper . . . a historian with a fancy for Confederate Gen. Robert E. Lee, and once held in high esteem by his employees. And Boyd Payton . . . the soft-spoken man who conducted the strike for the union.

And there were others, Mayor Carrol Singleton of Henderson, Attorney General Malcolm Seawell, Judge Raymond Mallard who presided over court cases arising from the strike, and a host of others either on the side of the union or management or haplessly in the middle. . . .

. . . The mills continue to produce, union members—limited to eight by court order—continue to picket the mill gates, and police continue to guard against possible violence. . . .

The end of the year does not bring into sight the end of the strike-caused situation.

In April of 1960, Harry Conn, writing for Press Associates, Inc., said in part:

Striking Henderson textile workers—dedicated to trade unionism with a fierce and a spiritual devotion—will not let their union die.

By any law of reason or logic . . . [they] should have been crushed to the point that only mourning and memory remained. It hasn't happened. If anything they are more militant, more determined and more solid than they were a year ago.

The strike . . . is in its 17th month. It's a lockout now with three shifts of scabs, yet less than 100 of 1,038 original strikers have crossed the picket line.

The strikers have fought the state troopers and the national guard who escorted strike-breakers into the plants. Some 200 arrests have been made and about 40 strikers have served time "on-the-roads."

. . . Three international union representatives and five strikers have been convicted of a conspiracy to dynamite part of a strike-bound plant. They maintain their innocence and charge a frame-up. Their case is being appealed to the U. S. Supreme Court.

. . . . TWUA has contributed $750,000 to the strikers while the rest of the labor movement has donated about $230,000.

. . . The time has passed when union radio broadcasts—sometimes three and four a day—kept members abreast of the news. Now, the local unions publish a weekly mimeographed paper called *The Freedom Fighter*.

"I'd rather listen to those broadcasts than eat," commented one woman striker.

One of the consuming interests of the members is political action. . . . Edith Peoples, secretary of the clothing committee . . . probably spoke for all the strikers when she said: "If everybody had been through something like this there would be no need for political speeches. . . . I can see right clearly now, what we've got to do and that is to turn things upside down politically in this state."

Strike or no strike, members have contributed 100 per cent to COPE. Some of the women picked cotton and tobacco and did other back-breaking jobs to earn enough to spare a buck.

The union has found jobs for some members out of the state, particularly in New England. The strikers are pretty well blackballed within a 100- to 200-mile radius of Henderson.

On November 22, 1960, the *Winston-Salem Journal* carried a Henderson-dateline story by Roy Thompson under the headline, "Bitterness Evident, But Not Defeat." He said, in part:

The two-year old strike ... is rarely mentioned on downtown streets.

But at night, gathered around the stoves in Henderson's mill sections, lean and bitter men curse the company as lean and bitter women and big-eyed kids sit around and listen.

At 7 A.M. and 3 P.M. and 11 P.M.—through glaring summer heat and biting winter wind—they march before the mill gates and carry their signs of defiance: "We Have Just Begun To Fight;" "We Support The Constitution;" "Slavery Is Illegal."

Once they'd have shouted curses at the cars. Shouted curses and thrown rocks and thrown tacks. . . .

Now ... [there are] only looks. Looks of bitterness and hatred and fear.

But not looks of defeat.

Most of the rest of the world that has heard of Henderson's strike says these people are beaten and their strike is all over but for the occasional shouting at union hall.

These people don't know they're beaten. . . .

Families have split asunder because one brother went back into the mills ... while another stayed on the street outside and carried on the fight.

Men have gone to prison. Some won't be back for years.

Children have listened to their elders ... and have learned to hate their Governor and their Mayor and their State Highway Patrol and their National Guard and their courts— . . .

There was a time when most could have gone back to work in the mills. Approximately 100 did. That's about one in every ten.

Others took jobs elsewhere in Henderson. And some moved everything they owned to other towns and cities in search for a job. . . .

David George ... continues to talk the good fight. "Meetings of the local unions," he says, "are being well-attended."

More than 400—if one believes the union figures, or 250 if one prefers anti-union figures—strikers have chosen to fight their fight on the picket lines if it takes all their remaining summers.

The Biased Courts of Henderson

As previously recorded, Vance County Superior Court Judge, William Y. Bickett, had issued a sweeping restraining order on February 3, 1959, against the union, its officers, and almost all of its active members.

For "violations" of this order, a total of 35 men strikers and ten women strikers were arrested (two of them were arrested twice). Sixteen of them were fined $100 and costs; 22 were fined $150 and costs; and three were fined $250 and costs.

Total fines in these 47 cases were an even seven thousand dollars. In addition, 25 of the 47 were given active jail terms ranging from ten days to 30 days. The 25 served a total of 560 days in jail.

Strangely, not one strike-breaker, company supervisor, or company sympathizer was ever fined or given a jail sentence for violation of the order, although there were numerous instances in which they were directly and actively involved in acts which violated the order.

Even stranger and more significant, was the action in Recorder's Court where the son of the company's attorney was the solicitor (prosecutor). Here, a total of 90 cases were recorded between February 16th and May 1st, on charges ranging from "Use of Profane Language" to "Engage In A Riot" and "Assault With A Deadly Weapon."

Involved in these 90 cases were seven strike-breakers with a total of 13 charges; two company supervisors with four charges; and 29 union members with a total of 74 charges.

The seven strike-breakers were found "not guilty" on eight of the 13 charges; two of their charges were "non-suited." In the other two, a "guilty" verdict for speeding was rendered in one, while the other was disposed of with a notation, "pending further action"—whatever that means. In the three charges against the two supervisors, one received a "guilty" verdict for "Disorderly Conduct." The other one was found guilty of "Assault With A Deadly Weapon." However, in both cases, the record showed—"Sentence to be given later."

Of the 74 charges involving the 29 union members, two "not guilty" verdicts were rendered. Other "guilty" verdicts brought sentences as follows:

4 — 30 days on-the-roads
   1 — 60 days on-the-roads
   2 — 6 months on-the-roads
   2 — 8 months on-the-roads
   4 — 9 months on-the-roads
   1 — 10 months on-the-roads
   4 — 12 months on-the-roads
   1 — 21 months on-the-roads
   8 — Suspended sentence — placed on probation
   5 — Fined $50 and costs — placed on probation
   1 — Fined $100 and costs — placed on probation

Eighteen of the 74 charges were "pending" as of May 1, 1959.

One or two specific cases will furnish an interesting comparison between the treatment of union members and others:

A strike-breaker was charged with five distinct and separate counts of "Assault with a deadly weapon." The charges were preferred by 18 different people, including two police officers who also charged him with speeding. He was found "not guilty" on all except the speeding charge.

A supervisor forced his way into a union committee meeting with an open knife in his hand and began slashing in all directions. He was arrested and charged with "forcible trespass, disorderly conduct, and assault with a deadly weapon." He was found guilty on all counts and was fined $50 and costs.

In the next case heard that day, a union member, charged with "possessing pyrotechnics" (two firecrackers) was found guilty and given a 14-month suspended sentence and fined $100 and costs. He was placed on probation for three years. A few days later, when he was seen with a group of strikers who were peaceably walking down the street, he was arrested, charged with violation of probation, and "sent-to-the-roads" for 14 months.

In another case, a state employee who had no connection with the strike, except that his wife was a member of the union, saw a group of people on a street corner, stepped out of his car "to see if his wife was in the group," and was promptly arrested. He was charged with "inciting to riot" and was sentenced to prison.

On April 23, 1959, the North Carolina Legislature passed a

"special" piece of legislation—"designed to control violence in Vance County." It provided "arrest power" for national guardsmen and set up special court procedures to "handle cases evolving from strike activity." The Council of State authorized $10,000 for a special session of Vance Superior Court.

A special judge, Raymond B. Mallard, and a special solicitor, Jack Hooks, were named to conduct the special court, although at the time of this action, only four cases were awaiting Superior Court action.

On May 4, 1959, Judge Mallard opened the special term and 58 cases were promptly transferred from Recorder's Court to Superior Court. The special term continued for five weeks.

The Conspiracy Arrests

On Friday evening, June 12, 1959, after a strenuous week of strike activity, including a great amount of time spent with reporters and photographers from *Look* magazine, I drove to Charlotte to spend a quiet weekend with my family. Little did I realize how the events of this weekend would change my life.

Early Sunday morning, June 14, 1959, I received, a telephone call from Charlie Ranes, president of the Harriett local union at Henderson. He advised that some of the strikers had been arrested on Saturday evening, but no one was sure of the number, their names, the charges, or where they were being held. He was positive that they were not in the county jail.

I agreed to call one of the union's attorneys, James Randleman, at Elkin, North Carolina and ask him to go to Henderson to investigate and render such legal assistance as might be necessary.

After speaking to Randleman, and receiving his assurance that he would go to Henderson promptly, I accompanied my wife and daughters to Sunday school and church.

After lunch, I decided to visit a friend who lived a few miles north of Charlotte. I had been at my friend's home for only a few minutes when my wife called and said she had just had a call from the Charlotte police department asking that she have me call the desk sergeant as soon as possible.

Assuming that the call had something to do with the reported arrests in Henderson, I decided to return to my home before making the call rather than involve my friend and his family in the matter.

While riding back toward Charlotte, with the car windows open, a pleasant breeze blowing in, and the radio playing, my world went spinning as the announcer stopped the music and said:

> We interrupt this program to bring you a special news bulletin. Attorney General Seawell has just announced in Raleigh that warrants have been issued for the arrest of Textile Union Director Boyd Payton; his assistant in the Henderson strike situation, Lawrence Gore, and Charles Auslander, the manager of the unions at Leaksville, Draper, and Spray. Mr. Seawell said that the warrants charged conspiracy to commit violence in Vance County. He also announced the arrest of four local union members in Henderson in connection with the same case. These men were named as Warren Walker, Calvin Pegram, Charles Abbott, and Michael Jarrel. Keep tuned to this station for further details. We return you now to your Sunday afternoon musical program.

Well, to say I was stunned is putting it mildly. My mind raced with a dozen questions. What conspiracy? What violence? How?—When?—Where? Who were these local union men?

The only one whom I knew by name was Warren Walker. How could I be involved in a conspiracy with men I didn't know? As for Walker, I only knew him as one of many who were usually available and willing to assist in handling the grocery unloading and distribution. I remembered that his wife was a member of one of the strike committees. I remembered, too, that Walker had spoken strongly in opposition to one of the proposed compromises on contract terms. However, I couldn't remember having had any more personal contact with him. I couldn't place Pegram, Abbott, or Jarrel at all.

I began thinking about Seawell. I had threatened to sue him for libel and defamation of character in connection with his calling me, in effect, a liar. The actual notice of such suit had been served on him just a few days before. Was the conspiracy charge simply a counter-move on his part to place me in an embarrassing position and possibly make it difficult for me to press the suit against him?

Then there was the hearing before the McClellan committee which was scheduled to be held within a few days. It could bring some red faces to highly placed state officials if we were successful in verifying our suspicions as to the role of the state in the business of union-busting. Were the conspiracy arrests an attempt to block those hearings, or at least to cast doubt on the union's charges? If so, I thought, I have to admire his cleverness in seeking to "kill two birds with one stone."

By the time I had reached home I had convinced myself that the arrests were simply another "play" in the union-smashing game which was being enacted in Henderson by the textile mill owners and their friends in state government. I could not believe that any serious personal threat was involved, but I was greatly concerned about the effect upon Kitty and the kids.

They were waiting, with anxious faces, when I arrived. The call from the police department, coupled with the earlier call from Ranes, had them thinking of all kinds of dire consequences for the people in Henderson whom they had grown to love and be concerned about through their visits there with me in the seven months during which the strike had been in progress.

They had not heard the radio broadcast and did not know about my personal involvement. When I told them, they stared at me in disbelief and sat spellbound with white faces, choking back the tears. Then, as if by some signal, they crowded around and nearly smothered me with hugs, kisses and tears, and words of faith and love.

I called the desk sergeant. He said, "We received word just after noon that two agents of the State Bureau of Investigation were on their way from Raleigh with a warrant for your arrest. We thought we should try to spare you and your family from having an unpleasant scene at your home on Sunday afternoon, so we arranged for them to come to the police station. We promised that you would meet them here. Just stand by there, and we will call you when they arrive."

I called one of our local attorneys, James Ledford. He was shocked, but agreed with my reasoning that it was only a strategy move by Seawell and constituted only another obstacle in the struggle to preserve the union at Henderson. He, too, was more concerned about my family than he was about me. He said he would arrange for a professional bondsman to be present with him when I arrived at the police station.

I tried to call Auslander at his home in Greenville, South Carolina, but learned that he was en route to Hendersonville, North Carolina, where he was to serve on an arbitration panel on Monday.

Kitty had prepared a wonderful meal. Patsy thanked God "for the food and friends, and all the goodness He had sent." We all choked down a few bites, but soon abandoned the effort and sat quietly waiting for the phone to ring. When it did, we all jumped as if a gun had been discharged.

At the police station, SBI agent Davis read the warrant which charged me with conspiracy to destroy the sub-station of the Carolina Light and Power Company in Vance County and the boiler room of the Harriett mill in Henderson by use of dynamite, as well as to burn the company's main office. I was directed to appear in Recorder's Court in Henderson on the following Tuesday morning.

The desk sergeant said, "What about the amount of the bond? I wouldn't think it needs to be high in Mr. Payton's case."

Both agents kept their eyes on the floor as one of them said, "The boss said it should be $25,000."

The sergeant said, "That's ridiculous—totally unnecessary—clearly out of proportion to the nature of the charge and the character of the person involved."

Ledford was furious. He said, "I never heard of anything so outrageous. I've had clients who were charged with murder and only held under bond of five-thousand. This is nothing more nor less than pure vindictiveness."

The sergeant left the room muttering something like, "We'll just see about this." He returned in a few minutes, and said, "The bond will be ten thousand dollars—not a penny more—and that's twice what it should be."

When I returned home, I called the hotel in Hendersonville and left word for Auslander to call upon his arrival. In a few minutes, Rene Berthiaume, one of my staff members in South Carolina, called from the hotel in Hendersonville. He agreed to advise Auslander of my instructions to meet me in Henderson on Monday evening.

I worried about not being able to reach Gore because he was

moving that weekend and had no phone. I had visions of him being arrested and thrown in jail before any of us knew about it, but there was no way to contact him until he returned to his assignment in Henderson on Monday.

The *Charlotte Observer* of June 15, 1959, carried the story under the headline: "Payton Gives Self Up." The Associated Press headline said: "Payton Surrenders, Auslander and Gore Still At Large."

On Monday afternoon, Kitty and I drove to Henderson and were told by several union members, who had been posted by Attorney Randleman on different street corners to watch for our arrival, that I should go directly to the Henderson Motel where Randleman was waiting. They advised that the grand jury had indicted eight of us, with Johnnie Martin having been added to the previous list. Randleman was reported to be concerned about the possibility of my being seen by the police or one of the Sheriff's deputies, or by an SBI agent, and arrested and jailed in lieu of the $15,000 bond which the Grand Jury had determined as being the correct amount to ensure my appearance in Vance County Superior Court the next day.

When we met Randleman, he told us that when he had arrived in Henderson on Sunday, he went directly to the jail and was amazed to see National Guardsmen, with drawn bayonets, patrolling in front of the entrance and denying admission to all.

He said the jailer and a deputy sheriff, who were among the group outside, talked with him and told of being dispossessed early that morning by National Guardsmen who advised that they were operating under orders from the attorney general. He said that it was not until nine o'clock Sunday evening (more than 24 hours after the initial arrests) that he and the jailer were permitted to enter the jail where he saw Walker, Pegram, Abbott, and Jarrel.

They had just begun to tell him, he said, of the events of the previous night when SBI agents arrived and ordered him out. He said he had tried every way possible to see the prisoners later on Sunday evening and on Monday morning, but was not successful until Monday afternoon, after the grand jury had met and indicted the eight of us.

Randleman suggested that we go to the police station immediately and arrange for posting of bond to put an end to the "arrest-on-sight" order under which law enforcement officers were operating in regard to me.

A representative of the National Surety Company (with whom Randleman had arranged for bond) was waiting for us, and papers were quickly signed to guarantee my appearance in Superior Court on Tuesday, June 16, 1959, at 2:30 P.M. Bond was set at fifteen thousand dollars, bringing the total to that suggested by Mr. Seawell.

No one yet knew the details of the charges nor the nature of the "evidence." The attorneys were anxious for my appearance in Recorder's Court on Tuesday morning so that they might request a "Bill of Particulars." Strangely enough, I was the only one scheduled for appearance in Recorder's Court. The bond which had been posted for the local strikers called only for their appearance in Superior Court on Tuesday afternoon. When Gore and Auslander arrived later in the evening they too were placed under bond only for appearance in Superior Court.

When union attorney William Nicholson and I appeared in Recorder's Court on Tuesday morning, much whispering was in progress between the judge, several lawyers, and the solicitor (son of the company's chief attorney). The solicitor finally called Mr. Nicholson to his desk and whispered to him for awhile. Nicholson was arguing that I had paid $500 for a bond to ensure my appearance there and I should at least be furnished with a "Bill of Particulars" and given a preliminary hearing.

The solicitor stood up, spread his hands in a gesture of "I have no choice in the matter," and announced: "The case of Mr. Payton has been taken out of our jurisdiction by indictment of the grand jury. He is scheduled to appear in Superior Court at 2:30 this afternoon."

At 2:30, the eight of us appeared in Superior Court and were formally charged in three separate indictments: "(1) Conspiracy to dynamite the power sub-station of Carolina Light and Power Company; (2) conspiracy to destroy the boiler room of the South Henderson mill through the use of high explosives; and, (3) conspiracy to destroy the main office of the Harriett-

Henderson Cotton Mills by burning."

Judge Bickett (the resident judge who had issued the original injunction against the union on February 12th) announced that the case would be continued to the next term of Vance County Superior Court, *either regular or special*, and that the bond of $15,000 for each defendent would likewise be continued for their appearance at such term.

Naturally, all of us had dozens of questions to ask of each other, of the attorneys, and of John Chupka, the General Secretary-Treasurer of the International Union who had flown from New York to be present for what he thought would be the beginning of our trial.

Arrangements were made for use of a room at a hotel in Norlina, a few miles north, because of the impossibility of conducting any private discussion in Henderson with the great interest engendered by the arrests.

The discussion at Norlina produced the following points of information:

Chupka: We believe that the conspiracy arrests are nothing more nor less than a further attempt on the part of the Textile Industry and their friends in state government to completely destroy the Textile Workers Union of America in North Carolina. We believe, too, that this is only a part of the greater conspiracy of the Southern textile manufacturers to rid themselves of all union influence in this part of the country. We know that if the union is destroyed or substantially weakened here it will only be a matter of time until we are faced with the same thing throughout the entire South. Therefore, I want you to know that we consider this a life-and-death struggle and we are prepared to use the full resources of the union in your behalf. We are arranging for Arthur Goldberg, our Washington attorney, to head up your defense. He will be assisted by Dave Feller and Hugo Black, Jr., and whatever local attorneys may be required.

Nicholson: The situation may be a little more serious than first thought. I think I'd be doing less than my duty if I didn't point that out to you. North Carolina is one of the few states where no overt act is necessary to constitute conspiracy. The law provides that when two minds meet to discuss or plan unlawful acts of violence, that, in itself, constitutes conspiracy regardless of the fact that no violence ever occurs. It has been denounced by many prominent legal minds as a law which permits the arrest and conviction of citizens whom the state wants to put behind bars but can't find any legitimate reason for doing so. However, it is still the law, and we must recognize the seriousness of the situation in which you fellows are involved.

Randleman: I have to agree with what Nick has said, but I'd like to know more about what actually happened before we jump to any conclusions. Let's go around the room and let each one tell his part of the story.

Walker: Well, let me tell you what this is all about. Some of us have been meeting with this "screwball" named Aaron that Auslander sent over here from Leaksville. We've been doing a lot of drinkin' with him and we've been doing a lot of talkin' and the SBI has a tape recordin' of everything that's been said. The only way I can figger it out is that Aaron is an undercover agent for the SBI.

He came to my house about ten days ago and invited me to meet him that night at the Brookwood Motel in Roanoke Rapids to talk about stoppin' production in the mills. He said Auslander had sent him. He also said he would have a bottle. I said, "Sure, why not, I'm not doing anything else, and I could sure use a drink or two." He told me that he had talked with Johnnie but he wouldn't do anything except show him where I lived.

Later, Johnnie came over and told me that Aaron had called and changed the meeting place to the South Hill Motel. I went up there and spent the evening with him. He did a lot of crazy talkin' about some secret way he had of makin' high explosives and about things he had blown up. I thought he was kinda' "nuts" but his liquor was good, and I didn't mind listenin' as long as the drinks kept coming. When I was leavin' he asked me to meet him the next night at the Brookwood Motel in Roanoke Rapids and bring Gore with me.

Gore went with me the next night and we did a lot more drinkin' and a lot more talkin'. (They got that on a tape, Gore, but it didn't turn out too good. They tried to play it for me Saturday night and get me to say who was talkin' but it was just a big jumble and I couldn't tell anything about it.)

We agreed to meet him again the next night, but on the way back Gore decided that he was crazy and we shouldn't have anything more to do with him. So-o-o, we didn't go up the next night. He was real upset and tried to call Gore, but got Payton by mistake. Or, anyway, that's what Gore told me the next morning when he asked me to go with him to see Aaron. Gore was "burned up" because Aaron had talked to Payton. When we met Aaron, he was complaining about Auslander not givin' him enough money for expenses. He said he had to get back to Leaksville but didn't have enough money to pay his motel bill. Gore said he could lend him twenty dollars, and he could have Auslander send it to Payton and Payton would give it to Gore.

That must have been the 5th, I guess. I didn't hear anymore until last Thursday. I guess that was the 10th. He came by the house and asked me to meet him at the same room at the Brookwood Motel. He wanted me to bring Gore, but I told him Gore didn't want anything more to do with him. Anyway, Gore was goin' to Greensboro to move his family. He kept beggin' me to come and I finally agreed.

When I got there, he was drinkin' and talkin' crazier than ever about all the things he had blowed up, but he had plenty of liquor and I stayed for several hours and we both did a lot of talkin'. They got that on a tape, too. When I was leavin' he asked me to come back the next night and bring two or three "of my buddies" with me.

Friday, we were down at the Fish Fry and doin' a good bit of drinkin'. I told Abbott and Pegram about Aaron wantin' us to come up. They was all for it, but Mike was with us and he was pretty drunk. We didn't want to leave him down there and we didn't want to take him home. So, we put him in the back seat and took him with us. He passed out on the way up and we left him in the car. He woke up later and come staggerin' in, but he didn't know where he was. Aaron was talkin' about Molotov cocktails and dynamite, and how we could blow up the power plant and the boiler room, and what each one was supposed to do. We agreed with everything he was sayin' and added a little bit here and there. They got all of that on a tape, and it sounded pretty bad.

He wanted us to meet him at the truck stop Saturday night at eight o'clock. He told each one what we was to bring and what we was to do. Pegram was supposed to drive his car and have Abbott with him. They was supposed to bring dynamite. I was to drive my car and bring the Molotov cocktails. All of us was supposed to get in Aaron's car and go to the power sub-station. Mike was supposed to follow in my car.

Well, we laughed all the way back to Henderson about him and his plans, but we agreed that we'd meet him just to see what he would do. Mike, though, said count him out, he was goin' to the movies.

Anyway, on Saturday evening, I drove to the truck stop. Pegram and Abbott arrived a few minutes later. I walked over to them and all hell broke loose. It seemed like a dozen men came from all directions and grabbed us and started pulling and hauling at us and tellin' us we was under arrest.

They tore both cars apart lookin' for dynamite and Molotov cocktails, but couldn't find anything and kept gettin' madder at us and shovin' us around. That stinkin' Aaron was nowhere in sight.

They put handcuffs on us and drove us to the highway patrol station. They made us strip and turn our clothes inside out. Then they took us to the SBI headquarters at the Cardinal Motel. They took us in separate rooms and questioned us. First one agent and then another one. They played them tapes and tried to get us to say who was doin' the talkin' on the tapes. They tried to make us admit that it was our voices. This went on 'till about three o'clock in the morning. About two o'clock, they brought Mike in. Then, about four o'clock, they took us to the jail. That's about it. I guess everybody knows the rest.

Auslander: Well, this thing has really gotten "screwed up." Let me tell you my end of the story. Sometime about the end of May, I talked with Harold Aaron about the Henderson situation and asked him if he would be interested in coming to Henderson, getting a job in the mill, and reporting to the union on conditions—number of strike-breakers, quality and quantity of production, supervisors' remarks and so on. He was a member of our union in Leaksville, but was discharged a long time ago and has been unemployed.

He said that he might be interested but would have to come to Henderson and look the situation over before giving me a definite answer. He said he would need ten dollars for expense money and would need a couple of names as contacts. I gave him the ten dollars and a slip of paper with the names of Johnnie Martin and Warren Walker on it. However, I kept seeing him around town every day for the next week or so, but couldn't get him to stop and talk with me. I finally concluded that I had been "taken for a ride" and he had made an easy ten dollars.

The next thing I heard about it was when Payton called and raised the devil with me about promising motel expenses for him. I never promised him anything. I didn't even know he was up here and I certainly never talked to him about blowing up anything.

Martin: I don't know that I have anything to add. The way Warren told it is about the way it was. Aaron talked to me about stoppin' production. He didn't say how he was plannin' to do it, but I got the idea that he was talkin' about usin' dynamite, and I told him I didn't want anything to do with violence. I never saw him after that first day, but he called me two or three times to give a message to Warren. I wish I had never seen or heard of him.

Johnnie was visibly disturbed and on the verge on an emotional display. (He had been ill with a heart condition.) Mr. Chupka said, "I think we should bring this conference to a close. I think it is important that we don't start finding fault or placing blame at this time. It looks like some foolish things were done, but it won't help for us to start fighting among ourselves. We are all in this together and we must do everything possible to come out of it together. I would suggest that we break it up now. Each of you go your own way and don't discuss this outside of this group. We will call you all together from time to time and keep you advised of developments."

On June 23, 1959, the chief justice of the North Carolina Supreme Court ordered that a special term of the Vance County Superior Court be held on July 13 for the purpose of trying the defendants. To preside at this special term, the chief justice appointed neither the judge who was regularly assigned for that judicial district for the regular term which was due to end on June 30, nor the resident Superior Court judge who had been assigned for the term which was to begin in October. Instead, Judge Raymond Mallard from the 13th Judicial District near the South Carolina border was appointed (The same judge who had just completed a special term in Vance County which is briefly described on page 52.)

Defense Attorneys

For the purpose of reviewing the facts and attempting to prepare defense arguments, the eight defendants met with attorneys either in a group or separately, on several occasions between June 16th and July 12th.

In addition to Arthur Goldberg and his assistant, David Feller, both of Washington, the list of attorneys retained by the union now included Hugo Black, Jr., of Birmingham, Alabama (son of U. S. Supreme Court Justice Black); William Nicholson, James Ledford, and Glen Ledford of Charlotte; and, James Randleman of Elkin, North Carolina.

Goldberg had assigned each of the attorneys to particular angles or aspects of the case and they were concentrating on review and study of cases involving these aspects which had been decided by the courts.

In order to secure a complete review of the situation a conference of all defendants, all attorneys, and TWUA Secretary John Chupka was held in Goldberg's Washington office on July 10th. As each one reported and was questioned by Goldberg and Chupka, an atmosphere of optimism developed and everyone began losing the worried look which he had carried for the month. Goldberg congratulated the attorneys on the work they had done and said he was satisfied with the preparation of the defense case. He said, "I think we have covered every possible angle. The only deficiency I can see is our failure to secure the services of an attorney from the Henderson area."

Nicholson reported on his effort to engage an attorney from Henderson and expressed the opinion that "local power pressures" were responsible for the failure.

Goldberg urged that efforts be continued to find, if not an attorney from Henderson, then one who was competent and well-known from the general area.

Someone named Hill Yarborough from the adjoining county of Franklin as the most competent in the area, but the consensus of opinion was that he would not accept because his brother was a member of the state legislature. Goldberg said, "Contact him as soon as you get back to North Carolina. Nothing beats a trial except failure."

* * * * *

Our wonderful neighbors on Wentworth Place in Charlotte began arriving early on Sunday, July 12th, to give us their best wishes, to assure us of their faith and confidence, and to pledge their support in any way possible, including appearing at the trial in a body to testify in my behalf.

We assured them of our gratitude for their concern and loyalty, but explained that we were confident of complete vindication and felt it would not be necessary to involve them.

After a family conference in which my daughters won their argument that all three should attend the trial with their mother, the five of us began the 200-mile trip to Henderson.

We were in good spirits and full of a special kind of warm and close feeling toward each other. Our family auto trips had always been pleasant and full of fun. This one was no exception. We laughed and joked and expressed little concern about the reason for this trip. Certainly, none of us could have imagined the unbelievable experiences with which we were to be faced during the coming ten days.

We arrived at the Vance Hotel about 6 P.M. and had supper with the Gore and Auslander families. A number of the strikers came by while we were eating to reassure us of their faith and to express their feeling of confidence in the outcome of the trial.

Soon after Kitty and I had returned to our room, about 8:15, the phone rang. Kitty answered and, with an expression of shock, handed the phone to me as she whispered, "Floyd Bowman wants to talk to you."

Cloak and Dagger Interlude

Floyd Bowman was a mysterious character who had appeared on the Henderson scene a few nights before the back-to-work movement was launched in February. He and/or his car with a Virginia license plate had been repeatedly reported as being near each incident of confrontation between strike-breakers and strikers, between police and workers, or between union sympathizers and company sympathizers. Our investigation of his background had revealed him as a former police officer in several Virginia towns. Reports were to the effect that he had served as the chief recruiter of strike-breakers for Harriett-Henderson Mills during its campaign to replace the striking former employees.

I was as surprised as my wife had been and couldn't believe it was really Bowman until he started talking. He said, "Mr. Payton, I've been wanting to talk to you ever since your arrest. I just heard a few minutes ago that you were in town and thought I'd call you."

"What did you want to talk to me about?" I asked.

He said, "Well, I can't discuss it over the phone. But I'd surely like to see you before your trial starts. I believe I have information which will be of great importance to you in your trial."

I said, "All right. Do you want to come to the hotel now?"

"Oh, no. I can't do that, I'm on duty at the South Henderson mill. How about you coming out here—alone? I'll meet you at the rear gate, near the mill office, at 9:30. You know where it is," he replied.

This was a real shocker to me. My mind raced with a dozen thoughts and questions, but uppermost was the fact that he was probably the one person who would know about the secrets which might be involved in our trial. I felt that I had to explore the matter further. So, filled with dread about going alone to the dark and lonely spot which he had designated, and full of suspicion about a possible trick, I nevertheless said, "Okay, I'll meet you at the rear gate at 9:30."

I called Dave George, my chief assistant in the strike situation and a long-time personal friend, and Jimmy Blackwell, the union's public relations director for the South.

Jimmy was strongly opposed to my keeping the date with Bowman. He was confident that it was some kind of trick which was designed to cause us more trouble rather than help us in any way.

Dave's greatest concern was for my personal safety. However, he agreed with my reasoning that the matter should be explored, and the only way to do that was to be at the rear gate at 9:30. He suggested that we call Charlie Ranes, local union president, and ask him to bring his son, Harold, a former city policeman, to drive me to the meeting place.

When Harold was told the story, he was strongly opposed to my going. He said, "They are guarding the mill with 30/30 rifles and they would like nothing better than an excuse for shooting you down like a dog. I won't have anything to do with it unless we tell the 'law' about it before we go."

It was decided that the two Raneses would take me to the home of Sergeant Cook of the state police and tell him the story. Cook's home was near the South Henderson mill. However, Cook suggested that the National Guard be advised, since all responsibility for "law and order" had been given to the Guard.

As we were leaving Cook's home at approximately 9:25, a National Guard patrol jeep was driving by, and we signaled them to stop. When the story was repeated to the three Guardsmen, they offered to drive me to the "appointment" but, feeling that this would defeat our purpose, I asked them to drive around the mill and be coming by the rear gate in about five minutes. They agreed.

With Harold driving his father's car, Charlie beside him, and me on the back seat, we drove to the rear gate and saw Bowman standing inside the wire fence in the shadow of some giant shrubbery. The car was parked opposite the gate, about thirty feet away from Bowman. Harold and Charlie remained in the car as I approached the gate with shaking knees, hesitant steps, and visions of rifle barrels pointing at me through the foliage.

Bowman swung the gate open, extended his hand, and said, "Come right in, Mr. Payton."

I said, "Oh, no. I'm not coming on company property. You can talk to me here. What did you want to tell me?"

"I have a lot to tell you, but you'll have to come inside. I can't keep standing out here," he replied.

The jeep rounded the corner and its headlights shone directly on Bowman standing in the open gateway and me standing a few feet outside. Bowman quickly pulled the gate shut and, looking past me at the approaching jeep, said, "I heard you are interested in getting information about quality and quanity of production in the mills."

I could have laughed at the irony in this remark if I had not been so scared. I said, "That was two months ago. It's rather late for that now. We have a few other problems."

Realizing that his last words could not have indicated the real reason for his call to me and convinced that a trap had been laid for me, I began backing away as the Jeep passed behind me.

Bowman called, "Think it over and call me Tuesday evening at the mill office. If you want that information, I can get it for you."

The Jeep had stopped some fifty feet below the gate at the entrance to the street. As we came alongside one of the Guardsmen called, "Everything all right, Mr. Payton?"

I said, "Yes, thank you very much."

As we drove into the street, all three of us heaved a great sigh of relief.

When we were back at the hotel and had discussed the incident, there was no doubt in any of our minds but that the call from Bowman had been part of an attempt to ensnare me, and that the appearance of the Jeep had crossed-up the well-laid plans. All were agreed that this was the first opportunity to tie-in the company to the promotion of the conspiracy charges and the first chance to confirm our suspicions that the company had much control over law enforcement and the courts in Vance County.

It was agreed that if newspapers carried the story of a company attempt to lure me onto company property it would support our contention that the conspiracy charges were a clear case of deliberate entrapment.

Blackwell quickly prepared a news release to be issued by either Chupka or Nicholson and we drove to the Lakeside Motel, some twenty miles away, where Chupka and the lawyers had obtained lodging for the sake of privacy and to be free of the "martial law" atmosphere existing in Henderson.

To our surprise and consternation, the attorneys expressed opposition to releasing the story to news media. In fact, Hugo was violently opposed and argued strongly that any publicity on the matter would only create an issue "extraneous to the trial proceedings" which would make our defense more difficult.

We could not understand his reasoning and argued just as strongly in favor of issuing the news release. However, Chupka finally said, "I suppose its up to me to settle this. I can see good points on both sides of the argument, but I know how hard the lawyers have been working to perfect their strategy for tomorrow morning, and I have to agree with Hugo that to have a new and unpredictable issue to deal with may force last-minute changes in plans and do us more harm than good. There is no point in hiring lawyers if we don't follow their advice. I think we should hold the release at least until we see what develops tomorrow."

The return trip to Henderson was driven in almost complete silence as each of us was engrossed in feelings of disappointment and frustration.

The Special Court

As court-time approached on the morning of Monday, July 13th, National Guardsmen patrolled the streets with fixed bayonets and the power to arrest civilians.

The courtroom was packed an hour before court was due to begin and a large crowd milled about the entrance.

Numerous police officers and sheriff's deputies, with guns and police clubs in view, circulated through the crowd and moved up and down the aisles of the courtroom.

Newspaper reporters and radio and television newsmen, along with their photographers, were much in evidence.

A *special* agent of the State Bureau of Investigation had been named to serve as bodyguard for the *special* judge.

A *special* solicitor (prosecutor) named Jack Hooks had been assigned to present the state's case. He was to be assisted by the regular solicitor, W. H. S. Burgwyn, Jr. Sitting with the two solicitors at the prosecution table, near the jury box, were three attorneys employed by the Harriett-Henderson mills. They were Robert S. Hight and Arthur A. Bunn of Henderson, and Charles Green of Franklin County. Their table was on the right side, facing the judge's bench.

Ralph Moody, assistant to State Attorney General Seawell, was also present and sat near the judge's bench with numerous papers and law books, but advised newsmen that he was "just a tourist."

Sitting at the defense table, on the left side facing the judge's bench, were attorneys William Nicholson, James Ledford, James Randleman. The union attorneys, David Feller and Hugo Black, Jr., sat on the front row of the spectators' seats.

The sheriff directed the eight defendants to take places on the side, to the left of the defense attorneys and facing the jury box rather than the judge's bench.

The old and dingy courtroom was very uncomfortable as two large, overhead fans lazily stirred the hot air.

The sheriff shuffled to the front of the room and intoned, "The special term of Vance County Superior Court is now in session. The honorable Raymond Mallard presiding. Everybody rise."

The judge took his place behind the bench and spent some time arranging papers. He then peered intently out over the courtroom, looked down at the attorneys, nodded several times, and glared at the defendants for several seconds.

It quickly became obvious that he felt a compulsion to verify newspaper stories which had described him as "a stern judge who demands an orderly courtroom" as he grimly launched into a recitation of the rules which would be in effect during the trial and the punishment which he would impose upon anyone violating those rules. His concluding words were: *"And that goes for every man, every woman, and every child within the sound of my voice."*

A few minutes later as he was conferring with defense attorneys, he angrily declared in a voice which carried throughout the courtroom, "If Payton says anything on the radio that can remotely be construed as criticism of this court, I will hold him in contempt and put him where none of you can find him."

Defense attorneys announced that they wished to present

several motions and desired the Court's instructions as to procedure. The judge snapped, "You can make all the motions you want to, but I want all of them before me at one time. I'm not going to rule on them on a piecemeal basis."

Counsel for the defendants filed the following motions:

1. A Plea in Abatement—asking that the charge of conspiracy be withdrawn on the grounds that no conspiracy had existed except that which was under control of the State Bureau of Investigation. Consequently, no unlawful activity could have occurred except by direction of the SBI.

2. That a Bill of Particulars be furnished to defense counsel as to the charges and the evidence upon which the grand jury indictment was based.

3. For a severance of the cases on the grounds that the defendants believed the state would attempt to introduce into evidence statements and/or reports which would be admissable only as to one or more of the defendants but which would prejudice the jury against all.

4. For a change of venue on the grounds that the defendants could not secure a fair trial in Vance County because of the bias and prejudice existing there as a result of the strike, the great amount of publicity, and the fact that the union could not obtain the services of a lawyer from Vance County.

The plea in abatement was denied; the motion for a Bill of Particulars was granted in part; the motion for severance was denied. On the motion for a change in venue, the judge called my name and ordered me to stand up. He asked me if I thought I could get a fair trial in Vance County.

When I replied, "No," he called each of the other defendants and asked the same question of each. When they had echoed my answer, he quoted from the General Statutes of North Carolina to the effect that the trial judge had authority to either move the location of the trial to another county or order the jury drawn from a different county.

He then directed counsel for the defendants to confer with the solicitor as to the county from which a jury could be selected because he did not intend to move the trial.

The reason for attorney Green's presence at the prosecution table became obvious as the solicitor promptly suggested that the jury be drawn from Franklin County and, although defense counsel argued that the same conditions existed in Franklin as had caused the question of a fair trial to be raised regarding Vance, the judge supported the solicitor.

The panel of prospective jurymen from Vance was discharged and a panel of 100 was summoned from Franklin. Court was recessed until Tuesday morning.

* * * * *

It was raining when we were leaving the courthouse and I asked my wife and daughters to wait until I brought the car from the service station across the street.

Two men in National Guard uniforms followed me across the street and into the little office. One of them introduced himself as Captain Pinnix and asked, "Do you mind if I ask you a few questions?"

When I said, "Not at all," he said, "Were you at the rear gate of the South Henderson mill last night about 9:30?"

I admitted that I had been there. He said, "Whom did you see there?"

I said, "I saw Floyd Bowman." I then related the full story.

When I had finished, the captain said, "Sergeant Cook called me after you had talked with him. He told me the story and said you were coming to see me. I didn't know why you hadn't come until the patrol boys made their report. I faced Bowman with it this morning. He's working for the company as a security guard. I told him he wasn't making my job any easier. I explained that the responsibility for maintaining law and order had been given to the Guard and, to me, that meant protecting Boyd Payton as well as John D. Cooper or any other person.

"At first, he denied that you had been there, but later admitted that you came to the gate and he talked to you through the fence. He denied that he had opened the gate, but my boys say they saw him standing in the open gateway. Would you state whether or not the gate was open?"

"I saw Bowman unlock the gate and I saw him swing it open," I replied.

"Will you testify to that if I get a formal investigation?" he asked.

I said, "I certainly will, and I'm sure that Charlie and Harold will, too. They were only 20 or 30 feet away."

The captain shook hands with me and thanked me. As he turned to leave, he said, "The wisest thing you ever did was to refuse to step on company property. I don't know what Bowman had in mind, but I feel sure that it wouldn't have been good for you if you had gone through that gate."

(I was never asked to appear at any hearing on this matter. No publicity was ever given to the incident and many of those involved felt that this was one of the gravest mistakes made in the entire affair.)

* * * * *

My wife and daughters were full of questions about my conversation with the Guardsmen which they had witnessed from the courthouse steps.

When I had completed the report to them, Kitty said, "Now, let me tell you about our experience. Mr. Nicholson came to me in the courthouse and said the judge was complaining because we were in the courtroom. He told me that the judge had said you had us there only to get the sympathy of the jury. I asked Nick if he thought we should leave. He said, 'Not on your life—would he rather see a family of hoodlums?' "

This affected me deeply. The love and devotion of my family has always been my prized possession. To be accused of "using" my family for personal motives was about the cruelest charge that I could imagine.

* * * * *

When court convened the next morning, with Attorneys Hill Yarborough, David Feller, and Hugo Black, Jr. at the defense table, it quickly became apparent that our objections to Franklin County had been well-founded as one prospective juryman after another was quickly disqualified because he had relatives working as strike-breakers in the Henderson mills; or had formed and expressed opinions as to the guilt of the defendants; or was otherwise unacceptable. The State automatically disqualified all who appeared to have any remote connection with unions or had been known to have any sympathies with the union's position in the strike. Defense lawyers naturally tried to exclude all who were known to have relatives working as strike-breakers or had expressed strong anti-union feelings.

As it became clear that the original panel of 100 would be exhausted long before the necessary dozen had been selected, the judge ordered an additional panel of 60 to be summoned.

During the examination of prospective jurymen, a remark by one caused the young daughter of Lawrence Gore to snicker. The judge stopped the proceedings, delivered a stern lecture to the spectators, and instructed the bailiffs to find the one who had caused the "disturbance" and bring him to the bench. The bailiffs roamed up and down the aisles and intently surveyed the faces in each row as everyone sat mute. When the culprit could not be identified, the judge warned that any further "interference with the work of the court" would result in more restrictive regulations.

* * * * *

When court recessed for lunch on Tuesday, my 13-year-old daughter, Nancy, waited for me as I stepped down from the "prisoner's box," and we walked from the nearly empty courtroom with our arms around each other's waist.

During lunch at the Vance Hotel, Attorney Feller informed us that when Nancy and I were walking together out of the courtroom, the judge had called to him, and had said, "See that—that's what I was talking about yesterday. He knows she's cute and he's just using her. But I'm too smart for him. I'll hold everyone in their places at the end of each session until the jury has left the building. They'll never see him with his family."

This spoiled my lunch completely. Nothing that had occurred in this unbelievable situation had depressed me as much as the news of the judge's attitude concerning my family. To demonstrate affection for each other had always been as natural in our family as eating or breathing, and to have this construed as a special "show" for this occasion was just too much. I could not believe that anyone could demonstrate such prejudice. It was most disturbing, to say the least, to realize that my fate in the trial was to rest in large part on this type of thinking.

A significant contrast was furnished during the trial when the judge's daughter, along with several of her classmates and an instructor from Meredith College, sat in the front row of the courtroom and, during a recess, photographers took pictures of her in an affectionate pose with her father at the bench while the wives and children of the defendants sat in awed silence and watched. My family could well appreciate his obvious pride in his lovely daughter, but it did nothing to relieve the pain of his reported remarks about them.

* * * * *

The original panel of 100 as well as the additional panel of 60 were both largely exhausted before noon on Wednesday with only five places having been filled. The judge was becoming even more irritable than previously demonstrated. As the question of still further panels being required was being discussed, a controversy developed which set the tone for the entire conduct of the trial.

As additional panels were being summoned, the Franklin County sheriff was apparently having difficulty in assembling the full panel requested. Because of this, the judge had requested an agreement from defense counsel which would permit questioning of prospective jurymen as they arrived without waiting for the full panel to be filled. They agreed to this. However, when he asked them to waive the sheriff's return certifying that the prospective jurymen were actually residents of Franklin County, they refused.

The judge called a recess and ordered counsel for the defendants to meet him in the clerk's office. There, according to a later report from those present in the clerk's office, he charged Mr. Yarborough with having breached his agreement concerning the certification. He ordered the reporter to make a special record of the matter and stated that he would report it to the North Carolina State Bar. He then charged that the attorneys for the defendants had failed to introduce Mr. Black in the proper manner and said that perhaps Mr. Black thought he was too big to require introduction to the court in the proper manner.

Mr. Black quickly assured the judge that he certainly did not feel that he was entitled to any special consideration and had not intended to violate the rules of the court. As the judge was turning to leave, he turned back, and said, "Not a single one of you have denied that Mr. Yarborough breached his agreement. If you want to be sons-of-bitches, then I can be a bigger son-of-a-bitch than all of you put together."

Additional panels of 60 and 35 were summoned to report on Thursday. Newspapers predicted that jury selection would be completed on Thursday because both sides would have used all of their challenges.

An episode occurred on Thursday which demonstrated that the judge's iron hand extended even beyond the walls of the courthouse.

A team of tree surgeons was cutting limbs from a tree near the courthouse and the noise from a power saw could be heard in the courtroom. The judge sent word that the noise should stop. The word came back to the judge that the saw operator had questioned whether the judge had power outside of the courtroom.

"Listen," the judge exploded, "if he goes back up that tree with that saw, he'd better take a lawyer with him because he'll need him when he comes down."

* * * * *

The 12-man jury, approved by both sides, was finally seated at 5:05 P.M. on Thursday. A fifth panel of 35 was summoned to report on Friday from which two alternates were to be selected. The full jury was empaneled at 11:15 A.M. on Friday, July 18th. Although the judge had given, as one of the reasons for using Franklin County jurymen that he wanted the members of the jury to be able to go home each night, he promptly announced to the newly empaneled jury that they would not be permitted to go home for the duration of the trial; would be quartered at the Little Hotel in Henderson; would be under constant guard of police Captains, J. W. Bowen and J. R. Wilkerson; would not be permitted to read newspapers, listen to the radio, or watch television; and, were prohibited from discussing the case among themselves or with anyone else.

The judge also announced that all spectators were prohibited from being in the hallways or on the steps used by the jurymen at the opening and closing of each session, and that all those in the courtroom were to remain in their seats until the jury had been escorted from the building at the close of each session.

To the bailiffs, he said, "I want you to keep a close watch and report to me if anyone so much as looks twice at a juror."

As the jurors were marched from the courtroom for the noon recess they looked even more dejected and browbeaten than the sick-at-heart defendants.

The entire atmosphere was one of extreme tension in which the judge plainly regarded himself as engaged in a contest with counsel for the defendants who represented all of the evil forces, while he was the defender of all that was right and good.

In this climate of apprehension, intimidation, awe and dread, the first witness was called at 2:10 P.M. on Friday. Apart from formal witnesses and corroborating testimony based on phone company records, the State's "evidence" consisted principally of testimony by various agents of the State Bureau of Investigation, and the testimony of one Harold Elzie Aaron who was finally identified in open court as a paid undercover agent of the SBI.

Aaron's testimony was largely based on notes which he admitted, on cross-examination, had been prepared in Raleigh, and to which he then had "added to and took away."

Walker, Pegram, Abbott, Jarrel, and Gore were implicated by Aaron's testimony that they had visited him at the Brookwood Motel in Roanoke Rapids, and their conversations had been recorded by SBI agents who had been secreted in an adjoining room.

Martin's implication came through Aaron's testimony that he had furnished directions to Walker's home and had delivered messages from Aaron to Walker.

Auslander was implicated by a conversation which Aaron had with him which, according to Aaron's story, had to do with damaging the Henderson mills but, according to Auslander, had to do only with Aaron getting a job in the struck mills to act as an informer for the union.

My implication came from Aaron's testimony that on June 4th, when he was trying to reach Gore by long distance telephone at the Vance Hotel, he was connected with me by mistake. He testified that when he had said, "This is the boy from Leaksville," I had said, "I know—don't say too much over this phone, it's going through a switchboard."

The State contended that this proved I had knowledge of the conspiracy which, according to the State, had been laid in Aaron's motel room. The State contended further that I had promoted that conspiracy by having Gore deliver twenty dollars to Aaron which [Aaron] said was the purpose of his call to Gore.

Cross-examination of State witnesses established that I was not registered at the hotel on June 4th; that telephone company records showed that Gore (not Payton) had talked on the call from Aaron; and that the twenty dollars was loaned by Gore to Aaron after specific plans were made for its repayment to Gore.

Actually, for the reader's clarification, the facts, as far as I was concerned were these:

(1) Auslander had suggested in April that we should have someone in the mills to give us information the same as the company had spies in our meetings. When I said that we had been unable to follow usual practice in this regard because of the strong feelings about strike-breakers among local workers, he suggested that he could probably get someone from Leaksville. Later, he had sent word that he thought he had found one or two who might be willing to fill our needs in this regard.

(2) Despite the telephone company records and the testimony of the hotel clerk that I was not registered on June 4th, *it was I* who answered the phone in the hotel room which we were using as an office. I *did* speak to a man who identified himself as "the boy from Leaksville." *I did say*—"I know." And *I did say*, "Don't say too much over this phone—it is going through a switchboard," just as we had been saying to everyone who called, because the telephone system was owned by the owners of Harriett-Henderson mills and we had reason to believe that our calls were being monitored.

(3) *I did* inform Gore about the call. Gore said, "That fellow is a real screwball. I'll go up to see him and tell him to go back to Leaksville and stay there." Later, Gore reported that he had talked with "that screwball," and he had asked to borrow

twenty dollars so he could return home. Gore said, "I loaned him the twenty but told him I'd have to get it back the first of the week because I would need it to move my family. He promised to send it to me through Auslander."

During cross-examination of Aaron, he admitted to having a police record in Rockingham County which included the following:

Case #6143 — Simple Assault; guilty, fined $10 and costs.
   #6144 — Profane and Indecent Language; guilty, 30 days "on-the-roads." (Sentence suspended on condition that he not be found in the state for a period of two years.)
   #6145 — Assault With Deadly Weapon; guilty, 12 months "on-the-roads" and fined $25 and costs. (Road sentence suspended on condition that he not be found in the state for a period of two years.)
   #9121 — Speeding; guilty, pay costs of $14.50.
   #9711 — Public Drunkenness and Assault; guilty, 60 days "on-the-roads."
   #9771 — Drunken and Reckless Driving; guilty, 6 months "on-the-roads."
   #9870 — Impersonating a Peace Officer; guilty, 60 days "on-the-roads."
   #9872 — Hit and Run; guilty, 4 months "on-the-roads."
   #9873 — Auto Theft; held under $2,000 bond for grand jury action.

Also established during cross-examination were the following:

(1) Aaron's room at the Brookwood Motel was reserved for him by SBI agents from June 3 to June 14. (2) He was free to use it at his will during that period. (3) Aaron had visited the Raleigh office of attorney general Seawell on June 11; had spent approximately 45 minutes there; had talked with the attorney general and received instructions from him; and, had driven directly to the Brookwood Motel from Seawell's office.

Much of the testimony of the other agents concerned statements made by Walker, Abbott, and Jarrel following their arrests. Such statements, if admissable at all, were admissable only against the persons making them, but the special prosecutor insisted in phrasing his questions in terms of—"What did he say next?" or, "What happened then?" This procedure blocked any objection by defense counsel until after the witness had answered and the jury had heard the inadmissable "evidence."

Defense counsel then requested the judge to instruct the witness to limit his testimony to the person making the statement being quoted or being referred to. The judge refused.

The defendants were thus reduced to motions to strike the testimony. The judge would, in most cases, dutifully intone: "Gentlemen of the jury, you will not consider the last statement of the witness. Dismiss it from your minds."

This occurred time after time until it would have required the mind of an Einstein to determine what was supposed to be retained in the minds of the jurymen and what was supposed to be dismissed. The Solicitor aggravated this situation on at least one occasion when he had the court reporter read back to the jury a prejudicial statement which the judge had just ordered the jury to dismiss from their minds.

During all of this, the judge kept defense counsel under constant threat of punishment for contempt. Counsel for defendants were spoken to sharply for stating grounds for objections, for rising when speaking, for verbally agreeing with the judge, for asking a witness on cross-examination for a "yes or no" answer, and for repeating the answer which a witness had given.

After the testimony adduced by the State on Friday and Saturday, in which tape recordings were mentioned on several occasions, it became apparent that these recordings were to be made a vital part of the trial proceedings even though everyone was agreed that the use of such recordings as "evidence" had been declared illegal by the Supreme Court of the United States.

On Monday morning, defense counsel made a motion that the State be required to produce the tapes referred to for inspection of counsel for defendants. The judge did not rule on the motion, but ordered defense counsel to confer with him at the bench. There, according to a later report of defense counsel, the judge said, "If you will stipulate that the defendants will not object to the introduction of a transcript of the tape recordings, and will waive any objection which they might have to the use of such a transcript instead of the recordings, I will request the State to let you read (but not keep) a copy of the transcript. Further, if you are concerned about the accuracy of the transcript, I will have the tapes played for you so that you can verify the accuracy for yourselves. In fact, in order to facilitate the comparison, I will get the copy from my car which the State furnished me, but which I haven't read."

Counsel for the defendants agreed to this procedure and court was recessed for this purpose. However, before the operation was concluded, a controversy developed when defense counsel refused to divide their forces so the trial and the tape inspection could both proceed at the same time. The judge ordered the trial to continue "with or without all of the defense attorneys."

The SBI agent who had made the tape recordings was called to the stand. He carried the tapes and the recording machine. The special solicitor instructed him to open the machine and explain how it worked. Defense attorneys objected to this display before the jury, but the judge overruled their objections. The witness continued his discourse on how the machine worked and how he had made the tapes in a room of the Brookwood Motel. While talking, he kept tossing the tapes from one hand to the other in the manner of dangling bait before hungry fish.

The special prosecutor then played his "ace card," as he said, "I have heard these recordings. They contain some matters which are not competent in evidence, but *we offer here the tapes and recordings. We offer them for use by the defendants if they desire, and we offer them in evidence to support the witnesses in this case who have testified about these matters.*" (Emphasis supplied by author.)

Attorneys for the defendants were stunned by this arrogant and audacious move. They realized that the purpose of the prosecutor's action was to force the defendants to object to the introduction of the tapes *in the presence of the jury*. They recognized that such objection would appear to the jurymen as withholding evidence.

After a whispered conference at the defense table, the motion was made objecting to the introduction of the tapes.

The motion was, naturally, promptly sustained by the judge while the faces at the prosecution table wore satisfied smiles.

Defense counsel moved for a mistrial on the ground that the entire performance was for the purpose of prejudicing the defendants' case by forcing them to object to the introduction of evidence which the State knew to be incompetent and had so stated. The motion was denied.

After a brief whispered conference at the prosecution table, the special solicitor said, "Your Honor, that concludes the State's case. The State rests."

For the second time in the matter of less than an hour, a bombshell had been dropped. No one had expected this development.

The defendants were faced with a decision as to whether any of them should take the stand in their own defense.

Uppermost in our minds and in the minds of our attorneys was the mistreatment of union-minded witnesses which had been experienced in this same court during the previous special term in which this same special judge and this same special solicitor had operated to convict all union sympathizers, plus the animosity shown toward the defendants and their attorneys during this special session.

In addition, our attorneys expressed the opinion that the State had failed to prove its case. Finally, they explained that our failure to present any witnesses would give us the right to both the opening and the closing arguments to the jury.

The decision was made to present no witnesses.

Defense counsel filed motions for non-suit and another one for mistrial. When these were denied, they made a motion for dismissal of the charges against Jarrel and me. They argued that, if any conspiracy existed, the evidence showed that Jarrel was not wanted in it and that no evidence had been presented to show that I had participated in it.

All defense motions were denied and final arguments to the jury were begun.

Defense counsel sought to show that no conspiracy had existed except that which was planned, promoted, and controlled by agents of the State Bureau of Investigation; that no violence or damage of any kind had occurred; that when the

SBI had arrested the men who, according to the State's chief witness, were on their way to perform acts of violence, not a single piece of evidence could be found to indicate that they were prepared, or had any intention, of committing any unlawful act; that Aaron was an unreliable witness who had a long record of law violations; and that he had demonstrated a yearning to "play policeman."

State and company-paid attorneys left no stone unturned to vilify the defendants. Although North Carolina law prohibits the prosecutor from commenting on the failure of defendants to testify, the argument of Solicitor Hooks before the jury included the following:

1. Nobody contradicted the witnesses for the State except the lawyers for the defendants.

2. Defendants were perfectly willing to talk until their out-of-state counsel got hold of them.

3. The defendants only denied the State's evidence by a plea of "not guilty."

4. Everyone who was in the conversations that made the conspiracy has testified but the defendants.

Attorney Green (company-paid) explained in great detail how Molotov cocktails are made and the effect of their use. Then he carefully explained how it had been named for the Russian leader by that name. "Molotov, Molotov, Molotov," he repeated, over and over, sometimes in a bare whisper and sometimes in loud and angry tones.

Finally, he stepped to the side of the jury box and turned, facing the defendants. His eyes roamed up and down the line of defendant faces for several seconds before he said, "Now, gentlemen of the jury, I want you to look at these men and decide, in your own minds, which one you think might have visited Russia and learned about Molotov cocktails." As he spoke, he kept wagging his forefinger at each one as his gaze moved from one to the other. However, when he came to me, he paused dramatically and held his finger steady, as he said, "Yes, gentlemen, I guess you picked the same one that I did."

He then launched into a denunciation of my character, belittled my church work, and labeled me a "wolf in sheep's clothing who professes to be a Christian but sneaks around in the dark of night planning to dynamite a power sub-station with never a thought of the new-born babies struggling for their first breath of life in incubators at the hospital."

Solicitor Burgwyn and attorney Hight concentrated on building Aaron into a great hero as they painted him as an "honest and trustworthy citizen of the State who believed in preserving law and order and was willing to expose himself to great danger in order to protect the good people of North Carolina."

Burgwyn described Aaron as a "brave man with real guts" and the defendants as "low-bellied cowards."

Hight said, "Aaron is the bravest man I know."

The final defense argument was presented by Hill Yarborough in a powerful and eloquent appeal which left few dry eyes in the courtroom as he beseeched the jury to consider the spotless record of the defendants as compared to that of Aaron, and the effect "on the families of these men if they are sent to prison for a crime that never happened."

The trial judge's charge to the jury consumed more than two hours. He recited, in great detail, the testimony of the State's witnesses on direct examination, but was much less explicit concerning the contradictory statements made by the same witnesses on cross-examination.

Guilty As Charged

The jury, after deliberating less than three hours, returned to the jury box and droned "guilty as charged" 24 times—three times for each of the eight defendants.

Defense counsel filed a motion to set aside the verdicts on the grounds of a mistrial. The motion was promptly denied.

The judge pronounced sentence immediately. The sentences imposed, and his remarks made it clear that, from the beginning, there had been no doubt in the judge's mind as to the purpose of the proceeding. This was further borne out by the fact that the sentences were based on our position in the union, rather than on degree of involvement in the "conspiracy." Gore, Auslander, and I were sentenced to six to ten years on each of the three counts. Walker, Pegram, Abbott, and Martin were sentenced to five to seven years on each of the three counts.

Jarrel's sentence was two to three years on each count.

The judge's remarks were significant and revealing. He needed no report or record of any kind. He needed no time for study or research. He simply said, "Fear has run rampant in Henderson and Vance County. *I don't know who caused it.* But it must end right here." (Emphasis supplied by author.)

In sentencing me, he ordered me to stand. He said, "I hope you will some day come to understand that the law is bigger than you, bigger than the union, bigger than any organization. The good people of North Carolina will not tolerate anyone holding themselves above the law. . . . Your lawyers have spoken about your good reputation—your church work—your nice family. . . . I say as a man thinketh in his heart, so is he. I say whatever good you have ever done has been cancelled by your actions here. I say a man is no Christian who harbors thoughts of violence—who must rule or ruin. . . . I have noticed your nice family and I feel sorry for them, but you should have been thinking of them when you were sneaking around at night planning these acts of violence.

"When I was here before, I heard the inflammatory speeches which you made over the radio and I have since read a copy of the script used on the weekend following adjournment of that court. I know you didn't make that particular one, but it was a vicious diatribe against this court and a plain attempt to set the union above the law. As the person in charge here for the union you must accept the responsibility." (Interestingly enough, no charge had ever been made and no evidence had been produced in the trial to link me in any way with any type of violence. Likewise, the radio broadcasts were never mentioned in the trial.)

The judge then ordered Auslander to stand and asked him where he was born. When Auslander replied "New York," the judge asked whether he had been sent by the union. "Yes, ten years ago," Auslander replied. The judge then loosed a tirade against Auslander, saying, in part, "Even though you come from New York and even though the union sent you, you are not above the law."

When the judge announced that bond "for Payton, Gore, and Auslander is set at $25,000: for Walker, Pegram, Abbott, and

Martin—$20,000; for Jarrel—$10,000," the bondsman complained that this would mean a total of $795,000, if the bonds were to apply to each of the three charges for each of the eight defendants.

After a brief conference with attorneys, the judge recalled the recorder and directed a change in the wording of his sentences to provide for the sentences to run concurrently rather than consecutively and requiring only one bond for each of the defendants.

As the sheriff's deputies were leading us from the courtroom for fingerprinting and photographs, I saw the judge in conversation with Attorney Black. An hour later, in the presence of my wife and Dave George, Black told me that the judge had said, "You almost broke me down with your tearful plea for your friend, Payton." Hugo reported that he had said, "It was a sincere plea, Judge. I think it is a shame to send him to prison on the kind of evidence which was produced against him." Then, according to Hugo, the judge had said, "Well, if I had been on the jury, I couldn't have found him guilty based on the circumstantial evidence regarding his participation." However, according to Hugo, the judge quickly reverted to character by reasserting his animosity toward me and referring to me in uncomplimentary terms.

Appeals

An appeal was filed with the North Carolina Supreme Court in September. As required by North Carolina law, the "case on appeal" was submitted to counsel for the State on August 25, 1959, but when the opposing lawyers were unable to agree as to what constituted the "official record," the matter, according to North Carolina law, had to be referred to the judge for settlement of the disputed points. The judge did not act until September 22, 1959, after meeting with and hearing arguments from both sides.

Incidentally, after the final session between the judge and the attorneys, on this matter, attorney Nicholson reported to me and quoted the judge as saying, "You may have me where Payton is concerned. I probably should have non-suited him in Henderson."

The North Carolina Supreme Court denied the appeal on January 15, 1960. In stating its opinion, the court reviewed the evidence at length, but failed entirely to deal with the most prejudicial matters relied upon by the defendants and plainly shown on the court record. On the other hand, when dealing with my involvement, the court relied on its own assumptions which were totally unsupported by the court record, to reason as follows: "Payton was the union agent in charge of the strike at Henderson and it was sufficient to show his participation in a plot conceived for the purpose of promoting his job of keeping the mills from operating."

One judge, Justice Bobbitt, dissented. He said, in part: "In my view, the evidence, as to Payton, is insufficient to support the verdict.... The crucial question is whether the circumstantial evidence is such that logical and legitimate inferences may be drawn therefrom to support the factual conclusion that Payton was a party to the alleged conspiracy.... In my opinion, the correct answer is, 'No.' "

* * * * *

A "Petition For A Writ of Certiorari" was filed with the Supreme Court of the United States on May 20, 1960. It carried the signatures of Arthur J. Goldberg, William M. Nicholson, Hill Yarborough, James B. Ledford, James J. Randleman, and Hugo L. Black, Jr.

This petition was asking only that the High Court grant a hearing and listen to argument from both sides for the purpose of reviewing the judgement of the Supreme Court of North Carolina.

The State of North Carolina filed an opposing brief asking the High Court not to grant such a hearing.

The decision, issued in October of 1960, was to the effect that the court had decided not to grant a hearing. Therefore, contrary to the impression of many, no "appeal hearing" was ever held by the United States Supreme Court.

At a conference in Goldberg's Washington office the day before the "Writ" was filed in May, Goldberg advised all of the defendants, in the presence of the attorneys, that he was confident that the High Court would grant a hearing when it reconvened in the fall. He remained equally confident throughout the summer months. However, in September, he told me privately that I should be prepared to go to prison, because he had little hope of a hearing being granted.

He explained that hundreds of requests for such hearings are filed each year and only five or ten per cent of them are granted. He said, "Twenty years ago, when everyone was concerned about workers' rights, your case would have been a natural for a hearing before the High Court but, today, many people believe that unions are too big and too powerful, and there isn't much public sympathy for the union's cause. Furthermore, you must realize that the Supreme Court is very reluctant to override a state court or criticise a state's laws unless it is a pretty clear case of violation of the U. S. Constitution."

As time approached for the expected (by me) denial of the "Writ," and I realized that our remaining hope was for "executive clemency" action by the governor, I began thinking about my contacts with Governor Hodges over the previous fifteen years.

I had dealt with him when he was president of Fieldcrest Mills, and we had, I thought, established a good relationship which was based on mutual respect and mutual understanding. On one occasion, I was invited to Natural Bridge, Virginia, to participate in a weekend conference of Fieldcrest supervisors when "sound labor-management relations" had been given a prominent place on the agenda.

Later, when he became "Governor" Hodges, he had appointed me to the "Governor's Safety Council," and I had participated in several conferences in his presence.

He had always been cordial and pleasant whenever we had met, even in the unpleasant and frustrating atmosphere which surrounded his mediation efforts in the strike situation.

I had always considered him as a person with high principles and motives and could not believe that he would permit this miscarriage of justice to actually send us to prison if he were aware of all of the facts.

I began preparing a document which listed the points that, in my opinion, demonstrated a clear case of "entrapment" by state officials for the purpose of destroying the union. In addition, I pointed up the circumstances, situations, and happenings which, to me, demonstrated beyond any doubt that we had not received a fair trial. I entitled this document, "You Be The Judge," and it was my intention to submit it to Governor Hodges the moment the "Writ" was denied.

However, I had not reckoned with the political situation. The race for the presidency, between Kennedy and Nixon, was described as "neck and neck." My associates in the labor movement and in political circles were constantly stressing the importance of Kennedy's election and the dire consequences of a Nixon victory.

It was pointed out to me, over and over, that any embarrassment to Democrats could possibly swing the election to the Republicans; that to carry North Carolina was extremely important to the Kennedy forces; that Governor Hodges was heading the "Businessmen For Kennedy" phase of the campaign and would probably be Kennedy's Secretary of Commerce; and that Arthur Goldberg was slated for appointment as Secretary of Labor and would be serving with Governor Hodges in the Kennedy cabinet.

On the state level, politics were also involved. Terry Sanford, who had won the Democratic primary for governor by defeating three other candidates, *including former attorney general Malcolm Seawell*, was expected to defeat the Republican candidate without difficulty. Sanford had been quoted on several occasions as saying he was convinced that the Henderson conspiracy case was a clear-cut case of "entrapment" which would not have been permitted if he had been governor. Furthermore, when he had met my wife and 21-year-old daughter at a political rally in Charlotte in September, he had been most sympathetic and had expressed hope for "the best of luck" in regard to the decision of the U. S. Supreme Court.

The "Writ" was denied on October 10, 1960, with Justice Douglas dissenting and with Justice Black not participating because his son was one of the attorneys of record.

After several soul-searching meetings with union officials and attorneys, it was decided that a "Plea For Executive Clemency" should be prepared which argued only for simple justice and did not criticise the state administration or the courts, although a group of Henderson women strikers had reported that when they had spoken to the Governor about irregularities in the trial and perjury of jurymen, he had said, "Nothing like that has ever been brought to my attention." It was also decided to attach some of the hundreds of letters from people in all walks of life who had written to express their concern and pledge their support.

This "plea" was presented to the Governor on October 20, 1960. On October 26th, Governor Hodges dispatched a telegram to defense attorneys and released copies to the press. In part, it read:

> The petition for executive clemency does not present any new evidence or information which was not available at the time of the trial. . . . If information had been placed before me showing that the defendants had not received a fair and impartial trial or showing that the defendants had been wrongfully convicted, *I would have had some basis for exercise of executive clemency* (emphasis by author).
>
> In addition to my own study . . . I have had the State Board of Paroles make an independent and thorough review of this case. In its report to me, the Board said, "There seems to be no doubt of guilt and had arrests not been made . . . there is every reason to believe that the dynamiting which was planned would have taken place. After a close study of these cases the recommendation of the Board of Paroles to the Governor is that no executive clemency be granted. . . . "
>
> I have earnestly endeavored to give this matter a completely conscientious and prayerful review. I regret that I must inform you that I cannot act favorably on the petition for executive clemency.

This telegram was interpreted by our lawyers as inviting the submission of full details. An emergency conference of defense and union officials was called for Saturday, October 29th, in Charlotte.

In the meantime, attorney Nicholson had been advised by the Clerk of Vance Superior Court, Henry Hight, that the eight men should report at the Vance Courthouse on Thursday, November 3rd, at 9 A.M. for surrender to the sheriff. In reporting on his conversation with the clerk, Nicholson quoted Mr. Hight as saying, "I pray to God that something may happen before then to make the surrender unnecessary."

At the Saturday conference it was decided that the material from the document, "You Be The Judge," should be drawn in the form of an affidavit from me, released to the press, and forwarded to the Governor by special messenger, as part of an "Amended Plea for Executive Clemency."

On Wednesday, November 2nd, Governor Hodges replied, "I have given careful personal consideration to the amended petition.... The request for executive clemency is denied."

* * * * *

The Charlotte Observer of Thursday, November 3, 1960, carried an article which I believe has a place in the story at this point:

In A Second-Floor Office, Unionist Fought And Lost
By VICTOR K McELHENY
Observer Staff Writer

A center of activities to try to keep Boyd E. Payton of Charlotte and seven other textile unionists from going to prison—as they will do today—has been a second-floor suite of offices above a restaurant on West Sixth Street.

It is the Carolinas office of the Textile Workers Union of America.

It is a place where TWUA staff man Red Lisk sometimes leans back in Payton's large leather chair, sighs that it's a rat race, and says, "We're all trying to give that last ounce of effort that will turn the trick."

It is a place where the secretary said she typed all weekend and where almost 1,000 letters asking Gov. Hodges to grant clemency were reviewed. Across Payton's desk came letters which contained passages like this:

"Dear Gov. Hodges ... I am sure you will agree with me that in the many years that both of us have known Boyd his participation in such an act is simply unthinkable ... Not only do I not believe it, but I am certain you do not believe it either...."

Ever since the U. S. Supreme Court refused Oct. 10 to review the eight convictions on charges of conspiracy to dynamite places in Henderson, where two TWUA locals went out on strike in 1958, lawyers and unionists have climbed the carpeted stairs looking at a smiling picture of John F. Kennedy, and turned left into Payton's office.

They have had two tasks:

—Trying to keep Payton and the others from going to prison.

—Planning how to run textile union affairs in the Carolinas in case Payton had to go to prison.

They went about their work in a determinedly calm and rational manner, talking about all possibilities, always reminding themselves that the Textile Workers Union of America was not about to go out of business.

Running through his mind were many thoughts:

—As a union leader, he could not, even at the brink of going to prison, seek to get himself cleared while other unionists were jailed.

—Gov. Hodges, a man with whom he had dealt in negotiations at Fieldcrest Mills and also in the Henderson strike, might feel friendly toward him and yet be subject to sharp political pressures.

—The work of the SBI under former Attorney General Malcolm Seawell and the conduct of the trial under Judge Raymond B. Mallard seemed to him motivated strongly by dislike of his union.

—Gratitude for the letters asking clemency and worry about his family.

Often during the last two weeks, Payton's wife Katherine has dropped by the office to chat with her husband, with visiting unionists and the secretaries.

Once Tuesday, she went into her husband's office and hugged him and said, "I must worry you being down here all the time."

Payton told her, "Sweety, you can come down here any time you want."

She said, "I'm no use at home."

And then she turned to a visitor, and said, "I feel like shouting in the streets."

Chapter II

PRISONS ARE NOT MADE FOR MEN

"I cannot send this man to prison because prisons are not made for men like him."

In this manner *The Charlotte Observer* of November 19, 1959, quoted a North Carolina judge in reporting on the trial of a trucking company executive who had been fined $100 after pleading guilty to charges of manslaughter, hit-and-run, and drunken driving.

The newspaper reported that, after the State's evidence, a parade of character witnesses had spoken in behalf of the executive and had described him as "a man of excellent character, active in the church, and in high standing in his home town." The judge was reported as saying, "If every man that came into court could prove they lived a life like you have lived, there would be very few men to go to prison."

Of special interest to me was the reference to "excellent character, active in the church, and in high standing in his home town," because when identical statements had been made in my behalf, just four months earlier, the judge who was then presiding not only failed to give any weight to them, but instead, launched into a bitter denunciation of my character, ridiculed my church work, belittled my reputation, and labeled me "a menace to the good people of North Carolina." He then meted out long prison terms to the eight members of the Textile Workers Union of America, including the author, who were standing before him.

When I first read the story concerning the executive, I was quite critical of that judge. I could not understand his reasoning. I thought this was simply another example of the "double standard of justice" which I had seen so often in my 20 years of experience as a representative of working men and women. However, at the end of my first twenty-four hours in prison, I came to the conclusion that the judge in that case was one of the wisest men in the state because, by that time, I felt that I had been thrown into a cesspool and that only by the greatest effort could I hope to keep my head above the filth and avoid sinking to the bottom, never to rise again.

It seemed to me that the sole purpose and major objective of all prison officials was to strip the new inmate of all pride and human dignity; to reduce his morale to the lowest possible level; to fill him with shame; and to make him look, feel, and act like a criminal at the earliest possible moment. I had also concluded, at the end of my first day in prison, that prison guards consider convicts only slightly better than animals and deserving of very little more consideration.

The reader, at this point, may be on the verge of concluding that the writer is an embittered, biased, and prejudiced individual who is writing a "spite story." Let me hasten to say that this is not the case. I am not embittered. I hold no grudge against any person. In my opinion, those who have the responsibility of administering the prison system are as much prisoners of the system as are those it is intended to control.

However, rather than continuing to state conclusions and opinions, let me lead the reader through nine months of prison life.

Eight Innocent Men

On November 3, 1960, after sixteen months of worry-filled days and nights during which every effort was made to avoid prison for a *crime that was never committed*, my seven associates and I were presented to the sheriff of Vance County by our chief local attorney, Mr. William Nicholson. He said, "Sheriff, I present eight innocent men to you this morning in accordance with our promise to the Court."

Of that morning in Henderson, I will let newspapers tell the story. The United Press International account, carried in most newspapers, said:

> Eight members of the Textile Workers Union of America (AFL-CIO) were committed to prison Thursday for conspiring to cripple operations of the Harriett-Henderson Cotton Mills, ending a 15-month legal battle.
>
> The defendants, including TWUA Carolinas Director Boyd Payton, surrendered to Vance County Sheriff E. A. Cottrell at 9 A.M. and were immediately transferred by automobile to Central Prison at Raleigh.

The men walked with their wives to the courthouse three and a half blocks from the Vance Hotel where they had a private breakfast with TWUA International President William Pollock, the union's secretary, John Chupka, and other officials. Emil Rieve, President Emeritus of TWUA and a Vice President of the AFL-CIO, was also present.

Payton, speaking for all eight defendants, told newsmen:

"There is no bitterness in our hearts. Neither is there any burden on our consciences."

Pollock called the imprisonment "the climax of a long series of injustices" against the workers of the cotton mills who went on strike two years ago in a dispute over arbitration privileges in a new contract.

Payton and the other seven—international representatives Charles Auslander and Lawrence Gore, and local members Calvin Pegram, Johnnie Martin, Warren Walker, Robert Abbott and Malcolm Jarrel, were convicted of plotting to dynamite a power plant transformer, burn the mill's office and blow up the boiler room at the mill.

Payton, Auslander and Gore were sentenced to six to ten years each, and the others, except Jarrel, each received five to seven years. Jarrel was sentenced to two to three years.

They were admitted to the prison receiving center at Raleigh where they will spend several days receiving medical examinations, aptitude tests and other processing. State Prison Director George Randall said the tests could require two weeks to administer before the defendants would receive permanent assignments.

The still unsettled strike against the cotton mills was filled with incidents of violence, including dynamiting, shooting, rock throwing and near-riots. State troopers were sent to the scene to reinforce local law officers and later the National Guard was ordered out by Governor Luther N. Hodges to restore order.

The union appealed the convictions and last month the U. S. Supreme Court refused to review the case. The defendants were ordered to surrender when the superior court received affirmation of the high court decision.

Shortly before the unionists began the walk to the sheriff's office, union attorney William Nicholson said, "As far as we are concerned the case is not closed. We intend to pursue every legal avenue" to gain their freedom. . . .

The unionists were met in the courthouse hallways by a crowd of people, mostly union sympathizers, who shook hands and wished the men well as they said good-by.

Traffic on the main street stopped as the men and their attorneys marched across the street in the middle of the block.

They were escorted to waiting sheriff's cars by deputies.

Mrs. Payton walked arm-in-arm with her husband . . . and told newsmen, "I've never been prouder of him."

Mrs. Payton said, "Our hopes were so high yesterday. We felt sure the governor would reconsider."

Hodges denied two petitions for executive clemency for the men. He turned down the second one on Wednesday. . . .

Pollock told newsmen the workers were "forced into a strike and that the state administration, influenced by mill owners and management, was against them."

"The conspiracy convictions which followed were obviously pressed to justify that course of action," he said. He urged the people of North Carolina "to raise their voices in behalf of these men."

Payton said the defendants did not consider "this setback the final defeat. Let this hour be one of dedication that the efforts to organize southern textile mills is a noble one that must be continued until it succeeds in bringing dignity, justice and better communities to working men and women. . . . "

This is the story which was carried in *The Charlotte Observer*, along with a picture of the tearful farewells of the men and their families. Other newspapers throughout the state carried substantially the same story. Most of them gave the story prominent headlines and carried several pictures.

None of them, however, reported the fact that top union officials and our attorneys were so filled with emotion that they had great difficulty in speaking, nor did any report the fact that the sheriff had tears in his eyes as he ordered us loaded into two police cars.

Textile Labor, the union's official publication, of course, gave the most sympathetic treatment to the story. Two pages from its November 1960 edition are reproduced on the following pages.

Clemency Denied:
Eight in Henderson Imprisoned

Eight TWUA strike leaders, convicted in July 1959 of conspiracy to dynamite the struck Harriet and Henderson Cotton Mills here, have begun serving terms ranging between two and 10 years in Central Prison, Raleigh, after denial of a long series of court and clemency appeals pressed in their behalf by TWUA. Heads high and protesting their innocence, the men presented themselves at the Vance County Courthouse here on the morning of Nov. 3 and were quickly transferred to Raleigh.

Hundreds of TWUA members, still carrying on their two-year strike against a union-busting employer, saw them off in an emotion-laden scene. Their ranks included General President William Pollock,

General Secretary-Treasurer John Chupka and President Emeritus Emil Rieve of TWUA.

Jail Terms Begin for Eight Henderson Strike Leaders

Pollock and Boyd E. Payton, TWUA Carolinas director and highest-ranking union official among the eight defendants, faced a battery of TV, radio and newspaper men at a press conference prior to the commitment proceedings.

Payton spoke in behalf of himself and his fellow defendants, Charles E. Auslander, Bi-County Joint Board manager; Lawrence Gore, TWUA representative; Johnnie Martin, Local 578 vice president, Warren Walker, Calvin Pegram, Robert Abbott and Malcolm Jarrell. All had been convicted on the testimony of an ex-convict in the hire of state police.

Their statement expressed appreciation to the many people in all walks of life who have helped them through their ordeal, and called upon TWUA members to continue their fight for "dignity, justice and a decent living" for textile workers.

Pollock called their conviction "the climax of a long series of injustices against Henderson textile workers." He appealed to "the many people of North Carolina who are greatly trouble by what is taking place here today to raise their voices in behalf of these men toward the end that this injustice will be remedied."

"TWUA," Pollock said, "has complete faith in the integrity of these men. We are deeply grieved at the hardships and sacrifices they are about to undergo. We know they will face their ordeal with the kind of courage that has always marked the struggle of textile workers for social justice."

Pollock said TWUA will continue to bend every effort to secure the release of the Henderson strike leaders.

Henderson Weeps, Struggle Goes On

Here it was, the day everybody hoped would never come.

Yesterday there still was a chance. Hadn't the Governor left the door open for clemency? He had asked for new evidence; it had been supplied. But late this afternoon the dismal news had come from Raleigh. Appeal denied.

Last night the eight men, their families and friends had gathered in a room at the Vance Hotel. The air was sodden with gloom. Mae Renn tried to perk things up.

"Let's tell some funny stories," she suggested.

A few gave it a try, recalling some humorous aspects of the trial. Despite the injustice of it all, there had been some laughs. The atmosphere lightened a little. Luther Jackson, who served five days in jail after a strike incident, stood up.

"I know these men," he began. "I brought two of them into the union. I was the sergeant of one of them. We went through D-Day together...."

His voice trailed off. He sat down, buried his head in his arms and sobbed.

Emil Rieve tried his hand.

"This has happened before and it will happen again as long as there is injustice against workers," he said. "I helped bury six labor martyrs myself. In fact, I assigned Charlie Auslander to the south. I took him away from a comfortable job in Massachusetts."

"I have no regrets, Emil," Charlie responded. "If I had the choice all over again, I would go."

Someone began singing "We Shall Not Be Moved." The rest joined in. Finally, the group dispersed for a few hours of fitful sleep.

Early this morning there was a breakfast. As the saying goes, the condemned men ate a hearty meal, Lawrence Gore washing it down with a medication for ulcers. There were brief speeches. Emil Rieve offered some words of comfort.

"After their persecutors are forgotten, history will know these eight men existed and that they tried to improve the lot of the little people."

John Chupka was next. "We hope this will leave an imprint on the consciences of all Americans," he said. "These men are not being punished for any crime. They are being imprisoned for what they believe in."

Bill Pollock got up. "We are here to pay respects to those who are making this sacrifice. We will continue our efforts to free them...."

Heavy with emotion, his voice broke and the tears welled up in his eyes.

"Forgive me," he closed. "I can't go on."

The silence was finally broken by Boyd Payton.

"None of us have any desire to be heroes or martyrs," he said. "We'd much rather go home to our families. But the struggle to build the labor movement is just as worthwhile as the sacrifices for Christianity. Let's hold our heads high and face this test with courage."

And they did. The men walked out into the jammed hotel lobby for a press conference. Pollock and Payton read statements. TV cameras whirred, flash bulbs popped. Soon it was over. The eight men and their families retired to a private room to say their farewells.

They returned to begin a slow walk to the Vance County Courthouse where the authorities awaited them. Hundreds outside silently followed them to their destination, a block and a half away on the far side of the railroad tracks. The men walked into the building.

Hesitant, at first, the crowd stopped outside. Then it pushed on into the main corridor, jamming all available space. The voice of the court clerk could be heard, calling the roll of the prisoners in alphabetical order.

"Abbott, Auslander, Gore, Jarrell, Martin, Payton, Pegram, Walker," he intoned. To most listeners, it was a roll of honor. Papers were shuffled and the sheriff and his deputies took over. They led the men through the rear entrance and finally to two police cars which were waiting to take them to Central Prison in Raleigh. Someone handed Bob Abbott a carton of cigarettes.

"Thanks," he said. "Give it to the strikers. I've got what I need."

As Calvin Pegram entered one of the cars, his mother tried to pull him out. "Hush up, Ma," he said. "Go home and put the kettle on the stove. We'll be back."

Nanny Hughes, who leads prayer at union meetings, was chanting, "Please, Jesus . . . Jesus, please." A woman began to sob, "This is the saddest day I ever did see in Henderson." There were tears on all sides. The police cars started off slowly.

Was this the end, after two years of heartbreaking struggle?

A quavering voice began singing "Solidarity Forever." Others picked it up and swelled it into a vibrant chorus, closing with "The union makes us strong!"

No, it wasn't the end. The struggle against industrial tyranny will go on.

*On-The-State**

The trip of fifty miles from Henderson to Central Prison in Raleigh, with four of us and two officers in each car, was uneventful. No one had been handcuffed and, except for our thoughts, the trip could have been called pleasant. Even the officers (who had been life-long friends with some of their passengers) tried to find things other than our destination to talk about. Personally, I spent most of the trip trying to read, with blurred eyes and a grateful heart, the Kays Gary column of the *Charlotte Observer* for November 3, 1960, which someone had placed in my hands at the courthouse:

---

* "On-the-state" is the expression used by inmates when speaking of a prison term. He will never say, "This is my second prison term." Rather, he will say, "This is the second time I've been on-the-state." Likewise, he will not say, "I've been in prison for two years." Instead, he will say, "I've been on-the-state for two years."

Wentworth ... Your Street?
... You Hope Not ... Not Today

Wentworth Place, Charlotte, could be the street where you live.

It is a quiet, middle-income street. It has 14 ranch houses, 35 children, almost as many dogs and a gorgeous pyracantha bush in the center of a circle at the end of the street.

The bush is directly across from 4501.

This is the house with the nicest yard.

It is the house where neighborhood parties are always held. It is the house most children go in and out of.

It is the home of the most admired family on Wentworth—a man and his wife and his three daughters.

Today the man, Boyd Payton, goes to jail.

Today, executive clemency denied him by Gov. Hodges, the TWUA labor leader still stands convicted of conspiring with seven others to dynamite facilities of Harriet-Henderson Cotton Mills.

Today you would not want to live on Wentworth Place.

Neighbors' Verdict ... It's Different

There is nothing there but sadness. There is no man, no woman nor child there who does not passionately believe in the innocence of Boyd Payton.

The trial has been held, the verdict has been given and in these columns no re-trial will be held.

But on Wentworth, among neighbors with strong anti-union feelings—neighbors who are attorneys and salesmen and contractors and housewives—there is but one verdict, "Innocent!"

Bill Miller, contractor, who has been in court to break up strikes on his company, says: "I would fight Boyd Payton if he tried to organize me, but I'll tell you this ... There is no man of higher integrity. He would not contemplate, let alone condone, violence. I cannot buy it and I will never buy it and I will do anything in his behalf. I've met a lot of nice people in this world but none more thoughtful and genuine day in and day out. He was railroaded in an effort to get rid of the union ... "

Said Mrs. Charles Lee: "I believe nothing but the best of Boyd Payton. His impossible convictions breaks my heart. He and Kitty and their three daughters are the kindest, most considerate, best people we've ever known. . . . Who do you think always had the time we didn't have to do things for our children ... ?"

With Each One, It's The Same

Then Mrs. William Foster: "The Paytons are the family yardstick all of us would like to measure up to, but never will. They love. . . . They do the neighborly things you'd like to do. They've always been that way. Boyd is our little Carol's second father, really...."

And Atty. Bill Grist: "If ever a man was innocent, Boyd is.... You have to know him...."

Atty. Russell Lowe: "I have only respect for him—the highest type of Christian gentleman, who never stoops except to lift, and I do not believe him capable of criminal involvement..."

Atty. Bill Poe: "Boyd is the finest neighbor I ever had and I cannot believe him guilty. I know him, you see, and..."

Gordon Golding: "I know it'd be easy for someone else to conclude, 'Those labor boys would do anything'... but you'll never find one who knew Boyd who'd say that. You don't meet many men that big, and when you do you don't forget..."

Mrs. C. W. Gallant Jr.: "I refuse to believe Mr. Payton capable of association with violence..."

Trembling voices tell you of the 30-year romance of Boyd and Kitty Payton and of the open devotion of parents and daughters.

It's Over... Only Kitty Smiles

They call Mrs. Payton "Two-Cake Kitty," because when she bakes one for the family there's another for a neighbor. They tell of Payton as the one man ready to take teen-agers bowling and to volunteer first for church work... of daughters who baby the smaller children on the street.

They tell of the night Boyd Payton told them all: "I swear to you, my neighbors, I knew nothing of any conspiracy...."

There is a 14-year-old named Kathy Storm who comes to a newsman with tears and a question: "Why? Why? Where is justice? Why can't somebody do something?"

Inside the Payton home Wednesday, messages by the hundreds piled up from clergymen, friends and men who have fought both with and against Payton in labor disputes. There were three offers to make the Payton house payments. And Kitty Payton, alone, was smiling—sure that "something will happen because it must happen."

It did not happen. It is over. Boyd Payton goes to jail.

Wentworth Place mourns.

We arrived at the gates to Central Prison about ten o'clock. After a brief delay while papers were examined, the gates swung open and we were driven "inside the walls." We were ushered into the main lobby where four or five guards and several men in prison garb were waiting. (It developed that the other inmates were being returned from road camps and were to be processed with our group.)

After some shuffling of papers by the guards and some

whispered conversation among them, one of them shouted, "All right, everybody up against the wall—half on one side, half on the other." Then, "Take off your coats, ties, shoes, and socks—lay 'em on the floor in front of ya'."

I happened to be the only one wearing a hat and, since no one had told me what to do with it, it was still on my head. A guard yelled, "Hey, you with the hat, take it off and lay it on the floor." When I had complied, he shouted, "Everybody empty pockets—lay everything on the floor in front of you."

By this time, we had quite an audience. Uniformed men looked in from several doorways, and several people in white clothes peered through the doors and windows into the lobby. We learned later that those with the white uniforms were clerks, kitchen employees, and hospital attendants, who were also inmates.

When our pockets had been emptied a guard bellowed, "Everybody turn around—face the wall—and reach high." Then we had our first "shakedown," as a guard passed his hands over every inch of our bodies and had us raise first one foot and then the other to see if we had anything taped to our soles.

We stood against the walls for what seemed like hours while the blood drained from our arms, and they became cold and numb as the guards searched through our belongings. From the corner of my eye, I saw cards and pictures from my billfold being tossed carelessly about and some papers from my pockets being thrown into a pile of trash which had been swept into a corner. I turned to protest, but was promptly ordered, "Keep your face to the wall and keep those hands up high—we'll take care of this."

Finally, we were ordered, "Turn around," and were shown a small pile of things which we could keep and a larger pile of things which would not be allowed. In the larger pile, I saw my membership cards, driver's license, snapshots and address book, scrambled in a heap. Toothpaste, shaving cream, bronchial medicine, a book, handkerchiefs, ball-point pen, pipe cleaners, postage stamps, and writing paper were also among the forbidden items.

A guard said, "Pick up your stuff in the small pile—put on your shoes and socks. Tell me what ya' want done with this other stuff. Your clothes will be sent to your home address—at your expense—you can send this other stuff along with 'em if ya' want to."

We were told that we would be allowed to carry no more than four dollars with us. I had four dollars and ninety cents. I was advised that the ninety cents would be placed in the prisoner's trust fund and I could draw it on Saturday. Then I was told that it would cost 79 cents to send my clothes home. Of course, I had no change. This seemed to irritate the guard as he fumbled about counting out one dime, two nickels, and a penny.

The prisoner's trust fund is the name given to the system through which an inmate or his relatives may deposit funds with prison officials from which the inmate may withdraw a specified amount each Saturday morning. The weekly limit was four dollars until January 1, 1961, when it was increased to five dollars along with the change in prison policy which prohibited packages from home. Considerable confusion seems to exist about this Fund in the minds of "free people" who are aware of its existence. Several visitors and even one of the workshop supervisors mistakenly believed that it was a fund established by Prison Industries from which inmates were paid for their work while in prison.

As some of the guards stuffed our belongings into bags, we were ordered through a side door to the prison yard. We were led across the yard while inmates in drab and ill-fitting clothes called out to us, "Welcome to your new home."

We entered a building where piles of clothing seemed to be everywhere. We were lined up and, as our names were called, we stepped forward to answer questions about home addresses, size of clothing, etc. (I have never been able to understand why they bothered, then or later, to ask about sizes, because no matter what size you gave, they always seemed to grab the piece of clothing nearest them and throw it at you. The big fellows usually got the small sizes and the little fellows the big ones.)

After some trading of clothing, taking tucks in some things and letting out tucks in others, we were finally outfitted with prison garb of patched and ill-fitting clothing in various shades of brown. This sombre color, we learned later, denoted "A-grade" inmates. We learned, too, that all new inmates were considered "A-grade" unless they were a "security risk." In this case, they would be dressed in gray.

We were then ushered through a door into a large shower room. A guard shouted, "Everybody strip and take a shower." When one of the fellows said he had just taken a shower that morning, the guard said, "I said *everybody* take a shower."

When all were bathed and dressed in our newly acquired clothes, we were a motley-looking group. It was a distinct shock to note how much we all looked like each other, and how much we looked like the men who had welcomed us in the yard a few minutes before.

We were marched to the extreme end of the prison yard, opposite to where we had entered, and into the last door before reaching the high prison wall. The "experienced" among our group advised that this was "detention," where all new inmates are held in quarantine pending classification and medical examinations. We were ordered to line up facing the wall and were given our second shakedown. The guard who had escorted us to this building gave some papers to the detention guard before backing out of the big door leading to the yard. The new guard unlocked a heavy metal door and began calling our names. As we answered, he motioned us through the open door and directed us down the grilled iron steps to the basement. When we were all together on the bottom floor, the guard called from the top of the stairs, "Everybody sit down." The floor was the only thing to sit on, so we sat down, cross-legged, and began to survey our surroundings.

The smell of unclean bodies, stale cigarette smoke and strong disinfectant burned our eyes and nostrils. Flies and roaches swarmed about us. On one side of the room, directly opposite from where we were sitting, were seven cells with upper and lower bunks. On the same level, but at the end, there were three more cells. Each cell had a toilet bowl and a small washbasin. On the second and third tiers were seven cells directly above those in the basement, but there were none at the ends where the big door occupied the space at one end and high windows occupied the space on the opposite wall.

Each of the cells was occupied by two men, except number

one in the basement and number seven on the second tier. Number seven on the second tier was empty, but locked. One of the "road gang" boys with us informed us that number seven was reserved for the clerk who was then being punished in solitary confinement, accused by a guard of "peddling" candy of undetermined origin. Number one on the first floor was occupied by only one man who sat on the side of his lower bunk holding his head between his hands and resting his elbows on his knees.

Most of the men in the cells facing us were calling to each other and making uncomplimentary remarks in vile and filthy language. The combination of oaths and obscene remarks was sickening.

About half an hour after we had been ordered to sit on the floor, a heavy metal tray was placed on the floor in front of each of us, and we were given a half-pint of milk.

The tray was made with recessed sections and contained three pieces of fatback, some brown beans, a little slaw, and some chocolate pudding. Two slices of bread lay on top of the beans. A large tablespoon was our only "silverware." We ate, sitting cross-legged and holding the trays on our laps, while battling the flies and roaches for our share. Then we lit "store-bought" cigarettes without realizing what this would mean to the men in the cells. A chorus of "Save me a drag on that duck" was heard. We learned that they were "rolling their own" with Bull Durham. We were loaded down with cartons of cigarettes which had been given to us in Henderson and which we had been allowed to retain. Opening our cartons, we began tossing packs into the cells. The men began talking with us and we learned that all of the cells were full, and we would be held in the basement until 8 P.M. when others would be "shipped" to make room for us. We were surprised to learn that these men knew all about our case and were able to identify all of us by name.

As the afternoon wore on, the cold floor became almost unbearable, and we were forced to move about. However, each time the guard came, he ordered us back to our places along the wall.

On one occasion, I walked over to cell number one where the

man was sitting on the side of his bunk—still holding his head between his hands. When I spoke, he jumped and turned startled, blood-shot eyes toward me as if he couldn't believe his eyes or ears. After a moment, he croaked, "Gotta, extry cigarette?"

As I was handing my pack to him, I noticed a man in one of the other cells vigorously shaking his head from side to side. When my pack was returned, I walked over to the cell from which the fellow had been motioning to me. He said, "You tryin' to get in trouble before you get started?"

I said, "No—why?"

He said, "That fellow is a 'dog-runner,' and nobody speaks to him or gives him anything. They never let him out of that cell. If they did, he wouldn't last five minutes."

I suppose it was obvious that I didn't know what he was talking about, and he continued, "You see, a 'dog-runner' is a convict who has helped to train bloodhounds to track an escaped convict. That's about the lowest thing a man can do, and once he's done that, his life ain't worth two cents among other convicts. You'd better not have anything to do with him 'less ya' want 'em to turn against you." I thanked him and walked back to my place by the wall with my mind in a state of shock.

Later, while talking to another inmate, I related the incident and expressed disbelief that a man's life could be so lightly held. He said, "You'd better wake up to the fact that you're in prison among convicts who expect to be here a long time, in most cases. They didn't get sent here for playing marbles on the sidewalk."

One grizzled convict with only two upper teeth (one in either corner of his mouth) was sitting on the floor of his cell, looking for all the world like a monkey as he peered through the bars. The others called him "Cal" and he seemed to be a favorite with them. Apparently he decided that we deserved to be entertained in return for the cigarettes, and he began telling stories. As I look back, I credit Cal with saving us from complete demoralization. He made us laugh when we thought there was nothing left to laugh about. He talked for hours about the experiences which had caused him to be in and out of prisons for thirty years and, with his slow drawl and humorous expressions, he kept the crowd laughing. Much of what he said could not be repeated here, but here is a sample of his more acceptable humor:

"Ya' know, fellers, I bin' readin' 'bout yer' case, an' I'd say they jus' ain't no justice." [After a moment of thoughtful silence, he said,] " 'Corse now, I'm glad they ain't, 'cause I'da bin hung long ago if they wuz."

Now take my las' time in court—they 'cused me of 'sault wit' intent t' kill—and speedin' at niney mile' a' hour—an' drivin' drunk an' leavin' th' scene of a' accident. Th' jedge said, "How do you plead?" My lawyer gets up an' sez, "Yer Honor, my client pleads guilty." Well, sir, I jumps up an' sez, "Now hol' on ther' a minute, I ain't pleadin' guilty—no sech thing." Ya' know what thet dern lawyer did? He jes' folded up his papers an' put 'em in thet little school book satchel an' sez, "Well, sir, then I must resign as your lawyer." Now, if thet wa'nt a fine kettle of fish. I jes' stood ther' with my face hangin' out.

Th' jedge sez, "Mister" (Yes, sir, he called me "Mister"). He sez, "Do you have anyone to speak in your behalf?" I sez, "Yer Honor, ther's only one man that kin say anythin' that might be favorable ta me." The jedge sez, "Well, goodness, man, you'd better get him around here. "I sez, 'Yer Honor, I got him 'round here—it's me."

He sez, "Then you are prepared to argue your own case?" Well, I stood there thinkin' 'bout thet. And then, I sez, "Yer Honor, ther's my poor ole mother sittin' back there—an' ya' know what? I betcha' I cain't even convince *her* thet I'm innocent. Guess I'll jes' have to th'ow maself on th' mercy-o-the-court." (I heerd thet once while I was waitin' to be tried in 'nother case.)

So, th' jedge sez, "Then you do plead guilty?" I sez, "Well, I'd ruther plead one o' them 'nolly prossies'." (Feller told me 'bout thet doen in South Car'lina. It means—I ain't gonna' say I'm guilty but I ain't gonna' argue agin' th' ev'dence they got on me.)

Well, the jedge sez to thet clerk kinda' feller, "Let the record show a plea of "Nolly Contendree". (Thets jus' th' same thing as a nolly prossie.) Then, he sez ta th' s'lister, "Proceed."

Well, sir, thet feller stood up there and read pages and pages of stuff 'bout all kinds o' bad things some feller had did, an' I got ta feelin' sorry fer thet feller 'cause it sure sounded bad fer him. I was bettin' ta' m'self thet he wuz gonna' git a life term. I started lookin' 'round ta see if I could see him. Ya' know what? There wa'n't a dern soul there but me an', all at once, it come ta me thet it wuz me he was talkin' 'bout. Boy, oh boy, I sure started feelin' sorrier and sorrier then.

Well, ta cut a tall tale short, when th' s'lister stopped readin', the jedge sez ta me, "Stand up." I din't feel much like standin', but I got up and he sez, "Do you have anything to say before I pronounce sentence?"

I sez, "Well, yer Honor, I don't believe I done all them things thet he read off'en thet paper."

The jedge sez, "Well, the report of the arresting officer said you were so drunk you could hardly stand up and that you staggered all over the place. Maybe that's why you can't remember."

I sez, "Well, I had a broke back—no wonder I couldn't walk straight. I tho't I'se doin' purty good to even stan' on my two feet. Fack is, I was s'prised ta be alive after hittin' thet tel'phone post."

Th' jedge sez, "It is my opinion, based on the evidence, that you were so drunk that afternoon and evening that you didn't know what you were doing. You hit your drinking companion with a tire tool and nearly cut off the top of his head. It is only a miracle that you are not being tried for murder."

Well, sir, thet kinda' stopped me. I hadn't tho't 'bout thet. I tho't ta maself thet it wan't th' top o' his haid 'cause I membered seein' his ear kinda' sliced off. But I 'cided I'd better not correck' the jedge on thet point.

Well, sir, he give me 20 ta 30 years.

During the course of this story we were interrupted two or three times by a guard coming to the top of the steps and calling out, "Everybody line up against the wall." He would count us and leave. It was a mystery to me why this was necessary because we were in the basement and surrounded by solid concrete walls. It was about 20 feet up to the only windows, and they had heavy iron bars across them. The only door was the heavy metal one through which we had entered and which the guard unlocked with a giant key each time he came in. The room was about 40 feet wide and possibly 50 feet long. The ceiling, above the third tier of cells, was about 60 feet above the basement floor.

Vaguely, I heard Cal droning on and on with his stories, but was lost in my own thoughts until he called to me and asked if I had ever "done time" in South Carolina. When I said, "No, this is my first," he said, "Well, ya' ain't missed nothin'; doen there th' cons ain't nothin' like up there. Now ya' look at me—I'm 'bout as ugly an' stupid-lookin' as ya'll see anywhere, but up here, ya' only see one like me now an' then—th' others all look purty good. But doen there in South Car'lina, they all look like me—jus' 'magine whole droves of 'em comin' at ya', an' all of 'em lookin' like me."

About this time, some men came in and again placed metal trays with food in front of us. We were given paper cups which one of the men filled with strong black coffee, for which we were most thankful because our very bones were aching from contact with the cold floor. Even the men in the basement cells were wrapping themselves in blankets while urging the guard, at every opportunity, to turn on the heat. However, each time they called out for heat, those on the third tier argued against it. Upon asking about this, we were shown the heater which was suspended at about the second tier level and it was explained that all of the heat went up and caused those on the third tier to swelter.

At 5 P.M., a guard and a clerk with a tally sheet came in. We were ordered to line up against the wall. (By this time our group, huddled together in the basement, had been increased by several as other new inmates were added during the afternoon.) When everyone in the cells and those in the basement had been counted, the guard and the clerk left. Cal explained that we had just been included, for the first time, in the official list of "guests at the Cross-Bar Hotel." He said that within a few minutes we would hear three short blasts on the prison whistle which would mean that all inmates had been counted and that the count tallied with the official record. Or, if we didn't hear the three blasts, the guard would be back to take a recount. Then, if we didn't hear the three blasts within another few minutes, we would hear the wailing of sirens which would indicate an escape. At exactly 5:15, the three short blasts (a sound that we were to hear morning and evening for many days to come) shattered the quarters.

Cal was still talking:

Ya' know, my ole gran'mother was from one o' this state's fines' fam'lies—an' wealthy, too. I guess she's spent twen'y-five-thousan' dollars tryin' ta git me out o' trouble. (Ya' know what?—I bin' runnin' from trouble all my life an' seems like I allus' run right inta troubl's arms.) Now what wuz I talkin' 'bout? Oh yes, 'bout gran'maw, she allus' wanted a son—jes' wanted a son so bad she could taste it, but she never had one. All her chil'ren was girls. Well, she fin'ly give up wantin' a son and started wantin' a gran'son. An' glory be, one day there I wuz. Well sir, she wuz jes' tickled to death with me, or so they tol' me. An' she couldn't do enuff' fer me. All I had ta do was jes' let on like I wanted sompin' and there it wuz. An' no matter how mean I wuz—she jes' kep' right on lovin' me an' doin' thin's fer me. One time—I guess I was 'bout eight—an' I wuz mean as a snake, she wuz complainin' ta my mamma 'bout what a bad boy I wuz, and mamma sez, "Well, ya' allus' wanted a boy an' ya' got one and ya' made him jes' like he is."

Well sir, ya' know I kinda' felt sorry fer thet ole lady. She looked at me a long time, an' sed, "Well, he ain't 'zactly what I had in min', but he is cute and mebbe he'll be a better boy when he gets older." But, ya' know, I never did. I jes' got meaner and meaner an' kep' gittin' inta more trouble, th' older I got. Yes sir, I guess twen'y-five-thousan' wouldn' cover what she's paid 'cause o' my troubles. An', ya' know what, I'se tryin' to think t'other day o' jes' one nice thing I ever did fer her an' derned if I could 'member even one.

He put his chin down on his chest and was quiet for several minutes.

I noticed that it was now dark outside.

Finally Cal started talking again, to no one in particular.

Ya' know, I had a jedge one time ta ask me ta name jes' one good thing I ever done in my life. He tho't he had me stumped, but I jes' reaches in my hip pocket, takes out my billfol', an' lays a pitcher o' my daughter doen in front o' him. An' I sez, "I made her and she's done more good fer more people already than mos' poeple do in their' whole lives an' she's only twen'y-two years old." Come 'ere, Payton, I'll show 'er ta ya'.

I walked over to his cell, and he handed me a picture of a very beautiful girl in a nurse's uniform. Written on the side was, "With love to my Daddy." With big tears of pride in his eyes, Cal explained how she had always been such a good girl—had always wanted to help other people—and was now a head nurse at an outstanding hospital in the state.

As I walked back to my place on the basement floor, I remembered a phrase which was to run through my mind many times in the weeks which followed: "There is bad in the best of us and good in the worst of us."

After a few minutes, I thought again of the fellow in cell number one and looked down that way. He was still sitting on the side of his bunk and still rested his chin in his hands. I felt great pity for him.

I wondered if the other fellows had been "handing me a line" about him and decided to ask Cal about it.

Cal verified the story, and when I asked if it was really true that he was in danger from the other inmates, Cal said, "Well, a dog-runner is lower doen than anythin' else—thet's 'cordin' ta a convict. Th' nex' lowes' thing is a 'rat'—thet's a con thet gits 'nother in trouble by squealin' ta th' screws. Well, jes' a week er two ago a rat had lighter fluid squirted on him an' his mattress an' they th'owed a lighted match in. Ya' kin figger' th' rest out fer yer'self."

At 8:00 P.M., a guard came in and called out several names. There was a lot of bustling and shuffling around in a number of the cells. When the guard stepped out of the room, everyone started calling to each other to find out who was leaving and where they were going. Some were being transferred to other sections of Central Prison, but most were going to the "shipping corridor" for transfer to road camps.

The guard returned in a few minutes and began unlocking cells. As each cell was opened, one or both of the occupants were ordered to line up at the door. When 14 had been lined up, another guard marched them away, and our guard began placing our group in the cells which had just been vacated.

Johnnie and Warren were placed in number ten in the basement; Lawrence was placed in number four on the second tier; Mike drew a stranger for a cellmate too and was placed in number five on the second tier; Robert and Calvin were placed in number four on the third tier. Charley and I were placed in number five on the third tier.

The shock which the smell had brought to our nostrils when we had entered the room in the morning was nothing compared with that of meeting the reasons for that smell on a first-hand basis.

The mattresses were full of holes, and the filling had sifted through the springs so that the bottom bunk and the floor were covered with a dirty brown dust. Larger pieces of dirty cotton as well as cigarette butts, torn papers, spilled tobacco, used paper cups, toilet tissue, dirty socks, and pieces of ragged clothing were littered about.

In addition, spilled food, coffee, and other liquids had apparently been mixed with the debris on the floor, so that in places there was a soggy mass of filth, and in other places, it had dried into a thick crust.

The bed clothing was still damp from the sweat of the last body which had reclined there. The army blankets were covered with great white splotches, which made them as stiff as pasteboard in spots. No pillows were in evidence. The stench was almost unbearable.

We tried as best we could with our bare hands to straighten the mattress and bedding and clean off a place big enough to lie down in but, before we had made much headway, the whistle blew and the lights went out in the cells, although the high center lights stayed on and shined through the bars into the cells.

We were shuffling around and talking in our normal voices when a man from the next cell whispered, "You fellows better not let the guard catch you or you'll spend your first night in the 'hole.' They don't allow talkin' after the lights are out."

The "hole," we learned, is the name given to the quarters used for punishing an inmate or keeping him in solitary confinement for one reason or another. Different versions of "the hole" were given by different inmates who had had first-hand experience with it. All described it as a small cell where the occupants were fed an evil-looking and evil-tasting concoction of ground liver and vegetables which is called "monotonous diet." The "sentence" could be from three to 30 days. Some said that all of their clothing had been taken from them, but others told of being allowed to retain their underwear. Some said they had a mattress and a toilet bowl and were permitted a light. Others insisted they had slept on a pile of dirty cotton, and that no toilet facilities were provided except the paper plate and the paper cup in which their food and drink were served. Each one was able to verify his version of "the hole" by the statement of another inmate, and it was a source of constant argument. It seemed strange to me that all were agreed that to avoid a trip to "the hole" was worth almost anything, but those who had been there exhibited a certain pride in this "accomplishment," and those who hadn't been there showed a certain kind of respect for those who had. "The hole" is the dreaded threat which is heard, over and over, every day of an inmate's life. An inmate who is reading in the mess-hall is never told "reading is not allowed in here." Rather, he is asked, "You wantin' 30 days in th' hole?" Likewise, an inmate who forgets to remove his cap according to regulations is never told, "Take off your cap." Instead, he will hear, "Yer' lookin' fer' 30 days in th' hole, ain't ya'?"

We stretched out on the bunks with all of our clothes on. The weakened springs sank with our weight until we were like a hot-dog in a bun. We soon found out that we couldn't stand this because of the heat. We were beginning to understand the complaints we had heard from the third tier about the heat while we had been freezing in the basement. Finally we were forced to strip to underwear.

As if by some signal, "lights-out" meant the appearance of what seemed like hundreds of cockroaches. Some were as big as quarters, but most were about the size of a dime. We killed them until we were groggy and finally fell asleep only to be wakened in what seemed like minutes by the lights coming on and someone yelling, "Coffee, coffee—have your cups ready."

We found two heavy, filthy metal cups hanging on the end of the bunks and barely had time to give them a quick rinse before an inmate appeared at our cell with a giant coffee pot. We tried to get our cups through the bars but found that they were too large. The inmate showed us how to hold the cups against two of the bars while he directed a stream of coffee between them. He said, "You fellows must be new 'on-the-state.' "

A few minutes later a Negro inmate shoved two of the metal trays through a slot under the cell door, and we watched, with a sickening feeling, as the bottom of the door (where cockroaches had been parading) leveled off the top of the mounds of food and dragged the bread off onto the filthy floor. We were sick and pushed the trays back through the slot onto the metal grill in front of the cells.

Soon we learned another part of the convict code, as a tremendous clatter of metal trays hitting the metal grill was heard. It was explained that no "good con" will ever miss the opportunity of showing disdain for the prison system, especially when there is no chance of being punished for it. Therefore, the "good con" will always shoot his tray back through that slot with much force so that it will make the greatest possible noise. "The guard knows he can't punish forty-eight at the same time, so he just ignores it, but it makes everybody feel better to let off a little steam."

By this time daylight was beginning to show and we could see the trees over the top of the prison wall, as well as some houses. We watched as the sun came up and turned the trees with their full dress of fall leaves into things of beauty. I was very lonely, homesick, and miserable.

Inside the cell it was horrible. The cell was about nine feet long and five feet wide. The bunks took up three feet of the width and six feet of the length. At the end of the bunk there was a small washbasin which could be approached either by lying on the bottom bunk and reaching through the opening under the top bunk or by sitting on the toilet and reaching down sideways.

The toilet was mounted on a block of concrete about two and a half feet square and a foot higher than the remainder of the floor. The total walking space was about two feet wide and five feet long, for the two of us.

The front of the cell was made completely of one-inch, round iron bars held in place by being welded into flat cross-bars about one foot apart. Half of the front was the door, which swung outward when unlocked by a massive key which the guard carried on his belt. The remainder of the cell was solid concrete.

Looking out the front, we could see no other cell. Directly across from us we could see only the opposite wall and the barred windows. Down on the second-tier level we could see a small, dark, recessed room which seemed to be added onto the corner of the building like a bay window. (We learned later that this was exactly what it was, and that it was used as a shower stall.)

As the morning wore away, we learned that we could communicate with each other by calling out the name of the person we wanted to talk with. When he answered, we'd yell our message over the voices of the others who were doing the same thing. I had been worried about Johnnie because of his heart condition, and I called to him in his basement cell to ask how he was feeling. I was greatly relieved when he brightly answered, "I'm all right now, but I nearly froze to death last night. Let's sing a union song." I started singing "Solidarity Forever." The other seven voices came through strongly from their various cells, and when I came to the chorus—several other voices joined in, until a guard opened the door and yelled, "Aw' right—that's enough of that—let's have some quiet in here."

After that, I called the roll each morning and was a little prouder of them each day as I witnessed their courage, their fortitude, and their good humor in the face of conditions and experiences which would have broken the spirit of many men.

The "run-boy" was sweeping in front of our cell, and we borrowed his broom to sweep out our cell. ("Run-boy" is the name given to the inmate who has been selected by the guards to be allowed out of his cell for the purpose of running errands and performing other duties at the guards' direction, including the feeding of those confined to their cells.) Then we lined the springs with newspapers to hold some of the mattress filling in place. From the bed clothing we shook out the "casualties" which had resulted from our rolling and tossing on the bunks while our "visitors" were searching for something to eat. Later, we "negotiated" with the run-boy for the use of his wet-mop and, using the water in the toilet, we were able, after a fashion, to scrub the cell. (The "negotiated rate" for use of the mop was four cigarettes.)

During the morning, we learned that we could order certain things from the "store-box" through the run-boy. We ordered Pepsi-Colas, candy bars, shaving cream, and tooth paste to replace what had been taken from us the day before. We were surprised that we could buy these items when new and unused tubes had been taken from us. The run-boy explained that there had been cases where new inmates had smuggled dope and paper money into prison by stuffing it into such tubes, and this was the reason for confiscating such items. ("Store-box" is the name given to the box-like prison facility from which certain allowed items may be purchased.)

Shortly after the run-boy brought our order, a guard came and told Charley that he was being transferred to the hospital. Since we had shared the cost of the shaving cream and tooth paste we decided that he should take the shaving cream and I should keep the tooth paste. However, an hour later, the clerk (an inmate) came and told me that Charley had sent the shaving cream back because it was plentiful in the hospital. "But," he said, "you can't have it until it is examined by the captain to see if he is smuggling anything to you." It was not until Sunday morning that I finally got it and had my first shave in some 78 hours. I couldn't remember ever having gone more than one day without a shave, and I had never shaved without a mirror. (Mirrors were prohibited on the grounds that they could be fashioned into a weapon to inflict injury on one's self or cellmate.)

Lunch had again been shoved through the slot under the bars and, again, the fried potatoes and chocolate pudding had been leveled, but I reached through the bars and caught the bread before it was dragged onto the floor. I ate the bread and washed it down with the strong black coffee.

The long afternoon dragged on as I paced up and down the length of the cell. Two steps alongside the bunk, left turn, half a step to the wall, left turn, two steps along the wall, left turn, half a step to the bunk, left turn, two steps alongside the bunk, etc., etc.

The run-boy came by, saw me walking, and said, "You'll probably be like my old man. He built two years in here and, when he got home, the first thing he did was untie the dog, knock down the pigpen, and tear down the fence around the chicken yard. He said nothing was ever supposed to be locked up around there again."

At four o'clock, supper was served. We learned that meal times were 5 A.M., 11 A.M., and 4 P.M. To our dismay, we also learned that the run-boy was not permitted to go to the storebox after 3 P.M., but we were pleased to learn that we could order Raleigh, Greensboro, and Charlotte newspapers each morning.

As I paused in my pacing to watch the changing colors of the trees as the sun was going down, I remembered Cal and wondered if he was still in his basement cell. I called to him and he promptly answered. I told him I had thought he had gone home, since I hadn't heard him all day.

He said, "Naw, I'm still here. I jes' bin' thinkin' all day. I got a letter from my mother an' she said she wuz awful glad th' jedge didn' give me life. I'm gonna' write ta her Sunday an' I'm gonna' say, 'Mamma, what makes ya' think twen'y ta thirty years don't mean life fer me?' She ask me, too, what my plans are fer my future. I'm gonna' say, 'Mamma, I ain't plannin' my future now, I'm plottin' it.' "

I asked him how he was fixed for cigarettes. He said, "I ain't fixed a'tall. I'm rollin' this dern Bull Durham, an' my throat feels like it's 'bout ready ta bleed."

I called the run-boy, gave *him* a pack of cigarettes, and asked him to take a pack down to Cal. A few minutes later, the run-boy came back and handed me a small, rusty, fingernail clipper. He said, "Cal said he wanted you to have this."

As soon as darkness had settled outside, the cell-block became a bedlam of wild animal calls, whistles, crazy singing, and combinations of oaths and vulgar remarks. Finally the guard unlocked the door, and yelled, "All right now, I want some quiet in here. It sounds worse than Dix Hill. If I hear any more of it, somebody's goin' to the hole." (Dix Hill is the state mental hospital.)

The noise was reduced to angry mutterings of what each one would like to see happen to the "screw," and the imaginations of some were fantastic. ("Screw" is the derogatory term given to guards by the inmates, but never used in the guards' hearing.)

Finally the "lights out" whistle sounded. I crawled up onto the top bunk. (With no cellmate, I had a choice, and decided that the top bunk might be a little less "populated.") I lay on my stomach for a long while and was fascinated by the activity of the roaches who were working like beavers to clean the food from the bottom of the bars. I don't know if roaches store their food like ants, but they reminded me of ants when they are carrying food to be stored. They came from somewhere above the door, sped down the bars in a steady procession and back up again. Of course, I couldn't tell whether they were the same ones coming back time after time or whether new ones were coming, eating their fill and leaving, but the parade continued on and on—some going up the bars and some coming down.

After a while, I turned over on my back and found that it was equally fascinating to watch their activity by looking at their shadows on the shadows of the bars, reflected on the rear wall.

I looked at my watch and noted that it was eleven o'clock. As I was hanging my watch on the corner of the bunk, a guard suddenly appeared in front of my cell and gave me quite a start, because I hadn't heard a sound except the snoring from the other cells.

He called me by name, asked me how I was feeling and explained that he had just come on duty and was making his "beginning-of-shift" check. He talked in a low voice about our case and expressed the opinion that public sentiment was in our favor and might force an early release for us. This was the first note of kindness or concern that I had heard from any prison official.

He left the third tier. A moment later, I heard some commotion on the second tier and heard someone running on the iron-grill walkway. I assumed that it was the guard. I could hear someone whispering below me, but couldn't tell what was being said.

In a few minutes, I heard more footsteps and the sound of jangling handcuffs. Then, I heard a cell door being unlocked, and "Come out of there, one at a time, with your hands in front of you."

Then I heard two sets of handcuffs being snapped in place and retreating footsteps. I was full of curiosity, but finally fell asleep.

When the coffee came the next morning I asked the run-boy about the incident. With no emotion and little interest, he said, "Yeah, the guard caught two fellows in the same bunk without any clothes on and took 'em to the hole."

Breakfast consisted of a hard-boiled egg, grits and gravy, stewed apples and peaches, and two slices of bread. The apples and peaches had been dragged over the top of the grits. I had reached through the bars to catch the bread, so I ate the egg and the bread. As the morning dragged along, I asked the run-boy about the possibility of a bath, some clean clothes, letter-writing, clean bed-clothing, and exercise.

He said, "You won't get a bath until next Friday or maybe Saturday—You'll get clean clothes whenever you get a bath—You'll get a clean sheet and a clean towel on Wednesday—You can write on Sunday. You won't get out of that cell until

Monday unless you get a visitor."

I said, "Don't they ever change these filthy blankets?"

He said, "Yeah, spring and fall."

Lunch of cold and greasy short ribs of beef, black-eyed peas, turnip greens and stewed pumpkin, was served at eleven. It looked as if they had tossed it all in the air at the same time and had caught it on the tray.

About two o'clock, a guard came, unlocked my cell, and said, "They want you up in the "back-hall."

I followed the guard down to the second tier and started toward the door. The guard said, "Not so fast there—stand up against the wall. I have to shake you down."

The guard at the door to the back-hall said, "You Payton?" I said that I was and he said, "You have a visitor."

He opened the door and I stepped past him. He said, "Hold it right there. I have to shake you down."

Finally I was allowed to see my wonderful friend, The Reverend W. W. Finlator, who had been such a source of strength and comfort during the long months of my difficulties. I was so glad to see him and so filled with emotion because he had thought to come when I needed him so badly that I couldn't speak. He seemed to understand, and just held my hand in a hard, warm grip. After a while we were able to talk, and he told me that he had talked by phone with my wife, that she and the kids were well, and that she would come to see me on Sunday. Then he offered a meaningful prayer and went out through the main entrance as I passed through the back door after another shakedown.

When I got back to detention, I was shaken down again before being locked in my cell. A few minutes later, a new cellmate was assigned to me. I will call him Winn.

Winn was really sour on the world, and he kept talking about what he was going to do to certain people when he completed his sentence. His story went something like this:

> Worked all summer for that stinkin' brother-in-law of mine—took care of his tobacco crop from beginnin' to end and never got a dime. Then he gets mad at me and kicks me out. When I asked him for some money, he says, "You know I won't have any money until I sell the tobacco." I knew that was a lie—he had plenty of money.
>
> I offered to settle a whole summer's work for fifty dollars so I

could go somewhere and get a job, but he says, "I ain't givin' you a nickel till I get paid for the tobacco." I coulda' killed him right there.

Anyway, I went to town and met a fellow and we had a coupla' beers, and I just got two blank checks and made 'em out for twenty dollars and signed his name to 'em, and got 'em cashed.

Well, I got me a job and met a good Christian girl and we got married. I was worried about them dern checks, and thought I better tell her about 'em. Nothin' would do her but for me to go down and see if I could straighten it out by payin' 'em off.

We was on our way down there when I was arrested and charged with forgery.

I was in jail for three months waitin' trial, and they wouldn't give an inch. My brother-in-law said I needed to be taught a lesson. The judge give me one to three years. One to three years for a lousy forty dollars. Dern that wife of mine—talkin' me into tryin' to do the right thing. This is what I get for listenin' to her. I shoulda' gone the other way.

Now she's pregnant and that's somethin' else to worry about. Dern it anyway.

When I get out of here I'm gonna' stomp that brother-in-law into the ground. I'm gonna' knock every tooth out, and I hope they go down his throat and choke him to death.

And, boy I'm gonna' do everybody I can from then on. There's no use tryin' to go straight. Nobody'll hire an ex-con.

I talked with him about the mistake he was making, and how he was young enough to build a new life for himself. I pointed out that he would have to change his attitude if he ever expected to get out of prison, to say nothing of staying out. After a week of my talking and a real nice letter from his wife, he announced that he was taking my advice.

Visiting Sunday

Sunday, November 6, 1960—the day my wife was coming to see me. After 28 years of married life, and only three days of separation, I was as excited as if it had been my first date.

Just after breakfast, Johnnie called to me and asked, jokingly, if I was going to Sunday School.

I said, "No, I guess not, but I have my lesson prepared." It was true, too. I had found a phamphlet in my cell which contained the International Sunday School lesson which was used at our church. In order to pass the time on Saturday, I had sketched out a commentary just as I would have done at home when I was to teach on Sunday morning.

Johnnie said, "Let's hear it." Several others started calling and urging that I let them hear it. The run-boy said, "Come on, Mr. Payton, I'll make everybody be quiet. We can sure use a little religion in this stinkin' hole."

Finally I agreed that I would ask the guard for permission to give it. However, when he came by and I asked him about it, I'm sure he wouldn't have been more surprised if I had asked to borrow his keys. His face turned red and he looked like he was going to explode as he stammered, "I don't know about that; I never heard of it bein' done before. They have services on Sunday morning in the chapel, but you fellows are not allowed to go. I don't know what they'd say about anything like that in here. I'll have to find out." He said nothing further about it, and it seemed to be forgotten by everyone.

At 12 o'clock, I was bathed and shaved as well as was possible, with a washbasin which only a contortionist could use and with no mirror. I was ready for my "date."

The run-boy had said that afternoon visiting began at one o'clock. When two o'clock arrived without any call to come to the visiting room, I began to worry and had visions of all kinds of trouble which might have befallen my wife.

At 3:25, the guard finally came and said, "Payton, you have a visitor."

After the inevitable shakedown when leaving detention and upon arrival at the back-hall, I was asked if I saw my visitor. When I said that I did not, I was ushered across the hall into another room. When I saw no one there whom I knew, the guard said, "There must have been some mistake. You'll have to go back to your cell."

As I was being escorted toward the back door, I saw my wife and Bill Finlator coming in from the outside. She hurried toward me with arms outstretched, and I was faced with a difficult decision. I wanted to take her in my arms, but I had been warned that any physical contact between a visitor and an inmate could mean punishment for the inmate and prohibition against visiting for the visitor. So, I held her away while I explained this to her. That wasn't easy.

We were then directed into the visiting room where I was

placed inside a large cage-like aisle, and she was directed along the outside until she was opposite where I was standing. We were permitted to talk through a wire-mesh screen for about 20 minutes. Then a guard called, "Time's up." My wife was ushered toward the front entrance as I was shaken down and told to go to the mail room for a package.

I had no idea where the mail room was, but found an inmate on the yard who agreed to show me. I was given a large canvas bag with my name on it after signing a form.

Back in my cell, I found what had been a beautiful big coconut cake which had been punched full of holes which I assumed was part of the testing for contraband. I also found a package of fried chicken, a bag of fruit, candy bars, peanuts, cookies, cheese and crackers, three cartons of cigarettes, two ball-point pens with extra fillers, two hanndkerchiefs, and a package of razor blades.

My poor darling, of course, had no way of knowing the conditions under which we were existing, nor the problem she had presented by her generous expression of her love.

I could see her in my mind's eye, in our kitchen, before daylight that morning, busily frying the chicken and baking the cake and pouring all of her loving care and kindness into it while she had visions of its being eaten "picnic-style" around a large table to which all of the "poor fellows" would be invited.

Little did she know that the mere volume of all the good things presented a problem of leaving no room to move in the small cell; little did she know that those "poor fellows" were locked tightly in their cells on three tiers, and they couldn't see me and I couldn't see them; little did she know that we had no knife or other tool with which to cut the cake; little did she know that it was imperative that everything not wrapped and sealed be eaten before "lights out" and the arrival of our nightly visitors.

By calling to my "rap partners" I learned, to my dismay, that they, too, had received packages and were faced with the same problem. ("Rap partners" is the inmate term for fellow prisoners who were involved in the same court case.)

Finally we enlisted the aid of the run-boy and kept him busy for more than an hour distributing the food throughout the entire cell-block and passing it through the bars to the eager hands of the happy occupants while their supper trays sat untouched.

When we had cleared away all of the "perishable" food except the cake, my cellmate had the brilliant idea of mashing his tobacco can flat and using it to cut the cake. We emptied his Prince Albert into a piece of waxed paper which had been around the cake, and he jumped up and down on the can. Then, he washed it, and we used it to crudely fashion chucks of gooey marshmallow and coconut-covered cake which we wrapped in toilet tissue and passed through the bars to the run-boy, who delivered them to the other cells.

Needless to say, crumbs and small pieces of food were strewn all over the cell-block, and we dreaded the lights-out whistle. When it came, our worst fears were realized. Where they had come single-file before, they were now arriving in columns of three and four. And, apparently, they had flashed the message throughout the entire prison.

Classification Examination

On Monday, November 7th, some 30 of us were taken from our cells and marched up the steps, in the same building, and told to sit on benches in one end of a large room surrounded by small offices over the doors of which were signs: "Station 1," "Station 2," "Station 3," and so on, up to and including "Station 8."

Every few minutes, a white-uniformed man (whom we later learned was also an inmate, but who looked very official that morning) called out a name, and one of the men would leave the benches and be directed to Station 1. After a while, my name was called, and I stepped to the desk at Station 1 where a record was made of height, weight, color of hair, color of eyes, and any identifying scars. Then, a set of numbers were placed on a bar which was attached to a chain at either end. The chain was placed around my neck so that the numbers rested on my chest while front- and side-view pictures were taken. After this, I was fingerprinted and directed to Station 2 with a card which contained the record made at Station 1. Here, another man asked questions about age, home address, names of relatives, etc., which he typed on the card which I had carried to him. Then I was directed to Station 3 where another man copied the information shown on the original card.

The next stop was Station 4, where I spent the remainder of the day filling in forms, doing spelling, reading, writing and arithmetic tests and answering 560 questions by checking "yes" or "no" and by checking another list of questions "true" or "false." (I learned later that all of this was part of the IQ and aptitude tests.)

As I was entering Station 4, Cal was coming out. He said, "I just finished thet I.Q. bizness and I think I made two points above a idiot."

Medical Examination

The next day, we were marched three or four hundred yards across the prison yard to the hospital where we were ordered to strip to the waist and line up along a wall. We were then taken to an office at the end of the long hall, where tests were made of our blood pressure and heart-beat, and where samples of blood and urine were taken.

As we turned from the first office, we were directed through another; as we passed between two inmates in white uniforms, one vaccinated us in the left arm while the other gave us a shot in the right arm. After this, we were again lined up in the first hallway and, as our names were called, we stepped forward for a chest X-ray.

The X-rays completed, we were directed to another hallway and lined up before a dentist's office. A very professional and efficient-looking dentist examined our teeth and called out his findings concerning each tooth to an inmate, in white uniform, who made a record of same. We were then herded into a small waiting room while the dentist recalled those whom he had determined needed immediate extractions.

When all extractions had been accomplished, names were called and, as we responded, we were directed into an office where we were questioned about physical complaints, ailments, disorders, previous illnesses, operations, and previous medical treatment.

Just before this, Charley had appeared, wearing pajamas and

bathrobe, and had informed us that his private physician had written a letter to prison officials which had resulted in his being placed in the hospital, where he had a clean bed and was permitted to drink fresh milk and watch television at will.

When I was called into the office to be questioned about complaints, etc., I started to explain to the clerk that I hadn't known about having my doctor write about previous illness and treatments. He stopped me and said, "You are lucky you didn't, believe me. And unless there is something seriously wrong with you, let me mark this card 'no complaints.'" I took his advice and thanked him for it, but I didn't realize then how weak a reward a mere "thank you" was for the favor which he had bestowed.

When the complaint cards had all been filled out, someone called out, "Everybody strip completely—everything off. Leave your clothes on the floor and line up against the wall."

For what seemed like hours, we stood, absolutely naked, with our stomachs against the backbone of the fellow in front. The guards seemed to think it was some kind of joke to keep urging "togetherness." A virtual parade of other inmates and guards went by, and there was considerable joking about the "new crop."

The door at the end of the hall was opened at least a hundred times while we were standing there and, each time, a cold blast of air whistled through the hallway causing us to shiver and become more miserable by the moment.

Finally I was next. As I stepped into the doctor's office, an inmate clerk made an examination of all body openings while the doctor was examining Calvin, who had been just ahead of me.

I heard the doctor say in an angry voice, "What's this about your stomach trouble?"

Calvin opened his mouth to answer, but the doctor said, "Suppose you let me do the talking. I'll decide whether or not you have an ulcer and I'll decide what kind of treatment you're going to get. But I'll tell you right now that you have a bad attitude—you're a smart-aleck—and you'd better change or you're going to be here a long time."

I couldn't believe my ears. I had been right behind Calvin all the time, and I hadn't heard him say a word which could possibly have been responsible for the doctor's anger nor his charge against Calvin.

The doctor told Calvin about some tests that he would be expected to take at a later date and turned to me with my complaint card in his hand.

He said, "No complaints, huh, Payton?" I said, "No, sir."

He said, "Feel all right?" I said, "Yes, sir."

He said, "Hold out your hands." I did so and he watched them closely for several seconds, then said, "Turn them over."

I turned them over. He watched them closely. Then he used his stethoscope on my chest and back. He asked, "Have you had a cold?"

I said, "Yes, sir, but it's about gone now."

He made some signal to the clerk and turned to the next patient. The clerk said, "That's all, Payton. You can dress."

When I returned to my pile of clothing, I saw my rap partners, who were seething with rage and humiliation as they recounted the insults which the doctor had heaped upon them.

It seemed that the doctor considered it a personal insult for an outside doctor to write a letter diagnosing an inmate's ailments or suggesting treatment. He was especially angry with the Henderson boys and Charley. He had given Johnnie a tongue-lashing for the entire group.

He had ordered Charley out of his pajamas and bathrobe, back into regular prison garb, and moved from the hospital to an "isolation cell." One of the inmate nurses reported later that the doctor had "raised the roof" about Charley having been assigned to the hospital in the first place. He was quoted as saying, "If he's looking for special treatment, I'll give him some."

The rest of us were then marched back to detention.

In reviewing the hospital experience, I had to admit that, aside from the indignity, it had been surprisingly thorough, efficient, and complete.

I Become A Run-boy

On Thursday, November 10th, I nearly jumped out of my skin at 4:00 A.M. when I was awakened by a guard shaking me.

He said, "Come on, Payton, we're going to use you as a run-boy. You'll have to go to the kitchen and help bring the chow."

I tumbled out of my bunk, dressed, and lined up against the wall in the hallway along with nine other inmates—five white and four Negro. After all of us were shaken down, we walked some 100 yards to the kitchen where we found large containers filled with breakfast for the 47 white inmates and the 31 Negroes in detention. We were also required to carry 78 heavy metal trays and 78 spoons.

As we were picking up the various items, I heard a big fellow whisper, "Let the 'big-shot' labor boss carry one end of the trays." I found myself maneuvered into that position. It was a back-breaking load during the trudge back to detention. Then we spread the containers of food on a long table and ladled it out to the metal trays which were carried to the inmates in the cells. However, before starting to fill the trays, four paper plates were filled with food, and the big fellow who had whispered about me, accompanied by a guard, carried these plates outside. The head run-boy informed me that the paper plates were for those in "meditation," and we should always try to give them a little extra when the guard wasn't looking. ("Meditation" is the name given to the isolation cells into which inmates are placed when they are suspected of having mental disorders or imaginary illnesses. However, the inmates generally contend that guards use it to punish in the same way in which the hole is used.)

When everyone had been served, the "chow-line boys" were permitted to take as much of what was left as they wanted for themselves.

I was surprised to find that when I prepared my own tray and did not spill one thing on top of another and did not have the top of my food leveled off by that bottom bar of the cell door, it tasted entirely different and was really not bad food.

When we had finished eating, it was our job to gather up all the trays, scrape the remains from each tray into a large garbage can, and carry all the equipment and any remaining food back to the kitchen.

Again, I found myself maneuvered into the position with the

heaviest load (the metal trays), while the big fellow carried the basket with a few slices of bread and made remarks about the "big shot" not having a bellhop to do his dirty work for him.

When we returned from the kitchen, the six of us had to sweep the grill runways in front of the cells, wipe up the coffee stains from the bars, and wipe the dust from the railings. Then four of the six were locked in their cells and the head run-boy and his new assistant (me) scrubbed the basement with hot water and strong liquid soap, carried the garbage to the incinerator some two hundred yards away, placed all the food scraps in barrels, and burned all the papers.

We were shaken down and the cans were carefully examined before we left detention. As we went through the gate leading to the incinerator, we were again shaken down, and the cans were again examined. When we returned to that gate with the empty cans, they were examined a third time, and we were again shaken down. We carried the cans to a platform at the corner of the cell-block and washed them with hot water.

The head run-boy explained very carefully and very seriously that this portion of the job needed to be done very thoroughly and should consume as much time as possible. I was duly impressed with his apparent concern, but did not understand the reason for it until he explained further that this was the only opportunity of the day for friends to inquire about those in detention. He said, "The run-boy can usually expect to pick-up a little change or a few cigarettes in exchange for information or for delivering a message."

Several men came by and pretended to be assisting in cleaning the cans while whispered conversations were held with the head run-boy, but I couldn't hear what was being said. When we returned the cans to detention, they were again carefully examined, and we were given a thorough shakedown.

While the head run-boy was taking orders for the morning papers, the guard supervised my move from cell number five on the third tier to cell number one on the second tier. He explained that cell number one was reserved for the two run-boys because it was closest to the guard's quarters. He explained, too, that it was unlocked at 4:30 A.M. and left unlocked until 9 P.M.

After the move had been completed, we went to the store-box for the newspapers which had been ordered by those in detention. As we delivered them to the cells, we took orders for items desired from the store-box. When I questioned the inefficiency of making the rounds of the cells twice and of making two trips to the store-box, the head run-boy said, "Don't be stupid—when you've been here as long as I've been you'll be looking for every excuse, too, to get out of this stinking hole for a few minutes."

This fellow spoke very well and seemed to have considerable education. He was tall and rather handsome. The others called him "Camp." I learned that his sentence was five to seven years, but never learned the nature of his offence. He was 28 years old and had served a previous sentence of one to three years. He had been on a road gang, but had been transferred back to Central Prison because of some question about his involvement in an attempted escape of other prisoners. He was "sweating-out" an investigation which would determine whether or not the term of his sentence was to be increased. I had a suspicion that his reason for selecting me as his assistant had much to do with the large package of good things to eat which my wife had sent. However, we became good friends, and he more than repaid me many times for the food and cigarettes which I shared with him.

Our next job was to clean the guard's washroom and toilet on the second tier. After this, and the distribution of the store-box order, it was time to go for the food for lunch. Once more I found myself maneuvered to one end of the heavy trays while the big fellow kept up a chatter of insulting remarks about "the big-shot labor leader." When we spread the food on the long table and the guard ordered me to handle the meat, the big fellow said, "Come now, children, pass yo' plates, an' the master will serve."

I walked over to him and said, "Look, Slim, I'm a real peaceable guy, and I'm not looking for trouble, but I'm giving you fair warning—*Get off my back, or I'm going to drop that coffee pot off the third floor on top of your head the first chance I get.*"

I fully expected a showdown right there and was greatly

relieved when a big grin spread over his face, and he said, "Man, ah' hears ya' talkin', and you'se sayin' it right. I'se jes' tryin' to see what kinda' man you was." He almost knocked the breath out of me with a hearty slap on the back. From that moment on, he and I were the best of friends, and he made sure that we took only our regular turns with the heavy load of trays.

After the trays had been gathered and everything had been carried back to the kitchen, we took the afternoon store-box order. When it was distributed, the guard sent us to the supply room. We carried a large carton of toilet tissue, a carton of soap, and two new mops back to detention.

Then, noticing that my ankles were swollen, the head run-boy suggested that I go to the cell and rest for an hour. He didn't have to ask me twice. I was really tired, and my vaccination was beginning to "take," with a big watery blister beginning to form on my left arm.

At four o'clock we served supper and, after taking the things back to the kitchen, we swept and scrubbed the floors and wiped the bars and railings. By this time I was about ready to drop from weariness and from a fever and headache which apparently were connected with the vacinnation and shots—everyone else who had a sore arm was also feeling ill. Strangely, the vaccination had not "taken" on any of the old-timers. When I mentioned this to Camp, he laughed and said, "You're not 'con-wise.' You should have spit on that scratch as soon as you got it and then wiped it off good, and you'd never know you had it. Why don't you take a shower and go to bed? I'll take care of anything that's needed."

Thoughts of that shower were all that had kept me going all day. I quickly stripped, washed my underwear and socks, hung them on a string which stretched from the head to the foot of the bunk, and paraded naked down the cat-walk opposite the cells to the little shower room in the corner.

I shall never forget that wonderful feeling when the warm spray hit my body. I thought of my own shower at home into which I automatically stepped each morning as soon as I was out of bed, without ever thinking of it as a luxury.

Then, as I soaped and rinsed and soaped and rinsed, I began feeling guilty because 40 pairs of envious eyes were fixed on me. I'm sure, though, that all would have agreed that I had earned it.

* * * * *

On Wednesday morning Camp advised, "This is clean-sheet day." Everyone stuffed his dirty sheet and towel through the bars. We gathered them up and carried them to the "clothes house." They were traded for clean ones which we distributed back to the cells.

Shortly after three P.M. (when the guards changed shifts) I stopped to get a drink at the fountain in the hallway. A heavy hand landed on my shoulder, and the afternoon guard said, "I'm only going to tell you once about drinking from this fountain. This is for the guards. Inmates are not allowed to drink from it. If you want a drink, bring your cup and fill it, but don't drink from the fountain."

I said, "I'm sorry. I didn't know. I've been drinking from it all day, and no one told me not to."

"I don't care what the other guards do or don't do. I'm tellin' you not to drink from the fountain," the guard retorted.

* * * * *

On Friday, November 11th, Camp received shipping orders. He was delighted because this meant that he was not to receive an additional sentence.

I became what was probably the greenest head run-boy in the history of Central Prison. The guard asked me who I'd like as my assistant, and I selected Lawrence. He moved in with me on the second tier. Both of us had sore and swollen left arms. Mine ached all the way to my finger tips. The secretion from the sore seemed to hold great attraction for the cockroaches while I was sleeping until I learned (from an old-timer) to put a strong rubber band around my left sleeve above and below the sore.

The next morning, the guard informed us that "this is clean clothes and shower day." He said that bundles of clean clothes were waiting for us at the clothes house. We found three giant bags. One was stuffed full of pants; one was full of shirts; and the third one was filled with underwear and socks. Together, we could carry only one bag at a time, and we had to make three trips.

Back at detention, we emptied everything on the floor and distributed everything, regardless of size, to the inmates. The place was a madhouse for an hour, with everyone trading sizes until each inmate had obtained, from what was available, the clothes which most nearly fit him.

As each man removed his dirty clothes to try on clean ones, he pushed the dirty ones through the bars of his cell. We collected them and piled them in the hallway.

When all had been outfitted, the guard began letting the men out of their cells, one at a time, to go to the little shower room. The guard watched from the doorway, and all the inmates watched from their cells. Of course, as each one paraded his completely nude manly charms across the catwalk, he was the object of ridicule or admiration, as the case might be. For the younger ones, a continuous chorus of wolf whistles was heard throughout their "performance."

Some were shy and embarrassed and tried as best they could to be modest, but others preened and strutted as if they were participants in a charm contest. All in all, it was quite a show, and everyone was in great good humor afterwards.

After we had served lunch, Lawrence and I had the unpleasant task of sorting all the dirty clothes and filling one bag with pants, another with shirts, and a third one with underwear and socks. We delivered them to the clothes house to be transported to the women's prison for laundering.

During the afternoon, it occurred to me that it might be interesting to learn the nature of the crimes for which the 47 white prisoners in this section were serving time. To my surprise, all cooperated, although I had been told that a "good con" never questions another inmate about his "rap." Perhaps they assumed that I had been instructed to secure this information.

When I completed the survey, I compiled the following data:

    2 for arson
    2 for murder
    2 for forgery
    4 for armed robbery
    7 for breaking and entering
    2 for grand larceny
    2 for carnal knowledge

    1 for assault on female
    2 for attempted rape
    2 for accessory to murder
    3 for manslaughter
    3 for embezzlement
    2 for assault with intent to kill
    1 for crime against nature
    2 for hit-and-run, drunken driving
    10 for conspiracy (including our group)

* * * * *

On Saturday, November 12th, I was given a choice of attending the movie in the auditorium or getting a haircut. I chose the haircut, and the guard gave me a "yard-pass." (Prisoners are not allowed on the yard without a "yard-badge" or a "yard-pass.")

I had been told that the barbers were also inmates, and that service was supposed to be free, but "it's a good idea to let the barber know in advance that you have something for him." Armed with a pack of cigarettes and a dime, I entered the barber shop in the corner of the clothes house. I was surprised to find a modern-looking (except for the fact that there were no seats for the waiting customers), three-chair shop, with professional-looking barbers. My second surprise came when I discovered that they all knew who I was and seemed to have detailed knowledge of our case.

When I offered the cigarettes, I was told that this wasn't necessary, and if I needed a friend or a favor at any time I had only to get word to one of the barbers. While I was getting my hair cut, our case was rehashed in great detail by the barbers and other "customers," and some strong opinions about North Carolina justice were expressed. It was amazing how they had been able to read between the lines of newspaper stories and deduce the actual facts in the case. Ironically, I found myself wishing that these men might have served on the jury in our case. Of course, they expressed violent hatred for the ex-convict who had been used by the state to entrap the eight of us.

This was my first experience with inmates who were not seen through bars and under the tight restrictions of detention. I was impressed with their intelligence, their seemingly well-adjusted attitude, and their friendliness.

As I was leaving the barber shop, a handsome young Negro stopped me in front of the chapel. He introduced himself in a well-educated manner, and said, "We have been very interested in your case and have been praying for you and your companions. We know that you don't belong here, but now that you are, we're looking forward to having you in our church activity."

I doubt that the reader can grasp the significance of the experiences just recorded unless he has personally experienced almost total despair and then, suddenly, found friendly faces speaking to him with kindness and genuine concern. To say that it was a wonderful feeling seems so inadequate to describe what that hour had done for my morale.

Back at detention, the guard said, "Right after lunch, I want that basement washed down with hot water, and I want the second and third tiers swept. You can't use water up there."

After lunch had been served, we stuck brooms through the bars on the second and third tiers and the occupants swept out their cells. When all of the dirt and debris had been swept onto the grilled walkway on the third tier, we cleaned that walkway and let the dirt drop to the walkway on the second tier. Then we cleaned that walkway and dropped everything to the basement floor.

The guard unlocked all of the basement cells (except number one) and ordered the occupants to place everything on top of the top bunk. While he herded the displaced inmates to a far corner, we proceeded to "blow out" each cell with water which was close to being steam. Lawrence manned the faucet end of the hose while I, in my dress shoes, manned the nozzle end.

The water ran thick and black. Hundreds of roaches floated with the flood across the floor and down the drain. The inmates from the upper tiers complained loudly that we were chasing all of the roaches up to them. I was soaked to my knees and the water sloshed from my shoes at every step.

Lawrence was ill. For ten days, he had been without the medicine which he had been taking every four hours since his return from a German prisoner-of-war camp. He had been X-rayed on Thursday, but had not been given medication.

After supper, I urged him to take his shower and go to bed, but he was more concerned about my wet feet and insisted that I get out of the wet clothes and take my shower first. Of course, I had no dry clothing; so, after my shower, I put the wet shoes back on, without socks, and performed the remaining chores in my underwear, while my shirt, pants and socks were draped across a mop-handle to dry. We needed no one to rock us to sleep when the lights-out whistle sounded at nine o'clock.

Sunday School In Prison

After breakfast on Sunday, November 13th, the guard said, "Payton, I understand you teach Bible class on Sundays when you are home. I spoke to the Major about it, and he says it's all right if you want to read the Bible and give a religious talk in here this morning."

I walked out on the catwalk facing the cells and said, "The major has given us permission to have a religious service in here this morning, but I don't want to force it on you men when you can't get away. How do you feel about it?"

There was a chorus of "fine," "good," "go ahead."

"Anyone object?"

One fellow in cell number two on the top tier said, "I don't believe in that stuff, but don't let me stop you. I'll wrap a blanket around my head, and you won't bother me."

I stood on the catwalk across from the cells, where all the men could see me. They crowded side by side to the front of their cells as I read Matthew 5:2-12. I then spoke for about 20 minutes. I looked especially at cell number two on the third tier and noticed that both occupants were pressed against the front bars, and neither had a blanket around his head. When I stopped talking, a number of voices called, "More, more." I read several selections from a little booklet, *The Upper Room*, which I had found under my mattress. Then I gave a short prayer. The cell-block remained strangely silent for a long while.

This was visiting day for Negro inmates. We could hear the loudspeaker calling those who had visitors, and we could hear the laughter from their cells directly back of ours. Apparently, many of them were receiving packages as we had on the previous Sunday, and the same kind of sharing was in progress.

As I thought of my visit, I could not realize that only one week had gone by. It seemed that I had lived a lifetime since then.

At lunch time, a guard gave me a supply of prison stationery with instructions to issue six sheets of papers and three envelopes to each inmate.

When I came to cell number seven on the second tier, the two young occupants began telling me that there was no point in leaving the writing material with them because they had no money for postage. Not being "con-wise," I foolishly told them that I would pay for their postage. As I turned from their cell, I saw one of them make a sign by placing one hand on top of the other and wiggling both thumbs. As I walked away, they began calling, in high-pitched voices, "Mother, Mother, Mother," but it meant nothing to me at that time. However, when I began collecting the letters for mailing, seventeen inmates gave me a sob-story about not having money for postage, and all knew of my promise to pay postage for the two in cell number seven. I paid 68 cents from my meager funds for those who claimed to have no money.

Later, I learned that the term "Mother" is an expression used by convicts to indicate an inmate who will fall for a sob-story and try to help another inmate out of his "difficulties." The "word" is passed from one inmate to another by the sign which I had witnessed in cell number seven. An inmate who will "Mother" one and all is held in contempt by the more experienced, and every effort will be made to "take him" at every opportunity. However, the inmate who learns to turn a deaf ear to the habitual poacher and "mothers" only a select group of "the more worthy" becomes that group's champion, whom all members of such group will fight to protect, defend, or promote.

Lawrence was still quite ill and was eating Rollaids by the handfuls, but he insisted on doing his share of the run-boy chores. I began worrying about whether or not I had done him a favor by selecting him as my assistant.

Calvin was also having severe stomach pains. Johnnie had developed a heavy chest cold. There was nothing I could do about Lawrence and Calvin except bring more Rollaids every time I came from the store-box. However, I was successful in having the guard move Johnnie and Warren to the second tier where it was not so cold and damp. Mike and Robert were fine and taking everything in stride. My admiration and respect for them rose by leaps and bounds. Mike had been notified that he was to be shipped to a county road camp to work as an electrician's helper. Calvin and Robert had also been notified that they were to be transferred to the shipping corridor, but they did not know any more. None of us had heard from Charley since we had seen him in the hospital.

On Wednesday, November 16th, the guard said, "This is the day for clean sheets and towels."

While Lawrence and I were engaged in this activity, the guard said, "Payton, the Classification Board wants you up front."

After the inevitable shakedown when leaving detention, I went to the front office where I was ushered into a small room in which several men sat around a conference table. Some were in uniform, and I assumed they were prison officials. Others were in civilian clothes.

A large, kindly-looking man was sitting in the center, directly opposite the seat I had been instructed to take. He introduced himself as the warden and began questioning me about my ability as a typist and my knowledge of office work. After everyone had been given an opportunity to question me, I was asked to wait outside. To my surprise, I found Johnnie, Calvin and Robert waiting there. I told them of my questioning in the small room and expressed the opinion that I would be assigned to an office job. However, after a few minutes, I was called back into the small room and was informed that I was being assigned to Road Camp 126 and would receive shipping orders the next day.

This was a real disappointment. I had hoped to stay in Raleigh where there was greater opportunity for contact with those who were seeking our early release and where there were jobs in which I could perform useful work in line with my training. And, frankly, not the least of my disturbing thoughts had to do with the stories I had heard of the horrors of "working on-the-roads" under constant "gun-guard" by brutal and illiterate guards and road foremen.

Unhappily, I trudged back to detention and the unpleasant

task of changing sheets and towels. The long afternoon was filled with more stories of road-camp unpleasantries, and several who had served time at Camp 126 attempted to brief me on who and what to expect.

Lawrence became deathly ill while we were serving supper. I found him on the floor of our cell with his head over the toilet bowl, trying desperately to vomit. I told the guard and he came in and examined Lawrence. He said, "I'll see if I can get him over to the hospital."

I stood in the doorway and heard him arguing with someone on the phone. "No, sir, I don't believe he is faking. Yes, sir, I saw him myself, and he's sick. No, sir, I don't believe he ate any supper. Yes, sir, he's down on the floor and screaming with pain. Yes, sir, I talked with him; he says he has an ulcer. No, sir, he has been trying to vomit, but nothing comes. No, sir, I don't see any blood. Yes, sir, I know that some of them are good at faking, but this boy is not faking. He's really sick. All right sir, thank you, sir."

The guard walked over to me, sweat streaming down his face and looking as if he had just finished a mile-long race. He was actually trembling as he said, "They're sending someone to take him to the hospital." For another hour, Lawrence rolled on the floor and screamed with pain. Then another guard came in and led him away. Lawrence walked in a doubled-over position, with sweat streaming from his face.

A few minutes after they had taken Lawrence away, a guard came in with a list of those who were to be shipped the next morning. My name was on the list, and I was told to have my personal belongings together and be ready to leave detention at four-thirty the next morning.

About half an hour later, they brought Lawrence back, and he promptly vomited some soda solution they had given to him at the hospital. Again, he began screaming and rolling on the floor in agony. I rubbed him and put hot towels on his stomach, but nothing eased his pain. He kept saying, "If I could just get that medicine they took from me."

When the guard came to lock us up at nine o'clock, I begged that he leave our cell unlocked so I could get to the main door in case of emergency. He said, "You know I can't do that. The major would have my scalp."

I then explained about the medicine which Lawrence had taken for years and which he had not been allowed to keep when he entered prison.

He said, "It has probably been destroyed, but he couldn't have it unless the doctor said so, even if we could find it. And the doctor won't come in until 7:30 in the morning."

With Lawrence still rolling on the floor and heaving in a desperate effort to vomit, I begged the guard to try to get him to the hospital again and to urge that they put him to bed there so someone could look after him. It was obvious that the guard was having a terrible struggle with himself. He knew that Lawrence was really sick and needed expert attention, but he dreaded another session with the major. Finally, his frustration turned to anger against me, and he said, "I've done all I can. Now you get in your cell and be quiet. The lights are supposed to be out, and if the major sees them on I'll get fired."

He slammed the door shut, turned the big key in the lock and went out, slamming the main door behind him.

I got Lawrence up from the floor and onto his bunk and kept putting hot towels on his stomach while tears of rage blinded me and dropped on him in a steady stream.

Apparently, the guard's conscience was bothering him because he came to the cell door twice, shined his flashlight in, and watched while I tried to calm Lawrence.

Finally, the hospital guard came again, and I was ordered out of cell and forced to stand in the hallway while he went in the cell to talk to Lawrence. (A prison rule prohibits a guard from entering a cell while it is occupied by more than one inmate.) After a few minutes, he came out and said, "Help him get dressed. I'll take him back over to the hospital."

He led Lawrence away, and as I climbed in the upper bunk I remembered that I was to be shipped out at 4:30 A.M. In my concern over Lawrence I had forgotten all about it.

I had just fallen asleep when they brought Lawrence back, still deathly ill, and again vomiting the solution they had given him. The nightmare went on until 11:15, when the night guard came on duty and saw me putting hot towels on Lawrence while he rolled and groaned.

Again, I was ordered from the cell while he went in and

discovered that Lawrence had been vomiting blood.

He became quite excited and rushed to the telephone. Within a few minutes, two other guards came and took Lawrence away. This time they took his belongings, and I was sure that he would be put to bed in the hospital.

I climbed to the top bunk again and was asleep almost before my head touched the sweater which I was using as a pillow.

About 12:30 A.M., I was awakened by the noise of the cell being unlocked and couldn't believe it when Lawrence staggered in and fell into the lower bunk.

The guard said, "They gave him a shot to knock him out. You'd better help him get undressed and in bed."

So, for another two hours, I helped Lawrence back and forth from the bunk to the toilet bowl and tried to keep hot towels on his stomach. He kept begging for more and hotter towels and insisted that they always helped at home, but I couldn't see that they were doing any good. However, I kept at it until my hands were raw from the scalding water, and his stomach looked like it had been cooked. Finally, he stopped throwing himself about and slept.

Lawrence was still sleeping when they came for me about an hour later and lined me up along the wall with ten others, including Johnnie. With each of us carrying our belongings in a gunny-sack or a pillow case, we were marched to the shipping quarters entrance next door. We were joined by 25 other inmates, including Calvin and Robert.

We were marched to the main dining hall where scrambled eggs had been prepared for us. This was my first experience in the prison dining hall. No one had told me that it was a rule to remove your cap upon entering. In fact, I didn't even realize that I was wearing a cap until, as I was about to sit down at a table with my tray, a guard bellowed, "Do you want to go to the hole for 30 days?" Startled, I stammered, "No, sir." He said, "Then take off that cap."

When I had finished eating and was ready to drink my coffee, from force of habit, I began filling my pipe. I was just ready to light it when I noticed one of the fellows behind the steam table making motions to me and shaking his head. In this way I learned that smoking is prohibited in the dining room. Later, one of our group told me that the guard had been watching me fill my pipe with an expression on his face which reminded one of a cat waiting to pounce upon a bird. (Weeks later, when I again entered the dining room, I saw "No Smoking" signs on the wall, but I didn't see them that first morning.)

When we had all finished our coffee, the guard said, "Let's go." We were marched to the visitor's room where we sat on the floor for nearly two hours.

One of the constant complaints of the inmates concerned the fact that those who are to be shipped are rousted out of bed at four-thirty in the morning to catch a bus which is scheduled to leave at 7:30, and the men are forced to sit or lay on the floor of the visitor's room for two hours. The inmates are convinced that this is done deliberately as part of the prison system theory that the purpose of imprisonment is to punish and that anything which makes inmates more uncomfortable is in line with the aims and objectives of the system.

The Blue Goose

Finally, a guard began calling names, and we were lined up against the wall and then marched singly to the "Blue Goose," which was waiting at the entrance. Blue Goose is the name given by the inmates to the bus which transports inmates to and from Central Prison and the various road camps. Some 40 or 50 men ride these buses, driven by inmates, each day, Monday through Friday. An armed guard rides beside the driver. The driver's compartment is completely separated from the passenger section, and there is no way to get into the passenger section except through the rear door which is padlocked from the outside with the guard carrying the only key.

The only fire extinguisher is located in front of the guard. In case of fire or accident, the passengers would be solely dependent upon the guard being unhurt and capable of assisting them. Otherwise, they would be as helpless as rats in a cage.

It would seem logical that if these men are such a menace to society that they must be transported in this fashion, they should not be allowed to work within a few feet of women and children in the yards of the homes along the highway. Incidentally, though, the trusted honor-grade inmates, and even those who have completed their sentence, are also transported by these same buses.

We were directed to place our belongings in the baggage compartment and to climb into the bus. The interior of the bus looked like it had been struck by a cyclone. There were two long seats running the length of the bus, on either side, and a row of single seats down the middle. The seats had, at one time, been covered with artificial leather, but most of it had been cut or torn away. The naked springs were sticking through in so many places that it was difficult to find a space large enough to sit on without being stuck by the heavy wire springs.

When our group of 35 had been crowded in, the rear door, with heavy bars, was bolted and locked. The glass on the front and sides was also barred.

A big, fat guard took his place beside the driver, and we rolled out of the prison yard amid bedlam. Most of the passengers were yelling vulgar and uncomplimentary remarks to each other about Central Prison and all those in authority. Most of them expressed extreme pleasure in regard to leaving the "Wall." We were hardly out of the prison yard before several of them "armed" themselves. This came as quite a shock to those of us who were having a new experience. The "arms" were a strange assortment of safety razor blades and long slivers of metal, sharpened on one end. They came from various hiding places around the windows, beneath the seats, and along the ceiling. The double-edged blades were fitted into empty book match covers and held between the thumb and forefinger to make a wicked-looking slashing weapon. The single-edged blades were held by some between the thumb and forefinger, but others held them between the knuckles of their closed fists. The metal slivers seemed to have been made from bolts or scrap metal and looked like short ice-picks.

With one eye on the guard, those who were armed made sure that everyone knew it by dancing around and making practice passes at the nearest ear, nose, or chin.

As we came to the highway and rolled smoothly through the open countryside, I marveled at how well the Blue Goose operated and how skillfully the driver handled it. As we picked up speed and seemed to be making 55 or 60 miles per hour, I began thinking of what our predicament would be in case of a wreck and/or fire. Then, as the insults became louder and several scuffles took place, I began wondering what one would do in case of a "free-for-all" slashing fray.

After a while I began thinking about toilet facilities and finally asked one of the fellows about them. He pointed to the left rear of the bus, and I saw a funnel attached to a pipe which ran down through the floor. Soon I saw it being used. However, accuracy at 55 miles per hour was next to impossible, and after the first hour, it became unimportant whether one went to the left rear or not.

One very old but very spry and cocky fellow, who chewed tobacco constantly and smoked all the cigarettes he could beg (without stopping his tobacco chewing), was holding forth in the center of the bus. He related the most vulgar stories I had ever heard concerning his "conquests" with the fairer sex, including his stepdaughter. Most of our fellow passengers listened to him with rapt attention interspersed with bursts of loud laughter. When he showed signs of slowing down, someone would ask him to repeat one of the juicer points of one of his stories, and he would oblige, "fer a smoke."

I tried to keep track of the roads we were traveling and the towns we were passing, but became completely confused by the use of what apparently were cross-country connecting roads. One of the passengers explained that the course of the Blue Goose was usually zigzag in order to reach the various prison camps.

As we stopped at the different camps, I tried to see an identifying name, but I was unsuccessful. At the second or third stop, Calvin and Robert were called out and loaded into a "boogey-cage" which had met the Blue Goose at that point. ("Boogey-cage" is the inmate name for the small pick-up truck which is equipped with a wire mesh cage around the truck bed and a rear door with metal bars, bolt, chain, and lock. It is used to transport a small number of prisoners between camps, to and from the work sites, etc.)

At another stop, some trouble developed with the motor, and mechanics worked under the hood for nearly an hour. While we were waiting, those in the front coaxed the guard into allowing the driver to take orders for drinks and candy bars, but it developed that only a few had any money. Those who did placed their orders and, within a few minutes, the rear door was opened, and the entire order was shoved in beside the funnel. Fortunately, the door was quickly slammed shut or surely some of the inmates would have been shot outside by the mad rush which followed. Johnnie and I hadn't moved from our seats, although I had ordered drinks for us, and he had ordered candy bars. We had quickly abandoned any hope of seeing either the drinks or the candy bars when we saw nearly all of the passengers converge, in a mad scramble, at the rear of the bus. We were greatly surprised, as the crowd moved back to their places, to have our drinks and candy brought to us by a fellow in gray clothes. He had been the first to arm himself and seemed to be considered a leader by the others. He said, "The fellow must have made a mistake when he took the order. He got one too many drinks. Now, he's ten cents short." I caught on quickly, fished a dime out of my pocket, and handed it to him as he handed our order to us. He had a sly grin on his face as he took the drink from a companion who had been holding it for him.

Around noon-time, after more zigzagging, we arrived at the Mocksville road camp. Johnnie's name was called and he left the bus. (The Mocksville camp is known as the "sick camp" where those are sent who have chronic illnesses. The story is that those inmates are only required to work enough to keep their quarters clean and take their turns in assisting with kitchen and dining-room chores.)

After another stop or two my name was called. I was surprised, because I knew that we could not be near Camp 126 at Lincolnton. Three of us were placed in a boogey-cage, and we started on one of the wildest rides I had ever experienced, over a partly paved and partly graveled road.

The boogey-cage had a narrow board, intended for a seat, fastened on either side, but we soon learned that it wasn't a good idea to try to sit on it while traveling at break-neck speed around the curves and over the holes in the road. We hadn't gone five miles until all of us had scraped the skin from our backbones, coming down after a hard bump and missing the narrow seat. Finally, the three of us stretched out full length on the floor and frantically clutched to each other and to the sides as we were tossed about.

We rolled into a prison camp yard and skidded to a stop beside two other boogey-cages. The lock and chains were removed from the rear door, and we were ordered out while one guard with a shotgun and another one with a revolver stood a few feet away.

One of the guards asked if we'd like to go to a toilet. (That wasn't quite the way he said it, but his words were very welcome.) When all three of us answered in the affirmative, he signaled the guards with the guns, and they moved to new vantage points while we were permitted, one at a time, to go behind a nearby building.

No one had mentioned lunch, although it was then after one o'clock. While the guards were talking a few feet away, I remembered two candy bars which were in my pillow case, and I dug them out and shared them with my companions.

After a few minutes, one of my traveling companions was placed in one of the boogey-cages standing nearby, and the remaining fellow and I were placed in the other one.

Our boogey-cage had wood shavings on the floor and, remembering our previous experience, we stretched out in the shavings rather than try to sit on the narrow seats. However, this driver wasn't in such a hurry, and the road was quite a bit better.

For the first time, it was possible to talk to my companion, and I learned that he was being transferred back to Lincolnton prison camp after several months at the Caledonia Prison Farm. He was elated. In his opinion, the Lincolnton camp was next to heaven when compared to Caledonia.

He knew everyone at the Lincolnton camp and gave me a preview of the life there, including a detailed description of the officers, guards, and inmates whom I was to meet.

At two o'clock we stopped in front of the Newton jail, and six prisoners, who were in great high spirits, were loaded in with us.

Amid much loud and drunken talk and a great amount of laughter, we rode the 18 miles from Newton to Lincolnton. We learned that they were being transferred to the prison camp because they had too many friends in Newton who kept them supplied with liquor through various ingenious schemes.

Prison Road Camp

Upon arrival at the camp, I found myself so sore and stiff that I had real difficulty climbing the steps to the captain's headquarters. After he had talked to us briefly and had examined our papers, we were escorted through a gate, across the yard, and into the main building.

A guard said, "Bags on the floor—take off your belts and shoes—leave them with your bags. Face the wall and reach high."

As I removed my belt, my trousers, which happened to be several sizes too large that week, started falling and were kept from dropping to my ankles only by a frantic grab, much to the amusement of the crowd. I solved the problem of how to reach high, as the guard had ordered, without having my trousers fall, by punching a finger through the rotten material and hooking a button into the new hole. I considered this quite an accomplishment.

The guard gave us a very thorough shakedown, including an extensive examination, in my case, of the mouth and dental plates. We were then herded into a tiny room where several inmates were lounging on three bunks, while others were lying on the floor beside a coal stove.

I was amazed to learn that this was the "sick room," and the inmates who were there had reported on "sick call" that morning because they were not able to go to work on-the-roads.

The room was filthy. It looked as if no one had made any effort to clean it in months. Coal was strewn on the floor for a radius of five or six feet around the stove, and ashes were rolling from the front onto the concrete floor. None of the bunks could be used as beds because of broken springs and pieces of wire sticking up. In fact, it was difficult to find a place where there was enough covered spring even to sit.

The fellow who was returning from Caledonia was greeted with enthusiasm by those in the sick room, and they had a grand time recalling old times and bringing him up-to-date on old buddies. He was extremely happy to be back, and they seemed just as happy to have him.

When we became tired of standing, we stretched out on the floor, and I listened to the conversation. I learned that the reason we had to leave our belts outside was that a former inmate had tried to hang himself while in the sick room. Also, the reason we were not allowed to wear shoes was that two former inmates had broken a window and escaped one time, and it was felt that lack of shoes would discourage any further running.

At five o'clock, the road-gang trucks began arriving and discharging the inmates who had been working that day. When the door to the sick room was unlocked, everyone made a dash up the hall. I started to follow, but thought I heard my name called from the opposite direction. I went toward the sound of the voice and stepped through a door onto the yard only to find myself staring into the barrel of a shotgun, held by a guard who had apparently been given a shock by my appearance. He yelled, "Get back in there. Don't you ever run up on me again like that or you'll get a dose of buckshot."

I turned, completely confused, and re-entered the building. I walked to my belongings which were still on the floor outside the sick room. A guard came over and said, "You Payton?" I said, "Yes, sir." He said, "Your number is 47." I assumed that this meant bunk number 47 and began looking for it.

Double bunks were arranged on either side of the large room in dormitory-style. A large table sat in the middle, and a big coal stove sat near the far end. Just over the entrance, a television set was suspended from the ceiling. To the right of the entrance, there were two large washbasins with four faucets on either side. Beyond that, on the side, were toilets and a shower room.

I finally found bunk number 47 and put my belongings on it only to have them promptly thrown to the floor by a scrawny and bewhiskered inmate who said, "Sorry, old man, you're in the wrong pew."

My boogey-cage companion noticed my confusion and said,

"Come on, you and I will have to make bunks behind the stove; there's nothing open."

I asked him about the "47," and he said, "Oh, that's your clothes number. Everything you wear here will be numbered '126-47.' You'll get two sets of clothes and change from one to the other every Saturday."

Just then the guard who had been holding the shotgun outside called to me from the hallway and said, "We want you down here."

I took my belongings and walked down to the bars where he was standing. He said, "Make up that number one bunk. We want you down here close to us." He handed me two sheets, a blanket, and a pillow case. I was glad to see a real pillow again.

I was having considerable difficulty trying to fix the bunk to look like the others, and one of the inmates kindly offered to help. He said, "I guess you haven't had much experience with prison life, have you, Mr. Payton?"

I was surprised at the "Mister" because I had been told that it was a sort of unwritten law that no inmate should be referred to as "Mister." However, throughout my prison experience, especially when I became a teacher in the prison school, it was not unusual for me to be called "Mister" by other inmates. And, on one occasion, the loudspeaker at Central Prison called, "Mr. Payton, report to the Major's office," even though, on another, when one of my young students said, "Good morning, Mr. Payton," he was taken from the breakfast line by a guard, and asked, "How in the hell does he rate being called 'Mister?'"

I was so grateful for his kindness that I couldn't speak, but I'm sure that my eyes conveyed the message to him. While he was helping me with "making up the bunk," he talked in low tones and explained, "They want you down here close so they can keep an eye on you—they don't want anything to happen to you. They're afraid of the newspapers. I heard that the captain was unhappy as hell when he heard you were coming."

In my confused state of mind, this conversation only served to confuse me further. I could understand the concern about newspaper publicity, but I could not conceive of any danger which I could be in which would require my being constantly watched while sleeping.

My newly found friend advised that it was his job to keep the cell-block clean and in order. The others called him "Hal." We became good friends and he coached me through those first confusing and difficult days while I was becoming acquainted with life in a prison road camp.

As we completed putting my bunk in order, a bell sounded. Everyone crowded against the door to the hallway. For the first time, I noticed another room, identical to ours, directly across the hall. However, everyone crowded against the door in that room was wearing blue clothes. Hal explained that the blue clothes denoted "honor grade," to which one could be promoted for good behavior.

The door across the hall was unlocked first, and the blue-clothed men were marched down the hall. Then our door was unlocked, and we followed the others across the yard to the mess-hall. Hal advised that if I had an ulcer I should go with him through the door on the left. If not, I should go through the doorway on the right. I entered the right-hand door.

Most of the blue-clothed men were already eating at long tables, with benches attached, on the left side of the room. The same kind of tables, on the right side, were rapidly being filled by the brown- and gray-clothed men. Three fellows at the end were placing food on the trays which each man carried. I found a vacant place for my tray and started to climb over the bench to sit, but was pushed aside by a young fellow with an ugly scar from his ear to the corner of his mouth. In fact, I was asked to move four times before I was able to begin eating.

Hal explained later that each one had his special place to eat, and would always insist on eating in that spot. He said, "You see, most of them carry something with them from packages received from home and they will only share with their special friends."

The food was very greasy, and tasteless. I felt very alone and miserable as the signal was given to return to the cell-block. We marched, single-file, following the blue-clothed men.

I climbed to my top bunk and stretched out. A guard took his place beside me. Only the bars separated us. He seemed to be studying my features intently. I tried a smile, but he remained stone-faced. I turned my back to him.

The TV set was blaring, but I could not see the picture because it was just above the foot of my bunk, and I was facing its side. A game of checkers was started on the big table, and a game of scrabble began on one of the bunks. Several men were cutting leather and shaping billfolds at the far end of the room while keeping one eye on the TV.

Hal explained that many of the men had become experts in this activity and had developed an on-going business relationship with novelty dealers who came to the camp regularly and bought the finished billfolds. He said that this endeavor was highly organized with one person handling the financial arrangements and hiring others to do the work. Each operation carried a piece-rate, and the most experienced could earn several dollars per week. It was a "closed-shop," and a new inmate could only get in on the operation by "buying" the place of one already in.)

Two young fellows were playing guitars and singing just below my bunk, but they could only be heard now and then during a moment of silence on television. Two or three were shaving, a few were washing socks and underwear, and two or three were under the showers. Across the hall, another TV was blaring, and the same kind of activity seemed to be in progress there. Guards walked back and forth in the hallway.

The TV program was "Tarzan," and Cheeta, the monkey, seemed to be a great favorite with the inmates. They roared with laughter and pounded each other on the back as Cheeta got into and out of one difficulty after another.

As I lay there, a hand clutching what appeared to be a comic book, came over my side of the bunk, and a voice whispered, "Don't let the guard see you reading this."

I opened the book and received a shock when I saw that it was an obscene cartoon booklet. This form of literature was strictly prohibited and, I had been told, meant 30 days in the hole if found in one's possession.

I sneaked a look at the guard, just four feet away. He was looking directly at me. I was sure that he had seen the book passed to me and was just waiting to see what I would do with it. Fortunately, I had my back to him. I slipped it inside my shirt and, looking as nonchalant as possible, slid to the floor and walked to the bathroom. Hal followed me, and said, "I saw that rotten bastard slip that thing to you. He couldn't wait to give you your first test. Here, give it to me, I'll get rid of it." I fished it out of my shirt and handed it to him. He tore it into small pieces and flushed it down the toilet. I started asking him about the significance of all this, but he urged me to go back to my bunk.

Later, he explained that it is part of the convict code to "test" every new inmate as to his reliability in supporting the inmates in their never-ending struggle to outwit the guards and frustrate the rules and regulations. He said that if I had made a scene which drew the attention of the guard, the men would have labeled me as a "rat," and they would have made my life miserable.

Back on my bunk, I found myself wishing that I had eyes in the back of my head. I undressed and crawled between the clean sheets. For the first time in my life, I thought about the comfort of a pillow and took time to be thankful for it as well as for my new friend, Hal.

I was very tired, and every muscle ached from the ride in the boogey-cage. Amid the din of television, laughter, and loud talk, I fell asleep.

Several hours later, I woke up facing the bars and found a new guard watching me. Everything was quiet as some 47 men in our section and approximately the same number across the hall slept peacefully.

Before I went back to sleep, I saw a young blond-haired boy hurrying to the bathroom and heard him vomiting. Some time later, I awoke again and noted that the guard was still in his chair directly beside my bunk. Again, I saw the blond boy going to the bathroom and heard him vomiting.

At 6:00 A.M. a bell sounded, and both cell blocks exploded into frantic, scrambling activity with everyone trying to get to the four toilets and the 16 washing spaces at the same time.

At 6:30 we were marched across the yard to the mess hall for a breakfast of grits and gravy with biscuits. There was no butter, no sugar, no milk, no cream.

As we were marching back to the cell-block after breakfast, a guard stopped me and asked if I had been furnished heavy field shoes before leaving Central Prison. When I said, "No," he said, "The sergeant said for you to 'lay in' today, and we'll try to get you a pair from the Dallas camp."

Therefore, when most of the men lined up for the road crews, I was herded into the sick room along with ten who were reporting on sick call, including the blond boy whom I had seen going to the bathroom during the night. Again we were ordered to leave our belts and shoes outside. I had anticipated this and had used a wire-centered pipe cleaner to fasten my pants together to keep them from dropping to my ankles.

The sick room was even more filthy than it had been the day before, and it was very cold, but one of the fellows cleaned out the ashes from the stove and soon had a fire going. A fellow in blue clothes had brought some small pieces of wood and some coal. Four or five of the fellows lounged on the broken bunks, and the rest of us sat or lay on the floor.

To my bewilderment, one of the fellows crouched down beside the toilet bowl in the corner and began poking a pencil in a crack along the wall near the floor. In a moment a rat ran out, and most of the fellows scrambled after it as it raced around the room. Finally it ran under the blanket of one of the fellows who was stretched out on the floor behind the stove. The fellow who had first used the pencil in the crack caught the rat by the tail and swung him around and around and then dropped him on the floor. The crowd howled with laughter as the "drunken" rat hopped, spun, and staggered about the room. Each time the rat would begin to get his bearings and start looking for a place to hide, he would be caught again, and the same procedure followed over and over and over. I became ill and forced myself to look through the window and not watch this depraved game.

At 11 A.M. the doctor was seen going into the cell-block, and in a few minutes a guard came to the door and called out a name. As each one came from seeing the doctor, another name would be called, until all, except myself, had gone out and returned with some tablets or cough medicine. However, the blond-haired boy was given nothing, and reported that the doctor had accused him of faking. When the last one came back, he said, "Somebody is going to the hole." He said he had seen the doctor hand a card to the sergeant and say, "This fellow is faking." The sergeant was reported as saying, "We'll see how he likes a stretch in the hole."

The approaching punishment was the main topic of conversation during lunch which had been carried to us by an honor-grade inmate. The stories continued throughout the afternoon.

One fellow told of not eating for 16 days while in the hole, and of losing 48 pounds. Another told how he had once astounded Central Prison officials by gaining 11 pounds while in the hole by having an arrangement whereby he could get food through the toilet bowl with the cooperation of a friend who was familiar with the sewage system. Still another story concerned the saving of body waste and throwing it in the face of the guard when he came in. This act of revenge had resulted in a beating with a blackjack.

In another story an inmate was laughing when he alighted from a road-gang truck. A guard had asked him what was so funny. When the inmate answered, "I just feel good today," the guard said, "A few days in the hole will change that." Then, several days later, when this inmate was released from the hole, the same guard asked, "Why are you looking so glum?" When the inmate replied, "Because that's the way I feel," the guard said, "Maybe a few more days in the hole will change your disposition," and he was returned to the hole.

About three o'clock, a big guard (the same one who had been holding the shotgun the day before) opened the sick room door, threw in the biggest pair of shoes I had ever seen, and said, "Here, old man, try these on fer size." He didn't wait to see how they fit and, although they were much too large, I said nothing about it. They became my work shoes, and it made me tired just to lift them. They rubbed blisters on my feet until I learned to stuff the toes with toilet tissue and to wear two pairs of socks.

As the time approached for the checking-in of the returning road crews, two guards took positions just outside the glass-windowed door to the sick room, rather than the customary single guard. This had no significance for me until Whitey said, "Oh, God, I was hoping they had forgotten about me," and the others began cursing the doctor, the guards, and the whole prison system.

When the sick room door was finally opened and all of us crowded toward the door, one guard said, "Everybody hold it just where you are." The other guard said, "Come on, Whitey, you know where *you* are going." He grabbed Whitey's arm and roughly steered him through the doorway and down the hallway away from the bunk room.

The remaining guard marched the rest of us to the bunk room door and herded us inside. Whitey's friends were in a bad humor and spent the time before the supper bell sounded by denouncing all those in positions of authority.

On-The-Roads

The next morning I lined up with the work crews even though several had told me that I was not required to go out without a sweat shirt and heavy coat. However, I was determined not to spend another day in that sick room. Furthermore, I did not want to give anyone an excuse for saying that I was seeking favored treatment.

So I became a member of a North Carolina convict road gang. I was assigned to the "ulcer squad" and took my place in the back of the boogey-cage for the ride to the work site. (It was explained to me that one of the road squads at each prison camp was designated as the "ulcer squad" to which those with ailments were assigned. Special rules as to treatment of these prisoners were supposed to be applied. No one ever told me why I was so assigned, but I assumed that it was because of my age.)

Canvas curtains on the sides of the boogey-cage flapped in the breeze, on the outside of the bars, as we rode the ten or 12 miles to our assignment. A guard rode in the small separate cage which was attached to the back of ours. A 30/30 rifle rested across his knees. A revolver hung from his belt. He was more than six feet tall and must have weighed about 200 hundred pounds. He was about 35 years old and quite handsome. He looked totally out of character, and I wondered why a man of his bearing would be found in such a position.

As we bounced along on the boards fastened around the cage

and intended for seats, the other members of the squad began my education as a member of the "gun-squad." They listed the "don'ts" for me as follows: (1) Don't let the guard hear you cussin' or you'll get 30 days in the hole; (2) Don't cross the road from where you're workin' or the guard can shoot you down for attempted escape; (3) Don't make any sudden moves like jumpin' or runnin' or stoopin' over like you was pickin' up a rock, or the guard can shoot you down; (4) Don't, never, approach within ten feet of the guard or he can shoot you down; (5) Don't stoop over to tie your shoe without gettin' permission 'cause the guard can say you was about to pick up a club or a rock and can shoot you down; (6) Don't try to go for a "crap" without gettin' permission and don't wait until the last minute 'cause the guard might not feel as urgent about it as you do; (7) If you do get permission to go for a "crap," be prepared for the foreman to be standin' over you with a revolver and be careful not to make any sudden moves or he can shoot you down; (8) Don't, never, speak or wave to anyone who passes, or you'll go to the hole; (9) Don't ever get more than ten feet ahead or ten feet behind the rest of the squad; (10) Don't ever pick up an apple or a nut without permission of the guard and don't ever take anything from anyone passin' by.

The foreman was riding in the cab with the driver. I was told that they were both employed by the highway department but were under the jurisdiction of prison officials while supervising prisoners. "The guard is the 'top dog'," they told me, "but both the guard and the foreman like to be called 'Captain'."

Two honor-grade inmates were in the cage with us. I was told that one of them would assist the truck driver, and the other one would carry water, serve milk to the ulcer inmates, and serve our lunch to us.

It was bitter cold in the cage, and the wind cut through my sweater like a knife. My teeth were chattering, and my feet, hands, and ears were aching from the cold before we finally stopped and were ordered out.

As I was climbing down from the cage, a big red-haired fellow handed me a heavy straw push broom and said, "This will be a little easier for your first day." However, the foreman noticed "the play" and promptly pulled the broom out of my hands, handed me a shovel, and said, "Naw ya' don't, ole man, yer gonna' handle a shovel."

I'm sure that he thought I wouldn't know which end to use, and I'm also sure that he was both surprised and disappointed when I took my place in the ditch and began throwing the mud, sticks, stones, and leaves out in perfect rhythm with the others. In fact, I kept at it until Big Red whispered, "Hey, take it easy. Come up for air, or he'll expect all of us to keep going like that."

At 9:30, one of the honor-grade inmates called us to a fire which he had built. He was holding a tin bucket half full of a liquid which looked like milk, and everyone dropped his tool and squatted on the ground around the fire while the tin dipper was passed from one to another. It was explained that regulations called for the ulcer squad to be given milk and a 15-minute break at nine-thirty each morning and two-thirty each afternoon.

When a dipperful of the white liquid was handed to me, I discovered that it was powdered milk with chunks of undissolved powder floating on top. Everyone was watching as I drank and then began trying to dislodge the gooey mass from the roof of my mouth. The group burst into laughter and one of them said, "This is the 'special treatment' which the state provides for inmates with ulcers."

Another one said, "Yeah, and the story in Raleigh is that this is the 'light work' squad, but we do more work in a day than any other squad."

At that moment I thought this was only the usual complaint, and that each of the other squads would probably claim that they worked hardest. However, upon checking later, I learned that the "light work" title was the standing joke of the camp, and the old-timers tried to avoid being assigned to the ulcer squad for this reason.

After the milk break, the foreman decided that a deep ditch should be cut through the heavy mud for about 75 feet to a point where the side road joined the main highway. It was back-breaking work for the next two hours.

I was surprised that I was able to keep my shovel moving as well as any of the others, and with no more apparent effort. In fact I was quite pleased with myself, because the foreman stood nearby, obviously watching my work in particular and hoping (I thought) for the first sign of weakness on my part.

Just before noon, the course of our ditch was blocked by a large rock and three of us with shovels climbed out of the ditch while the other two shovel-men struggled with the big rock. As we stood watching, the foreman said, "Come on, ole man, get down in there and see what you can do with that rock."

I was sure that I could do no more than the others were doing, and I was furious at his derogatory use of the term "ole man," but I said nothing and got down in the mud to wrestle with the rock. After a mighty effort, we were able to slide it sideways enough so that all of us could get at it, and we were able to lift it out of the way.

When we climbed out of the ditch it was nearly 12 o'clock and the truck driver was taking orders for lunch drinks. I asked him to bring me a pint of milk and a small cake from the store near where we were working.

The foreman overheard my request to the truck driver and called, "No cakes, old man. Nothin' but drinks." One of the fellows whispered, "You shouldn't have said it so loud. That bastard won't let us buy anything to eat if he knows about it."

One of the honor-grade inmates was dishing cold brown beans and cold yams from two metal pots onto paper plates. He also placed two slices of bread on each plate. The first fellow to take one of the plates yelled, "These damn beans have worms in 'em again." He tossed his plate into the nearby field. The others took their plates but scraped the beans back into the pot. They filled up on bread and yams. I ate the two slices of bread and washed them down with milk.

After lunch we crossed to the ditch on the opposite side of the road and began working our way back to where we had left the cage that morning.

Sometimes, for a distance of 50 or 75 feet, we would do heavy shoveling of muck, sticks, leaves, and other debris. Then we might walk for half a mile with no shoveling to be done while the broom men swept the edge of the pavement with their heavy push-brooms.

Soft-drink bottles were numerous, and each time one was

sighted the men would swear and grumble in low tones. I didn't understand the reason for their agitation until it was explained to me that, until recently, they had been allowed to collect these bottles and have the truck driver redeem them at the nearest store for two cents each. The total was then divided equally among the crew, and this was the only source of income for most of them and their only hope of getting ready-made cigarettes, a soft drink, or an occasional candy bar. They were bitter because the foreman had stopped this practice, but they religiously kept account of the number they might have had and kept multiplying the number by two. Then they would divide by ten and would become angrier with each new total. In addition to the money value of these bottles, they had served to provide some interest in the day's work and had taken away some of the drudgery. Each newly found bottle had brought a little excitement and a moment of pleasure into an otherwise dull and hopeless day. Now, each bottle which they were forbidden to touch was another cause for frustration, bitterness, and unhappiness, all of which turned into a consuming fire of hatred toward prison officials, courts, judges, and the state administration.

My first reaction was that this was a small thing for grown men to become so concerned about, but later I realized that it was just one more source of irritation, added to a thousand other seemingly senseless rules, regulations, and restrictions which plague the convict every moment of every day.

At 4:30 the foreman motioned the truck driver to pull ahead of the squad, and we were ordered to line up for the count. I could not understand why ten men had to be lined up in two columns of five each in order to get a correct count until I learned that many of the guards and foremen had almost no education and found it really difficult to count ten men who were even slightly scattered.

We arrived back at the prison camp at about five o'clock after a bumpy and windy ride in the boogey-cage. Each man was thoroughly searched before entering the main cell-block where everyone was trying to crowd in at the washbasins to clean up for supper.

At 5:30 we were marched across the yard to the mess hall.

The biscuits were very good, especially after a little fellow named Jimmy had slipped some butter to me.

Back in the cell-block, TV was the big attraction for most of the men, but some played checkers, dominoes, or scrabble. I spent most of the evening writing to Kitty until "The Untouchables" program came on. Then I was fascinated by the great interest of my cellmates in the program and was somewhat shocked when they cheered the criminals and denounced Eliot Ness. They sat spellbound, with open mouths, as the story unfolded on the screen and actually held their breath during the more tense scenes. Each time the break came for the commercial, a dozen arguments broke out over the tactics used by the criminals, and a dozen theories were advanced on ways the criminals could have outwitted Ness and avoided capture or death.

Surprisingly, after a hot shower, I was not nearly as tired as I had expected to be. I slept well and felt good the next morning except for some soreness of muscles and stiffness of joints.

This was Saturday, and no one was required to work. When we were going to breakfast, an honor-grade inmate stopped me and asked if I was expecting visitors on Sunday. I said, "Yes. The warden at Central Prison said he would notify my wife of my transfer."

He said, "That's what I thought, and I've got new clothes for you and have pressed them. After breakfast everybody will come to the clothes house for clean clothes. You make sure you are last in line."

As I ate my breakfast of soggy pancakes and fat-back, I thought of the new clothes, and it was amazing how much brighter the world looked.

As instructed, I waited until I was last in line for clean clothes and was pleased when he handed me a carefully folded bundle containing new dark brown pants, a new brown shirt, new undershirt, new shorts, and new socks. The shirt was starched and ironed to perfection, and the pants had a sharp crease. Everything was stamped "126-47."

When I got back to the cell-block with my new clothes, I found a guard waiting for me beside my bunk. He said, "Better fix your bunk like the others if you don't want to go to the hole."

I had straightened the sheet and blanket on my bunk before going to breakfast and had been careful to make it look like I had seen the others the day before, with the white sheet folded back so that the blanket was covered. To my surprise, all the others were now completely covered with the brown blankets. Mine was the only one which was white. I quickly changed mine to correspond with the others. As soon as the guard had gone, I asked one of the fellows why the bunks were brown today when they had been white yesterday. He seemed to think this was a very funny question and laughed for a moment before replying in a loud voice, "My Gawd, ain't you never been on-the-state before? Don't ya' know the bunks are s'posed to be white when we're out workin' and brown when we're here lollin' 'round on 'em?"

I was glad to learn that we were not required to change clothes until Sunday morning. I wanted mine to look starched and creased when Kitty and the kids arrived on Sunday.

At about eight o'clock, two guards came in and started calling out names of those who had money on deposit in the prisoners' trust fund. As each name was called, that person went to the bars and received his money. The limit was four dollars per week, but very few drew that amount. Some drew three dollars, some drew two, and some drew only one. Most of them didn't draw any. My name was not called; and, when I inquired about it, I was told that my money had not been transferred from Central Prison, and that I would not be allowed to draw anything until the following Saturday.

The cell-block was a bee-hive of activity with several different groups feverishly cutting, shaping and lacing billfolds as if their lives depended upon it. Dominoes were being played at one end of the big table and, in addition to the players, a large group seemed overly intent and unusually interested in the progress of the game. As the morning wore on, and one after another "lost interest" in the game and grumbled about being broke again until next Saturday, I realized that the game wasn't exactly the kind of dominoes that the kids and I played at home.

Upon closer study, I learned, too, that the checker game in progress at the other end of the table had some peculiar twists that caused one player after another, along with his group of supporters, to leave the table angrily muttering about "rotten luck."

Only the scrabble game which had been relegated to the top of one of the bunks seemed to be "legitimate."

By lunch time only the scrabble players, the billfold makers, and a small group of the domino and checker players were at all happy. The majority were glum and sullen.

During the afternoon we were permitted the freedom of the yard until four o'clock, and a lively game of volley-ball was soon in progress. Another group took turns with the one set of horseshoes. Three young fellows who were shooting baskets at a ring mounted on a backboard invited me to join them, and I did.

After supper we were again locked in the cell-block and TV occupied most of the men until 11 P.M. However, a scrabble game remained in progress, and I found myself becoming the arbiter in heated arguments over whether or not a certain word was a "word." At first, I was reluctant to become involved, but soon realized that this was being interpreted as aloofness, and some resentment was beginning to be shown toward me. Then I began expressing an opinion, when asked, and was constantly amazed when my opinion was accepted without question by both sides. A violent argument which had seemed on the verge of erupting into physical combat a moment before would subside with a "yes" or "no" from me, and the game would calmly continue.

During the evening, I became aware of Jimmy watching me from his bunk, two bunks away from mine. Finally I smiled at him and, as if he had been waiting for this signal, he came to the side of my bunk and said, "Mr. Payton, I have some shoe polish, and I'd like to shine your shoes before your family comes tomorrow." In almost the same breath, but in a tone that implied a special bond between us, he said, "I'm from Charlotte, too."

I assumed that he was trying to earn a dime and began explaining that I hadn't been able to draw any money and was completely "broke," but he looked as if I had slapped him, and I was sorry for what I had said. In a plaintive voice, he said, "I didn't want to be paid." He looked so forlorn that I hastened to assure him that I'd like very much to have him shine my shoes. His face lit up like a light bulb, and he began scrambling around getting his polish and rags together. I explained that my shoes were in pretty bad shape from the scrubbing and garbage handling at Central Prison. He said, "I'll make 'em look like new." And he did.

Although I didn't know it then, I had just become a "pigeon." (This is the term used by inmates to denote an inmate who has been "adopted" by another inmate. An inmate who is believed to be in a position to grant favors, such as cigarettes, soft drinks and candy, will find himself adopted by one or more of the other inmates. When more than one is interested, each will try to outdo the other in rendering service and/or protection to the adopted inmate in an effort to become the favorite and induce the pigeon to dismiss the others.)

A few minutes later, the big red-headed fellow who had tried to give me the broom the day before, came over and said, "I got plenty of room in my locker for your stuff. You won't get a locker for several days, and you won't keep your stuff very long if its not locked up."

I thanked him and explained that I didn't have much to lose. He said, "Yeah, but your folks will bring stuff tomorrow, won't they?" I agreed that they probably would and that I would appreciate using his locker to store part of it. That was his signal to gather up my belongings and put them in his locker.

Again, without knowing it, I had become a pigeon for the second time. And, before bedtime, I became a pigeon for the third time when another big fellow, whom they called "Hitler" because of his marked resemblance to the German dictator, came over and informed me that he had room in his locker for any excess I might have after my family had visited. I thanked him and told him how much I appreciated the kindness being shown to me.

I learned later that the "con-wise" inmate would have selected one of these fellows and would have dismissed the others but, not knowing this, I tried to return the kindnesses of each without showing any partiality. During the days which followed, I found myself almost smothered with favors, as each of them tried to impress upon me the importance of their friendship to me.

As it turned out, it was fortunate that I was stupid in this regard because there were many times during the days which followed that I needed all three of them, especially the extra pairs of eyes. In addition to the constant "testing," I found that I was resented by a group of five or six who had gained a reputation as "real rough." They seemed determined to see me in some kind of trouble which would cause me to be punished. They talked openly about "cutting the big-shot down to our size." They tried every possible way to involve me in an argument and were constantly trying to prove their superiority to me in one way or another. Each day saw a tug-of-war between those who were trying to get me in trouble and my new friends who were trying to keep me out of it. Prohibited items such as knives, obscene literature, extra clothing, dope pills and, once, a whiskey bottle, were planted under my mattress, but were always discovered by one of my friends, rather than by the guards.

Sunday, November 19th, was a beautiful day. The cell-block was filled with much good humor as nearly everyone was busily engaged in "sprucing-up" for his visitors, wondering whether certain members of the family would come, and trying to guess what good things would be brought.

After a lunch of fried chicken at 11:30, everyone crowded to the windows to watch for their people. I was surprised that some families were already arriving because I had been told that visiting was not scheduled to begin until one o'clock, and we were not to be permitted on-the-yard until that time.

By 12:45, the parking spaces were nearly all filled, and families were lined up on the outside of the fence which enclosed the prison yard. Each inmate had his visitors spotted and, when the cell door was finally unlocked, there was a mad scramble to get to the spot opposite where each man's people were waiting. Inmates were required to stay behind a railing about four feet from the fence. The families were pressed tightly against the fence on their side.

An inmate told me an unbelievable story about the reason for the separation of four feet. His story was verified by several others. He said that inmates were once allowed to press against the fence on their side as the families were allowed to do so on their side, but this practice was discontinued when the couples became too amorous and caused considerable embarrassment to the more inhibited.

I had not seen my family arrive while watching from the cell-block window and, when I had walked full length of the fence without seeing them, I began to worry about whether or not they had received word of my transfer. I had visions of them waiting for me at Central Prison in Raleigh. However, as I neared the end of the fence closest to the highway, I saw them drive into one of the few remaining parking spaces and watched them filling their arms with bags and bundles and boxes. I waited for them near the gate and informed them about giving their names to the sergeant and leaving the packages with him to be checked for contraband. Then we found a vacant place along the fence and finally were able to visit. At first we were so filled with emotion that no one could speak, and we just devoured each other with eyes full of love and devotion. Then everyone started talking at once, and the time raced by.

Ironically, the fellow on my left was doing a life-term for murdering his wife, and the fellow on my right was doing 20 years for raping his stepdaughter. I had some difficulty with my feelings. It wasn't shame, but I was pretty unhappy about my loved ones being subjected to that kind of situation. I believe that was the closest I came to being embittered throughout the entire prison ordeal.

A good friend from the Carpenter's Union came by and offered the full support of his union. He told my wife that she had only to call if he or his union could be of service or assistance.

We were permitted to continue our visit for the full three hours. It was really wonderful until the time arrived for the painful parting.

While we were visiting, the sergeant had checked all the packages and had them carried to me. The willing hands of several inmates helped me carry the "loot" to my bunk.

Most of those who had had visitors also had packages. Fried chicken, huge slices of home-cured ham, cookies, cakes, pies, candy, apples, and oranges were being shared with those who had not had visitors. When the supper bell sounded, and we were marched to the mess hall, it was like leaving a banquet table to go looking for a hot-dog stand. Apparently, however, those in charge of the menu had been through the experience of "Visiting Sunday" before. Nothing had been cooked, but some slices of cheese and canned meat were available for anyone who might be interested. Nearly everyone just drank coffee and waited impatiently for the signal to return to the cell-block.

The evening was spent giving each other bits of news which had been gained through the visits and storing the loot. All the lockers were bulging, and everyone was in a gay mood.

My "friends" had been able to store all of my things only by taking all of their belongings out of their lockers and leaving them on top. A guard came in and surveyed the piles on top of the lockers. He said, "You fellows know you can't leave that stuff there when you go to work in the morning."

Red said, "Yeah, we know. We were wondering if we could take Whitey's stuff out of his locker. He won't be using it for awhile."

The guard said, "I'll ask the sergeant."

He came back in a few minutes with a key and unlocked Whitey's locker. He said, "All right, Payton, this is your locker. We'll find another one for Whitey when he's ready for it."

Hitler said, "Why don't we leave everything in the lockers just like it is and use this locker for all our other stuff?"

I, of course, was aware of the reasoning behind his suggestion, but was not really concerned about how much of my food they ate, and raised no objection when they crowded their belongings into Whitey's locker.

On Monday, the boogey-cage headed in a different direction from that taken on Friday, and the fellows informed me that we would be "cutting right-of-way." They said, "You'll catch hell today."

When I climbed down from the cage, the foreman handed me a "bush-axe" and said, "You cut in number four position."

A "bush-axe" is a tool made like a hook and fastened to a handle about four feet long. The inside of the hook is sharpened and is used to cut small brush and weeds by swinging it somewhat as a mower would cut wheat with a scythe. The outside or back of the hook is also sharpened and is used to chop heavier growth, as with an axe.

I had no idea what was meant by "cutting in number four position" until Big Red said, "Just watch me and do what I do; I'm number three."

Little Jimmy was number one, and he took his place at the far edge of the right-of-way, about 15 or 20 feet from the edge of the road, and started swinging his axe, cutting a path four or five feet wide. As soon as he had taken two or three steps, the number-two man stepped in and started swinging, with his axe cutting another path four or five feet wide. His axe seemed to just miss Jimmy's heels on each swing. As soon as the number-two man had taken a couple of steps, Red went into action, and I followed him, with the number-five man swinging nearest the road and at my heels.

As we cut our way through brush, small trees, vines and briars, I soon realized that this was quite different from the shovel job which I had handled without difficulty. It was real "hard labor." Briars caught at my clothes, branches slapped me across the face, and my feet became entangled in vines. The sharp blade behind me kept swishing within inches of my heels, and the foreman kept urging me to move closer to Red's heels.

The first patch of brush kept us swinging for nearly an hour. I was ready to drop when I finally cut my path through and crawled up the bank to the roadside. Fortunately for me, we then came to a long stretch where the road had been cut through a hill, and high banks rose on both sides. There was room only for Jimmy at the top of the bank. The rest of us just walked along swinging now and then at a straggling weed or small brush.

Then we came to a place where the road had been built up, and the ditch was some 15 or 20 feet down the bank. As number-four man, I was able to cut my patch by standing on the edge of the bank and swinging my axe back and forth like a pendulum. This was not nearly so tiring, especially after I got the knack of turning my axe at the end of each swing and having it cut both ways, with the momentum from each swing providing the power. However, even so, when the fellow came with the powdered milk at 9:30, and the foreman signaled for the break, I gratefully dropped to the ground and drank a full cup of the white liquid between gasps for breath. Even though the day was quite cool, my shirt was soaked with perspiration.

Before noon, I was more tired and miserable than I could ever remember having been in my life. My hands, arms, face, and legs were covered with dozens of briar scratches, and my wrists were swollen twice their normal size. I couldn't remember ever being so hungry. I kept looking at my watch and examined it closely two or three times to see if it was still running. Finally, the truck driver came to ask if anyone wanted him to get drinks, and I ordered a quart of milk.

Cold brown beans and a spoonful of cold spaghetti were dished out on the plates and handed to each of us. The beans were only partly cooked and the spaghetti was like rubber. Neither was salted. However, one of the honor-grade fellows had a fried peach pie for each one of us. Big Red had brought a large bag of peanuts from my supply, and I had brought six Hershey bars. We divided everything among the ten of us. When the guard wasn't looking, we dumped our plates in the ditch and threw dirt over our lunch.

The afternoon was much like the morning, only more so. By the 2:30 "milk break," I was staggering, and every muscle in my body was aching. I just dropped in my tracks and sat while the others drank the powdered milk solution.

When the foreman called, "Awright, les' go," I debated on just sitting still. I wondered what punishment they could give me for refusing to work that could be worse than the punishment of the work itself. However, Big Red grabbed my hand and pulled me to my feet, whispering, "Stay two steps behind me and I'll get most of yours."

For the next hour, Red worked in a low crouch, and his swing spread out over his path and most of mine. I just stumbled along behind and dazedly chopped at the foot or so of my path which he was missing. We thought the foreman wasn't paying any attention, but found that we were wrong when we came to the next patch to be cut, and he said, "Les' see ya' take the lead through there, ole man." The "lead" was in a ditch into which sewage from several houses was draining, and I found myself wading in slimy, evil-smelling muck as my axe cut through the weeds, briars, and vines, and the muck splashed up into my face.

For the first time in my life I felt blind rage and hatred, and I believed that, also for the first time in my life, I would have been capable of doing physical violence to another human being. I prayed for strength with which to swing the axe and for will-power to keep me from swinging it around the neck of the hateful foreman.

When I had been swinging steadily for about a half-hour, one of the honor-grade fellows slid down the bank and said, "Let me get a little exercise, Mr. Payton." He took my axe and cut through the remaining 15 or 20 feet.

The foreman hadn't said anything during the performance of the honor-grade man, but as we climbed up the bank, he growled "If you're so dern anxious to work, mebbe' we oughter get ya' some brown clothes tommorer." (This was a threat to demote him from honor-grade to A-grade, but it apparently went no further.)

It was 4:30, and the truck was waiting. I had real difficulty climbing into the boogey-cage and doubt if I could have made it without the helping hands of my companions. They were furious about my "initiation" and swore all the way back to camp. I was too tired even to talk and sat limply on the bench without even making an effort to ease the spine jolting which resulted from the bouncing of the truck over the rough road.

Upon arrival at camp, after the cold and bumpy ride from the work site, I found that I had "charley-horses" where I didn't know there were muscles, and it took real effort to crawl down from the cage.

Tuesday and Wednesday were much like Monday as we continued to cut right-of-way, and it was a nightmare, wading in muck and mire while briars tore at my clothing, and vines entangled my ankles and sometimes threw me to the ground. I was constantly amazed that I was able to get through each day and then was able to get out of my bunk the next morning and line up for another day of hard labor.

Thursday was Thanksgiving Day, and we were not required to work. After breakfast we returned to the cell-block and just loafed around until time for lunch. When we entered the messhall for lunch we found trays loaded with roast turkey, mashed potatoes, peas, and yams, already placed along the tables. Pitchers full of coffee were standing in the middle of each table, along with cream, sugar, plates of biscuits, and great chunks of butter. The captain was standing in the center of the room when I arrived. Apparently, he had given an order for everyone to remain standing.

As I approached my usual eating place, the captain motioned me over to his side. Then, in a loud, but pleasant, voice, he said, "Fellows, since this is Thanksgiving Day, I think we should give thanks to God for this food and for our many other blessings. I'm going to ask Mr. Payton to do that for all of us."

I was taken completely by surprise but managed to offer what I hope was a meaningful (to the men) prayer of thanksgiving. Several of them spoke kindly to me about it later.

The food was really good, and everyone enjoyed it. The captain ate with us and laughed and joked with those nearby. The "silence-during-meals" restriction had apparently been waived, and everyone was talking and laughing. A festive mood prevailed, and all seemed to have laid their cares and troubles aside, at least for this hour.

After lunch, we were permitted freedom of the yard until 4:30. Volleyball, horseshoes, and basket-shooting occupied the time of most of the men. As for me, I was too sore and stiff to move quickly and enjoyed just sitting on a box in the warm sun and reading newspaper clippings which Kitty had mailed. The reader may find them to be an appropriate part of the story. They are reproduced on the following pages:

A Tug at the Conscience
By Charles Clay

(Editor's Note: This is the first of a series on the Henderson strike conspiracy case).

Should Boyd Payton be in prison?

In the long months of legal proceedings that sent him there, only one high placed jurist—Associate Justice William H. Bobbitt of the North Carolina Supreme Court—said no.

But the fact of Boyd Payton's imprisonment still tugs at the conscience of many fair-minded North Carolina people just as it brought tears and sobs from some of the humble cotton mill workers who followed him in the ill-fated Henderson strike and then watched him walk through the gates of Central Prison here.

Payton, North and South Carolina director of the Textile Workers Union of America (AFL-CIO), went to prison for 6-10 years along with seven other men after their conviction on charges of plotting to dynamite cotton mill property during the Henderson strike.

The eight were convicted by a jury in a courtroom where emotions were as potentially explosive as the dynamite none of the convicted union leaders and cotton mill workers actually ever obtained or tried to use.

They were convicted on the testimony of an unemployed former cotton mill worker from Leaksville who has a personal history of law-breaking and drunkenness and whose sudden civic consciousness and concern for restoring law and order and ending violence in the strike-torn town of Henderson was at least strange.

Instead of taking its normal course in the court channels, a special term was set for the trial in July, 1959. This meant it came while the violence from the crumbling strike was still fresh in the minds of people everywhere and while National Guard bayonets were still required to keep the peace at Henderson.

Harold Elsie Aaron, the unemployed worker from Leaksville, took money from and then wove the State Bureau of Investigation's net about the alleged dynamite plotters at the trial.

Except in the case of Payton, where the evidence was thin and circumstantial, the net was woven tightly.

Aaron said some liquor was involved in the plotting he testified about. However, his testimony was carefully framed to avoid giving any impression that it was drunken talk the alleged conspirators were indulging in in the bitter atmosphere of the strike that violence and hence State intervention had doomed to failure.

Aaron said Charles Auslander, a TWUA official who went to prison with Payton and the rest, approached him on or about May 25, 1959 at Spray during the height of the strike violence and suggested putting the mill out of operation.

Before he saw Auslander again, Aaron said, he reported the plot to John Cooper Sr., owner of the mill.

Aaron also said he reported his conversations with Auslander about putting the mills out of operation to a State highway patrolman. The SBI contacted Aaron shortly and he went to work for it.

The SBI put Aaron up in a "bugged" motel room in Roanoke Rapids where conversations between the accused plotters and Aaron were put on a tape recording.

On the strength of these recordings, the SBI said it obtained confessions from three of the imprisoned men—Warren Walker, William Malcom Jarrel, and Robert Abbott. Walker and Abbott had been arrested along with Calvin Ray Pegram on June 13.

Later indictments were drawn against Payton, Auslander, international TWUA representative Lawrence Gore, and Johnny Martin, an official of the TWUA local at Henderson.

Reading from a notebook he'd kept, Aaron said they talked over a plot to dynamite mill facilities with Gore and Walker in the motel room on June 3.

On June 9, Aaron said, he talked about it there with Walker, Jarrell, Pegram and Abbott.

Aaron brought Payton into the SBI's net this way:

He said he made a telephone call to another union official in Henderson and the voice on the other end of the line said, "This is Boyd Payton."

Aaron said he replied, "This is the boy from Leaksville."

Aaron said Payton replied, "I know," without mentioning Aaron's name.

Aaron said he told Payton he was broke and had to go home, that he was disturbed because Gore and Walker had not met with him the night before in Roanoke Rapids as planned.

Aaron said Payton told him he'd have Gore contact him and that later Gore did so and gave him $20.

However, Justice Bobbitt said in his dissenting opinion that there was nothing in this conversation sufficient to prove Payton had knowledge of a dynamite plot.

The records of several telephone calls Aaron said he made to union leaders in connection with the plot were introduced in the case but the call in which Aaron said he talked to Payton was listed as a call to Gore, not to Payton.

Payton, as the leader of the strike, cast his lot with the other seven although the evidence against him was weaker. None of the imprisoned men testified at the trial. They all pleaded not guilty.

A group of defense lawyers tried hard to discredit Aaron. One of the lawyers said the State had gone out and gotten "an ordinary drunk and a thief and called him the truth" in the case against the union men.

After the jury chose to believe Aaron, Superior Court Judge Raymond Mallard gave all eight union men stiff concurrent prison sentences on each of three counts against them.

—*The News and Observer*, Raleigh, North Carolina, November 20, 1960

The Final Crushing Blow
By Charles Clay

(Editor's Note: This is the second in a series of articles on the Henderson strike conspiracy trial.)

Boyd Payton, leader of the violence-ridden and ill-fated cotton mill strike in Henderson in 1959, went to prison on a court decision that could have gone either way.

Associate Justice William H. Bobbitt's dissent in the State Supreme Court's decision in the case attests this.

And, legal technicalities aside, Boyd Payton and seven other textile union men were convicted and sent to prison in a courtroom atmosphere stonily hostile to them and their cause in the bitter strike.

The strike itself, of course, had already been doomed to failure by a combination of violence that virtually put the town under martial law and an implacable mill management.

But the trial at which Payton and the others were convicted of conspiring to put the Harriet-Henderson Cotton Mills out of operation with dynamite served as the final crushing blow to organized labor in the vital strike.

Boyd Payton went to prison protesting his innocence although he had chosen to rise or fall with his fellow unionists at the trial despite the fact that the evidence against him was questionable to many North Carolinians if not to a majority of the State Supreme Court.

Since the emotional atmosphere has cleared with the end of the violence, the question of whether justice was served, particularly in Payton's case, has been raised in several quarters.

The union men were convicted on testimony by Harold Elsie Aaron, an unemployed onetime textile worker himself with a police record, who said he took about $300 from the State Bureau of Investigation for expenses incurred while setting a legal trap for the unionists.

Aaron testified that he had been convicted of assault with a pistol and that he served time for taking a police car and impersonating an officer.

"... When first I came out of the service I was convicted of being drunk quite a few times," Aaron told the court.

Just why Aaron decided to report the alleged plot to the authorities never was made convincingly clear. He made vague statements at the trial about reading of the violence at Henderson and thinking that it ought to be stopped.

Defense attorneys sought to show that Aaron had a grudge against Auslander because Auslander, as the TWUA leader at Spray, hadn't processed a grievance Aaron had against the Fieldcrest Mill at which he once worked.

Aaron denied he had a grudge against Auslander but admitted he had gone without success to Auslander about arbitration of his grievance against the mill.

Aaron, who was put up by the SBI in a Roanoke Rapids motel room "bugged" to record conversations and where the trap was sprung, brought Payton into the plot through a telephone call.

The plot as such never was mentioned in the alleged conversation between Payton and Aaron, nor was Aaron's name mentioned. He said he referred to himself as "the boy from Leaksville at Roanoke Rapids" and that Payton replied, "I know."

The question of what Payton might have meant by that simple, two-letter sentence is raised in Justice Bobbitt's dissent to the State Supreme Court's decision last January 14.

Bobbitt said the evidence was competent only to show that Payton knew Auslander had sent Aaron to Henderson "for some purpose incident to the strike."

Judge Bobbitt added:

"The crucial question is whether the circumstantial evidence is such that logical and legitimate inferences may be drawn therefrom to support the factual conclusion that Payton was a party to the alleged conspiracies ... In my opinion, the correct answer is, 'No.' However strong the suspicion, it seems to me that supposition and conjecture must be invoked to reach such factual conclusion.

"Of course, if we could assume that Payton then knew the facts disclosed by the evidence now before us, there would be no doubt as to the sufficiency of the evidence as to him. But there is no evidence that he had such knowledge at the time of his telephone conversations with Aaron and Auslander.

"Activities incident to the strike were many and varried. Conceding the sufficiency of the evidence to support a finding that Payton knew Aaron had been sent by Auslander to the Henderson area *for some purpose* incident to the strike, Payton's guilt or innocence depends upon whether he had knowledge of and was a party *to the (particular) conspiracies alleged in the bills of indictment*. In my view, *the evidence*, as to Payton, is insufficient to support the verdict." The emphasis is Judge Bobbitt's own.

One other member of the seven-man State Supreme Court, Justice Carlyle Higgins, did not participate in the court's decision.

—*The News and Observer*, Raleigh, North Carolina, November 21, 1960

What the Climate Meant
By Charles Clay

(Editor's Note: This is the third in a series of articles on the conspiracy case in the Henderson strike.)

Was Boyd Payton's only crime that of being a union leader?

Payton, now serving 6-10 years in prison, says it was.

As leader of the violent Henderson cotton mill strike, Payton went to prison recently along with seven other union men.

They were considered by friends of labor to be casualities of a labor dispute that dealt a crippling blow to the cause of workingmen which Payton had served so long.

Although Governor Hodges has twice refused to pardon or grant clemency to any of the men, it is a case that has begun to trouble the conscience of many North Carolina people.

The troublesome thing, of course, is not only the comparatively weak circumstantial evidence against Payton himself. It is also the climate in which the alleged plot was hatched and in which the union leaders and cotton mill workers were tried and convicted of conspiring to dynammite mill property.

The climate, of course, was anti-organized labor but what did that mean in this particular case?

When the men were arrested, National Guard bayonets ordered out by Governor Hodges kept a bitter peace in Henderson where the strike lingered on although the mills were operating without the strikers, some of whom had undoubtedly worked all their lives in the mill.

The local union's back and the strike were broken for practical purposes. John Cooper, the mill's elderly owner whom Governor Hodges accused of blasting the Governor's own efforts to end the strike, had not only gotten his mills back in operation despite the strike.

Cooper had also succeeded in terminating the contract his employes had worked under for years by adamantly refusing to permit outside arbitration of his workers' grievances.

Governor Hodges said Cooper "intentionally or otherwise misled all of us. . . . "

Violence that certainly could not be tolerated still seemed inevitable in the Henderson situation. In the end, it cost the strikers public sympathy and inevitably set the stage for the State to move in.

And under former Attorney General Malcolm Seawell, one of the most aggressive chief legal officers the State has ever had, the State Bureau of Investigation moved in quickly and effectively along with the National Guard and the Highway Patrol to restore order.

At times, at least, it appeared that Seawell might be waging a "personal vendetta" against Payton, as Payton was to charge later.

Seawell accused Payton of a "hoax" when Payton reported violence against him. In the course of a running exchange between them, Seawell also called Payton a liar.

If any of the violence actually was instigated by people friendly to the mill's cause which the violence served so well, it never was brought to light or proven.

Testimony at the trial disclosed that Harold Elsie Aaron, the unemployed Leaksville man who became the SBI's informant in the conspiracy case, conferred with Seawell about the supposed plot at Seawell's offices here before he made any charges. The SBI, of course, is a wing of the Attorney General's office.

Judge Raymond Mallard ran what reporters described as a "very tight" court during the trial. He refused to allow one of the defense attorneys, Hugo Black Jr. of Birmingham, Ala., son of a liberal member of the U.S. Supreme Court, to stand up when asking questions.

Mallard and Black had several icy exchanges during the trial. And Judge Mallard also gave the defendants a sharp dressing down after their conviction.

He said Payton "does not now deserve to be called a leader" while Payton's wife and three teen-aged daughters wept at the outcome of the trial.

Judge Mallard also inquired of defendant Auslander's origin in a revealing moment at the end of the trial.

When informed it was New York, the judge said:

"Unions are all right but we don't need unions that feel they are above the law. Even though you came from New York and even though the union sent you, you are not above the law."

Clearly the judge spoke truth about the law. The message between the lines which spoke of a distrust of outsiders and unions was just as clear.

Before the trial was over, even the State Revenue Department got into the act against the union men.

In what could only be regarded as over-eagerness to do its part, the Revenue Department levied the State's business license tax upon two out-of-State attorneys who went to Henderson to help defend the union men.

They were Black and Dave Feller, an AFL-CIO attorney from Washington, D. C. The two were given their money back after Revenue Commissioner James Currie got a requested reminder from Seawell that the State doesn't levy the tax against attorneys who make "isolated appearances" in this State.

Before he left the State, Attorney Feller spoke of the "industrial adolescence" of North Carolina and the South.

Shortly before the union men went to prison John Cooper's son of the same name was placed in its "Hall of Fame" by the publication Textile Reporter. That publication cited as a reason Cooper's role in the strike.

—*The News and Observer*, Raleigh, North Carolina
November 22, 1960

'Plot' Marred Clean Slates
By Charles Clay

(Editor's Note: This is the fourth and last in a series of articles on the Henderson strike conspiracy case.)

Before the violent strike came, Johnnie Martin had worked in the Harriet-Henderson Cotton Mills at Henderson for 40 years, since the age of 12.

Martin is 53 years old, married but childless and was a sweeper in the mill making $40 a week before the strike and his conviction along with seven others on conspiracy charges.

When he went to prison this month to serve 5-7 years, Johnnie Martin was concerned most about his standing in his community. Like the other seven imprisoned union men, he had no criminal record before the strike.

To a prison interviewer, Martin talked about his "spotless citizenship record which he had maintained over a lifetime of living in the same community."

Martin "presented his crime story as though he had no knowledge of the happenings at the Henderson mill strike and especially the charge in which he was committed," the interviewer said.

On the strength of testimony by an informant with a considerable police record, Martin and the others were convicted of conspiring to dynamite mill property. (Under North Carolina law, conspiracy is a meeting of minds to commit an unlawful act. It does not require commission of the alleged act, which was the case in the alleged Henderson plot.)

Martin, who has a fourth grade education, is a member of the fundamentalist Free Gospel Mission Holiness faith and according to prison records attended regularly with his wife.

After 40 years in the cotton mill, Martin suffers arthritis and high blood pressure and has a work rating in prison which prevents him from hard labor that would endanger his life.

Martin and the other four laborers who went to prison with the three union leaders are typical of the workers in a North Carolina cotton mill town.

Warren Walker, who also got 5-7 years, is 39 years old, married and has two children in high school. He worked in the mills 16 years and was a foreman. During the strike, he went to work in the Vance County tungsten mine to provide for his family but his chest was crushed in an accident two weeks after he'd been there.

Walker served in the National Guard in 1939 and in 1940 went into the Army. A non-drinker and Baptist, according to a prison report, he saw 19 months of combat duty in Europe as a squad leader. He attained the rank of sergeant.

Walker "feels that the connection with which the SBI agents associated him with dynamiting was due to the fact that he was an active and loyal union member," according to his prison interview.

Malcolm Jarrell, 24, got the lightest sentence, 2-3 years. Earlier, he had been convicted of engaging in a riot, a misdemeanor, in connection with strike violence at Henderson and was sentenced to eight months. Only he among them is not officially recorded as a first offender.

Jarrell went into the Army in 1956, served three years and was honorable discharged as a specialist fourth class. He lived with his mother, Mrs. Maud Jarrell, who is separated from her husband.

Robert Edward Abbott, 22, has an above-average I.Q., according to prison records, but only a sixth grade education. He married

Patricia Weaver when she was 16, had worked in the cotton mill four years as a doffer. The son of a tenant farmer, Abbott also worked some on the farm.

Abbott told prison authorities he was about drunk when the alleged plot was talked about in the room "bugged" by the SBI to record conversations the workers had with the paid informant, Harold Elsie Aaron.

Aaron had testified some liquor was involved but his testimony was designed to refute the suggestion that the prisoners were drunk at the time.

"His memory is very vague as to the conversations that took place," the prison interviewer said of Abbott.

Calvin Ray Pegram, 23, was married this year to Betty Askew, 21, between the time of his conviction in the summer of 1959 and the time he entered prison for 5-7 years this month.

Pegram also was a doffer in the mills where he'd worked five years. He is the son of a textile mill foreman and has a fifth grade education.

Pegram said Aaron was "very liberal with both food and drink" in the bugged motel room where the SBI trap was sprung.

The three union leaders—Boyd Payton, 53, Charles Auslander, 49, and Lawrence Gore, 43—were given 6-10 year sentences. Like the workers, they went to prison claiming innocence.

Aaron fingered Auslander as the one who originated the alleged plot. Auslander claims he was "framed," that the reason he contacted the unemployed Aaron was to get him to go to work in the struck but operating mills and to relay information to strike leaders.

A native of New York, Auslander attended college for two years, at Fordham and New York University. He was "raised under better than average economic circumstances," according to prison records. He is married, the father of three children and a Catholic.

He has been a Textile Workers Union of America (AFL-CIO) administrator since 1946.

Gore, a native of Columbus County, has an eighth grade education, an above-average I.Q. and rose from a doffer in a mill to an organizer for the TWUA. He draws 30 per cent disability pay from the Government for wounds he received in World War II in Europe, where he was captured by the Germans in 1944.

Shrapnel wounds left one of Gore's hands partially paralyzed. He also has ulcers from his diet in the POW camp.

He is married and has five children.

Payton, Carolinas director for the union and the strike's leader, left a job with the Celanese Corporation of America in 1943 to become a union official.

He was convicted at the conspiracy trial on thin circumstantial evidence about a telephone conversation with Aaron in which no dynamite plot was mentioned. One justice of the State Supreme Court, William H. Bobbitt, said the evidence was not sufficient to convict Payton.

None of the imprisoned men testified at the trial in a decision to leave the matter with a jury, which took Aaron's word in the case.

However, Payton has said that during events at the time of the alleged conspiracy, he asked Auslander to try to find a worker to "plant" in the mill for information purposes.

Payton said he thought Aaron referred to the "plant" when he spoke of himself as "the boy from Leaksville."

Payton, married and the father of three teen-aged daughters, was an active church member in Charlotte, where the union has headquarters. He taught a Sunday School class in his church.

He is now working the roads under a gun in Lincoln County.

—*The News and Observer*, Raleigh, North Carolina
November 23, 1960

Payton Case Discussed
Labor Chiefs See Governor's Aides

Two high-ranking national labor officials paid a call on Governor Hodges' office Tuesday to discuss the case of Boyd Payton, Carolinas director of the Textile Workers Union of America now serving a six to 10-year prison sentence.

They were James Carey, president of the International Union of Electrical Workers and vice president of the AFL-CIO, and Arthur Goldberg, general counsel of the industrial union department of the AFL-CIO and special counsel to the AFL-CIO.

Governor Hodges' administrative assistant, Robert Giles, said the two discussed the Payton case with him and Harold Makepeace, the Governor's private secretary, for about 30 minutes. Gov. Hodges is in South America.

The labor leaders made no official requests to the Governor's office concerning Payton, Giles said. "They were just in to talk to us generally about the case," he said.

Payton and seven other union members recently began serving prison terms after being convicted of plotting dynamite violence in connection with the long Henderson cotton mill strike.

Giles said he explained to Carey and Goldberg that Gov. Hodges has twice denied requests that he grant the eight unionists executive clemency. Giles said he also pointed out that under the State's parole laws the eight men would be eligible for parole after serving one-fourth of their sentences.

Goldberg was one of the union attorneys who presented the Payton case to the United States Supreme Court.

The State Supreme Court upheld the convictions of the eight men and the U. S. Supreme Court refused to hear the case on appeal.

Cause for Speculation

The appearance of Goldberg and Carey on the Tar Heel scene showed that labor looks on the Payton case as a cause celebre.

Goldberg was a close advisor to President-elect John F. Kennedy before the Democratic National Convention last summer and helped line up labor support behind Kennedy. More recently he has been mentioned as a possible appointee to the post of attorney general in the Kennedy administration.

Prisons Director George Randall said Tuesday that Payton is assigned to road work in Lincoln County. Randal said Payton has a "B" work rating, meaning that the labor leader does not have to do strenuous work.

—*The News and Observer*, Raleigh, North Carolina
November 23, 1960

VICTOR RIESEL: INSIDE LABOR
New 'Sacco-Vanzetti' Case to Haunt JFK?

Almost unnoticed, a "Sacco-Vanzetti" case is stalking John F. Kennedy into the White House. It will take a latter day Solomon to solve this problem for the new administration.

Involved are eight imprisoned men who were popular leaders of a union long active in New Deal political campaigns.

These men, officials of the Textile Workers Union of America, have been in North Carolina's Central Prison at Raleigh for a few weeks. Now they are being dispatched to state work camps. From these compounds they are moved, shackled and guarded into road gangs almost daily. One of the eight is an organizer extremely popular inside labor. He is Boyd E. Payton, a TWUA vice president, now swinging a pick and shovel on the highway.

There are seven other Textile Union officers who were jailed along with Payton. Four weeks ago, he and his colleagues surrendered to serve terms ranging from two to 10 years. Payton, a friend of most of labor's national chiefs, could serve as many as seven to eight years on the road gang. These are the heaviest prison sentences to hit labor officals in years. The charge was conspiracy to dynamite installations of the Henderson Mills, Henderson, N.C.—still on strike. There was no explosion.

NO EXPLOSION, that is, except on the part of the Textile Workers who have been attempting to get a pardon from Governor Luther M. Hodges, whose term expires at year's end. Gov. Hodges, it has been unofficially "announced" will be John F. Kennedy's Secretary of Commerce. Until the Henderson strike he was high in labor's esteem. He started as a mill worker himself. Later as an industrialist he was one of the first in the Carolinas to encourage collective bargaining with the TWUA.

Up until the night before the eight labor men surrendered to

Central Prison, the national union leaders hoped for a word of executive clemency from Gov. Hodges. It didn't come. There were harsh words that night at the farewell dinner in the Vance Hotel, Henderson, N.C. Two men high in national labor councils, union president William Pollack and the equally influential president-emeritus Emil Rieve (one of the founders of the CIO) privately denounced the Governor.

It was their opinion that the eight men were being punished more for union activity than for violation of the law. It was pointed out that there had been no dynamiting. Boyd Payton, it was said, is an active church lay leader—and now is organizing Sunday School classes in his prison camp.

EFFORTS WERE MADE to contact Hodges but he had left with the Governor's group for Latin America. Then came word that President-elect John Kennedy would name Hodges as Secretary of Commerce.

Soon former CIO leaders, Walter Reuther and Jim Carey as well as Arthur Goldberg were asked to contact Sen. Kennedy or his close advisors to intervene with the incoming Cabinet member. Slowly, behind the scenes there began to build up sentiment for a national fight which would make "labor martyrs" of the eight in campaigns reminiscent of the Mooney and Billings and Sacco-Vanzetti cases.

A few days ago the Textile Workers met. They called on all unions to start public drives for the freedom of the Carolina eight. The TWUA chiefs asked their colleagues to make this the first order of business at all "future conventions."

Slowly the embarrassing spectre of a Sacco-Vanzetti cause celebre is beginning to loom over the labor scene and may stalk noisily through the early days of the new Presidency.

—New York *Mirror*, November 23, 1960

* * * * *

On Friday, we again cut-right-of-way, and I thought the day would never end. Just after four o'clock, when we had finished a particularly difficult strip of briars and vines, we all thought we had finished for the day and started placing our tools in the truck.

The foreman, who had been sitting on a large rock, came running toward us, yelling, "What th' hell ya' think yer doin'—it ain't quittin' time yet—git yer tools and git yer asses on up that road. I'll tell ya' when it's quittin' time."

With angry mutterings, we trudged another 50 yards, taking an occasional swipe at a stray weed or small bush. When we were ordered to line up for the count, everyone was in a bad humor. Making sure he didn't hear them, they called the foreman some choice names on the way back to camp.

A tasteless supper did nothing to improve dispositions, and our crew spent the evening thinking up and talking about situations in which they'd like to see our foreman. Some had vivid imaginations, and it was good that they weren't free to carry out their expressed desires. It was good, too, that we had Saturday and Sunday for rest and for tempers to cool before facing the foreman again.

After breakfast on Saturday, one of the inmates opened a "barber shop" in the center of the cell-block and did a brisk business. I watched for awhile and noted that he was quite good. I noted, too, that some of his customers gave him a pack of cigarettes or a quarter, while others gave only a dime or a candy bar, and some simply said, "Thanks, I'll see you later." The amount or kind of payment seemed to make no difference to him. He took real pride in his work and gave everyone his best "professional" service. I finally took my place in the waiting line and got a fine haircut.

Speaking of pride, I was often amused, and sometimes saddened, at the efforts of inmates to "show off" their particular accomplishment. It seemed that each one had found something that he could do better than anyone else could do, and he was always looking for an opportunity to demonstrate his prowess. One fellow was the champion checker player, and he delighted in showing each new inmate how good he was. Then, when others were playing, he would drive them crazy by mapping out their strategy for them.

Another fellow was the champion weight-lifter, and he was constantly lifting everything in sight; another one had been the state prison heavyweight boxing champion. He was always trying to get someone to spar with him. He delighted in reminding one of the other inmates about a certain fight of his which they had witnessed. He would insist that they recount each detail and would become quite irritated when they omitted one of the points which reflected well on his ability.

Still another was good at doing flip-flops and handsprings. Without warning, he would come flipping head over heels, down the full length of the cell-block. This was always a signal for another inmate to flip upside-down, and go walking around on his hands with his legs flapping in the air.

All of them, apparently, had an exaggerated impression of my education and knowledge. They had great respect for this, but each one felt impelled, it seemed, to prove to me that he was better than I in something else. Sometimes it was a very childish thing, and I was saddened by their feeble attempts to obtain recognition, status, or respect.

* * * * *

On Saturday afternoon, I had a visit from secretary-treasurer John Chupka, and attorney William Nicholson. They told me of the conversation which had been held among the Governor's secretaries and Arthur Goldberg and James Carey, concerning possible clemency action. They said that one of the Governor's secretaries had indicated that the Governor was inclined to take favorable action, but "needed something upon which to hang his hat." The secretary asked, they said, "Would Payton be willing to submit to a lie detector test?" Mr. Goldberg had replied, they reported, "I don't know, but its worth exploring."

Mr. Chupka said, "What do you think of the idea?"

I said, "I am opposed to it. From what I've seen of justice in this case, I'm afraid of a trick. I can't see how the state could afford to have me win such a test. Furthermore, after sitting through the trial and hearing the testimony and, after reading and rereading the transcript of the trial, I doubt that I could separate, in my mind, that which I knew on a date 18 months ago from that which I have learned since that time."

Mr. Chupka said, "I think you are probably right; it would be a long-shot gamble." After some further conversation of a general nature, they departed, and I returned to the cell-block to worry about whether or not I had made the correct decision. I was very depressed because of the hopelessness of the conversation with my visitors.

During the evening, I reread all of the letters (more than 40 of them in some 23 days) which I had received from Kitty and my girls. They were a wonderful tonic. They were so full of faith, confidence, hope, and love, that I was made ashamed of my weakness and despair.

On Sunday, I wrote to Kitty and said, "What a beautiful Sunday morning. I'm thankful just to be alive today and to know that I have your faith and love. We have just returned from Sunday School in the mess-hall. A lady and a young man came from Lincolnton. He played the piano, and one of the honor-grade boys led the singing in a strong, clear voice. I enjoyed it very much."

After a good dinner, we were allowed freedom-of-the-yard until 4:30. I shot baskets for awhile and pitched two games of horseshoes.

Back in the cell-block, a guard informed me that two of the A-grade boys had been promoted to honor-grade, and I could have either of their bunks. I chose an upper bunk beside a window in the center of the room. A strong light just overhead made it possible for me to read and write at will.

Little Jimmy was now in the next bunk, and he was quite pleased about my move. However, I wasn't so sure that this part of the change was good, because his open devotion to me was beginning to be almost too much. It was impossible to move without having him at my heels, and his "willing slave" attitude was embarrassing. I tried to explain this to him but only succeeded in hurting his feelings. When he thought he had displeased me, he would sit watching me with a mournful expression. Then I would feel sorry and smile at him and he would come bouncing back for all the world like my cocker spaniel when the first kind word was spoken to him after a scolding. Jimmy was actually two people. On the road, as lead man of our squad, he was hard as nails and completely his own master; but in the camp, he was like a small child whose greatest desire was to be loved.

After leaving Lincolnton, I was told that Jimmie had been forcibly seduced shortly after he became an inmate, but then had "really fallen in love" with his seducer and was heartbroken when the relationship was ended by the release of his "loved-one." My informant insisted that Jimmie's ultra-friendliness toward me was designed to fill the void which had been created in his life. However, this whole story came as a shock to me because, looking back, I could not remember any instance which would have given support to such intentions.

* * * * *

We continued cutting right-of-way, and it was almost too much for me. My ankles were swollen, and my right hand became infected from one of the many briar scratches. Once, when I swung at a small tree, it bounced back, hitting me across the left eye and cutting a gash in my cheek. Within an hour, my eye was closed with swelling. The foreman noticed it, and said, "S'afternoon ya' kin' handle one o' th' forks. Ya' better lay in tamorrer and see th' doctor."

During the evening Big Red, Hitler, Little Jimmy, and I were eating salted peanuts. A nice-looking young fellow was watching from his bunk. He said, "You fellows are driving me crazy with those peanuts. Would you sell me some?" I said, "No, but I'll give you some." He came over with cupped hands, and I filled them from the bag. He thanked me and said, "I'll give you something if my family comes to see me Sunday."

Death of Escapee

On Thursday, December 1st, as I was returning from breakfast, the sergeant stopped me, and said, "You stay in today and help Hal. If the doctor comes, you'd better have him take a look at you."

We were finished with the cleaning by lunch time and were sitting on the table talking. Hal asked how I was treated by the other members of my work squad. I said, "Fine, they've all been wonderful, except that older fellow. He doesn't seem to like me at all. In fact, he doesn't seem to like anyone. He's about the meanest and most hateful inmate I've met."

Hal laughed, and said, "You can't tell me anything about him. He's my old man and, I agree, he's the meanest man on God's green earth."

I was embarrassed. I said, "You mean, he's your father?"

He said, "Sure, but don't let it bother you. I have a helluva time standing him myself most of the time."

Just then, a guard came in and ordered us into the sick room. This caused great consternation among those already there. They kept watching through the glass door as two guards entered the cell-block and began a systematic search of all bunks and lockers. They kept saying, "Something's up—the screws are lookin' fer somethin'."

The watchers reported that the guards were making a pile in the middle of the floor of extra underwear, socks, and other items which they were finding under the mattresses. The consensus was that some inmates would be sent to the hole. However, in the midst of the cell-block shakedown, the sergeant went running in and spoke, excitedly, to the guards. They ran out with him, leaving the pile in the middle of the room. A few minutes later, some commotion was heard from the back yard. The "experts" expressed the opinion that the dogs were being placed in one of the prison trucks. This meant that there had been an escape.

Curiosity was just about killing everyone, but there wasn't a sound from outside our sick room quarters. The entire camp seemed to be deserted. Some of our group began calling to the honor-grade inmates who were supposed to be in the kitchen preparing supper, but they got no answer.

After another hour had gone by, one of the road squads came in, but only eight, instead of ten, were marched into the cell-block. Speculation was rife in the sick room as to who was missing from that particular squad. It was clear that this was the squad from which the escape had been made, and it appeared that two of them were missing. However, there was no agreement in the sick room as to the identity of the ones who were missing. As each tried to recall the names of those on that squad, and concluded that the missing ones were so-and-so, others would argue against the conclusion. Excitement ran high and tempers were hot. The greatest anger involved the fact that no one was paying any attention to our group in the sick room. Guards and honor-grade inmates were now dashing up and down the hallway, but we were ignored completely. We were held in the sick room until almost six o'clock. Long after all of the road gangs had been checked in, our door was unlocked and we were permitted to return to the cell-block where we found a strange and sullen silence prevailing. Some groups stood around several of the bunks and talked in low tones. The tension was terrific. The failure of the doctor to arrive and the shakedown of the cell-block seemed to have been forgotten completely. Most of the pile in the middle of the floor had disappeared, amid angry mutterings.

After a while, Big Red moved over to my side and whispered, "Red ——— was shot and killed by a guard when he and Joe tried to run. Joe got away, and they have the dogs after him. That dirty, rotten bastard didn't have to shoot to kill," he sobbed.

When I asked him to describe the one who had been killed, he said, "You know, the fellow you gave the peanuts to last night. Remember, he said he'd give you something if his family came next Sunday? They won't be coming now. That dirty, rotten. . . . His voice trailed away. He was genuinely stricken with grief. Most of the others seemed to be likewise affected.

The supper bell sounded. Several extra and strange (to me) guards lined the way to the mess-hall. We ate in complete silence. When one boy dropped his fork it sounded like a gun shot, and 200 angry eyes turned in his direction. The captain, the sergeant, and two guards stood stiffly by the door until everyone had finished eating. They watched each one closely as we filed past them to return to the cell-block where the small groups again took positions around a few of the bunks.

About seven o'clock, a guard called my name and motioned me to the front bars. When I was close to him, with only the bars separating us, he whispered, "You'd better get a shower and shave tonight, you're gonna' ride at five in the morning." When I began asking questions, he shrugged and walked away.

While I was standing there, wondering about the significance of his remark, another guard (carrying a bundle of letters and papers) came into the alleyway and began calling out names. Strangely, no one moved to get his mail, except me. I got a package and four letters. As I carried them back to my bunk, I was surprised that no one crowded around as they had been in the habit of doing.

After reading my letters, I showered and shaved. As I was returning to my bunk, I noticed that the television sets had not been turned on. Both cell-blocks were as quiet as a morgue. Everyone was standing beside his bunk, and all appeared to be waiting for something. Every face was tense and sober.

I asked one or two, "What's going on?" They didn't answer. I tried to get the attention of Jimmy, but he ignored me. Finally, walking over to Big Red, I said, "Tell me what the score is. Why is everyone acting this way?" He whispered, "The guard who brought the mail is the one who killed Red. All of us had agreed that if he brought the mail nobody would take it from him."

I said, "Gee whiz, that puts me in a fine spot. Why didn't someone tell me? I didn't know he was the one."

Red said, "You're all right. Everyone knows that you didn't know."

I said, "Well, why is everyone so quiet and tense now; they act like they're waiting for something to happen."

He said, "You're so right. They're waitin' to see who's goin' to the hole for refusin' to take their mail. That's what they call insubordination, ya' know."

They didn't have long to wait. In just a few minutes, the sergeant came to the bars and called out eight names. He said, "Come on, let's go. You know where."

The eight quickly lined up at the door, and two guards marched them away. I tried to fathom the system used to select those who were to be punished. I was sure that more than eight names had been included in the mail-call. I was sure, too, that Jimmy's name had not been called, but he was included in the group which had been marched away. However, no one would talk about it. Even Big Red said, "They have their reasons. Let's forget about it. Just be glad you weren't included."

The men in the cell-block continued to stand around quietly. No one moved to turn on the TV. After a few minutes, Whitey appeared in the hallway, and the cell-block came to life. Everyone crowded down to the bars to give him a welcome. A guard came and unlocked the door. Whitey staggered in, looking like a corpse. His long blond hair stuck out in all directions. His ears were completely covered with hair. His face was chalk-white behind a stubble of blond whiskers, and his eyes were sunken behind protruding cheek bones.

Everyone crowded around him and began giving him things to eat. I remembered the package which had just arrived for me. I gave it all to Whitey, and he nearly choked as he began devouring the fruit in great bites. He explained that they had been forced to release him from the hole to make room for those who had just been sent there. "Even then," he said, "some of 'em had to be taken to the Newton camp."

About nine o'clock, the major entered the hallway. I walked over to the bars near where he was standing and asked if I could speak to him. He came to the bars. I told him what the guard had said about being ready to ride in the morning and asked if he knew where I was riding to. He said, "You've been called back to Central Prison, but I don't know why. It might mean a transfer there, or it might mean that you are going before the parole board. I suggest that you take all of your things with you. You won't be coming back here."

I spoke of my concern about my family coming to Lincolnton on the following Sunday and not knowing that I had been transferred to Raleigh. He said that I should write to my wife, and he would see that the letter was promptly mailed. I hurriedly scribbled a note to her, and handed it to him, with thanks.

As I climbed up on my bunk, most of the fellows came over to shake hands and give me their best wishes. Big Red said, "Be sure to wake me before you leave in the morning."

Back to the "Wall"

At 4:30 the next morning an inmate, returning from the bathroom, shook me and whispered, "The guard said to tell you you'd better get dressed."

I washed and dressed as quietly as possible while a chorus of snores came from the various bunks. I gathered my belongings and stuffed them into a pillow case. I hadn't intended to awaken Big Red as he had asked me to do, but when I returned from washing he was sitting on the side of my bunk. We talked in low tones while waiting for the guard to come for me. I told him how much I appreciated his friendship and the many favors he had done for me.

He said, "Heck, don't be thanking me. Knowing you has been one of the bright spots of my life. I'm gonna' miss you like hell."

At five o'clock, the guard who had first told me about leaving came to the cell-block door and motioned me out. He led me to the kitchen and told one of the cooks, "fix some eggs for this fellow." For the first time since leaving home I had *hot* eggs, "sunnyside up," instead of cold, greasy ones which had been fried hard as leather. I also had hot biscuits with *butter*. The two cooks came and drank coffee with me.

My guard was having breakfast in the adjoining guards' dining room. He seemed to be in a fine humor as he joked and laughed with the cooks. As we were leaving the kitchen, another guard called to my guard: "Don't you think you'd better give him a blanket? He doesn't have a coat, and he's gonna' be pretty cold in that cage."

My guard said, "Naw, he'll be all right." As we continued walking across the yard toward the entrance, he was grumbling, "Somebody's always tryin' to run somethin' that ain't none of their business."

We went through the office, and he picked up a folder with my name on it. Then we proceeded to the parking lot where I was locked in the back section of the boogey cage. I sat shivering on the narrow seat while the guard tried to get the motor started. When the battery would no longer turn the motor over, I was taken from that cage and placed in another one. After several minutes of grinding the starter, without results, the lieutenant came down from the office and suggested that they try to push it, but my guard said, "Why don't I just take him over in my car?"

The lieutenant agreed, and in a few minutes, I was riding beside the guard with his heater blowing hot air against my legs. When I started to speak about the "lucky break" for me in having the motors refuse to start, the guard shook his head from side to side and gave a meaningful wink. He explained that he would only take me the 18 miles to Newton, and the Blue Goose would pick me up at 7:30.

We soon arrived at the Newton camp and I was locked in their sick room. It was an exact replica of the one at Lincolnton and was like an icebox. However, I found some pieces of wood and some coal in the corner and soon had a fire going in the small stove.

It was 6:30, and the Newton inmates were going to breakfast. The captain stopped by and asked if I had had breakfast before leaving Lincolnton. Several of the inmates stopped at the door and asked about the incidents at Lincolnton which had caused the visit to the Newton hole the night before.

Promptly at 7:30, the Blue Goose rolled to a stop at the camp gate, and I was led from the sick room and ordered into the rear of the bus. The guard on the bus said, "You sit up front where I can keep an eye out for you."

The trip was dull and uneventful except when we stopped at a prison camp about noon and two young men in blue clothes brought a boxful of sandwiches and a large coffee pot with paper cups. Unlike my last experience on the Blue Goose, the fifteen fellow passengers were quiet and sullen. Everyone seemed to be in a bad humor. When one fellow, returning to his seat from the funnel, stumbled over the feet of another he was roughly shoved across the bus where he cracked his head against the bars, and was roundly cursed by two or three. He stumbled to the rear and sat wiping blood from his forehead. I went to the funnel and stopped to say a word to him, but the guard signaled from the front for me to return to my place next to him with only the glass partition and bars separating us.

We arrived at Central Prison about 3 P.M. After a very thorough shakedown, I was assigned to cell number seven on the fifth floor of the main cell-block.

I was told that this area was known as "shipping corridor" and that inmates assigned there are kept locked in their cells while waiting for some decision to be made about their future, either by prison officials, the parole board, or the courts. Regular inmates are prohibited from entering that section without specific instructions.

The cell was considerably larger than those I had occupied in the detention section. It had double bunks fastened to the wall on one side. There was a washbasin, a toilet bowl, and two steel wall cabinets at the back end. The walking space was about three feet wide and eight feet long, but the bunks could be lifted up and fastened flat against the wall, almost doubling the walking space.

The bunks were simply plates of iron with six rows of holes bored in them every four inches. Each bunk had a lumpy cotton mattress, a pillow, and a blanket. Both bunks had been slept in, and the occupants had left the bed clothing in a tangled pile on the floor in the corner of the cell. Dirty socks, torn underwear, pieces of newspapers, old magazines, and a greasy sack which contained a piece of moldy meat loaf and a slice of bread, were mixed with the bed clothing. The floor was littered with cigarette butts, peanut hulls, and pieces of food.

My cellmate was a young textile worker from Greensboro who said he had known me through the union in one of the Cone mills. He was 19 years old and nice-looking. He seemed to be well above the average inmate in education and breeding, but was very quiet and withdrawn.

We began trying to straighten and clean up the cell. Roaches ran in all directions as we scraped and dragged the debris to the front of the cell where we hoped it would stand a better chance of being noticed by a guard and ordered removed. We had salvaged the bed clothing and had vigorously shaken it before making up the two bunks.

Just as we were finishing our housekeeping, two metal trays were slipped through the slot beneath the door. To my surprise, Camp (my run-boy buddy from detention) was one of the feed boys. He said he had been brought back to Central Prison because some new information had been discovered about the attempted escape in which he was suspected of having been involved. He was again "sweating out" an investigation which could result in his sentence being increased.

Our trays had two slices of bread which the bottom of the cell door had dragged over into the chocolate pudding, and the juice from the brown beans had been spilled over the rice. However, we both ate everything in sight, and it wasn't until later that I thought about how unappetizing the tray looked. Camp brought extra coffee twice and stayed to visit as long as possible.

On Saturday morning, we were taken from our cell and, along with 30 or 40 others, were marched to the clothes house and shower room. We were permitted to take a shower and were given clean clothes. The clothes were ragged and faded, but we were thankful that they were clean.

When we were back in our cell, I noticed two fellows edging their way along the row of cells and furtively watching the front of the hallway where the guard was stationed. My cellmate informed me that they were male prostitutes. I could not believe the shocking stories which he told about them, and others like them, until I saw them "servicing" the occupants of the adjoining cell. The sight made me ill. I had heard of such things but had never expected to witness them with my own eyes. It was a revolting experience, and I had great difficulty in putting it out of my mind.

In the afternoon, a guard came to my cell and said, "You're wanted up front." He directed me through the corridor to the front office where I found Warren, Charley, and Lawrence in conference with two of our union officials and one of our attorneys. They had not known that I was back at Central Prison until so advised when they had asked to see the other three.

It was good to see them all. We were allowed to be together for nearly an hour. Warren and Charley seemed to be doing all right, but Lawrence looked like a ghost. He said he had "gone through hell" since last seeing me. Warren said that he had been the head run-boy in detention since the day after I had been sent to Lincolnton. Robert and Calvin were reported as working on-the-roads out of the Sanford camp, but doing well. Mike was reported as having been promoted to honor-grade so that he could be transferred freely between camps for use as an electrician's helper. Johnnie was said to be quite ill at the Mocksville camp.

* * * * *

I was again in trouble concerning finances because my deposit in the prisoner's trust fund was still in Lincolnton, and I was not permitted to draw my weekly allowance. However, it wasn't serious because the next day was visiting Sunday for white inmates. I knew that Kitty and the kids would bring everything I needed.

It was wonderful to see my family. They all looked like angels. We were permitted to visit through the screen for the full hour. Kitty sat in the middle, Sandra was on her left, Nancy on her right. Patsy stood just behind her mother, straining to hear everything said.

To our surprise and great joy, when the guard called "time," he said, "Payton, you can go down to the end and kiss them goodby if you want to." If I wanted to! Of course, I wanted to. In fact, I had just been thinking that I'd give almost anything to be able to touch them. I scrambled over the feet of a dozen other inmates and got to the end of the screen where I was allowed to kiss each of them and hear the words of love which each whispered in my ear.

When I turned to leave, the guard said, "Did you like that?"

I said, "I surely did. Thank you very much. I didn't know it was allowed."

He winked and said, "Well . . . you have a real nice family, and I couldn't see any harm in it. You're supposed to go to the mail room now to get a package."

My cell-mate couldn't believe his eyes when I opened my package. He said, "Boy, you must have a nice wife." I said, "She is about the nearest thing to an angel that you will find on this earth."

He looked very sad and wistful. Finally, he whispered, as if to himself, "I wouldn't be here if anybody had ever cared about me. I never get a visitor and nobody ever writes or sends anything to me."

I opened the hot-water faucet and let the water run until it was very hot and made two cups of hot chocolate. Then I opened a package of cheese, and we made a little party with cheese and crackers, candy, peanuts, cookies, and fruit.

The Parole Board

On Monday morning, December 5th, I was taken from my cell and escorted to the front office where I met Mr. Matthews, chairman of the Board of Paroles, and his assistant, Mr. Hepler. Mr. Matthews said, "The Governor has asked us to review your case and we had you brought in from Lincolnton so that we might talk to you to see if you have any information which we have not considered. You should feel free to say anything you want to—this is off the record."

I asked, "Have you read the document entitled 'You Be The Judge' which was sent to the Governor?"

Mr. Matthews said, "No, I haven't."

I said, "Well, if you could get that and read it, you would have the full story. It is in great detail, and it gives numerous reasons to justify clemency action."

Neither of them made any comment and both avoided meeting my eyes. I said, "I can only repeat some of the points made in that document. First, the Governor has said, 'The extent to which the criminal laws were violated, and by whom, was decided by the trial jury.' However, it seems to me that in order to evaluate the action of the jury, certain extenuating circumstances must be considered. For instance, I think that considerable weight should be given to the atmosphere in which the trial was held. The fact that we were engaged in a long and bitter strike which had caused strong feelings and intense emotions in Vance County certainly played a large part in the thinking and in the deliberations of the jury. Likewise, the fact that the union was involved in much controversy with state officials which had been given great publicity throughout the state, did not promote an atmosphere which was conducive to a fair and impartial trial by those who were under the control of those who were involved in the controversy.

"I think, too," I said, "that some special consideration should be given to the police record of the man whose testimony was used by the state to build its conspiracy case against us. It is inconceivable to me that the testimony of a man with that kind of law-breaking record should be used as the sole proof for convicting eight men whose records of moral character were above reproach throughout their previous lives.

"Furthermore," I continued, "it seems to me that any fair-minded appraisal would have to give serious thought to the fact that, if any conspiracy existed, the state's agents were in control of it at all times, and no damage could have been done through such conspiracy without the knowledge and consent of these agents. The facts, of course, are that no damage was done. The facts, too, are that when the men were arrested at the truck-stop, their cars were literally torn apart by SBI agents, and nothing was found to give the slightest indication that they had had any intention of committing any act of violence."

As I paused for a moment of thought, I suddenly got the impression that neither of my listeners were even slightly interested in what I had been saying. A feeling of hopelessness descended upon me. In desperation, I blurted, "The Governor quoted you as saying, 'There seems to be no doubt of guilt and, had the arrests not been made, there is every reason to believe that the dynamiting which was planned would have taken place.' How could you make such a statement when there was no evidence of any kind of explosive to show any intent of dynamiting, and when newspapermen who sat through the trial, a Justice of the State Supreme Court, and a Justice of the United States Supreme Court have all expressed doubt about guilt? What information did you have that they didn't have which made you so positive of guilt?"

No one spoke. They sat stiffly, looking down at the table between us. The silence became uncomfortable. Finally, Mr. Matthews said, "Would you be willing to take a lie detector test?" In almost the same breath, he said, "You don't have to give an answer today."

I said, "I think it is unfair to ask me to take such a test when attorney general Seawell has publicly stated that the results of lie detector tests depend upon the person giving them and can be made to show any desired results. Furthermore, I can't understand how a lie detector test would provide any basis for clemency action if the document 'You Be The Judge' hasn't done so."

Mr. Matthews said, "Well, if you change your mind, let us know."

Back in my cell, I tried to recall all that had been said and tried to find a reason for the lie-detector proposal. I couldn't see how the state could afford to let me win such a test, and I couldn't see any purpose, from their standpoint, in suggesting it.

Lunch was served, but I was too deeply engrossed in thoughts about my experience with the parole board to eat anything. I simply shoved the tray back through the slot under the door. My cell-mate had been transferred, and I was alone.

* * * * *

The weather had turned very cold, and a broken window opposite my cell allowed the cold wind to blow directly into my cell. I sat on the edge of the bunk with two blankets wrapped around me and was thoroughly miserable, both physically and mentally.

A few minutes after one o'clock, a guard came to the front of my cell and said, "They gave you the works up front, didn't they?" I had spoken to no one about my experience with the parole board and wondered how he knew anything about it. And I didn't know whether he was trying to be friendly or trying to get some information from me. Cautiously, I said, "Yes, but I guess everyone has his job to do and he has to do it the best way he can."

He said, "You're a hot potato; they don't know what to do about you. You were smart to refuse that lie test. They can make those tests come out any way they want them to."

I said, "Oh, so you know about that?"

He said, "Sure, it's been on the radio. Everybody's talkin' about it. It'll be in the evening papers in big headlines—'Labor Leader Refuses Lie Test.' I'd bet on that."

To say that I was surprised and angry would be a gross understatement. I felt that I had been tricked and that state officials had deliberately planned the lie test proposal, hoping that I would refuse it and give them an opportunity to give publicity to the refusal, thereby easing the pressure of public opinion which was increasing in our favor.

About three o'clock, a friend from detention brought a copy of *The Raleigh Times* and, sure enough, there was the headline, "Payton Refuses Lie Detector Test." The story gave a complete account of my "off-the-record" conference with the parole board officials. My friend was furious and had some choice names for everyone connected with the state administration.

I wrote to Kitty and gave her my version of the day's developments. I said, "Apparently, vengeance and vindictiveness are not yet satisfied." Then I wrote to the chairman of the parole board and complained about the unfairness of his action in giving publicity to the conference after telling me that the conference was off-the-record. I concluded by saying, "You have now placed me in a position where I have little choice but to agree to the test in order to erase the implication that I am fearful of the test because of guilt."

The next day I received a letter from the parole board chairman. The letter had apparently been written upon his return to his office after seeing me on the previous day. It confirmed the fact that I had been offered an opportunity to submit to a lie detector test and advised that the offer would remain open until Thursday noon, December 8, 1960, "if you change your mind." *Significantly, however, attached to the letter was a note which said, "I didn't mean to mislead you yesterday when you asked about the document, 'You Be The Judge'—I had read it."*

In the afternoon, I was called to the front office for a visit with my minister friend, Bill Finlator. It was amazing how he always arrived when I needed him most. He was a real tonic for my depressed spirit and my feeling of frustration as he held my hand in his strong warm grip and offered a meaningful prayer which renewed my hope and faith. Then, as in all of his visits, we smoked two or three of his cigarettes and engaged in interesting and pleasant conversation about things other than my personal problems.

As he was leaving, a guard advised me that I had another visitor and should stay in the visiting room. A few minutes later Jimmy Ledford, one of our attorneys, came in and asked for my version of the conference with the parole board officials. When I had finished my story, we discussed the various angles for some time. He agreed that I had been placed in a bad position by the publicity, and that if I continued to refuse to submit to the test it would be construed as an indication of guilt, at least by certain people. It was finally agreed that I should advise the chairman of the parole board that I had no fear of the test and was willing to submit to it, but desired a delay until the attorneys could discuss, with parole board officials, the details of plans for giving the test and report them to me. He said he would also talk to parole board officials before leaving Raleigh.

The following day newspapers carried the story that I had changed my mind about taking the test, and an extension of the deadline for acceptance had been granted at the request of our attorneys.

The next morning I was selected by the guard to assist with

feeding the other inmates in the shipping corridor, and I was glad to get out of my icebox cell and be able to move around. The broken window had not been repaired, and I had been wearing all of my clothes around-the-clock as well as keeping two blankets wrapped around me most of the time. Fortunately, I was still alone in my cell and could use the bed-clothes from both bunks.

While returning from the kitchen with the breakfast food, I saw Warren getting food for those in detention. We had only a moment to talk, but I was able to tell him of the latest developments. He agreed that I had little choice but to take the test after the publicity and said, "I'm not worried about you not passing the test if they are honest about it, and, win, lose, or draw; it can't put us in any worse position than we are now." He also said he had been told that he would probably be assigned to a job inside the Wall and not be sent to a road camp at all.

When I was locked up again after helping to serve breakfast and scrubbing the corridor, I decided to clean the cell and spent most of the day at it. We were kept locked in our cells each day from 6:30 A.M. to 4:00 P.M., and lunch was brought to us by a crew from detention. Four of us were turned out to serve breakfast at 5:00 A.M. and again to serve supper at 4:00 P.M.

The Shipping Corridor

Life in the shipping corridor was like that poem about ships that pass in the night. Only six of us were permanent. Two were being held for observation and daily interviews because of some indications of mental disturbance. Both had been convicted of sex crimes. Two others had been sentenced to life imprisonment, but were being held in shipping corridor to be available for possible appeal hearings. The fifth man had been convicted on a charge of manslaughter after having had the unfortunate experience of being engaged in a fist-fight in which his opponent was knocked down, hit his head against a concrete curb, and died.

Each evening, some 25 or 30 new faces were brought to the shipping corridor, and the next morning most of them would be gone. Now and then two or three would be held over for an extra day or two, but the usual stay in the shipping corridor was only overnight and, of course, the occupants of the cells had no interest in cleaning or otherwise concerning themselves about the condition of the cells. In fact, it seemed to me that each one made a special effort to add to the filth and disorder which he found. The shelves and doors of the wall cabinets were deliberately ripped away; the metal drinking cups were battered into many different shapes; and papers, old clothing, and pieces of food were strewn about or kicked into a pile in the corner.

The regular cell-blocks were below and beyond shipping corridor, and the inmates from these cells were permitted to go to the first floor to watch television in the evenings. We could hear the music and dialogue but could not see the screen. This could be very frustrating if one allowed himself to become interested in the dialogue and tried to follow the story.

One of the fellows being held for mental observation fancied himself an accomplished tap dancer and nearly drove the rest of us crazy with his constant tapping out what he considered "tunes" on the metal bars, while he kept time with his feet and sang in a weird, off-key voice. When he tired of this, he would do what he called "bird and animal imitations" and worry the others close to distraction by insisting that we try to identify the sound.

The cold wind continued to blow into my cell from the broken window, and all of my requests to have it repaired were ignored. I had developed a heavy cold in my chest and head, and my lips were covered with cold blisters. I hung a blanket on the bars in front of my bunk, but the wind blew the bottom of the blanket out until I got the idea of tying it down with the strings from my shoes.

On Saturday, December 10th, a new guard came to my cell to advise that I had visitors in the front office. When he saw the blanket on the bars and found me sitting on the bunk with the ear-flaps down on my cap, he became angry, and said, "There's no sense in this—I don't care what they say—I'm moving you up front. Bring your stuff with you."

I quickly gathered all of my belongings and put them in cell number two on my way to the front office. I saw at once that another cleaning job would be necessary, but I was glad to be away from the frigid cell number seven.

When I got to the front office, I found two of our attorneys, Nick, and Jimmy Ledford. They informed me that they had just returned from a conference in Goldberg's office in Washington with all eight of our attorneys and top union leaders. The conference had been called to discuss the matter of the lie detector test. They said the attorneys felt compelled to advise against my submitting to the test because of my emotional and physical condition; and because, it was generally agreed, the person giving the test could get whatever results he desired. However, both agreed that our only immediate hope for early release lay in my taking and passing the test; that all other approaches had failed; that there was no other plan under consideration which offered as much hope for success; that my passing the test would benefit the other seven as well as myself; and, finally, that my failure to submit to the test would, in view of the publicity already given to it, be construed as an indication of guilt.

I had the impression that the attorneys were hoping I would agree to the test, but could not, or would not, say or do anything to force that decision upon me. They showed me two newspaper releases which had been prepared at the Washington conference. The first explained why I insisted upon submitting to the test against my attorneys' advice. The second was to the effect that I had decided not to submit to the test upon the advice of attorneys. I felt that I had no choice but to agree to the test and so advised them. They were obviously pleased; both gave me a bear hug and slapped me on the back after saying they were proud of me and were betting that I would pass the test with flying colors.

After agreeing that they would ascertain the details of arrangements for the test and keep me advised, they left. I was returned to my new cell to find that I had a cell partner. Within a few minutes two guards came and marched all of us to the clothes house and shower room for our weekly shower and clean clothes. There were about 40 of us, since a large group had been brought in for the weekend as part of a mass transfer between prison camps.

The weekly shower was quite an experience. We were

marched to a window opening into the shower room. As each piece of dirty clothing was removed it was passed through the window and exchanged for a clean one, but the clean ones had to be held in one's arms and not put on until after the shower. As each man was completely outfitted, he tried to find a dry place to leave his clothes while he was under the shower. There was much good-natured jostling for the choice spots. Everybody was in great good humor. Jokes and singing were the order of the day as spray from 40 shower nozzles pelted 40 bodies of all shapes and sizes.

The tiled shower room was clean and smelled strongly of disinfectant. It occurred to me that this was about the happiest time of the week, and it came as somewhat of a shock to realize that something taken for granted all of one's life could be considered so wonderful.

Clothing sizes were given little consideration, and much trading was necessary to get something approaching a correct fit. One fellow whose middle I could have encircled with my hands had a pair of shorts big enough for Jackie Gleason and was insisting that they be altered to fit. The fellow at the sewing machine doubled the waist-band over and sewed it. When the skinny fellow put the shorts on, he looked like he was wearing one of those split skirts, and everyone had quit a time kidding him.

As we were being marched back to our cells, the guard stopped the line and ordered several into the barber shop for a haircut. I asked if I could get one, but the guard said, "You don't need no haircut."

* * * * *

The next morning, Sunday, December 11th, I again helped with the feeding and got a real break when we ran out of eggs and I was sent back to the kitchen for more. I was able to order them "sunnyside up" instead of hard and greasy, and the "chow-line" boys (including me) really enjoyed them. By 6:30 A.M. I had washed, shaved, cleaned my teeth and done my laundry, and I wondered how I could possibly get through the long no-visiting, rainy Sunday. My cellmate kept whistling a mournful tune and I was reminded of one time when I was about ten years old and went to visit my aunt on her farm. Her son kept whistling "There's a Long, Long Trail A-winding," while the rain spattered on the porch roof, and I was so lonesome and homesick that I insisted upon being taken home before dark.

At 8:00 A.M. the run-boy brought the paper which I had ordered earlier, and I read the story about the lie detector test proposal.

At 11:00 A.M. I was called by the guard and advised that I had a package at the mail room. My wonderful wife and daughters, knowing what a long day it would be, had arranged for a package of fruit, nuts, candy and cigarettes to arrive with the morning mail. I also received four letters—one from each of them—and the day was brightened considerably. After reading the letters, I lay on my bunk for hours and thought about the 28 wonderful years I had spent with Kitty, a patient, understanding, and ever-loving wife who was like a solid rock to cling to when the storms were roughest. I remembered a song that we had often sung together and which had a special meaning for us. I hummed and thought of the words.

My cellmate said, "You're feelin' kinda' sentimental, aren't you?" I admitted that I was and then I talked quite awhile about my home, family, and friends. When I stopped talking, he said, "Now, do you mind listening to my story? It won't be as happy as yours."

I told him that I would like to hear his story. It went something like this:

"I've been in love with the most wonderful girl in the world since she and I were both 17 years old, but I've been married for nine years now to a she-devil. Boy, was I stupid! I thought this blonde was a real hot sketch, and I stepped out on my real girl-friend. Finally, the blonde became pregnant, and I agreed to marry her until the baby came. My girl-friend had a nervous breakdown and nearly died. Then I learned that I hadn't been the only one with the blonde, and I wasn't sure that the baby was mine. Boy, I was about ready to blow my brains out.

"The baby finally arrived. It was a boy and couldn't have looked any more like me. I was crazy about him and so was my wife; and, for about a year, we got along real good. I could have been happy except that every time I thought of the way I had treated my girl friend I got cold chills up and down my spine and became sick at the stomach. She'd been taken to one of those rest homes.

"Then I got laid off at the plant and couldn't find another job. When the unemployment checks ran out, and I still couldn't find a job except for a day now and then, my wife turned into the meanest woman I ever knew. She never spoke to me unless it was to give me hell about something. She wouldn't cook a meal and wouldn't clean the apartment. At first she took good care of the boy, but she finally stopped doing even that, and I had to do everything—clean, scrub, wash dishes, do the laundry, take care of the boy, cook, and do everything else that was done. She would go out every night and stay until after midnight—then, stay in bed until noon the next day. The only time I had to look for a job was during the afternoon because I had to care for the baby until she got up.

"I finally got a job on the night shift. It was a good job, and I was making more money than before, but my wife and I were finished. She didn't want any more to do with me, and she had lost all appeal as far as I was concerned. The boy was the only thing we had in common. He was really cute as he began saying things and then began walking. I'd have given everything I owned or ever expected to own if my first girl friend had been his mother. By the way, she was back home and looked real good. I had seen her a few times, but she was always with her mother, and I didn't have a chance to talk to her. I had been told by mutual friends that both of her parents hated me with a passion.

"It was a hell of a way to live. I was about as unhappy as it was possible to get. I cooked my own meals, cleaned the apartment when it got so bad I couldn't stand it, did my own laundry, and paid all the bills. My wife never spoke to me unless she had to and paid no more attention to me than if I hadn't been there. When I tried to give her money, she would throw it on the table and leave it there, but when I left it on the table for her in the first place, it would be gone the next day, and the boy always had plenty of food and clothes. And she didn't stay in bed late. She was always up and dressed before I got home at 7:30 each morning.

On my nights off, she would sleep on the sofa in the living room. My only happiness was for a couple of hours each evening when I could have the boy to do with as I pleased from the time I got up from my day's sleep until his bedtime. She never raised any objection and never asked where we went or what we did.

"I don't know how long I could have gone on like that. It just wasn't human. No man could have stood it for very long.

"One day when the boy and I were walking across the ball field, my old girl friend was sitting on a bench by herself. She called to me, and we walked over. She was as pretty and sweet as ever and talked so easy and natural, as if nothing bad had happened between us. She held the boy on her lap and talked "little boy" talk to him. He liked her at once. She told me how cute he was and how much he looked like me. Then she told him how wonderful his father was and how he should always try to be like his father. By golly, I never heard anything like it. She was tearing my heart out, and I was sure that hers was in the same shape, but she kept talking as calmly as if she had been talking about last winter's snow.

"To make a long story short, we met in the ball park every day when the weather was nice. When it wasn't, we would go to the movies, and she would find us, or she would go first, and we would find her. All we ever did was hold hands, except once when the boy went to sleep on her lap, and I kissed her two or three times—long and hard but, boy, we were really in love, and both of us were achin' for the other one.

"When the boy was about three years old, I decided that I had to take the bull by the horns and try to get things straightened out. I thought about it for a week after I had made my decision and planned each word that I would use. I didn't think she would object too much to a divorce if I would agree to pay enough for her to live on, but I wanted the boy, and this wouldn't be easy, I figured.

"When I finally got around to talking to her about it, she didn't say a word until I had finished. Then she really knocked me for a loop when she said, very quietly, 'I've been expecting that—here's my proposition—I want five thousand dollars and no strings after that except the right to have the boy for one day each week while I'm in town or for one month in the summer time if I don't stay in town.'

"Well, I didn't have five thousand cents, to say nothing of dollars, but I decided then and there to get it by hook or by crook. And I tried, too. That's why I'm doing 18 years for armed robbery. I haven't seen my wife or boy since I was arrested—I don't even know where they are—but my girl-friend came to see me in jail, sat through my trial, and never misses seeing me every visiting Sunday. She says she is waiting for me. Imagine that—we'll both be 44 years old when I get out, and that will be 25 years we've been waiting to be together. How do you like that for a true sob-story?"

I tried to think of something appropriate to say, but I couldn't do anything but shake my head and breathe a silent prayer of thankfulness for the steadfast love of my wife and kids, as well as for the years of happiness which had been mine. That night he was transferred and I never saw him again, but I have often thought of his story.

On Tuesday afternoon, I was called to the front office where my good friend, Bill Finlator, reported on some interesting conversations which he had been having with influential people who felt that the state was looking for a way "to get off the hook" of public criticism. He felt assured that I would win the lie detector test, and that this would make it possible for Governor Hodges to grant clemency before he left office in January. He said, "I'm hoping and praying that you will be completely vindicated and that the injustice done to you will serve to rekindle a great crusading spirit which will make it possible to organize the entire South."

When I returned to my cell I was surprised to find a C-grade inmate as my new cellmate. It was unusual to find a C-grader celled with an A-grader, and it was especially surprising in my case because everyone knew that I was being held there to be available for the test. In addition to having an unusual number of visitors at this time, I was being used as one of the feed boys. This meant that my cell was opened several times each day to let me in and out. C-graders were held under close supervision, were seldom allowed to have contact with other prisoners, and their cells weren't supposed to be opened unless an extra guard was present.

I was suspicious. I thought he had been "planted" to observe me or to try to get information from me. As he talked, displaying superior intelligence and vocabulary, my suspicions were strengthened. His clean, neatly creased clothing and his concern about getting the cell cleaned did nothing to lessen my feelings. I resolved to be doubly careful about expressing any opinion which might involve me in any further controversy with state or prison officials.

* * * * *

Before daylight the next morning, as I was helping to carry the breakfast from the kitchen, another inmate stumbled against me in the hallway; and I felt a tightly folded piece of paper being pressed into my hand. Quickly, I slipped it into my watch pocket and followed the others back to the shipping corridor, hoping that the kitchen guard hadn't seen the note passed to me and that I could avoid a thorough shakedown until I had read and destroyed the note. (Passage of messages between inmates was strictly prohibited.)

There was no chance to read the note while out of the cell and under the guard's constant observation. I was just as concerned about allowing my new cellmate to see me with it. That piece of paper was like a red-hot coal, and I worried about it all morning. Each time a guard approached, I felt sure he knew about it and was coming to "arrest" me. Finally, about two o'clock, my cellmate went to sleep on his top bunk. I crawled as far back on the lower bunk as possible, fished the note out of my watch pocket and read it. It was from Charley. He was concerned about the failure of the lawyers to keep us advised of developments and about Lawrence being so ill and not receiving proper medical attention. To my surprise, he didn't mention the lie detector test.

As soon as I had finished reading the note, I flushed it down the toilet. Of course, there was no way to get an answer to Charley even if I had been inclined to take a chance on it.

When I turned around, my cell-mate was lying on his side and watching me. For an anxious moment, I thought that he might have been watching as I destroyed the note; but he didn't say anything. I was soon to learn that it wouldn't have made any difference if he had seen me. He was in a talkative mood; and as I listened to him, I began to lose my suspicions. I even found myself liking him.

He certainly was a welcome change from most with whom I had come in contact. It was obvious that he was from a good family, well educated, and well read. He talked intelligently about the world situation, about politics, baseball, football, and organized labor. Apparently, he had kept abreast of developments in our case and, by reading between the lines of newspaper accounts, had formed the opinion that state officials had planned entrapment for the eight union men in order to assist the company in smashing the union; to avoid the embarrassment of the libel suit against the attorney general; and to promote the latter's future political ambitions.

I was anxious to learn the reason for his C-grade status, why he was considered a maximum security prisoner by the guards and a sort of hero by other inmates. However, I had learned that one inmate never asked another inmate about such things.

I was glad to have someone to talk to. It had now been more than a week since I had agreed to take the lie detector test and five days since my attorneys had promised to advise me as soon as the arrangement details were completed. I had heard nothing from anyone and was quite disturbed by the complete silence. My cell-mate said officials were deliberately delaying the matter, keeping details a secret as a form of torture and hoping that I would be a nervous wreck when the test was finally given.

To add to my concern, a letter from my wife informed me that the attorneys had left Charlotte for Raleigh the day before to work out details of arrangement for the test. Twenty-four hours had passed since then, and I couldn't understand why I had not been advised of the results of any conference held concerning the test, especially when such a conference would have been held only a few blocks from the prison.

The Lie Detector Test

Thursday, December 15th started out just like any other day. The guard called me at 5:30 A.M. to go to the kitchen for the breakfast for the 22 men who were in shipping corridor that morning. We had Rice Krispies with fresh milk, rice with gravy and, of course, the ever-welcome coffee. After breakfast and the clean-up chores were completed, I began writing my third and final letter of the week to Kitty. I said, "Do you realize that it has been six weeks today since I kissed you goodby in Henderson? Sometimes it seems like a life-time, but then I can remember each detail so vividly that it seems like only yesterday. The boys here have a saying, 'Let me up,' when someone is giving them trouble. It means, 'I've had enough.' Well, I'm saying this morning, 'Let me up.' I've had more than enough."

I had had no advance warning and no word from my attorneys when, at 11:00 A.M., I was ordered from my cell by a guard who said, "Let's go get you some court clothes. You're gonna' take that lie test."

I was led to the clothes house and was given a white shirt, blue denim trousers, and a blue sweater to replace my ragged and faded brown clothes. Not having had a bath for a week, I asked if I could take a shower. The guard said, "No, not today." I hadn't had a haircut for nearly three weeks and asked permission to stop in the barber shop as we passed its entrance. The guard said, "You don't need no haircut." When I asked if I could get my street shoes from the storage room to replace the heavy, size 13, field shoes, the guard pretended not to hear, marched me back to my cell, and locked me in.

After about an hour, another guard came and said, "You're wanted up front." I was somewhat subdued by the gruff attitude of the guards and by the fact that I knew none of the details concerning the test, but I was not worried or nervous. My first misgivings came when, for the first time in my life, handcuffs were snapped on my wrists. My spirits sank completely when they fastened a heavy strap around my waist and between my legs and attached the handcuffs to it, so that I couldn't quite stand straight and couldn't raise my hands above my waist. I protested the treatment, but was told that it was "prison regulations." (This is the procedure used when transporting the most dangerous or mentally disturbed criminal.) I thought of withdrawing my agreement for the test and asking to be taken back to my cell, but was forced to go on by thoughts of headlines screaming: "Payton Turns Yellow" or "Payton Gets Cold Feet." So, without comment, I allowed the major of the guards to place me in the back-seat of a prison car. An honor-grade inmate was at the wheel; and, as the major stepped back into the warden's office for a few seconds, the driver said, "You're a dern fool for agreeing to that test. You haven't got a chance to win it. They can make it come out any way they want it, and they can't afford to let you win it."

Before I had a chance to reply, the major took his place beside the driver and said "Justice Building." We started moving toward the front gate. The major noticed the difficulty I was having trying to strike a match to light a cigarette and reached back to assist. No one spoke as we rolled through the gateway and entered the stream of traffic on the city street. I knew nothing of any arrangements made for the test, although my wife had told me that our attorneys had been promised full details before the test was given. Within a few minutes, the car was eased into a parking space in front of the Justice Building where, to my dismay, I saw several newspaper photographers waiting on the sidewalk. In addition to the many other emotions which I had experienced in the previous hour, I was now almost overwhelmed with anger as I realized that only the parole and prison officials knew of the date for my test and that they had informed the newspapers. I sat for a long moment fighting to get control of my emotions and debating the consequences of refusing to leave the car. My mind was in a state of turmoil as I thought of the shame and heartache of my wife, daughters, and friends when they saw pictures of me in the ill-fitting clothes and the "desperado harness." I had a great urge to throw myself on the floor and hide from the cameras but, again, thoughts of screaming headlines calling me a coward and labeling me "guilty" forced me, but not without a great effort, to drag myself from the car and across the sidewalk. Pedestrians stepped gingerly away from what must have appeared to be a most dangerous criminal.

As I was led into the building and down a long corridor, I looked frantically for one of our attorneys or some other friendly face, but I saw none. The major directed me into a small room on the left and removed the handcuffs and the harness. He ordered me to sit in a chair which had been placed against the wall on one side of the room, and he sat directly opposite, about four feet away, with his revolver hanging loosely at his side. I soon realized that we were sitting in the State Bureau of Investigation's display room which seemed to serve as the entry to the SBI laboratory. The walls were covered with what I assumed were exhibits from cases handled by the SBI. One case was filled with Ku Klux Klan hoods and other paraphernalia relating to activities of this organization. A number of display cases containing samples were mounted along the wall—samples of various narcotics and detailed explanations concerning each. There were several weapons and other objects which I did not recognize hanging from nails on the walls.

As we sat quietly and waited, a virtual parade passed between the major and me, as numerous people who appeared to be Justice Department personnel suddenly found that they "had business" in the SBI headquarters.

We had entered the room at one o'clock. The "prisoner" was thoroughly observed until about 2:30, when a man came in waving a copy of the controversial trial record in our case. He introduced himself as a polygraph expert from New York City. He explained that he had been engaged by the North Carolina Board of Paroles to administer a lie detector test to me. He apologized for being late and blamed the delay on "a thorough study of the record."

I began complaining about the newspaper men and photographers being at the entrance when I had understood that no publicity was to be given to the test. He said, "Yeah, I questioned that, too, but parole officials said your attorneys had set it up." (This comment only increased my growing suspicions that the test results were "planned," because it would have been utterly ridiculous for my attorneys to have exposed me to such cruel and humiliating publicity.)

He informed me that he would have his equipment set up within a few minutes and would be ready to begin the test. He went into the next room, and I was left to worry about whether he had any information about our case except that which was in the record—a record which contained, of course, only the "evidence" against us.

There was still no word from our attorneys. The parade of observers had stopped. The major sat quietly and stiffly. The room was hot and still. It was now apparent that no one would explain anything to me, and that I was strictly on my own.

About 2:45 I was escorted into a small room. The "expert" began a lecture about what made him an expert. It was obvious that he had a very high opinion of himself, was enjoying himself immensely, and was in love with his machine which he patted affectionately and referred to as "Old Betsy." He explained that it was the very latest in polygraph equipment and that it might lead to a judicial re-evaluation of polygraph procedures which would make results of such tests admissable evidence in court. I remembered the statement which the North Carolina attorney general had made more than a year earlier: "I've had some experience with polygraphs, and it depends on the man operating the machine. The lie detector is not admissable evidence; not even the Labor Relations Board accepts it."

The "expert" continued his discourse about his qualifications and about the unfailing accuracy of his machine. He said, "If you think you are smart enough to fool Old Betsy, I'd advise you to back out before it's too late." He questioned me about a similar test which I had taken in 1959 to disprove "hoax" charges made against me by the attorney general. He said, "Don't think you can fool my machine just because you passed that test in Washington. There's as much difference between that equipment and mine as between day and night."

He said, "Of course, now, it's a pretty good gamble, isn't it? You don't have anything to lose. Six to ten years is a long while, and it's worth taking a chance to try to cut it down, huh? If you win, you're a hero—if you lose, well, you're no worse off than you are now. You have nothing to lose. It's still just six to ten. Ha, Ha, Ha!"

Finally he began reading questions which he had apparently prepared previously and which he said he planned to use in the test. He said that I could object if I felt the questions were unfair, and that I could suggest rephrasing. I did object to two or three of the questions, but found it difficult to re-word them without appearing to be evading the issue, and I felt that this only strengthened what I considered his preconceived opinion that I was guilty.

About 3:15, I was seated in a chair beside a table upon which the machine rested, and several gadgets were attached to my body. In adjusting the attachment to my left wrist he used the hated trial record to prop up my arm. This sadistic act only served to heighten my suspicions that I had agreed to take a test which I would not be allowed to pass.

Throughout the test he needled me about thinking I was smart enough to beat "Old Betsy." When I lost my temper once and made an angry remark which caused the recording needle to jump and make crazy lines, he laughed uproariously and said, "That wasn't quite fair, was it? I'll have to cut that part out." He also kept accusing me of moving and charged that I was deliberately trying to influence the machine, although I sat perfectly still, in his full view, without moving.

Each chart seemed to run for ten or 15 minutes. He would then take the chart out of the room and be gone for what seemed like hours while I, still strapped to the machine, had visions of him and the SBI men in the other room fitting the chart to correspond to the "evidence" which they had used against us.

By the end of the second chart, I knew that I had no chance of passing the test. "Old Betsy" became a monster, and I was torn between a great desire to get away from it and a greater fear of the consequences of doing so.

Once, after an especially long wait between charts, he returned with a cup of coffee and joked with "Old Betsy" about the necessity of keeping up his strength to prevent my outwitting the two of them. At no time did he offer me a drink or inquire as to my personal comfort, although it had been nearly five hours since I had entered the building.

Finally, at 6:45, I was unstrapped and allowed to go to the men's room. Then I visited with my lawyer for a moment while the major stood a few feet away. The attorney told me that he had been in the building all afternoon but had not been permitted to see me before the test. He said, too, that he had learned only that morning that the test was to be given that day and had not been advised of any details of the test arrangements. The polygraph expert told me that it would take several days to prepare the report showing the results of the test.

At seven o'clock I was again handcuffed, strapped up with

the maximum security harness, and led through the group of reporters who were waiting in the lobby. Several tried to talk to me about my physical condition and how the test had gone, but I was hustled into the prison car and driven back to Central Prison where my blue "court clothes" were exchanged for my regular browns before I was returned to my cell.

My cell-mate was full of questions about my experience. As I told him of my treatment and expressed the opinion that I had never had a chance to win the test, he tried his best to cheer me up by telling of others he had known who thought they had failed a test of one kind or another until the actual result was announced in their favor. I appreciated his good intentions and his genuine concern for my welfare, but I couldn't shake the conviction that my failing the test had been a foregone conclusion.

I was completely exhausted and more forlorn and miserable than I'd ever been in my life as I ate a few bites of the cold food from the supper tray which had been saved for me.

The News and Observer of Friday morning, December 16, 1960, gave front-page treatment to the test experience with emphasis on a horrible picture showing me in handcuffs and harness.

Payton Goes For Lie Test

A handcuffed, dungaree-clad Boyd Payton entered the justice building in downtown Raleigh today to take a lie detector test.

Payton, Carolinas Director of the Textile Workers Union of America, is serving a six to 10 year prison term for conspiracy in connection with violence in the long, bitter strike at Harriet-Henderson Cotton Mills at Henderson.

Payton was offered an opportunity to take a lie detector test a week ago but refused on the advice of his attorneys. Later, however, he insisted that he take the test and arrangements were made secretly.

It was understood that someone not directly connected with the State Bureau of Investigation would administer the test.

The offer to Payton for a lie detector test was made by Johnson Matthews, Chairman of the State Pardon and Paroles Board.

Payton, who has been confined at Central Prison here, alighted from a prison department car and was accompanied by a guard. He walked slowly into the justice building facing the State Capitol.

About 7:00 P.M., Friday, a guard stopped in front of my cell and said, "So, you didn't get away with it, did you?" When I asked what he meant, he gleefully explained that it had just been announced over the radio that I had failed the test. He seemed to think it was a great joke and stood laughing at me and taunting me through the bars. When he finally became discouraged about his failure to get me involved in an argument and walked away, my cell-mate expressed some choice ideas about what he would like to see happen to guards in general and especially to those who seemed to take special delight in the misery and unhappiness of other human beings.

After an almost sleepless night, I was up and dressed at five o'clock. Anxiously, I waited to be sent to the kitchen for the breakfast food so that I might get the morning papers from the store-box. *The News and Observer* story was typical:

Lie Test Failed By Union Leader
By DAVID COOPER

Carolinas textile union director Boyd E. Payton failed his lie detector test, the State Board of Paroles said Friday.

Payton took the test here Thursday in an attempt to prove his innocence and gain freedom from prison.

Results of the examination were made public by Johnson Matthews, chairman of the State Board of Paroles, in a letter to Governor Hodges.

"The Board of Paroles does not recommend executive clemency for Boyd E. Payton," Matthews said in the letter to Hodges.

Payton is serving a six to 10-year prison term levied after he was convicted with seven other union members of conspiracy in connection with the long Henderson textile mill strike.

'Attempting Deception.'

Cleve Backster of New York City, who administered the six-hour-long lie detector test to Payton, said the tall union leader "was attempting deception" when he answered questions during the examination.

Backster said it was his further opinion that "Payton had definite knowledge of, and did directly or indirectly authorize the specific acts outlined in the conspiracy charge against him."

Backster's conclusions were contained in part in Matthews' letter to the Governor and in full in his report to the paroles board, also released to the press and sent to Hodges.

Unless new developments arise in the case, Payton will have to serve at least one-fourth of his minimum sentence. This would make him eligible for parole in about 16 months. He and the other seven unionists entered prison in October after legal attempts to overturn their convictions failed.

In his report to Matthews, Backster said: "It is also the opinion of this examiner that Boyd E. Payton deliberately attempted to distort his polygraph (lie detector) charts by movement and other concentrated efforts to produce extraneous results."

The test was administered in the offices of the State Bureau of Investigation. "There was nobody in the room but the examiner and Payton," Matthews told newsmen.

Payton had first declined to take the examination, offered to him by Matthews on Dec. 5 after Payton had written Hodges a letter again asserting his innocence.

Then last weekend Payton decided to take the test—over the objections of his attorneys, one of his lawyers, William Nicholson of Charlotte, had said.

In his report, Backster said, "The very latest and most refined polygraph equipment was brought from our New York City testing and research laboratory and used during this examination."

Of Payton's condition during the tests and his response, Backster said: "Special technique procedures indicated that subject was not overwrought to a degree that jeopardized the interpretation of his charts. Additional techniques clearly indicated ideal basic reaction capability throughout his entire series of tests."

Backster added: "Non-typical movement patterns obvious to the experienced polygraph examiner, were exhibited periodically throughout subject's charts. These were rendered insignificant by proper repetition of any question in the vicinity of such irregular tracings."

12 Questions Asked.

The New York examiner listed 12 questions and answers by Payton as the most pertinent given during the examination.

In the answers Payton said he had no knowledge of the alleged conspiracy and denied any association with the plot.

Backster said, "In the opinion of the examiner, subject showed strong and consistent unresolved reaction to each of the above listed pertinent questions, when he gave the answer indicated."

"In the opinion of examiner," Backster said in his conclusions, "after careful analysis of all charts, Boyd E. Payton was attempting deception when he gave each of the answers indicated next to the pertinent questions listed above. Based on the restricted scope of the pertinent questions asked, in regard to the specific conspiracy in question it is the further opinion of this examiner that Payton had definite knowledge of, and did directly or indirectly authorize the specific acts outlined in the conspiracy charge against him."

Prior to the testing, Backster said, Payton signed a "statement indicating complete willingness to undergo a polygraph examinater and authorizing this examiner to render the results, and opinions expressed in regard to these results . . . "

Matthews included a copy of the release statement he said was signed by Payton in making public the results of the test.

Payton Helped.

Backster said he formulated questions for the test with Payton's help. "each of these questions were (sic) agreed upon as being completely fair and unbiased by Payton who was allowed to make suggestions, help formulate, and give his approval of the final version of the question concerned," Backster said.

Backster said equipment used in the test "indicated and recorded relative changes in blood pressure, rate and strength of pulse, breathing pattern, and galvanic skin responses."

"As an additional assurance of accuracy three completely independent polygraph techniques were utilized, each acting as a cross-verification of the other two," the examiner said.

Details of the case surrounding Payton's conviction were supplied to him by Matthews, Backster said. "The principal issue covered by this examination involved possible knowledge or authorization of plans to dynamite the Vance County Power Company sub-station; plans to burn the Henderson Mills main office; plans to dynamite the Henderson South Mill boiler-room; all to have occurred on or about June 13, 1959," the examiner said.

Payton's lawyers had twice petitioned Governor Hodges asking him to grant the big, balding union leader and the other seven men executive clemency. The Governor, acting on the advice of the paroles board, had denied both requests, but said he would consider any new evidence brought forward.

In his letter to Hodges, Matthews said, "With further reference to Payton's letter requesting executive clemency on the grounds of his innocence, no information has been developed in our recent second review of this case which would seem to justify executive clemency."

List of Questions.

Backster listed the 12 "pertinent questions" and Payton's answer to each as follows:

"Prior to arrest in June, 1959, did you know for sure of the existence of a plan to dynamite the Vance County Power Company sub-station? (Subject answered. 'No.')

"Prior to your arrest in June, 1959, did you directly or indirectly authorize the dynamiting of the Vance County Power Company sub-station? (Subject answered 'No.')

"During June, 1959, did you intend to directly or indirectly make money available to pay for the dynamiting of the Vance County Power Company sub-station? (Subject answered 'No.')

"Prior to your arrest in June, 1959, did you know for sure of the existence of a plan to burn the Henderson Mills main office? (Subject answered 'No.')

"Prior to your arrest in June, 1959, did you directly or indirectly authorize the burning of the Henderson Mills main office? (Subject answered 'No.')

"During June, 1959, did you intend to directly or indirectly make money available to pay for the burning of the Henderson Mills main office? (Subject answered 'No.')

"Prior to your arrest in June, 1959, did you know for sure of the existence of a plan to dynamite the Henderson South Mill boiler room? (Subject answered 'No.')

"Prior to your arrest in June, 1959, did you directly or indirectly authorize the dynamiting of the Henderson South Mills boiler room? (Subject answered 'No.')

"During June, 1959, did you intend to directly or indirectly make money available to pay for the dynamiting of the Henderson South Mill boiler-room? (Subject answered 'No.')

"On or about June 4, 1959, at the time you talked to Harold Aaron over the Vance Hotel room telephone, were you aware that he was part of a plan to dynamite the Henderson South Mills boiler room? (Subject answered 'No.')

"Have you answered truthfully each question on this test about the June 13th dynamiting conspiracy? (Subject answered 'Yes.')

"Are you withholding any information whatsoever about the June 13th dynamiting conspiracy? (Subject answered 'No.')"

Private School Director.

Matthews had identified Backster as an expert with over 13 years experience in the lie detection field. "He was the best we could find in the country," Matthews said.

Backster is director of the National Training Center of Lie Detection in New York, a privately-run organization that trains polygraph operators. He is also president of Backster Associates, Inc. of New York, an outfit that sells the machines. Backster had had previous experience with Army Counter-Intelligence Corps, with civilian intelligence agencies, The Keeler Institute in Chicago, and as a consultant to the Office of Secretary of Defense, Matthews said.

—*The News and Observer*, Raleigh, North Carolina
December 17, 1960

Payton's Attorneys Say He's Innocent

CHARLOTTE (AP) — Attorneys for Boyd E. Payton said Saturday that results of a lie detector test given the imprisoned union leader "have not shaken our faith in his innocence."

They also said that in their opinion "findings of the polygraph are not conclusive."

Payton, Carolinas director for the Textile Workers Union of America, underwent a lie detector test in Raleigh Thursday. Results announced by the State Board of Paroles. Friday said Payton flunked the test.

The union leader, convicted with seven others of conspiring to destroy facilities at the struck Harriet-Henderson Cotton Mills in Henderson in 1959, is serving a 6-10 year prison term. He has steadfastly maintained his innocence and underwent the lie detector test in an attempt to prove it.

In a statement, Payton's chief attorney, W. M. Nicholson of Charlotte, said:

"As an attorney who advised against the proposal I must reiterate the sound reasons we advanced for Payton to reject such an ordeal. We said the test had no legal standing, that its findings are not accepted as evidence in the courts of North Carolina, that there are intangible and emotional factors making such a 'test' subject to grave doubt and against logical acceptance.

"Malcolm B. Seawell, ex-attorney general who was active in the Henderson case, has rejected the theory of legal acceptance of polygraph results. He has expressed his opinions on the abilities of the operators of such devices.

"As attorneys we were surprised that the State Board of Paroles made Payton the proposal to undergo such a test. We pointed out that even under ideal conditions the results are legally inconclusive. In this instance we drew attention to the lack of ideal conditions created by the great emotional stress under which Payton has lived during the trial, the appeals and his many weeks of imprisonment."

Nicholson said that Payton was "cooped up" for nearly six hours in a small room at the SBI headquarters. "He arrived there from Central Prison in handcuffs, with newsmen and photographers on hand to cover his arrival."

Nicholson said he talked with his client briefly in the corridor after Payton finished the test. "Its results were plainly evident both in his physical appearance and responses during our conversations.

"It is our considered opinion that the findings of the polygraph are not conclusive. They have not shaken our faith in his innocence nor altered our belief that eventually he will be vindicated of the charges under which he is now imprisoned," Nicholson's statement concluded.

—The News and Observer, Raleigh, North Carolina
December 18, 1960

Union Hits Payton Test

CHARLOTTE (AP) — The general secretary-treasurer of the Textile Workers Union of America said Saturday "it appears the State of North Carolina is going to extraordinary efforts to justify its past actions in the Henderson textile strike case."

John Chupka of New York, in a statement issued through TWUA Carolinas headquarters here, said union officials "cannot help but believe" that a lie detector test for Boyd E. Payton "was designed to nullify the mounting nationwide interest of those who are convinced that an injustice has been done.

"We are apprehensive," he said, "that the episode is a continuation of state efforts to discredit our union."

Chupka referred to a polygraph test given to Payton, Carolinas director for the union, earlier in the week. State paroles officials said Payton, now serving a prison term for conspiracy to damage facilities at the Henderson mills, flunked the lie detector test.

Chupka said the polygraph test "should be considered together with all the other lengthy and complex factors surrounding the Henderson conspiracy trials.

"When such a yard stick is used, it appears to us that the state of North Carolina is going to extraordinary efforts to justify its past actions in this case," Chupka said.

The TWUA secretary said Johnson Matthews asked Payton to undergo the lie detector test if he wanted to prove his innocence.

"It is disturbing that the chairman of the Board of Paroles persisted in his proposal and had it carried into effect even after the strong advice given Payton by his attorneys to reject the offer and outlining their sound reasons therefor."

—*The News and Observer*, Raleigh, North Carolina
December 17, 1960

The Kays Gary column of December 17, 1960 carried the following comment:

Boyd Payton says he didn't agree to take a lie detector test at first because of (a) advice of attorneys and (b) a May, 1959, statement of the then attorney general, Malcom Seawell. Asked by newsmen what he thought of Payton's successful appearance behind a lie detector in a rock-throwing case, Seawell said: "I have some experience with the polygraph (lie detector), and it depends on the man who is operating it."

Among those still pressing for Payton's release are evangelist Billy Graham and author Harry Golden. Writes Graham:

"I think he's one of the outstanding union leaders in the South but more, one of the outstanding citizens of North Carolina. From the evidence I have in hand, he no more deserves to be in prison than you or I."

—*The Charlotte Observer*, Charlotte, North Carolina
December 17, 1960

On Sunday, December 18th, Kitty and the kids came to visit as soon as permitted after 9:00 A.M. It was wonderful to see them, but so frustrating to be forced to speak through the screen in low tones and guarded words when we were bursting to talk about the test and its aftermath. And then, of all times, our visiting time was cut to 30 minutes because of the crowded conditions. It seemed that we had hardly finished saying hello when the guard called time. I tried to dictate a statement about my treatment before, during, and after the test; but there was so much to explain and such great pressure for time that I felt I had only succeeded in further confusing my family.

Kitty told me of dozens of calls, letters, and visits from people who were furious about the terrible picture of me being taken for the test in handcuffs and maximum-security straps. She said that she had hidden the paper from the kids that morning, hoping that by the time they came home from school she would have found some way to explain this further evidence of "man's inhumanity to man."

She also told me of having met with Billy Graham and Harry Golden, in Mr. Golden's office, on the previous Thursday and of first learning there that I was taking the test that day. She said that Billy Graham had written to her and that Mr. Golden had talked with her several times. Their expressions of kindness, faith, and hope had been largely responsible for her ability to bear up under the burden of constant frustration and disappointments.

She told me of their discussion about the kind of appeal they intended to make to Governor Hodges and the proper timing of their visit. When they had agreed on the following Monday, Billy Graham called the Governor to ask for an appointment. The Governor informed him that I was then taking the test. Billy quoted the Governor as saying, "I don't know why he agreed to take that test. I've been wanting to do something." (News of this statement came as a real surprise in view of the fact that the Governor had rejected two clemency petitions which were presented to him just six weeks earlier; that he had ignored the document, "You Be The Judge," which set forth the entire case in minute detail; and, the final irony—the Governor's secretary had been the one to suggest the lie detector test to Arthur Goldberg.

* * * * *

On Monday, December 19th, two of our attorneys came and we spent an hour discussing the test and the predicament in which it had placed us. Although no solution was found, I felt better knowing that someone outside of the prison knew my side of the story. However, I was really disappointed when they told me that Billy Graham and Harry Golden had postponed their planned visit to the Governor to plead for clemency action in our behalf. The test had apparently served another of its purposes. It had blocked this approach which had been given publicity and had evoked expressions of public opinion to the effect that support from these two men would carry great weight with the Governor.

* * * * *

On Tuesday, I was pleased to receive a letter from Mr. Golden in which he explained the reasoning behind their decision to postpone the conference and said, "Billy Graham, in speaking to me this morning, asked me to say for him (and I say this for myself anyway) that you should not construe this as abandonment in any sense and that we are as convinced of your innocence today as we were last week."

Another bright spot of Tuesday, December 20th, was a report that a television newscaster had criticized my treatment and the methods used in regard to the test. He was quoted as saying, "Payton was subjected to treatment previous to the test that would have thrown anybody, and especially an innocent man, into such a state of emotional tension and disturbance that it's a wonder the machine was able to operate at all."

* * * * *

After assisting in the feeding of breakfast to 47 men on Tuesday, I was returned to my cell. The C-grader was still my cell-mate. He began telling me of his difficulties with the law. I had been anxious to hear this story for the previous nine days but had not violated "the code" by asking about it.

His story went something like this: At the age of 18, just after graduating from high school, he and his best girl were returning from a dance. Another couple was in the back seat of his car. They had all been drinking throughout the evening and continued to pass a bottle of liquor between them as they laughed and sang while traveling at high speed through the early morning hours. Suddenly, a sharp curve loomed ahead. The boy applied the brakes; the car went into a skid and hurtled over a high embankment. My cell-mate said that he regained consciousness three days later and learned that the other three had been killed instantly, and that he was charged with manslaughter.

Later he had been tried and found guilty. He was sentenced to from three to five years in prison. He had entered prison in 1950 and had escaped five times, for which he had been given additional sentences totaling eight years. He had just recently been returned from his sixth escape, during which he had slugged a guard, stolen a prison truck and a private car, and shot his way through two road blocks, critically injuring three officers before being captured at a third road-block. For this, he had just been sentenced to a total of 40 years and was now being held in Central Prison pending the expiration of some kind of time limits and a decision by prison officials as to where he might be held with the greatest prospect for maximum security.

The Literacy School

In the afternoon of December 20th, a guard came to my cell and said, "Get all your stuff together. You're supposed to report to the major's office."

I hurriedly gathered all of my belongings and stuffed them into a gunny sack. When we arrived at the major's office he said, "Leave your stuff here and come with me. You've been assigned as a clerk in the school." He handed me a badge and explained that it gave me "yard privileges," including eating in the main dining room and visiting the library, the chapel, and exercise areas. The wording on the badge was "Transit—B.E.P.—098-234—Brickmason School." The major explained that it was only a temporary badge and that a permanent one would be issued later.

He escorted me through the gate which led to the industrial area of the prison yard and then took me to the second floor of the first building. There he introduced me to the supervisor of vocational education, Mr. Vernon Powers, a man whom I liked at once.

As soon as the major had departed, the supervisor explained that being his clerk would be the least of my duties. He said that most of my time would be devoted to teaching the literacy classes which were also his responsibility. He explained that only seven inmates were then enrolled in literacy classes, and that he had made no effort to build up enrollment because he had no one to assist him with the teaching. He had to spend almost all of his time teaching brick masonry.

Jokingly, he said, "I hope you don't get into the same trouble that my last clerk did."

My eyes questioned him and he continued, "He was teaching the boys how to make home-brew in the back of the classroom instead of how to read and write. That was almost a year ago, and I haven't had any help since."

I assured him that he wouldn't have the same problem with me. Before quitting time at 4:30, he and I were good friends and remained so for the months to follow. He was one of the finest men I have ever known.

Upon returning to the main prison yard, after lining up with several hundred other men at the "work gate" to be shaken down, I heard my name called over the loudspeaker with instructions to report to the major's office. There I was given my belongings and was assigned to cell number 13 on the fifth floor of the main cell-block. It was a two-man cell, but no one was assigned there with me and I lived alone for several days.

When I had stored my possessions in the wall cabinet and repared my bunk, I returned to the prison yard. It was wonderful to be able to move about with comparative freedom after the many days of close confinement.

The Mess-Hall

A long line was forming in front of the main dining hall. I took my place at the end of the line. When the supper whistle sounded, the line started moving across the yard, under the long porch, up the stairs to the second floor, and down the full length of the porch to the main entrance. Upon questioning the disappearance of the Negro inmates, I was informed that they had their own dining hall "around in the back."

As I entered the dining hall, I saw a large metal rack which held hundreds of metal trays. A sign on the end of the rack said, "Take As Much Food As You Want But Eat What You Take. Waste Of Food Will Not Be Tolerated."

Taking a tray from the rack and selecting a fork, metal cup, and a spoon (no knives) from a metal tub, I dipped some beef stew from a large container on the table and filled the largest compartment of my tray (no dishes). Then, moving along the steam table, I took a spoonful of beans, some bread pudding, and a slice of bread.

Guards directed us to the tables. There were about 40 of them with room for ten at each table. The first men were assigned to the first table, the next to the second table. By the time all the tables were filled, the first men were finished; the tables were cleaned promptly; and the procedure was repeated until everyone had eaten. A big metal pitcher of coffee as well as quart-jars of salt, pepper, mustard, vinegar, and "blackstrap" syrup stood in the middle of each table. On either side of each table were wooden benches. The tables, also made of wood, were covered with a grayish vinyl material which gave the appearance of marble.

One of my table-mates, sensing that this was a new experience for me, informed me that the guard would insist that every bite be eaten. He told me that if I had anything left on my tray I should scrape it off in my hand and hold it under the tray until I got to the tub where each inmate was required to rinse off his tray by swishing water over it with a long-handled brush. He said, "If you have anything in your hand when you reach for the brush, just accidentally let your hand go on down in the water; the guard won't notice." He seemed to think this was an important thing to know, and I was duly impressed. It wasn't until some weeks later that I really appreciated his advice when I witnessed an "arrest" because a young inmate had scraped into the garbage tub a whole fish which he claimed had not been cooked. It was reported that he was given 30 days in the hole for this infraction.

The Strange Case of Boyd Payton

To many the strange case of Boyd Payton will seem more settled than ever following the negative results of a lie detector test in Raleigh last week.

To others who abhor the polygraph's invasion of privacy, or who firmly believe in his innocence, or who naturally have sympathy for the underdog nothing much has changed.

Did Boyd Payton conspire to dynamite the Vance County Power Co. sub-station and engage in other destruction of municipal and mill property?

Courts from the lowest to the highest have failed to overturn a jury's verdict that Payton did participate in such conspiracy with his lieutenants, now also serving prison terms. Some jurists, among them Associate Justice William Bobbitt of the N. C. Supreme Court, say the case involved too much circumstantial evidence; they doubt that the courts proved Payton guilty.

Now comes a failing grade on a lie detector test to bolster the case against the Charlotte labor leader.

One must immediately wonder: Why did he submit to the test? The chairman of the State Paroles Commission interviewed Payton on December 5 to determine whether or not he had any new information or facts to present in connection with his case. He did not, according to Chairman Johnson Matthews. But Matthews went on at that time to suggest a lie detector test administered by an outside expert. "The paroles board," Matthews later wrote, "has on several occasions in past years arranged for prisoners to take lie detector tests in cases where a prisoner persisted in efforts for executive clemency on the grounds of complete innocence of the crime for which he was convicted."

On the advice of his attorneys Payton at first refused. Even former Attorney General Malcolm Seawell, who confronted Payton with his most damaging public accusation and stood by it without challenge, shared doubt about the usefulness or accuracy of the polygraph examination.

But later Payton, for reasons best known to himself, decided to take the test. Perhaps he recognized that the Paroles Commission's public announcement of his first refusal compromised his position. Perhaps, whether guilty or not, he decided he could beat the machine.

He did not. The report of the New York examiner, using latest equipment, did not equivocate. It positively concluded that "Boyd E. Payton was attempting deception" and that "he had definite knowledge of and did, directly or indirectly, authorize the specific acts outlined in the conspiracy charge against him." It added that he "deliberately attempted to distort his polygraph charts by movement and other concentrated efforts to provide extraneous responses."

Nobody, even the polygraph needle, can measure the motives of Boyd E. Payton. They can see the effect. But they can only surmise the cause.

And there lies the secret of the Payton case. It has attracted national attention because the man who now holds power over his future is a cabinet member of an administration widely recognized as a friend of labor. The very labor attorney, Arthur Goldberg, who sits with Commerce Secretary Luther Hodges in President-elect Kennedy's cabinet, was in Raleigh recently to plead Payton's innocence.

But is he innocent? In an emotion-packed atmosphere, involving deeply felt convictions about man and society, the courts have rendered justice as they saw it. Now man-made machines of the electronic age confirm the court's judgment.

But who really knows?

—*Greensboro Daily News*, December 21, 1960

The Main Cell-Block

At 5:30 the lock-up whistle sounded; and we were marched to our cells—Negroes to the left section, whites to the right. The "all-clear" whistle sounded to indicate that all inmates had been counted and found to be in their proper places. We were now free to do as we pleased until nine o'clock.

My new cell was filthy, and I spent the evening sweeping with rolled newspapers. The bunks were fastened to the wall by hinges, and I learned that I could fasten the top one up so that I could sit upright on the bottom one. Each cell had a toilet bowl, a washbasin, and two wall cabinets. A fellow in the next cell advised that I should try to get transferred to one of the lower floors where the cells were cleaned each day by a regular cleaning crew of inmates.

The Schoolroom Guard

The next morning, after breakfast and the sounding of the work whistle, I went to the schoolroom, but was promptly ordered out by a guard. He said, "Yer' supervisor ain't here yet and you ain't allowed up here without him bein' here. Don't let me ketch ya' here again when your supervisor ain't here or you'll git yer ass throwed in the hole."

I tried to explain that I hadn't known about such a rule, but he interrupted and said, "You go up to the major's office and tell him I chased yer ass outta' here cause yer supervisor ain't here."

I went to the major's office and reported as instructed. He said, "He did right, and you'd better remember it in the future."

I said, "Well, what should I do now. How am I to know when the supervisor does arrive?"

The major said, "Keep watchin' for him and don't go down there till you see him there first."

I left the major's office and stood alone in the empty prison yard feeling as if I had been marooned in the middle of a desert. However, within a few minutes, I saw a group of inmates being marched toward the work gate. My supervisor was behind them. I was greatly relieved to see his smiling face and hear his friendly greeting. When I told him of my experience, he said, "Why, they knew where I was. I was in the major's office just a few minutes ago and arranged to borrow these men from detention to do some cleaning."

When we were back in the vocational school office, I began typing some forms which the supervisor had requested. The guard who had ordered me to the major's office came in and said, "Now, so's ther' won't be no misunderstandin', I wanna' tell ya some things. Ya' already know ya' ain't s'pose to come in this buildin' less'en the supervisor's here. Now, I wan' ya' to take a good look at where yer sittin'. Yer right in the winder and in plain sight of the major. Yer jes' like in a goldfish bowl. They can see everything you do from the major's office, but ya' can't see them watchin' ya'. If I let ya' git away with anything, it's my ass; and I ain't plannin' on losin' my job over you. If anything goes wrong in here, I'm holdin' you responsible; and yer ass is goin' to the hole. Ain't nobody s'pose to be in this office 'cept you and the supervisor. If I ketch anybody else in here, their ass and yers too is goin' to the hole.

"Another thing," he continued, "if I ever find anything in here that ain't s'pose to be in here, yer' ass is goin' to the hole; and I ain't gonna ask who brought it in. Yer s'pose ta see it ain't brought in here. An, sumpin' else, see that toilet right behind where yer' sittin? And, see that sign that sez 'Employees only?' Well, that don't mean you. If I ketch ya' usin' it, yer' ass is goin' to the hole. Yer s'pose to use the same one as the niggers use at the end of the hall."

I hadn't said a word while he had been talking, although I was seething inside. By a real effort, I managed to remain quiet until he went out and closed the door to the office. I was almost overcome with rage, and I felt like hitting something with my fists which I realized only then were closed so tightly that my fingernails were cutting into the palms of my hands.

I didn't realize the significance of his closing the door to the office when he left until sometime later when the students informed me that he had gone to the classroom after delivering his tirade to me. He had said to the inmates there, "Ya' got a new teacher, and I jus' wann' tell ya' all—he ain't runnin' nothin' 'round here. He's jus' a convict like you, and you ain't to take no orders from him. If he gets uppity with me, he'll find his ass in the hole just the same as any of you, education or no education."

The Prison Yard

I sat for a long while after the guard had left the office and stared through the window, not really seeing anything. Finally, I remembered what he had said about my being in a goldfish bowl, and I began to survey my surroundings. I found that I had a good view of the greater part of the prison yard.

To the extreme right, I could see part of the recreation field with its volley-ball court and baseball diamond. Beyond that, I could see the guard's station mounted on top of the east wall. Just below the guard's station and slightly to the right, I could see a heavily barred gate, large enough to drive a truck through.

To the left of this opening, I could see part of the hospital in the southeast corner; and I remembered that the main entrance to the prison was at that corner. Much nearer, I could see the old red brick building which housed the library in front and the hobby shop in the back. The second floor of this building, I had been told, contained the basketball court.

Just to the left of the library was the entrance to the dining hall; beyond that, the kitchen and the administration offices. Straight ahead, I could see the main cell-block which filled the entire section to the west wall. Away around to the left, I could see the guard's station mounted on the west wall. High above the wall and cell-block was the big, metal water tank which supplied water for Central Prison.

Down below the west wall guard's station, and directly in front of it, was the chapel, a new red brick building which looked like a rose among thorns. Beside the chapel and nearer to my vantage point was the building known as the clothes house which also contained the white and Negro shower rooms, the white and Negro toilets, and the white and Negro barber shops.

About 50 feet directly in front of the chapel, and about 200 feet in front of my office window, stood the headquarters of the major and the captain of the guards. From this office, I had been told, the operation of the prison was administered. The warden and the prison director had little knowledge of the decisions made there.

Nearer to me and around to my left I could see the incinerator and a small building in which kitchen and dining hall garbage was kept in barrels to be transported to the prison farm for hog feed.

Directly down in front of my window was the work gate with its guard station standing alongside. Beside the guard station, in an area some 30 or 40 feet square, there was a garden plot around which inmates had stretched wire and trained rose bushes to grown. A small, homemade windmill was mounted on a high post. On two other posts were small bird houses.

Just as I finished my survey of the prison yard and turned to resume typing of the forms, the supervisor came in and advised me that I was supposed to go to the clothes house and exchange my brown clothes for white ones. He explained, "All inmates who are assigned to the hospital, the kitchen, or the dining hall, and all clerks, are supposed to wear white clothes; and they are allowed to take a shower and get clean clothes each morning between nine and ten."

This was really good news, and I lost no time in heading for the clothes house. However, when I came to the gate to the main prison yard, the guard refused to pass me through. He said, "You ain't got no white clothes on, and nobody told me yer a clerk. I can't let you through without a pass from your boss."

So I had to go back to the school to ask my supervisor for a pass. He said, "While you're up there, ask the major for a permanent badge, and it will allow you to go through any gate at any time—except the ones to the outside," he laughingly concluded.

After taking a shower and being outfitted in new white duck trousers, a new white shirt, white socks, and a white "doctor's" coat, upon which I pinned my new permanent badge, I felt like a new person. As I passed through the gate to the work area, the guard who had gruffly ordered me back for a pass a few minutes before now joked, "Hi, Doc. When you gonna' perform your first operation?"

The Prisons Director

Back at the school I resumed typing of the forms, but within a few minutes, was called to the front office for a conference with the prisons director, Mr. George Randall.

He said, "I've just had a chance to read your record and study your background, and I wanted to talk with you. You see, everyone here doesn't have a background like you and I have. You may think that some of our rules are unnecessary and too harsh; but you must realize that there are some bad actors here. We have to make the rules to handle them, and the good ones have to suffer with the bad ones. We can't make any exceptions to the rules."

"I've never asked for any exceptions to be made for me, and I don't expect any," I replied.

"I know you haven't," he said, and then quickly added, "I didn't mean to imply that you were. In fact, our report on you from Lincolnton states that you complained about nothing and worked several days when you could have stayed in."

After a brief pause, he continued, "What I really wanted to say is that you can be a force for good in here or you can be a force for trouble. You are a leader and the men will listen when you talk. This places a great responsibility on you, but knowing the kind of person you have been, we think you will want to be a force for good. At least, we are hoping that you will."

He paused, apparently choosing his words carefully. I waited. Finally, he said, "An awful lot of people have taken an interest in your case. You have a lot of friends who think you've been done an injustice. Some of them are quite influential, but I don't have to tell you that there are others who feel otherwise. It's not my place to judge and I can't express an opinion either way. I'm not here to offer any apologies, but I do want you to know that I'm sorry for any unnecessary hardship or embarrassment which you or your family have been caused. I don't want you to feel that you have been persecuted.

I spoke of the degrading experience of being taken to the Justice Building in the "desperado harness." He said, "That wouldn't have happened if I had been here. Handcuffs are prison regulations, but harness—not in your case.

"General Waynick of the North Carolina National Guard called this morning and said he'd like to come to see you this afternoon. When I jokingly told him that he wasn't on your approved list of visitors, he said he was still the head of the National Guard and could blow this place off the map if he wanted to do it."

I said, "I'd like very much to see General Waynick. I've known him for years and value his friendship highly. As for any influence I might have on the men here, you can rest assured that I have no desire to create any controversy or trouble. I've had enough of both to do me for a lifetime."

"I'm sure you have," he replied. "The final thing I wanted to say is that I consider your imprisonment a rare opportunity for us to gain an insight into prison operations and inmate behavior that wouldn't be possible in any other way. I want you to feel free to give me your comments and reactions at any time. Write to me whenever you feel like it, seal the letter, and leave it at the mail room or give it to the major or the warden. It won't be opened until it gets to me, and anything you want to be confidential will be kept that way."

When I came from his office, I found the line forming for

lunch and took my place at its end.

Prison Mail-Call

At twelve o'clock the loudspeaker blared, "Mail-call on the back porch." Everyone crowded around as an inmate loudly called out the names on letters which he took from a wire basket. A guard stood alongside. When an inmate answered as his name was called, his letter would, in some cases, be thrown at him, while in other cases the letter would be carefully passed down to the person who had answered. When my name was called, three letters were carefully passed to me while another fellow was still trying to get his, which had been thrown and had dropped to the ground amid dozens of feet. I questioned the person nearest to me about the different treatment. He gave me a scornful look, then said, "Ain't you ever been 'on-the-state' before?"

When I shook my head in the negative, he explained, "Ya' see, most fellows in here don't have money on the outside and nobody to deposit any for 'em—so they try to get some kind of racket. This fellow has th' mail racket; and, if ya' want to get yer mail in good shape, ya' pay him fifty cents a week. Likewise, if you want good clothes, ya' pay the clothes boy fifty cents, else ya' get rags. Likewise, if ya' want ta' change cells, ya' pay the cell clerk a dollar. Same thing goes fer appointments with the doctor or the dentist. Ya' don't get on the list 'less ya' pay the clerk."

I said, "But I haven't paid anybody and I just had my mail handed to me. I also got new clothes this morning."

He said, "Yeah, but they figure that you will. Just try not doin' it and see what happens." I learned that he knew what he was talking about.

Returning to the school at 12:30, I found two new students waiting to enroll. One was a Negro, age 57, who said, "I ain't never learned to read and write—they say you can teach me." The other one was white, age 20. He said he had quit school in the third grade.

Within an hour, the Negro was writing his name after tracing it several times on a sheet which I had prepared. The white boy was adding and subtracting on a prepared third-grade test sheet.

Both were quite pleased with themselves.

At three o'clock, I was called to the front office where I spent a pleasant hour with General Waynick, commander of the state National Guard. He had brought a carton of cigarettes for me. He said, "I just felt that I couldn't go through this Christmas week if I didn't come to see you and try to give you a word of encouragement. A lot of fine people have great faith in you and are working hard to see that you are completely vindicated. I'm sure you won't be here long, but I know how difficult it must be for you and your family at this particular time of year." I learned later that he called Kitty that evening and was very kind.

* * * * *

At suppertime, while waiting for my coffee to cool, I was thinking about something Kitty had said in one of her letters and decided to re-read it. A heavy hand landed on my shoulder and a gruff voice said, "Ya' wanna' go to th' hole?—Ya' ain't allowed to read in here." Thus, I learned of another rule.

* * * * *

The next morning, I carried my newspaper through the work gate and up to the school office. The guard had shaken me down at the gate and had said nothing about the newspaper, but when I got to the office, the supervisor said, "You're not supposed to bring newspapers to work with you. The guard in the tower saw you with it and reported it to the major. The major just called me and told me about it. He said you should leave it in the library after this."

A few minutes later, the guard in charge of the school came in and asked, "Payton, didn't you know you're not supposed to bring newspapers down here?"

"No sir," I replied, "I didn't know it until a few minutes ago."

He said, "Well, we've all caught hell about it. I didn't see ya' with it and the guard at the gate didn't notice it, but the guard in the tower saw it and reported it to the major. You let that happen again and you'll find your ass in the hole."

When I went back through the work gate for my shower, the

guard there said, "Did you take a newspaper to work with you this morning?"

I said that I had and explained that I hadn't known about that rule until my supervisor had told me when I got to the office.

"Well, did you have it hid?" he asked.

"No sir, I was reading it right up to the gate and had it in my hand when you were shaking me down," I replied.

He said, "Derned if I saw it; but the guard in the tower did and reported it to the major and he's on my ass about it."

I said, "I'm sorry. It won't happen again."

The mail at noon brought letters from Kitty and each of the kids as well as a copy of a letter which Patsy (my oldest daughter and a senior at Queens College) had written to the Governor.

Just before quitting time on Thursday, December 22, 1960, we were informed that the work area would be closed until the following Tuesday because of the Christmas holiday. This was a real disappointment to me. While in the school, I could keep busy and forget my own problems by becoming involved in the problems of others. I dreaded the long, useless hours stretching ahead over Friday, Christmas Eve, Christmas Day, and Monday.

* * * * *

Friday was even longer, drearier, and more useless than I could possibly have predicted. The cells were opened as usual at 6:30 A.M., and we marched to the dining hall for a breakfast of creamed, chipped beef. Then just nothing—until lock-up time at 5:30. We were not permitted to return to our cells during the day. Those who had enough "seniority" to rate a place in the hobby shop were busy there, but there were only about 30 places. Some went to the library, but this only had accommodations for 30 at the tables, and possibly 20 extra chairs. Some 30 or 40 could huddle together on benches underneath the dining-hall porch, and another 40 could find chairs on the first floor of the cell block. The remaining four or five hundred wandered around looking for a place to sit down or just stood, sat, or laid on the concrete portion of the prison yard.

Christmas Eve—1960

On Saturday, I wrote a special letter to Kitty. I believe it has a place here.

My Darling:

This is the night before Christmas; and I am sitting here in cell 13 of Central Prison thinking about other Christmas Eves which I have known and trying to imagine what this one is like at my home, without me.

I am remembering 28 wonderful years of married life in which Christmas has always been the happiest and most wonderful day of the year for which we planned and prepared for months in advance and, upon which all our love for each other was expressed in piles and piles of gifts—never too expensive and usually useful, but always, many of them, with each item wrapped separately in fancy paper and tied with bright ribbon with such loving care.

I remember the first seven years when there was just the two of us and we would decorate the tree on Christmas Eve and be very secretive about placing each other's gift under the tree before going to bed. Then, on Christmas morning, before breakfast, how we would spend a wonderful hour opening packages and exclaiming over the contents with each newly unwrapped gift being another excuse for hugs and kisses. (She is, you kids know, as near to being an angel as God ever put on this earth.)

I remember 1939, when Patsy had arrived a few months before Christmas and how she was fascinated on Christmas morning by the unusual activity and sights. Then, 1943, when Sandra was adding her share of happy sounds on Christmas morning. And, 1945, when Nancy was holding her own in adding confusion which always began before daylight on Christmas morning. The hugs and kisses which had been a standard when there were only the two of us were now greatly multiplied, and by the time the last package was opened—we were nearly exhausted but all would be full of the joy of Christmas.

Today, I've prayed several times that God will give you strength and courage to face this Christmas morning without allowing your grief at my absence to completely destroy the joy of Christmas.

Here at Central Prison, the day before Christmas dawned crisp and cold as some seven hundred of us were turned out of our cells to hurry to the dining hall for pancakes and side meat.

After breakfast, some went for a shower and clean clothes. Others went to the warm and cozy library to read the newspapers, but the great majority returned to the cell block and huddled in groups or sat alone. At 8:55, the loudspeaker announced that a movie would begin in five minutes in the auditorium. It wasn't much of a movie, but the room was warm and we had chairs to sit on.

Mail call was announced at eleven o'clock. While I was still reading my mail the loudspeaker called me to the front office where I found Bill Finlator waiting. When I expressed surprise and gratitude that he had taken time out of such a busy day to come to see me, he said, "What could I be doing that would be more important than visiting with you on this day before Christmas?"

At about two o'clock, the loudspeaker announced that the warden had a package for each inmate. We gathered in the yard to receive a sack which contained nuts, candy, oranges, apples and three packs of cigarettes. A few minutes later, I was called to the mail room where I was given your wonderful package with all the things you know I like best.

Despite all that I've reported above, I'm ashamed to say, I only felt more depressed and sorrier for myself until, as I sat in a corner of the cell-block with my own sad thoughts and looking, I suppose, very forlorn, an inmate who had been friendly to me on several occasions sat down beside me, and said, "I know how you feel—I can remember my first Christmas in prison. I thought I would die that day of loneliness and almost wished I could, but this will be my ninth one here and it doesn't hurt as much anymore."

Suddenly, I felt very ashamed. Especially when I realized that he had no hope of ever spending another Christmas with his family. I said a prayer and asked God to forgive me for being so self-centered. I asked Him, too, to help me console and cheer those around me who were less fortunate than I and had more reason to despair than I had.

For the first time, I noticed that the spirit of Christmas was all around me. Hardened criminals, representing every conceivable crime, were being kind to each other and were calling out "Merry Christmas" to each other as they passed in the yard or corridor instead of the usual oath or insulting remark. Even the guards smiled some and were tolerant with the habitual pranksters and trouble-makers. I wondered, with a shock, if this had been evident all day and I had failed to notice it. . . .

As time draws near for "lights out," I am strangely at peace with the world, I feel no shame because I know I do not deserve this punishment, but I am not embittered toward those responsible for it. Truly, this is the magic of Christmas— Peace on earth—Good will to men.

Christmas Day

On Sunday morning, Christmas day, at ten o'clock I went to the chapel, where a Mrs. Doaks and her two sons (both in their forties) told stories about the birth of Jesus; and a Mrs. Garrett read, beautifully, an account of the life of Jesus. I was told that they had been coming to Central Prison each Christmas for more than 20 years.

As they were leaving, one of the sons shook hands with me, and said, "There are a lot of us who think there is something rotten in Denmark about your case and we hope to get to the bottom of it—keep your chin up."

For Christmas dinner, we had roast turkey, ham, hot rolls, dressing, mashed potatoes and gravy, with cake and ice cream for desert.

In the afternoon I attended a meeting of the Brotherhood of St. Andrews and became a member. I learned that members of this group came to the prison chapel on Sunday afternoons and it had been largely through their efforts that the new chapel had been built. I learned, too, that the prison group was considered a chapter of the Brotherhood and that the inmate leaders of the chapter were responsible for the first half-hour of each program and were to have speeches, or readings, or songs by inmates before the program was turned over to the visiting group. Negro and white inmates participated equally in the programs, although the audience was segregated.

After the Brotherhood meeting, I was asked to write a letter to a young fellow's wife for him, and we went to the library where everyone else was writing letters. (Forms and envelopes for inmate letters were distributed at noon each Sunday. The limit, per week, per inmate, was three and they had to be ready for mailing before six o'clock on Sunday evening.)

When I had finished the first letter, two others asked me to write letters for them, and I did but in each case I urged them to enroll in the school so that they could learn to write their own letters in the future. Thereafter, most of my Sundays were spent writing letters in the library, and enrollment in the school increased each week until I had a total of 69 students. It was a tremendous source of satisfaction to see a full-grown man first learn the letters of his name, then the complete alphabet, then how to join them together to form words and how to put the words together to form sentences—finally, to see their first letter to a loved one, or to hear them haltingly read their first letter from a loved one, or perhaps an item from a newspaper which had caught their interest. I found this very rewarding. I often thought that it was almost like being blind and then suddenly being able to see, and I'd try to imagine what it would be like to know nothing of the great world to be found in the pages of books, magazines, and newspapers.

* * * * *

On Tuesday, December 27th, I was very glad to return to my job in the school. I spent most of the day preparing an enrollment form. We had learned that most of the new students were reluctant to give exact information about their lack of schooling and we had learned, too, that they resented being questioned about it. Therefore, it became important that we devise a system whereby all would be made to feel that they had equality; or, at least, a system in which their inadequacy would be shown only on a cold, silent paper and not paraded before the other inmates.

In order to approach this objective, I prepared a standard enrollment form which requested certain information about each new student. As each new student appeared for enrollment, he was given a copy of the form and, in an off-hand way, I'd say, "Don't worry about filling all of it in—your name is the important thing."

Actually, the form was prepared so that the questions became more difficult as they progressed; and the number of questions answered would give a fairly good indication of the extent of the enrollee's schooling. In this way we could determine where to begin our assistance to each one without referring to it as "second-grade" or "third-grade." And more important, if an enrollee had announced that he had finished the fourth grade, but was able to do little more of the form than to fill in his name and address, it was a secret that only he and I knew. And, if questioned, he could always say, "Aw', I didn't bother filling in all that stuff—the teacher said my name was all that was important." Of course, those who could fill in the form completely did so without question. Those who could not even fill in their names were no problem. They were quick to say, without apparent embarrassment, "I ain't never learned to write my name."

I wondered about this. Why would a person who couldn't read or write at all be completely honest and unashamed about it, while the one who could hardly write his name would insist that he had finished the fourth grade, and the one who had barely finished the fourth grade would insist that he had finished the seventh?

I searched for the answer to this question because I thought it might be an important key to the whole pattern of human behavior, but I never arrived at a definite conclusion. The nearest I came to an answer, as I remembered the attempts of those at Lincolnton to prove themselves superior to me in some way, was that it was a matter of status—a desperate need to feel important or, at least, to have others think of them as important.

* * * * *

Wednesday, Thursday, and Friday were much like Tuesday—lights on at 6:00 A.M., turned out of the cell at 6:30, line up for breakfast, to work at 7:30 after a quick reading of the morning papers, a class from 7:30 to 8:30, office work until nine, shower and clean clothes, another class from 9:30 to 10:30, office work, lunch at 11:30, mail call at 12 noon, a class from 12:30 to 1:30, another one from 1:30 to 2:30. . . .

Some students came only one hour each day. Others, who were assigned to dangerous jobs and required to "take-a-break" of one hour after each hour on duty, came to school during each hour away from their job. Still others, who were on night duty or who were free between meal hours, came for two or three hours either in the morning or in the afternoon. There was no way to arrange a regular schedule of attendance or classes. We never knew which students were coming at any particular time.

It was my job to assist those who came, whenever they came, with whatever each one happened to be studying. At one moment I would be explaining the difference between a capital letter and a small letter; two minutes later I would be helping the one student who was studying second-year high-school mathematics or the one who insisted on studying European history. By pure coincidence there were times when five or six who were studying the same thing would find themselves together in the classroom. Mr. Powers had urged me to keep a watch for these occasions and try to "have a class." He felt that this was of great value to the "students."

The last hour of my work day was spent with reports and record-keeping. At 4:30, the work area became deserted; the gate was closed and locked.

* * * * *

When I joined the others to watch television on Friday evening, I took some letters with me to re-read. A self-styled "tough guy" saw my letters and began telling all who would listen, "Letters from home ain't no good. They do more harm than good. You can't live in here and on the outside, too. It's better you don't hear nothin' from outside. If my folks was to write to me, I'd tear it up without readin' it. I say if you got time to do you'd better just concentrate on doin' it and forget about everything else. Letters from the outside just pulls and hauls your insides and makes doin' the time just that much harder. Letters ain't no good, Payton, I'm tellin' you."

As he ended his speech, he tried to grab my letters. I held to them and only a corner of one envelope tore loose in his hand, but this was enough to make me as angry as I had ever been, and I got to my feet prepared to defend my letters at all cost. Just then, a quiet voice, but one full of authority, said, "You ever touch another of his letters and I'll break every bone in your body. Now, everybody sit down and watch television before we all get locked up." Everybody sat down.

The voice had come from the same inmate who had befriended me on several occasions—the one who had made me so ashamed of myself the day before Christmas. To me he said, "Don't let him kid you—he'd give his right arm to get letters like you do. All of us would."

A little later, when the chair beside me became vacant, one of the inmates I had known in detention sat down beside me and said, "I'd like to show you a letter I got from my wife today."

He handed it to me, and I read a beautiful letter filled with love and faith and hope and heart-breaking loneliness. She had ended it by quoting their five-year-old daughter as saying, "Mommy, if I told those men in Raleigh that they could have Rusty, do you think they would let Daddy come home?"

With tears rolling down his cheeks, he explained that Rusty was her dog that she loved above just about everything else in the world.

Prison Payday

On Saturday, December 31st, we had the usual Saturday morning breakfast of pancakes and side meat. Then those who had money on deposit in the prison trust fund lined up for their weekly "pay" of five dollars.

As we were edging toward the "pay" window, I noticed, for the first time, that the guards were carrying night-sticks. I asked the fellow behind me if this wasn't unusual. He said, "They usually carry them on Saturday morning—pay day."

I didn't understand the connection and said so, but he seemed reluctant to talk further about it. I remembered that a "good con" never presses for an answer. However, before the day was over, I had my answer. I saw numerous inmates with bloated faces, bleary eyes, and lolling tongues become mean and hateful as the day wore on.

On one occasion, when I went to the yard toilet behind the clothes house, I stumbled into a group of wild-eyed, slobbering inmates who resembled nothing more than a pack of wild dogs. One of my students who happened by hustled me out and urged me not to go there alone on Saturday morning. He explained that dope and whiskey could be bought in Central Prison any time an inmate "had the price," but they usually had it only on payday.

New Year's Day, 1961

I wasn't sorry to see the end of 1960; and, as we were turned out of our cells at 6:30 to welcome the dawn of a brand new year, it seemed that the air was fresh and clean and that we had a whole new world filled with hope and promise. My family would visit me today, and I was filled with visions of their lovely faces with love and concern and faith showing through their tears of welcome and their tears of parting. I tried to list in my mind all the things I wanted to say to them. I was anxious for them to see me in my starched white clothes for the first time after the times I had been so ashamed of my faded brown rags.

After breakfast, I went for a shower and clean clothes. Then I sat in the library for an hour reading the newspapers. I expected the family before noon because we had decided that the visiting crowds weren't as great in the mornings, and we could have greater assurance of having the full hour of visiting time. However, I was surprised when promptly at nine o'clock the loudspeaker called, "Boyd Payton—report to the back hall. You have visitors."

I stepped into the visiting room, allowed the guard to shake me down, and moved to the spot opposite those beautiful faces, sending their messages of love through the wire screen just as I had pictured them. What a wonderful sight they were! They told me they had left home at 5:30 in order to be first in line when visiting hours began.

Although our hopes for my early release were at low ebb, they had apparently caught the same feeling which I had about the unhappiness of 1960 being behind us and the new year being filled with hope and promise of good tidings. The happy hour went entirely too fast; there was not nearly enough time to share all of the little stories we had for each other or to answer all of the questions which came from both sides of the screen. Again, the parting was very painful; and, for an hour, my heart seemed to be choking me as I returned to the yard and sat on the concrete in the sun. My back was to the chapel where the Negro inmates were conducting their worship service. (The arrangement was that the white inmates had morning worship service on the Negro visiting Sunday; the Negro inmates, on the white visiting Sunday.)

Because of the earlier ruling prohibiting such items, this was the last visiting day that food packages could be brought to inmates. The explanation for this ruling had been that this practice afforded an opportunity to smuggle contraband into the prison and made it more difficult to control vermin.

There was much grumbling as each man completed his visit and was called to the mail room to get the package which had been left there for him by his family. General comments were to the effect that the ruling had two purposes, neither of them in accord with the official explanation. First, the inmates complained, "They did it to make it a little more unpleasant for prisoners"; and, secondly, "They did it to force the inmates to buy more at the prison store-box so it would show a greater profit."

(I doubted that either of these points were well taken. However, I did feel that complete prohibition of packages from home was not only unnecessary, but was, in fact, a real detriment to rehabilitation because it cut another tie with home and family. These ties, I believe, are an important part of any program of rehabilitation. I could understand the prohibition of home-cooked foods, but felt that the reasons given by officials would not apply to factory-packed food in small quantities; and they certainly couldn't be the reason for forbidding cigarettes and tobacco from home.)

My family had told me about the wonderful things they brought, and I couldn't understand why I hadn't been called to the mail room.

The whistle for lunch sounded; and we marched to the dining hall for fried chicken, mashed potatoes with gravy, green peas, hot rolls, cake, and coffee. As I was leaving the dining hall, several fellows said, "You'd better get to the mail room; they've been calling you for a half hour."

I went directly to the mail room and found the guard there in a very bad humor. He said, "What'sa matter with your ears, Payton, didn't you hear us calling you?"

I tried to explain that I had waited on the yard for an hour and a half expecting such a call, had not heard it, and had gone to lunch where the loudspeaker could not be heard.

"Oh, so you think we should drop everything and take care of your stuff as soon as it arrives," he said, sarcastically.

I said, "No, sir, I don't expect that at all. I'm sorry if I caused you any trouble."

"You ain't gonna' cause me no trouble. The next time you don't come when you're called you just won't get your stuff, that's all," he said. He shoved two gunny sacks into my arms; I left quickly, carrying the bags which my family had told me contained a plentiful supply of all of the things I especially liked.

The mail call was announced as I was carrying my packages to the cell block, and four letters from my loved ones quickly erased the gloom of my encounter with the mail-room guard.

The Brotherhood of St. Andrews was to meet that afternoon at two o'clock. As a group of us stood in front of the hobby shop, we saw one of the inmate nurses pushing a wheelchair across the muddy baseball diamond. The chair contained another inmate who was paralyzed from his waist down. Several willing hands assisted with getting the chair into the chapel as the nurse explained that the crippled fellow had been asking for weeks to be taken to a Brotherhood meeting.

Mr. Charles Morton gave a splendid talk, and we sang several hymns. After the meeting, Mr. Morton stopped to talk with me. He said, "I've followed your case closely and have been anxious to meet you. I just wanted to tell you that you shouldn't be ashamed about being here. The shame is on others, not you."

We helped again with the wheelchair and were pleased to see the happiness of the crippled fellow. Several had tears in their eyes, and again I was reminded, "There is good in the worst of us and bad in the best of us."

The Long Wait

Monday, January 2, 1961, was still a holiday for the supervisors and this meant no work and no school for the inmates. One of our good neighbors had given Kitty some jelly to bring to me. I took it with me to breakfast and put it on the table while urging those near me to share it. Like magic, a quarter-pound of "contraband butter" appeared in my lap and, with one eye on the guard, we all enjoyed the hot rolls.

At one o'clock the loudspeaker announced that a variety show would be presented by "local talent" in the auditorium. Everyone attended, and the performance was quite good. The first half was hillbilly singing, playing and jokes; the second part was a minstrel show. The members of the orchestra were dressed in tuxedoes, and each one sat behind his little stand upon which were the the letters CP, standing for Central Prison. The master of ceremonies was the head inmate nurse in the prison hospital, and he wore a white coat and dark dress trousers. He was excellent, as was one of the saxophone players and three tap-dancers. Several of the skits in which three of the fellows dressed like girls were really clever, and they received the greatest applause and plenty of wolf-whistles. Frankly, it was a much better show than many I've seen on TV; and it served a real purpose in brightening what was otherwise a very dull day.

* * * * *

Tuesday, January 3rd. I was really glad to be back at work, and all of the students seemed equally pleased. Several new ones came to enroll, and the assignment of lessons and the tests to determine capabilities made the morning pass quickly.

When I returned from lunch on Tuesday, I found the classroom almost filled and thought, for a moment, that business was really picking up. However, a few minutes later, two young men in street clothes came in and informed me that they were from North Carolina State and had been coming to the prison school each Tuesday and Thursday to teach high-school math to this specially recruited class composed of those who had completed grade school. They were splendid with the fellows and made a real worthwhile contribution to the prison educational program.

* * * * *

Wednesday went well, and my spirits were quite high as we moved toward our cells at lock-up time, but as I came to the corridor leading to my cell I began stepping on peanuts which had been spilled on the floor, and my spirits took a nose-dive as I realized they must have been taken from my cell. My worst fears were confirmed as the cell doors opened, and I stepped inside mine. The lock had apparently been picked on my wall cabinet, and everything which my family had brought on Sunday was gone. In addition, my letters, cards, and newspaper clippings were strewn about; some of them had been dropped into the toilet bowl.

As I was retrieving my letters, the guard came by while taking his count and asked me what had happened. When I explained, he told me to make a list of all that was missing; and he would report it to the major. When he had left the corridor, the fellow in the next cell called to me and said, "Look Buddy, let me give you some advice. You ain't gonna' git your stuff back, and you'd better not make too much fuss about it if you don't want to git all the fellows down on you. They want to watch television tonight; and, if you make a big stink about your stuff, the major will keep everybody locked up. Take my advice and play it down. You can git along without that stuff, but you'll have a rough time if the fellows git it in for ya'. I'm tellin' ya', it ain't worth it."

So when the guard returned for my list, I said, "Let's just forget about it. I didn't lose very much, and it's not worth making a fuss about."

He said, "O.K., if that's the way you want it; but I've already reported it to the captain. He may not want to let it drop. You'd better have some good answers ready if he decides to question you."

When the others went down to watch television, I stayed in my cell and worried about what I would say to the captain if he called me for questioning. However, I needn't have been concerned because no one mentioned the matter again, but it was rumored that inmates in the hospital were buying cigarettes for ten cents per pack.

* * * * *

Saturday, January 7th. I was approached by an inmate who said, very secretively, that he could get a lock for me that couldn't be picked. When I expressed interest, he whispered that I should wait for him at the entrance to the cell-block; he would drop the lock in my pocket as he brushed past me. He warned me that I should ask permission to return to my cell and leave the lock there rather than take a chance on being caught with it by a guard.

I learned later that his secrecy was "part-of-the-act," of building me up for a double charge for the lock, and that nothing would have been said if I had carried it about in plain view; but he was a good actor and I was duly impressed.

I waited for nearly an hour, while those who had money on deposit in the prisoners' trust fund were drawing their weekly allowances. When he finally came and I had gotten the lock safely to my cell, I ran to the pay window; but I found that it had just been closed. A guard advised that the captain might give special permission for me to draw my allowances when the pay guard went to the hospital to allow inmates there to draw their allowance; but when I asked the captain, he said, "Naw, we can't start that." So, I reconciled myself to getting through the next week with only 53 cents. However, as we were leaving the auditorium, after seeing Jerry Lewis in "Sad Sack," I had several offers of loans, "without interest." When I questioned the "without interest" angle, it was explained that several inmates operated a "loan agency" and charged interest of 25 cents per dollar, per week. When I asked a friend why so many had offered to lend me money without interest, he said, "They figure that's good insurance. They know you'll have money every week, and they know you'll pay back anything you borrow. They'd like you to feel obligated to them when they are broke some week and ask you for a loan."

In the afternoon an inmate suggested that I go with him to the chapel to meet a young student minister from Wake Forest Divinity School. He explained that the young man came every Saturday to visit with inmates who were confined to the hospital, after which he would meet with any who cared to come to the chapel to talk with him. I went and thus learned to know, and soon to love, Don Daughtry. Thereafter, I looked forward with eagerness and pleasure to Saturday and spent every possible moment talking with Don about world problems, ethical practices in business and in labor, race relations, equality under the law, and politics. Then, sometimes, we talked about the importance of loving and of being loved; of kindness, and of the need for understanding and communication between men and between nations. He was a good man and was deeply and sincerely concerned about men as human beings and about how their human dignity and self-respect might be maintained even while in prison. He was highly respected by all of us who knew him and was a real source of comfort to the men who brought their problems to him each Saturday afternoon.

* * * * *

Sunday, January 8th, was visiting day for Negro inmates; this meant that white inmates were in charge of chapel activities. At 8:45, six girls and four young men from Wake Forest Divinity

School came to conduct worship service. Don Daughtry was in charge. A very pretty girl who reminded me of my daughter, Patricia, sang beautifully; and a young minister named Wilson delivered an excellent sermon.

*   *   *   *   *

Tuesday was a good day at the school. Several new students enrolled, and everyone was taking a real interest in learning. However, between three and four o'clock, when the room was very crowded, a big fellow parked himself at one of the tables and just sat there, doing nothing. I had been warned that he was a "bad actor" and should not be crossed. As tactfully as possible, I said, "Mac, don't you want to do some spelling with these fellows?"

With eyes blazing, he snapped, "I can make up my own mind about that. I don't need you to tell me anything."

"I wasn't trying to tell you anything," I answered. "I was inviting you to join with us."

He jumped up, shook his fist under my nose, and yelled, "I'm sick and tired of bein' told what I can do and what I can't do. I have to take it from the 'screws,' but I'll be goddamn' if I have to take it from another con! You ain't nothin' to me. Unnerstan', just nothin'." With that, he swept the papers and books from my table and ran from the room, slamming the door behind him.

Several of the men moved their fingers in a circle around their ears to indicate that the fellow was mentally unstable.

I dismissed the incident from my mind and continued with the spelling lesson. When the class was leaving, two or three stopped to warn me that I could expect further trouble from Mac. "Don't let him catch you alone with your back turned to him," they advised.

I didn't take the warning too seriously until I had closed the classroom and was leaving the building. When I came to the end of the hall, he was waiting in the corner and stepped out, blocking my way. I moved to the other side and started by him but, again, he blocked me, and said, "You think yer' better'n me jes' cause ya' got some education. I still say *you ain't nothin'*. Hear me, *you ain't nothin'*—and I think I'll jes' teach you a thing or two."

With his fist he took a swing at the side of my head, but I ducked under the blow and ran down the steps, hitting only every fourth or fifth one. When I landed on the first floor, the supervisor was waiting with the lock in his hand. He said, "I was looking for you. You dern near got locked in for the night." As Mac lumbered by without looking at either of us, the supervisor raised an eyebrow and asked, "Did you have any trouble up there?"

I said, "No, not really. Everything is all right. Let's get out of here before both of us get locked up."

We walked together to the main prison yard. Mac was standing alone by the dining-room entrance. As the supervisor left me, I continued walking toward the cell-block. Mac fell in step beside me. Out of the corner of his mouth he snarled, "You breathe a word of what happened up there and I'll break every bone in yer body."

Out of the corner of my mouth I said, "Look, Mac, I don't want any trouble with anyone. I'm not saying anything more about it. It's closed and forgotten—now get off my back. You go your way and I'll go mine."

For the next two weeks, Mac came to class every day, but refused to participate in any of the activity. He just sat and glared at me and sometimes laughed sneeringly when one of the students expressed appreciation for some help I had given. He presented a real problem, both to me and to the other students, but I held my temper and tried to ignore him. On the second Sunday following the original incident, he came to Sunday School and sat at the opposite end of the pew in which I was sitting.

Mr. Charles Morton of Raleigh was the teacher, and he brought an inspiring and emotional message which caused several to move to the front and pledge themselves to lead a better life. Without my having noticed, Mac had moved over beside me and suddenly reached over and took my hand in a warm and strong grip. I returned the grip and, as I looked at him, I found him smiling, but with tears in his eyes. Neither of us spoke, but later he passed me as I was standing in the chow line and gave me a friendly slap on the back. We were friends thereafter.

* * * * *

On Wednesday, the supervisor was called home just before noon due to his wife's illness, and the school was closed for the day because of the rule that inmates were not allowed to attend classes unless a "free-man" supervisor was present. I spent the afternoon in the library preparing for the talk I'd been asked to give at the Brotherhood meeting on the fourth Sunday of the month.

It was warm and cozy in the library. Several tables with chairs were arranged in the center of the room, and the walls were lined with books. Most of the books were quite old, but some of them were excellent selections. The encyclopedia section and the Bible section were very complete.

Two inmates were in charge behind the counter where they kept records of the books and magazines borrowed. Books could be taken from the library for one week, but the magazines had to be read in the library and returned to the counter. Greensboro, Charlotte, and Raleigh papers could be read standing at the counter; but they could not be taken to the tables or removed from the library. Inmates who received their home-town newspaper through the mail donated back-copies to the library. These papers were kept on file in one section and could be read by other inmates, provided they were not removed from the holders.

* * * * *

On Thursday, January 12th, another inmate was assigned to my cell. (I had been paying the clerk fifty cents each week for the "privilege" of not having a cell-mate, but had not paid for that week because of not having drawn any money on the previous Saturday. I was being taught a "lesson.")

The top bunk had to be lowered to its sleeping position, its mattress had to be taken from my lower bunk and replaced on the upper one, and one side of the wall cabinet had to be cleaned out. In addition, my new cell-mate never stopped talking: "I ain't got nothin' to live for—ain't nothin' good happened to me in the last ten years, and nothin' good is gonna' happen from here on.

"My first wife died in childbirth while I was in service, and I didn't even know about it until they were both buried. I didn't care if I never came home, but my old man got me out of the army because my mother had lost her mind and had to be taken to Dix Hill. Then he was killed in an automobile accident and I was left to run the farm by myself.

"Dad had let the place run down because he was spendin' everything he had tryin' to find out what was wrong with Mom. I worked like a dog tryin' to pay off the debts and was doin' purty good. Then I met this girl and we got married.

"She wasn't the best lookin' girl in the world, but she was real good to me and she was a good worker. By golly, she was as good as another man and worked right with me, besides keepin' the house real good until she got pregnant. Then, she was real sick most of the time, but she had a big healthy boy and was soon her old self.

"We was crazy about him. Boy, he was cute until he was about five months old. Then, he got something wrong with his head and finally lost the sight in both eyes. The doctor said he had some kind of growth that pressed on his optical nerves. He said an operation might correct his eyes, but it might cause him to be weak-minded the rest of his life. Anyway the operation would have to be done in Baltimore, and it would cost plenty. That's what got me in trouble. I knew a fella' that run a gas station and I knew where he kept his money. I was desperate to get money quick for the trip to Baltimore and I decided to get it from the gas station. Jus' my luck—the owner was returnin' from a party at two o'clock in the morning and jus' happened to stop by the station.

"There I was, caught red-handed. I didn't mean to hurt him, but I had to try and fight my way out, and I hit him too hard with a wrench. Now I'm doin' ten years for manslaughter. My baby is still blind and my wife is almost crazy. See what I mean about havin' nothin' to live for. I ain't worth the powder to blow my brains out."

* * * * *

A cold wind and rain made Saturday, January 14, a miserable day. As usual, we were turned out of our cells at 6 A.M. and stood shivering in the rain while waiting for the breakfast line to move under the shelter. After breakfast, we lined up for "payday." I made sure that I was there early and soon had all my "debts" paid. After reading the newspapers in the library, we went to the auditorium and enjoyed having the warm place to sit down while watching an old movie.

After another unpleasant experience of standing in the chow line for short-ribs with rice, we sat huddled together on the floor of the cell-block waiting for supper and lock-up time. Because everybody was thoroughly miserable and begging for the comparative comfort of our cells, the captain ordered supper served at four o'clock and allowed us to go directly to our cells after eating.

I tried to write some to Kitty, but my cell-mate just never stopped talking, and it was impossible to concentrate on anything else. He had had more unhappy and unpleasant experiences than anyone I'd ever known. Finally, I became so depressed that, before seven o'clock, I undressed and went to bed.

* * * * *

Sunday, January 15, 1961—Visiting Day for white inmates. Kitty and the kids were there early and my name was one of the first called when the visiting room was opened at nine o'clock. We had a full hour together (separated only by the wire screen), but it seemed like only a few minutes, and we didn't get to say half the things we wanted to say. They were so beautiful and so full of love. When they had gone, I found a quiet spot in the corner of the cell-block and spent another two hours reliving that hour—repeating to myself what each of us had said and remembering each expression I had seen on their faces.

At two o'clock the loudspeaker called me to the mail room, and a guard gave me a lecture because my family had left me a package which contained forbidden items. He said, "Now look, Payton, I ain't gonna tell you this again. You ain't no different than any other prisoner; and you ain't allowed to receive a new pipe, new socks, a new pen, and this shaving cream. You can have the tooth brush and the razor blades, but nothin' else. If you want to give me 33 cents, I'll send this other stuff back to your home; and you'd better tell your wife not to bring this kinda' stuff again."

* * * * *

Monday, January 16th, we were awakened at the usual time and were ready to leave the cells for breakfast at six o'clock, but the usual whistle didn't sound for the cells to open until 7:25. As my cell-mate and I were speculating aloud about the reason for the delay, an old-timer in the next cell explained that it was because of the heavy fog. He said, "They have a strict rule not to allow inmates in the yard unless all of the guards on top of the walls can see all of the guards on the other walls."

* * * * *

Wednesday, January 18th, I wrote to Kitty and said, "Well, I finally got out of that cell number 13 and away from that talking machine of a cell-mate. I am now in number five on the third tier. This is a four-man cell with an upper and lower bunk fastened to the wall on either side and with four wall cabinets, a washbowl, and a toilet in the middle. The walking space is about ten feet square, and everything is a big improvement over what I have known before. One of my new cell-mates is the fellow I mentioned in my Christmas Eve letter as having been here for nine Christmas Eves. He is the one who arranged for my transfer to his cell when a vacancy occurred. He has been such a good friend to me on several occasions, and I am very pleased to be with him."

Another of my new cell-mates was a young Indian fellow who was a star pupil in the school. The third was about 40 years old and was about to complete a three-year term for "drug transportation."

They were quite interested in and enthusiastic about the television show "Bonanza" and decided that the four of us should be "the Cartright family." The older one (my friend) was to be "Pop," I was to be "Big Hoss," my student was to be

"Little Joe," and the other one was to be "Adam." (These are the names I will use in referring to them hereafter.)

Pop was about 60 years old and was serving a life-term. He was the custodian of the third tier of cells. It was his job to clean those 21 cells and the corridors each day and to see that each cell had soap and toilet tissue. He was solidly built and weighed about 200 pounds. He was an expert in Judo and, by demonstrating his ability to defend himself on two or three occasions when called upon to do so, had gained the open respect of all who knew him. It was often said of him, "He is as strong as an ox and as quick as a cat." But, invariably, any discussion about him would end with a statement to the effect that he was one of the kindest of men and a person to whom anyone could turn when in need of help. He was probably the best known and most generally liked inmate in the entire prison system.

He was fairly well educated and had made a particular study of legal procedures, criminal codes, and penal systems. He was a constant "thorn-in-the-side" of prison officials because of his willingness to serve as spokesman for any inmate whose rights were violated.

He had been in the hole once at a road camp and twice at Central Prison. It was generally agreed that Pop was "a marked man" to whom the guards gave "special attention" and in whom they found special delight in reprimanding or punishing. There was hardly a day when he was not involved in a "cause" for some inmate which kept him on the brink of being sent to the hole. It was always for someone else, not for himself, that he risked the displeasure of the guards and other prison officials; and it was probably this fact alone that saved him from punishment on many occasions. The guard had to consider not only the effect of the wrath of Pop's friends, but also the wrath of prison officials if Pop managed to "beat-the-rap" by citing facts, figures, codes, and rules which were irrefutable.

Pop's first experience with the hole (according to his account, but verified by other inmates) came as a result of his reporting to high prison officials a disgraceful incident at one of the road camps. All the inmates except Pop and one other man had become deathly ill from being fed spoiled food, and their cries of pain were ignored by the guards until they began breaking the windows. Pop and the other inmate had not eaten in the mess hall that evening because Pop had received a package of food from friends and had shared it with the other inmate.

As one after another of the inmates became violently ill, Pop and his friend tried to administer to them, in between anguished calls for help. When the doctor finally came, it was Pop and his friend who carried each inmate from his bunk to the hallway where the "examination room" had been established.

Pop's letter to high prison officials resulted in an investigation which uncovered deplorable conditions regarding lax and unsanitary handling of food. The road camp officials were severely criticized, and the food steward was discharged. Pop was promptly transferred to another camp and spent nine days in the hole "as a troublemaker."

His second experience with the hole came at Central Prison when he was charged with violating the regulation which prohibits the removal of food from the dining room.

Pop's story, verified by others, was as follows: He had made friends with the pigeons which abound inside the walls of Central Prison. They seemed to know him and to recognize him as a friend. They would follow him about and would eat from his hand when he brought them bits of bread or, sometimes, popcorn or peanuts which he bought for them at the store-box.

On this particular day, Pop had half of a slice of bread left on his tray when he finished eating, and he slipped it inside his shirt. Another man also had a half slice left and told Pop, "Give this to your pigeons, too."

As he was about to leave the dining room, Pop was roughly seized by two guards, and gleefully escorted to the front office where he was charged with "Violation of prison regulations by removing a quantity of food from the dining hall."

After three days of solitary confinement on death row, he was "tried" and sentenced to "3 to 30" days in the hole.

Ironically, in order to apprehend this "dangerous pigeon feeder" and to make sure that he was properly confined, the two guards had been forced to abandon their assigned posts. And while they were occupied with this "crucial mission," a fight erupted on the yard, a fight in which an inmate was stabbed to death.

Pop's third trip to the hole was the culmination of weeks of a persistent campaign by two guards to "show that smart-aleck old man who's runnin' things 'round here." (Pop had incurred their special animosity by proving them to be liars in regard to statements they had made about a young Negro inmate.)

After two weeks of being reprimanded at every turn and of being assigned to the most disagreeable jobs, the breaking point came one night when Pop was ordered from his cell, after he was undressed and in his bunk, and told to scrub the large concrete area in front of the cell-block. "And don't just squirt some water on it—use soapy water and a broom," he was told.

When he protested this unfair and unnecessary assignment and proclaimed that he intended putting a stop to his mistreatment by informing the warden of the fact that a certain guard was stealing state shoes and selling them to inmates, he was promptly arrested, charged with "deliberate lying," and placed in solitary confinement on death row, pending trial.

At the "trial," both his story of mistreatment and his proof that the guards were dealing in stolen shoes were ignored, and he was given the usual "3 to 30" days in the hole.

On the second day of his "sentence," the two guards entered the hole, searched Pop, and tore his mattress apart. Although it was well-known that Pop didn't smoke, and that he was, in fact, allergic to the smell of tobacco smoke, they charged him with "smoking in a restricted area" after having "found" two partly burned matches.

He was transferred to the "dark hole" and spent 28 days in a cold, damp cell without any clothing or bed clothing, without light, without ventilation, and with only a pile of dirty, evil-smelling cotton waste for a bed. His only food during the ordeal was the foul-smelling and evil-tasting monotonous diet. His toilet facilities consisted of a rusty and filth-caked commode which was located in the dark by following the stench rising from it.

On the one occasion, when he was visited by the prison chaplain he complained about intense suffering from acute gastritus and begged for some mineral oil; the chaplain joked about it and said, "You'll be all right; nature will take care of it."

When Pop was finally released, he had lost 28 pounds; and, for weeks, he became violently ill after every meal.

* * * * *

Little Joe had also had experience with the hole on two occasions, both at road camps. The first time he spent 60 consecutive days in the hole, although there was supposed to be a rule prohibiting more than 30 consecutive days there.

He said that all of his clothing, except his shorts, was taken from him; and these were what he wore for the entire period of confinement. He did not have a bath, shave, or haircut during the 60 days and ate nothing but the sickening, monotonous diet.

Other inmates verified Little Joe's story and testified that his weight dropped from 180 to 130 pounds, and that his eyes were "just like two holes behind cheekbones which seemed to be pushing through his skin."

The reason for Little Joe's punishment is a good example of why inmates believe that prison officials get a sadistic pleasure from making life as miserable as possible for every inmate and from deliberately causing infraction of rules to give an excuse for punishment.

Little Joe had just been transferred to this camp. No one had explained that the signals at this particular camp were given by the blowing of a horn which sounded much like any regular auto horn. Joe heard the horn that first morning but, thinking it came from a car on the nearby road, he paid no attention to it, pulled his blanket over his head and went back to sleep. When he finally woke up, hurriedly dressed, and ran to the mess hall, a guard said, "You should know the rules—no breakfast when you are late."

Several pitchers of coffee were still sitting on the tables. Joe said, "If I can get some coffee, I can make it without breakfast."

The guard said, "*I said no breakfast—that includes coffee.*"

Joe returned to the cell-block where other inmates were preparing to leave for road work. A guard said, "You buckin' [refusing to work], huh?"

Joe said, "No, sir, but I'd surely like to have something in my stomach before going out with the road gang."

The guard said, "We've got a good cure for buckin'. We'll see what you think about it after 30 days in the hole."

Shortly after Joe and two others had been placed in the hole, an honor-grade inmate came by and whispered, "Dig a hole under the back wall and I'll slip you some chow."

They took turns digging with their bare hands and within a few hours had worn most of the skin from their hands, but they could see daylight and were eventually able to get a hand and arm through the opening. However, their efforts were wasted when the honor-grader decided to "get himself in good with the captain" by tipping him off about the opening. The captain promptly had the opening filled and doubled the original sentence.

Little Joe's second experience with the hole was at another road camp where he served 30 days for "insubordination." The charge of insurbordination was lodged when he was found in an "off limits" area of the prison yard, according to a rule about which he was told only after his arrest.

This time he was allowed to wear his regular clothing, but not permitted a bath, clean clothes, a shave, or a haircut for the 30 days.

Little Joe was 26 years old. He had already served eight years and, according to a complicated and confused record of convictions and additional sentences for attempted escape, he still had eight or nine years to serve.

Adam had never been in any trouble while "on-the-state." He was a quiet fellow who worked as a member of the prison paint crew. He had a reputation as an excellent workman, but a "loner." He had previously served 30 months for "robbery by force."

* * * * *

Sunday, January 22, 1961. This was the day I was to be the speaker at the Brotherhood meeting in the chapel. I had entitled my remarks, "The World's Most Powerful Forces."

I spoke of the development of the atom bomb and other forces of destruction usually considered the most powerful forces in the world. "However," I said, "I believe the forces of love, kindness, and understanding are more powerful than all of the forces capable of destruction."

I spoke of the great need and desire of all mankind for love, kindness, and understanding, and listed the gains and advantages which would come to our civilization if love, kindness, and understanding were the motivating forces in relationships between men and between nations.

The talk seemed to go quite well. I was told that the crowd was one of the largest ever to attend a chapel meeting. A group of Raleigh churchmen were present and were very kind in their remarks. More important to me, however, was the reaction of the inmates. I had practiced my theory with some of those who were considered the most hardened criminals. In every case, once they became convinced that I had no trick up my sleeve, I found something decent and good under each toughened hide which might have led to a brighter future for that individual and for society if that spark of decency had been nurtured and cultivated by love, kindness, and understanding, rather than seared by the flame of hatred, scorn, and/or unconcern. Therefore, it was a rewarding experience for me when a large number of inmates waited outside to shake my hand and speak a word or two of appreciation.

* * * * *

Monday, January 23rd, was a very cold day in which we stood in line with chattering teeth while waiting for breakfast of fatback, grits and gravy; lunch of brown beans with chili; and, very spare spare-ribs with kraut for supper. We begged the captain to lock us up as soon as we had finished supper. He finally agreed.

* * * * *

As happened many a time, an especially bad day was followed by an especially good day. The icy wind had stopped blowing when we left our cells the next morning, the eggs had been scrambled in butter, we had good beef stew for lunch, and chicken and dumplings for supper.

While I was eating supper I heard my name called over the

loudspeaker and the announcement that I had a visitor. I knew it could only be Bill Finlator because of the unusual time. (Only a minister or an inmate's lawyer would be admitted so close to lock-up time.)

It was so good to see him, and it was wonderful to be allowed to visit in the small conference room without bars or screen between us. While we were talking, the lock-up whistle sounded; I began worrying about the consequences of being locked out of my cell and being required to go to the major's office to explain. However, it was so pleasant to be with my faithful friend and to listen to his words of encouragement that I decided to say nothing.

When he had said goodby, I hurried to the cell-block; but upon reaching it I was amazed to see all of the inmates from my tier standing in a group outside their cells. Someone explained that there was a defect in the mechanism which controlled the opening and closing of the cell doors on number three tier. Just a minute after my arrival, all the doors rolled open and we went to our cells, with no one noticing that I had been late.

* * * * *

Wednesday, January 25th, I received "permission" to attend prayer meeting. This was important. Those who are approved to attend prayer meeting are not locked up at 5:30 but, instead, are permitted to go to the library. Some sing, some read, and some tell stories until 7:30 when the guard comes to march everyone to the chapel to meet a group of church people from Raleigh and have an hour and a half of speaking, prayers, and singing hymns. A young Presbyterian minister was the speaker on this occasion, and he was excellent. I was very pleased about being approved to attend prayer meetings.

* * * * *

An experience at the school that day seems worth recording here. One of the "students" who had a reputation for being tricky came for his spelling lesson. As he took his seat he carefully fixed a list of words on the floor between his feet. I assumed that he had somehow obtained a copy of the words which I had been using and intended copying them on his test paper. Instead of following the order of the list I began skipping about. He was almost standing on his head trying to find the word on his list to correspond with the one I had just called. Finally, in desperation, he said, "You ain't goin' 'cordin' to the book."

I said, "No, I'm skipping around so you can't copy from that list you have on the floor."

He laughed, and said, "Dog-gone, you'se too smart fer me, I'se jus' wantin' to make a hunert jus' onct." Later, on the yard, he came to me, and said, "I bin thinkin' 'bout me tryin' to fool you today—an' ya' know what? I wasn't foolin' you, I'se foolin' me."

* * * * *

Thursday, January 26th dawned with sleet pelting the windows. When we left the cell-block we found the prison yard covered with ice. We slipped and slid to the dining hall and learned there that there would be no work because the supervisors could not travel the slippery highways. Later, we were told that there would be no mail and no newspapers for the same reason. What a long, miserable, and useless day as we huddled together in groups wherever we could to keep out of the foul weather. How welcome was the lock-up whistle at 5:30.

* * * * *

One of my pupils had become interested in European history and kept me busy pronouncing "Liepzig," "Luxembourg," "Zurich." I asked him why he didn't study American history and spend his time on things which would help him when he got out of prison.

He said, "Europe is no farther away for me than my home town. I'll never see either one of them. As for time, I've got 30 years of it. I can start with ancient history and still have time to get up to date before I have a chance of getting out of here."

* * * * *

Sunday, February 5th. This was another visiting Sunday, and my family was there promptly at nine o'clock. They looked so wonderful—cute little Nancy trying so hard to keep smiling through the wire screen while her heart was breaking; sweet and lovely Sandra blinking away the tears and whispering, "I love you"; the charming Patsy, so ladylike and grown-up, but still looking like the little girl who became so angry when her tricycle was broken beyond repair by one of the neighbor's children; and, finally, my wonderful wife—so brave and glowing with love, encouragement, and faith, and trying not to show her heartache. How proud I was of all of them.

* * * * *

February 14 (Valentine's Day). I received lovely cards from Kitty and the kids, as well as from several others. This gave me an idea for the beginners' reading class in the afternoon. I would make up verses about various members of the class, write it on the blackboard, then ask the person involved to read it aloud. They were enthusiastic and were thrilled when they finally deciphered all of the words and were able to read it straight through. This may not appear to be so great an accomplishment as recorded here, but it should be remembered that these were men ranging in age from 18 to 67 who had not been able to read or write their own names just six weeks earlier.

* * * * *

February 17. Two college students came to the school with the major. He introduced them and explained that they were to help with the classes every Friday afternoon. I introduced them to the "students" and was amused when the "bug" on European history began asking them how to pronounce some of the words. They thought he was trying to play a joke on them. Then, a few minutes later, they looked at each other with disbelief when one of the newer "students" asked, "What is the difference between 'T-H-I-N-K' and 'T-H-A-N-K'? Ain't they almost the same thing?"

* * * * *

Monday, February 20th, brought a wonderful visit from my long-time friend, the Reverend Charles Webber, director of the Department of Religion for the AFL-CIO. He said he had been in Raleigh for a speaking engagement and felt that he could not leave without seeing me. He repeated what he had once written to me—"I feel that part of me is in prison with you, and I shall never feel completely free while you are here." His visit and his kindness were great tonics for my morale.

* * * * *

Tuesday, February 21st, was also brightened greatly by a visit from Frantz Daniel, the assistant organizing director of the AFL-CIO. He had also spoken at the conference which had brought the Reverend Webber. Frantz expressed considerable irritation about the lack of an active campaign to secure our early release. He felt that it was a mistake to assume that leaders of the state and federal government would see that the injustice was corrected without continual pressure of public opinion.

* * * * *

Wednesday, February 22nd, brought an unpleasant experience which affected me for several days. I had, from time to time, noticed several inmates who were badly maimed, some with pretty horrible facial scars; but I had never had close contact with them. Certainly, I had never noticed that most of the inmates were careful about selecting their places in the chow line to avoid eating opposite the worst of these unfortunates. I always just took my place at the end of the line without looking to see who was ahead of me or who lined up behind me. This day I followed the same procedure and found myself eating opposite an inmate who had lost most of his chin and had an ugly-looking hole where his upper lip and nose should have been. Saliva and particles of food dripped from his face as he sucked and gulped his food. I was filled with pity, but try as I might, I could not finish my meal. Not wanting to embarrass the poor fellow by showing the revulsion which I was feeling, I pretended to be more interested in drinking than eating and tried looking at my other table-mates. To my surprise, six of the ten had some kind of deformity.

When I mentioned the experience to my cell-mates that evening, they were surprised that I hadn't learned to "count ten in front and ten behind" before getting in the chow line.

* * * * *

Thursday, February 23rd, saw five new enrollees of the school; also, I was asked by the supervisor to do a survey on the amount of interest in night classes. Forty of the first 50 contacted indicated real interest.

* * * * *

Monday, February 27th. A fellow sat beside me at breakfast of leathery, cold eggs, and said, "When I get home and ever complain about my eggs, I hope my wife slaps my face off."

* * * * *

Thursday, March 2nd, was a real red-letter day. The Reverend Clair Cook of *The Christian Century* came to see me and advised that he had been assigned to do a story on the Henderson strike and the resulting prison experience. We were allowed to visit in the private conference room for an hour and a half. While we were talking, Bill Finlator arrived, and the three of us had a wonderful visit. The prison chaplain, Reverend Jackson, brought them both in and had apparently been responsible for permission to use the private conference room.

* * * * *

On Friday, March 3rd, we began giving special attention to "phonics" in the school. The students who were just learning to read and write had great difficulty in understanding what letters to use to make the proper sounds. I finally worked up a simple set of rules about vowels, consonants, syllables, tenses and singular and plural.

It was amusing, even though pathetic, to see fathers and grandfathers pursing their lips to make the proper sounds and trying so desperately to understand.

Once, when I had explained that the singular and plural of "sheep" and "deer" were exactly the same, an old fellow said, "Then it don't make no differences how many sheeps I have, I still just spell it s-h-e-e-p."

I said, "That's right."

He said, "What about mules?"

* * * * *

On Saturday, March 4th, I was having trouble with an old hip ailment and had difficulty getting up and down steps. The biggest fellow in Central Prison (six feet, two inches and 270 pounds) had become one of my best friends. He and I did quite a lot of friendly teasing and playing of innocent jokes on each other. As I was standing in the yard on my one good leg, he came close behind me, threw out his great stomach and sent me sprawling on the concrete. When he saw what he had done and learned about my sore hip, he was greatly concerned and made quite a fuss with his apologies and offers to help me up the steps to the dining hall. Then, at lock-up time, he waited at the cell-block door to see if I needed help to get up the stairs to the third tier.

* * * * *

Sunday, March 5th was visiting Sunday again, and my family was there promptly at nine o'clock. They were a wonderful tonic; and, for the first time, Patsy's husband was allowed to come into the visiting room with them. My request to the prison director that he be placed on my "approved visitor" list had been granted.

When I returned to the yard from the visiting room, Pop met me and, with great elation, began describing my family in detail. Naturally, I was surprised because I knew that he could not have been near enough to the visiting room to see what they were wearing, the color of their hair, the expressions on their faces, which he kept talking about. He teased me for a while about his "radar mind," but then explained that he had climbed up the painters' scaffold in the cell block, to an opening in the partition which permitted him to look down into the visiting room. He was very pleased with his accomplishment and talked about it for days.

* * * * *

Monday, March 6th, saw the school rooms repainted and a new desk and swivel chair for the "teacher." The supervisor had decided that it was easier for me to run to the office to answer the phone three or four times each day than to run to the classroom 30 or 40 times each day to answer questions.

I learned that "test papers" evoked great interest among the "students," and I prepared a series of tests for the various grades. Some of the men would take several days to complete one test, while others would be able to do one each day. They would leave the completed test paper and I would grade them and place them in their individual folders. They were delighted to see their names neatly typed on the folders and raced to the filing cabinet each day to see what grade I had given them. My standard greeting when I'd meet one of them on the yard was, "How'd I do on that test?" They seemed to think that I should remember each one's grade at all times.

I'd sometimes think if they had shown one-tenth as much interest in school at the proper time, they probably would never have come to prison. But then, as I heard some of their stories, I decided that my first observation had been unfair.

One young fellow told me that, since he was six years old, his mother and father had both been in prison. He had lived with seven different relatives in 13 years—the last of whom he had crippled for life while attempting to defend himself from a severe beating with a hot poker. Hence, his present prison sentence.

Another one told me about his stepfather, a demented religious fanatic, who whipped the boy every time he caught him reading anything except the Bible, refused to allow him to attend school after the third grade, and kept the boy locked in a closet whenever he saw the truant officer approaching.

* * * * *

On Tuesday morning, March 7th, when the cells were opened and I came to the bottom of the stairs, I found an inmate who worked in the diet kitchen waiting for me. He always attended prayer and Brotherhood meetings and we had been friendly. This morning, he really looked haggard as he pulled me to one side and said, "I have to talk to you—I haven't slept for two nights and I'm nearly crazy."

Briefly, his story was that his first wife had given birth to two children while he was serving four years in the Army. He had divorced her upon his return. Then, after three years, he had married his present wife. They had two children (18 months and three months.) He had never seen the baby because he had become involved in dope transportation while his wife was pregnant, was arrested and sentenced to two years in prison. He had entered prison two months before the baby was born.

His first wife was now telling some rather embarrassing and somewhat degrading stories about him. They had come to the attention of his present wife. While he had been eagerly anticipating her visit on the previous Sunday, she had been seething with suspicion, hurt pride and anger. Consequently, they had spent their visiting hour arguing and exchanging charges and counter-charges. She had left with a threat to take the children where he wouldn't be able to find them, and said she never wanted to see him again.

He said, "If I lose her and the kids, I just don't have anything to live for, and it doesn't make any difference whether I ever get out of here."

I felt sorry for him, but didn't know what to say or do. It was time for me to go to work, and all I could say was, "Let me think about it and we'll talk some more this evening."

He said, "Will you pray about it, too?" I promised that I would and did, but still didn't know that I had an answer for him when we met again at 4:30. However, I began talking and words kept coming—"You know, I believe that we usually reap what we sow. You were disturbed because she asked you questions about things which you'd rather forget. You became angry because she was angry. You both said things in anger that should not have been said, and you are now sorry for what you said. I'll bet she is just as sorry as you are.

"You are now sick with fear of losing her," I continued, "and I'll bet she feels the same way. You fear that she has lost faith in you. You are wondering whether her love is strong enough to survive the hardships and the loneliness which you see ahead. You desperately need something to hold on to. You feel that your wife and children provide the only basis around which you can build a life of happiness and contentment for *yourself*.

"Have you ever stopped to think that she is facing the same problems and has the same fears which you have? Don't you think she desperately needs something to hold onto just as you do?

"I can't tell you what you should do, but I can tell you what *I* would do. If she is the worthy and worthwhile person you say she is, I would crawl on my belly to prove my love for her and that her faith in me was justified. I would do most anything to assure her of my faith in her and to give her hope for the future.

"Give her love and kindness and she will return love and kindness to you. Show faith in her and she will show faith in you."

As I talked I could see the tenseness and anxiety leaving his face and, when I finished, he was smiling, but there were tears in the corners of his eyes.

He shook my hand, and said, "You've given me a Bible for my future and I'm writing to my wife about it tonight." The next morning he showed me a beautiful letter. A week later he showed me his wife's answer, which was all that he (or I) could have hoped for. I felt good from head to toe about it.

* * * * *

The *Raleigh News and Observer* for March 2, 1961, carried a story which was headed, "Man Who Lost Feet in Prison Will Get $4,500." Several of the inmates knew the story and told how the man had been confined to an isolation cell for 12 days during a particularly cold spell in January of 1935. They said his feet had frozen on the third day; burst on the sixth day; and his toes began dropping off on the ninth day. His feet had to be amputated and the state outfitted him with artificial feet. The prison department paid him $20 per month until 1953 when the legislature authorized the prison department to make a lump sum settlement up to $4,500. The payment of the $4,500 had been delayed because of questions concerning a guardian or trusteeship for him.

The story prompted many stories of prison brutality and the indifference of prison officials and guards to the physical well-being of convicts. One of the hospital attendants told me of an inmate who was in the hospital with an incurable bone disease—it was generally agreed that he had less than six months to live. He had been eligible for parole consideration for some time, but no action had been taken by the paroles board because of his condition.

He had received a letter from the Veteran's Administration advising that a bed was available at a Veteran's Hospital if and when he was paroled from prison.

The prison doctor had made his rounds and, as he was leaving, the veteran inmate called to him, and said, "Doc, I have a paper here that says I can go to the Veteran's Hospital if I can get out of here."

Almost without turning his head, the prison doctor said, "Oh, yeah! You can probably get one that says your bowels will move regularly, too."

The attendant said he felt like smashing his fist into the doctor's face as he left the room with a sarcastic laugh.

Pop told about his transfer to a road camp in the mountains in the fall of 1956 where he was given a size 13 pair of work shoes (he usually wore size 10).

Several days later as he was climbing down from a boogey-cage the toe of one shoe caught on the bottom of the cage while his other foot slipped on the icy step. He fell and was knocked unconscious when his face crashed into the truck bed.

When he was revived, he found that several teeth were missing and his right arm was injured.

He was taken to a doctor in a nearby town, where he was treated for his head and face injuries, and X-rays were taken of his arm.

After several days of intense pain, without any report on the X-rays, Pop began insisting that something be done to determine if a bone was broken, but his complaints were ignored.

After two weeks of suffering and protesting, he was allowed to see the prison doctor, but was advised that he should seek permission to be taken to a private hospital (where he would be required to bear his own expenses).

The warden finally ordered the prison doctor to have new X-rays taken, and they showed the arm fractured in two places. The facture was set, the arm was put in a cast on the fifteenth day following the accident.

* * * * *

On March 9, 1961, *The News and Observer* carried a story which was headed, "Butner Inmate, 30, Dies Of Heart Seizure On Job." The story quoted the prison's director as saying that the man had died "while sorting apples" and that he had been given this "light work" because it was known that he had a heart condition. However, other inmates reported *that the apples were in gallon cans weighing six pounds each* and the "sorting" involved lifting and handling cases containing ten of these cans.

* * * * *

On March 11th, while waiting in the pay line, I heard loud and angry talk at the head of the line. The guard was saying, "The next time you don't answer that loudspeaker when your name is called, I'll put you where you can do a lot of sleeping."

As the inmate turned from the window I recognized him as an acquaintance who worked as a night nurse. As he was passing, I asked him about the loud talk at the window. He explained that his name had apparently been called the day before while he was sleeping and no one had told him about it until the mail room was closed. He had just made the mistake of asking about the call while he was getting his "pay." (It was the same guard and the same window, but the guard insisted that the package which had arrived on Friday could not now be delivered until Monday.)

Later in the day, one of the ward attendants told me of an incident which he had witnessed that morning in the hospital. He said, that the wheelchair inmate (whom we had assisted in getting to a Brotherhood meeting) had developed chills and a fever following an injection. The inmate nurse had become quite concerned and had made repeated attempts to have the doctor examine the man.

Finally, the doctor entered the ward, and the nurse assumed that he was coming in response to his pleas on behalf of the paralyzed man. When the doctor walked by without glancing to either side, the nurse ran after him, and asked, "Aren't you going to look at ———? He's really in bad shape."

Without breaking stride, the doctor said, "He's just scared.

He'll be all right—and if he isn't, so what?"

* * * * *

March 18th was a cold and rainy day. To make it more gloomy in our cell, Pop was nowhere in sight at lock-up time and the "grapevine" reported that he had been "arrested" and sent to the hole. One story said that he had "bucked the chow line" (slipped in ahead of those already in line). Another story said that he had slipped some extra cookies into his pocket.

Four days later, he was released and told us the charge had been "bucking the chow line," but when he had explained at his trial (after three days in isolation) that he had been forced out of line by a rush of other inmates trying to get in out of the rain, his punishment was set at "extra duty for four weekends" instead of the hole. ("Extra duty on weekends" means no movie on Saturday morning, and being available at all times for errands or duties assigned by the guards.)

* * * * *

On March 22nd, William Pollock, general president of the Textile Workers Union of America, came to visit and we were allowed to meet in the conference room of the warden's office. He was very kind in his expressions of concern about my welfare and that of my family. He assured me that the full resources of the union would be used to secure our release and indicated certain hopeful aspects. It was good to see him and get direct news from the union, but I was troubled by the implication in one of his statements that it might be necessary to transfer me from North Carolina after my release from prison. I worried about this and its effect on my family which was now so firmly rooted in Charlotte among wonderful friends and neighbors.

The day following Mr. Pollock's visit, my long-time friend, Dave George, came to see me. (Dave had been an assistant in the Henderson strike and had taken my place as the striker-leader when I could no longer serve.) My request to the warden to have Dave added to my approved list of visitors had apparently been granted. His visit was a real morale booster as he spoke frankly of the activities being planned to secure our early release and was critical of the "hush-hush" policy which had been established in regard to statements and actions. He felt strongly that more publicity should be given to the entire episode and that those segments of the labor movement which wanted to take protest actions should be urged to do so instead of being discouraged. Dave reported that he had proofread the manuscript of Dr. Clair Cook for the *Christian Century* story and was very pleased with it.

* * * * *

On Sunday, April 2nd, after a wonderful visit with my family, I read an article on prisons by Miss Doris Betts of the *Raleigh News and Observer*. She wrote, "In 1960, more adults were confined in American prisons than ever before in the nation's history." She asked, "What is to be done with and for this part of our population? Can we permit it to become larger and larger? . . . What are we willing to spend to prevent crime or to return to society men [from prison] who can live there without further criminal acts?"

This started me thinking about the shortcomings of the prison system as I had seen it in operation. I was forced to conclude, as I had done earlier—but now more positively—that *prisons manufacture criminals and promote crime rather than curb it*. I wondered if anyone had ever stopped to think, when expounding the theory that meaninfgul work is a necessary part of prisoner rehabilitation, that the trade of making license plates can only be practiced in another prison.

I thought of the fact that Prison Industries in North Carolina pays five dollars per day to the prison department for each day's work by an inmate, and that this requires every prison official to guard against a lost day on the part of any inmate, even at the expense of the inmate's physical well-being.

I recalled an instance where an inmate who had been seeking dental attention for weeks was called to the prison dentist's office at 7:30 A.M., had 12 teeth extracted and was ordered back to work before eleven o'clock.

On another occasion, I knew an inmate who lost two fingers in a machine, spent three days in the hospital and was ordered back to the same machine. When he protested, he was sent to the hole for 30 days. This had prompted me to inquire about workmen's compensation and/or insurance protection for employees of Prison Industries. I was told that neither was provided.

What is true of Prison Industries at Central Prison is also true at the county prison camps where the highway department pays five dollars per day to the Prison department for the services of each inmate assigned to "work on-the-roads."

As to the literacy school at Central Prison, it was supposed to play an important role in rehabilitation. In theory, it was "open" to all inmates who desired to further their education. In practice, however, this laudable principle was given a low rating compared with the "more important" principle of assuring a profitable operation for Prison Industries. Furthermore, some of the guards openly stated that it was a waste of time for those inmates who could already read and write to spend more time in school.

For nearly a year, prior to my assignment there, no one was assigned to assist the inmates who wanted to study except when the vocational instructor could spare a few minutes from his full-time job of teaching brick masonry. Only seven inmates of a potential of 900 were enrolled, except for the two afternoons each week when the college students came to teach mathematics.

Within 30 days after my assignment, 172 had signed up to attend classes, but only 50 were enrolled and only ten had been given permission to leave their regular jobs for more than one hour per day to attend school. Many reported, "I'd sure like to learn something while I'm in here, but it ain't worth gettin' my boss down on me."

Despite the fact that it is generally agreed among those interested in rehabilitation that no other single factor could mean more to the future welfare of the inmate than to make it possible for him to rise above the educational status which he knew before entering prison, no encouragement was given to the inmate who expressed a desire to attend school, and no incentive was provided for those who did attend. In fact, it was an accepted fact among the inmates that "goin' to school" was not a popular idea among the guards and was actually discouraged by the supervisors who came each day from the outside and had their success or failure measured by the production charts.

During my eight months in the school I saw 17 grown men learn to sign their names for the first time. Then, with each passing day, I saw their outlook on life changing as they were able to read a letter from home for the first time, or struggle through a newspaper story whose headline had caught their interest.

One day I inquired in a class how it could be possible for them to grow up in this day and age without learning to read and write. One said, "Mom and Pop both worked and they didn't know or care whether I went to school or not."

Another one said, "My dad never went to school. He said he didn't see no sense in it, 'specially when a kid was big enough to work."

A young Negro and an Indian gave identical answers: "There was about 50 or 60 kids in the school and only one teacher. She didn't notice whether I was there or not. I 'spect she was glad when I wasn't."

"Hero" of Henderson

On the morning of April 9th, when I came from my cell to the prison yard, Warren was waiting for me and was excited about radio reports concerning the involvement of Harold Aaron in some kind of shooting incident in Martinsville, Virginia.

We ate breakfast as rapidly as possible and were first in line when the newspapers arrived. The headline in *The Charlotte Observer* was: "Strike 'Informer' Held In Shooting." The AP story, datelined at Martinsville, Virginia, gave the following account:

> Harold Elzie Aaron, the undercover informer whose testimony sent eight textile union officials and members to jail in the Henderson, N. C. strike, was charged Saturday with malicious wounding.
> Aaron was arrested shortly after 1 A.M. at the Gardner Lee Motel ... where the shooting occurred.
> He was charged with shooting John Layton Pulliam ... of Danville, Va.
> Aaron was released on $2,500 bond, for appearance May

15... in Henry County Court for a preliminary hearing.
Henry County Chief Deputy Sheriff Raymond Smart quoted Aaron as saying he shot Pulliam by accident when the Danville man came to his motel room and refused to leave when asked.

Smart said Aaron was in the room with a 17-year-old Henry County girl when Pulliam, who was occupying an adjoining room alone, came in. The deputy quoted Aaron as saying he took a .38-caliber revolver out of a brief case and gave Pulliam a punch in the stomach with the weapon.

The pistol discharged, the bullet striking Pulliam in the right groin. Aaron drove him to Martinsville General Hospital, where he underwent an operation before dawn and was in satisfactory condition Saturday night....

On Monday, April 10th, *The News and Observer* carried an editorial with the heading, "New Reason For Scrutiny." The text follows:

> Nobody, of course, expects an informer in a criminal case to be a paragon of virtue. Still the additional evidence of the far-from-perfect character of Harold Aaron, whose testimony sent the Henderson strikers to prison, cannot increase the State's confidence in the righteousness of the convictions it got.
>
> A former union man who was given money by the SBI to pretend to be a partner of union men in an alleged proposed dynamiting, Aaron's part in this business was never pretty. Now a shooting in the middle of the night in a motel room, where he had a seventeen-year-old girl, reflects further on Aaron's character.
>
> This was a case in which no dynamiting took place. It was a case in which this man Aaron, with State funds, helped prepare the alleged plot in order to betray those whom he involved in it.
>
> Of course, no dynamiting or plotting to dynamite can be tolerated in North Carolina or any other civilized community. Guilty men should be punished. Still any verdict of guilt based upon the testimony of a paid informer, who was given money to arrange entrapment, deserves special scrutiny. This new incident involving the informer provides added reason why the conscience of North Carolina should be troubled in this case.

On Tuesday, April 11th, newspapers quoted attorney general Wade Bruton as saying that Harold Aaron was not an undercover agent for the State Bureau of Investigation as he (Aaron) had claimed to be when arrested in Martinsville. However, notwithstanding this denial by the attorney general, under whose direction the SBI functions, the SBI director Walter Anderson admitted on Wednesday that Aaron had been paid at least $1,100 by the SBI for his services as an informer.

The week from April 9 to 15 was filled with reports of radio and television statements as well as newspaper articles and many "letters to the editor." Most of these reports were favorable to our cause and urged that our case be reviewed. The entire population of Central Prison seemed to be as much interested in the Aaron shooting case as were the eight of us who could be most directly affected. Each one seemed to feel duty-bound to get each scrap of information to us at the earliest possible moment. Of special interest to the inmates was the Kays Gary column of April 15. I had 11 copies of it before 9 A.M.

Write Hero Of Henderson Care Of Martinsville Jail

—Kays Gary

"The bravest man I know."

This was the tribute prosecutor Robert Hight had for Harold Aaron more than a year ago.

True, Aaron's testimony had just sent Boyd Payton and seven other union men to the penitentiary in the Henderson dynamite conspiracy trial.

But it was a peculiar tribute, just the same. The only thing Aaron had heard from prosecutors for most of his adult life had been ugly charges of his guilt on charges of assault, assault with deadly weapon, drunkenness, reckless driving, theft, larceny of an auto, impersonation of an officer, etc.

BUT THIS TIME Aaron, as a paid informer of the State Bureau of Investigation and with at least $1,100 of taxpayer funds in his jeans, was to bask in the role of Hero for the State.

As defense attorneys indignantly challenged acceptance of this man's testimony as truth, Aaron could afford to properly wear the martyr's cloak. A handsome young man, he wore it well as prosecutor Hight grandly pronounced him, "The bravest man I know."

When, in cross-examining Aaron, the defense asked why he had called mill owner John D. Cooper to warn him of a plot, Aaron indicated his nature of compassion and non-violence by replying: "Because if I hadn't told him, somebody might have got killed."

THE PORTRAIT of the new Aaron was enough to bring tears to a salvationist's eyes.

Then, last Saturday night, "The bravest man I know," living it up in a Martinsville, Va., motel room with a 17-year-old girl, embarrassed his champions.

When a second man in the room refused to leave, Aaron pulled one of two pistols he happened to have in his possession and shoved into the man's belly. He also pulled the trigger. The man fell . . . seriously, though not mortally, wounded.

POLICE TOOK Aaron into custody, whereupon he promptly advised them that he is an undercover agent for the S.B.I.

But in North Carolina, as new flurries of indignation arose for review of the Payton case, authorities for the state begged to disagree with handsome Harold.

This time, they said . . . This time, Two-Gun Aaron, "The bravest man I know," had done an awesome thing.

He had done gone and told a lie.

Now the indignant flurries of mid-week are over.

This is Saturday.

And Boyd Payton is still doing 6 to 10.

Aaron's preliminary hearing resulted in his being bound over to the Grand Jury in Henry County, Virginia. He was indicted and the case was brought to trial on July 18, 1961. After some lurid testimony, Aaron was fined $100 and ordered to pay the court costs. The prison grapevine carried many reports of "secret conferences" and "deals" between North Carolina and Virginia officials in regard to "soft-pedaling" the prosecution. We, of course, had no way of determining the truth in any of these reports, but it was reported later by those who had attended the trial that little effort was made to build a strong case against Aaron and that it was obvious that the greatest consideration was given to bringing the trial to the earliest possible conclusion.

"Payoff" For Visit To Doctor

I had been having some difficulty with dizziness and had nearly fallen two or three times when I stood up quickly from a reclining or sitting position. I had been trying for several days to get an appointment with the prison doctor, but had not been able to get the "cash" to the inmate who prepared the appointment list. When I finally covered this detail I was promptly called and received an expert examination which showed that my blood pressure had dropped from 148 to 100 since entering prison. The doctor suggested that the starchy diet might be responsible. He ordered medication for me and advised me to buy as much juice as possible from the "store-box."

* * * * *

On April 19th, I was visited by Mr. John Rapp, a polygraph

expert from Buffalo, New York. He had been engaged by the union to analyze the polygraph examination given to me on December 15, 1960. He questioned me for more than an hour after advising me that he had already spoken to state officials, attorney Nicholson, and my family. He also said that he had studied the court record and carefully reviewed the text of the negative report issued in regard to my test.

He explained that his purpose was simply to evaluate the previous examination as conducted, and not to attempt to reach any conclusion as to my innocence or guilt.

Of course, he gave no indication to me as to what his report would contain. However, after leaving prison, I was given a copy of his report to the union. It covered nine pages. His conclusion was: "This was not a proper or fair examination. The positiveness of Backster's statement that Payton attempted deception on all relevant questions is not supported by the evidence. If Payton had had absolutely no knowledge of the events of the conspiracy, he could not have "passed" this examination, conducted in the circumstances, at the time and in the manner in which it was conducted."

* * * * *

April 21st—my 53rd birthday; April 22nd—my wife's 53rd birthday. These two days had always meant much to us and called for special celebrating. This year, they were most difficult days to live through as we were forced to "celebrate" with prison bars and 150 miles separating us. I was most depressed for days before and days after. Furthermore, it seemed that just nothing was happening to break the monotony of prison routine or to lift our hopes for early release. The attorneys had visited us and had spoken about some activities designed to promote early release, but their vagueness about dates and other details did little to lift our spirits.

In order to demonstrate the depth of depression which seemed to have descended on everyone in Central Prison, let me report on the two incidents which provided the greatest excitement among the inmates during this particular period.

One of the many cats at the prison had apparently given birth to seven kittens at a spot just outside the prison gate. For some reason, she had decided to bring them into the utility room in the rear of the chapel. She had several hundred spectators as she carried each kitten in her mouth through the bars of the gate, deposited it gently in her new home, and returned quickly for another. The fellow who usually sold baseball and football "pool" tickets quickly made up tickets for betting on the number of kittens she would eventually bring. He sold them for 25¢ each and did a brisk business. As she brought each kitten, those who held the ticket number corresponding to the new total begged her not to go for another one. Then, as she ignored their pleas and dashed out through the gate again, those to whom this meant that they had lost gave vent to their feelings by angry curses while those "still alive" cheered. The "show" lasted for more than an hour and about 20 of the inmates were several dollars richer.

As the crowd was dispersing, someone noticed thousands of honey bees swarming over the high wall and forming a great ball by landing in a small tree beside the "Meditation" building.

Everyone had a remark about the stupidity of the bees in coming to prison of their own volition. The fact that they had selected the spot near "Meditation" was of special interest and served, the inmates said, to prove that the bees were in need of mental treatment.

* * * * *

Mother's Day, May 14th, an announcement was made over the loudspeaker that roses were available on the back porch for anyone who wanted to wear one in honor of his mother. Most of us went and found two large boxes of red and white roses. No one seemed to know who had brought them, but they were beautiful and a great morale booster. I thought there must be a lesson somewhere in the way everyone wore their rose so proudly and talked of pleasant memories involving their mothers. The chapel services were well attended and everyone seemed to be a little more human and kind to each other throughout the entire day.

* * * * *

I was still having some trouble with dizziness and had nearly fallen from my upper bunk on Wednesday morning. Since it was prayer-meeting night, I did not return to the cell until after 9 P.M. When I did, I found Little Joe sitting on my bunk and "looking like the cat who had swallowed the canary." The lower bunk was neatly made up with my bed clothing and all of my belongings had been transferred to the lower shelf. Little Joe said, "I'm not takin' any chances on you fallin' out of that top bunk and crackin' your head and not bein' able to get me through the sixth grade before you leave here. I traded bunks with you."

* * * * *

On May 23rd, prison director Randall called me to his office. He was very kind in his remarks about the work I was doing in the school. We talked for several minutes about the operation of the prison (his problems and responsibilities and inmate behavior). Then, he said, "The real reason for my asking you to come in was to tell you that Mrs. Gore called about her husband being ill at the county camp, and I have ordered him transferred back here and assigned to the dining hall."

* * * * *

On May 26, 1961, the executive council of the union voted in New York to end the strike at Harriett-Henderson Cotton Mills which had begun on November 16, 1958.

I was called to the warden's office in the afternoon and was told that a reporter from *The News and Observer* had been given permission to submit a list of questions to me concerning the ending of the strike, and that I could reply by writing if I was so inclined. I agreed and was escorted to a side office. After a few minutes, the warden brought a list of the questions to which I quickly wrote answers. The warden asked me to wait until he determined whether or not the reporter needed any clarification. When he returned, he said, "He wants to know if you think the ending of the strike will have any effect on the Governor in reducing your sentence. You can answer any way you want to, but I'd be a little careful on that one. I wouldn't lean it either way." I said, "I don't believe there is much relation at this time between the strike and our being here. I can't see how the ending of the strike at this late date would have much effect one way or the other on the Governor's action."

* * * * *

May 28th was a difficult day. This was graduation day at Queens College in Charlotte and a very important day in the life of my eldest daughter, Patsy. My thoughts were with her all day and, in my mind's eye, I watched as she marched in looking so pretty and ladylike; and I was so proud of her as I pictured her crossing the stage to receive her diploma. Once again I had difficulty in avoiding all-consuming bitterness.

* * * * *

On May 31st I was elected prayer leader by a vote of the inmate group. This meant that it was my responsibility to arrange and conduct the prayer service each Wednesday, certify to the major the names of those expressing a desire to attend prayer meetings, and secure his approval for their attendance as well as to give him a report each Thursday morning on the attendance and the program. It also meant that requests for special prayers were channeled to me and that I could meet with the person making the request; either alone or in the chapel with others who had asked for special prayers. The chapel was a very wonderful place in the midst of so much that was beastly. It was always clean and orderly—warm and cozy in the winter and cool and pleasant in the summer. Many told me (and I experienced it myself) that they thought of the chapel as a place of refuge, and that only there did they feel safe and secure. Only there could they cast off the fears, worries, frustrations and heartaches which are the constant companions of the inmate.

* * * * *

On June 3rd, the Caledonia prison camp baseball team came to play against our Central Prison team. Charley was their manager and he, Lawrence, Warren and I had quite a reunion. Charley, Warren and I had lunch together and had a lot of fun complaining to the "waiter" (Lawrence) about the service: the "soiled tablecloth," the "tarnished silverware, etc." Then we were herded *outside the walls* to the baseball field where we could see cars going by on the highway and see *free people* strolling by. This was great after five months of seeing only high and thick stone walls in all directions. Armed guards were still much in evidence surrounding the field, but somehow they didn't seem as formidable.

* * * * *

On June 4th, a new "student" enrolled. He was 57 years old and had never written his name. He promptly asked for a "times table like John has." I couldn't understand what he meant until he explained, "You know, it tells you how much two times four is." He was anxious to be doing arithmetic problems as his cell-mate was doing. He said, "I don't wanna fool with readin' and writin'—I just want to learn to count." However, when I explained how important reading and writing was in learning to count, he agreed to try it only "if you'll give me one of them books about the Brown family. My cell-mate had a book like that and I enjoyed hearin' 'bout all the things that family done."

* * * * *

That was the day my oldest pupil, age 67, was waiting for me in the hallway. He said, "Mr. Payton, my aunt has died and left me several thousand dollars. I don't have nobody who cares about me and I don't care about nobody as much as I do about you. I want to give you some of that money if you won't be insulted and will tell me what I have to do so the trustee will let you have it." I was deeply touched, but told him that I couldn't accept his money. He looked very disappointed and said, "I thought you'd say that, but I wanted to offer it to you, and I want you to know that if you ever do need it all you have to do is ask. You know where to find me. I ain't never goin' no place but here." (He was serving a life-term.)

* * * * *

On June 5th, we had a visit from two of our attorneys and two union officials who were managing the campaign to secure favorable action from the Governor on our petition for commutation of sentences. Warren, Lawrence and I were greatly enthused when we were called to the visiting room because rumors had been flying via the prison grapevine that the Governor would act in a few days to reduce all sentences to time already served. However, our visitors could give us no assurance in this regard, and we were very depressed when we returned to the prison yard. Rumors persisted about our early release. Some of the inmates worked outside of Central Prison on "work release" jobs in and around state offices and the Governor's Mansion. They were returned to their cells each evening, and each one had a story about what he had overheard concerning favorable action which the Governor had decided to take in our behalf. Even some of the guards relayed stories ("from friends close to the Governor") which indicated that our prison days were numbered. Despite this optimistic atmosphere inside the prison, we received no encouraging word from the outside and continued to "sweat it out" dreary day after dreary day. It was very strange and very frustrating to hear hopeful stories several times each day from inmates and guards, only to have those hopes dashed each time a report was received from those upon whom we were depending for our freedom.

* * * * *

For several days, at Mr. Powers' suggestion, I had been "breaking in" the young inmate who had been designated to take my place in the school if and when the Governor did take favorable action on our petition. He was rather well educated and had taught in the Ohio state prison school. The "students" liked him, and I was pleased to know that they were to be in what I considered to be "good hands." However, he decided to escape by concealing himself in the vacant spare-tire compartment of a large truck which was about to leave the prison yard. Apparently no one had seen him climb into the truck, and we knew nothing about the incident until we heard the escape siren shortly after the lock-up whistle had sounded. All were held in their cells and television viewing was cancelled as guards patrolled the corridors and counted and recounted the inmates. Curiosity as to the identity of the escapee was at fever pitch for more than an hour. The "grapevine" revealed that it was my replacement. Calls came from all over the cell-block to the effect that I could not now be released because I would have to stay to break in a new "teacher." The escapee alert was cancelled about 9:30 P.M. It was explained to me that this meant that the escapee had been recaptured. The next morning we learned about the truck and the fact that it had been driven outside of the walls; but the driver had backed it against the wall in such a way that the rear doors could not be opened. Therefore, although the escapee was free from the prison enclosure, the "wall" was still holding him securely on the outside. The noise made in his efforts to get the truck doors open had caught the attention of a guard, and he was quickly brought back inside the prison and placed in solitary confinement. I never saw him again.

Harry Golden's Letter

On June 10th, I received a copy of a letter which Charlotte author Harry Golden had written to Governor Sanford on June 1st. I believe it deserves a place in this story, and I am quoting it, verbatim, below:

Charlotte, N. C.
June 1, 1961

Governor Terry Sanford
State Capitol
Raleigh, North Carolina

Dear Governor:

We had been previously advised to see you about an appeal for the release of Boyd Payton after the adjournment of the State Legislature, when you could give more time to the petition.

I'd like to brief you now on what has gone before.

Early last December Rev. Billy Graham and I made an appointment with Governor Hodges who was most receptive to our solicitation to speak in behalf of this petition.

A few days before our scheduled visit to Raleigh, we learned of the "results" of a lie detector test. The publicity said that Boyd Payton had "failed." After discussing this with Governor Hodges we cancelled our appointment. May I hasten to add that the concellation was not because we had lost faith in Boyd Payton's innocence, but rather because of the facts of life. The attendant publicity would have undoubtedly had some effect, and we decided to put off our plea for some time in the future.

I would like to dwell a moment on the lie detector test. Even to a layman, this seems highly irregular. I can't imagine what prompted Mr. Payton to agree to taking a lie detector test. But neither can I imagine responsible government suggesting and carrying out such a procedure with a man who had already been convicted. I am not ready to say that the offer was an entrapment, but such a suggestion to a man *after* his conviction means that authority itself was questioning the sovereignty of its course; because if the announcement had been, "Boyd Payton Wins," then every man in the penitentiary, no matter how many years he still would have had to serve, would have demanded a lie detector test. Is this not so? And does not this whole procedure belong in a Gilbert and Sullivan Operetta?

My interest in the matter is based entirely on the fact that I am a Tar Heel in love with this community. I am a member of the Radio and Television Artists Union, and the only other connection I have with Boyd Payton's organization or any trade union in the U. S., directly or indirectly, is that the entire AFL-CIO gives me $9.00 a year for three subscriptions. (The National Association of Manufacturers gives me fifty times that much for a subscription.)

I have read the entire testimony at the trial of Boyd Payton. Billy Graham and I went over it thoroughly; and, at our own expense, engaged an attorney to advise us on some of the legal points. I have come to this conclusion; that the prosecution witness, Aaron, might have continued his testimony as follows:

'After I hung up on Boyd Payton, I called, one after the other, Billy Graham at Montreat, Harry Golden in Charlotte, and Terry Sanford at Fayetteville, and told them what I was going to do, and each of these men said, "That's fine." ' On the basis of Payton's conviction, the court would also have had to convict Billy Graham, Golden and Sanford.

As you know, Governor, Billy Graham is now in Manchester, England, and will be out of the country until the end of July, after which I suspect he will take a long rest. He left with me, however, an authorization to speak for him and a letter to you when the Reverend W. W. Finlator and I receive the appointment for this plea. (The Roman Catholic Church would like to send a priest along, and we will give you his name eventually.) Billy Graham also told me that if you thought it necessary, I should make an appointment the day before with the long distance operator, so that he could particpate in this plea over the phone while we are in your office.

I know how simple it is for a jury or the abstracct "public" to say "away with him," and how much more difficult it is when the issue is put up to one man. We are doing you no favor. But *you* will have to do it; either release Boyd Payton or decide that he must finish his term.

I think Boyd is a man of great courage. It takes a little thinking to understand this. To seek "mercy" might be considered an acknowledgement of guilt. That is why I believe Payton is made of sterner stuff. Tom Mooney was offered his freedom many times on the basis of mercy, but he refused it for he said he did not bomb the Preparedness Parade in San Francisco and he wanted vindication. Payton understands what terrible soul-searching there must be for a state to say, "We have done an injustice." This is not a simple matter. Tom Mooney came out an old and broken man and died.

Boyd Payton is a man of wisdom. He has agreed that we should plead for "mercy." Thus he pays honor, as I do, to the established authority of government; and that his vindication must come across the years through his own actions, research, investigation, all of which should come about if he receives this "mercy" without a frontal "attack" on the institutions of his state. Eventually, I am sure, as are Billy Graham and Mr. Finlator, and a host of others, that this vindication will come, not because the state engineered a frame-up, but because the state is often imposed upon by —— the false witness.

If you set the appointment, would you please also notify Mr. Finlator? In any event, we will be guided by your wishes in the matter.

Sincerely yours,

Harry Golden

CC: Mrs. Boyd Payton
    Arthur Goldberg
    Rev. Finlator
    Kays Gary

Billy Graham
H. D. Lisk
Julian Scheer

The Christian Century Article

A copy of *Christian Century* which carried an issue date of June 14, 1961, came (surprisingly) through the regular prison mail system. It carried the article by Dr. Clair M. Cook, which I read several times with mixed emotions. The title "Boyd Payton: Saintly Scapegoat" was surely a misnomer when applied to me, and it gave me real concern. I had hoped, too, that the article would have given greater attention to the other seven. This had been an extremely "sore spot" with me. We had made a special effort from the beginning to discuss and plan and speak in terms of all being involved, and emphasized that "no one is more important than the others"; but, invariably, newspapers referred to it as "the Payton case." However, aside from these points, the story was factual and well-written, and I was hopeful that church people would respond to it. My reaction to the story was also a feeling of thankfulness for family and friends, and it made me feel very humble.

The prison chaplain did nothing to lessen my concern about the points I'd questioned when he stopped by the school with a copy of *Christian Century* and expressed the opinion that the story would not help toward securing early release because "it is too one-sided."

Several unhappy days and sleepless nights were spent until the "work release" inmates reported that the Governor's office staff had been enlarged and was working overtime to answer the letters resulting from "that church paper story."

Hope For Freedom

The News and Observer for June 21, 1961, carried the following interesting and significant headline and story.

Industrialist Backs Move To Release Boyd Payton

Spencer Love, president of big Burlington Industries and top spokesman for the American textile industry, has written Gov. Sanford recommending clemency for Boyd Payton, the textile labor union leader now serving a prison sentence for conspiracy growing out of the bitter Harriet-Henderson mill strike.

Sanford, now in Hawaii at the National Governors Conference, is studying a report of the State Paroles Commission about Payton's case. Paroles Commissioner Johnson Matthews visited Sanford the day before he left for the two-week trip to deliver a report and discuss Payton's situation.

Industry Leader.

The fact that Love has joined in the appeal for clemency reportedly indicates that organized labor has won over a responsible industry leader to its position that the Henderson strike and the imprisonment of Payton and other union members creates an antagonistic climate in the textile industry that is good neither for labor nor management.

It also adds strength to the belief that Sanford will act either to free Payton or reduce the six-to-ten-year sentence he is serving.

Many Letters.

The Governor's files are packed with hundreds of letters recommending such action.

The appeals have come from those in high places.

Secretary of Labor Arthur Goldberg, who serves with Love on a presidential committee on labor-management relations, visited Gov. Luther Hodges in the summer of 1960 to discuss the Payton case. Hodges was also attending a National Governor Conference at the time. Goldberg at that time was general counsel to the AFL-CIO.

Goldberg reportedly has discussed the Payton case with Love at meetings of the presidential committee, and suggested that the antagonisms brought about by the Henderson strike and the Payton imprisonment should, if possible, be removed in the interests of both management and labor.

Other labor leaders and Congressmen friendly to labor have written in Payton's behalf.

Church groups have increasingly joined in the appeal for Payton's release. Most recently, in an article in the *Christian Century*, a liberal nondenominational weekly, Payton's case was reported.

Billy Graham, the evangelist, and Charlotte author-editor Harry Golden have joined with Raleigh's W. W. Finlator, pastor of Pullen Memorial Baptist Church, in requesting a joint meeting with Sanford to make a personal appeal for Payton. They are expected to see Sanford after he returns from Hawaii.

Payton is now in Central Prison, where he is working as an instructor with illiterate prisoners.

Six other union members convicted with Payton of conspiring to blow up a power plant and other facilities of the Henderson mill are also serving sentences. One has been paroled.

All eight were convicted in the fall of 1959 after the bitter strike had been on for more than a year.

They went to prison early last fall after appeals to the State and U.S. Supreme Court failed.

Monday, July 3, 1961, was filled with reports about action the Governor was about to take in reducing our sentences. One report was to the effect that a conference of administration leaders was to be held at 2 P.M. and that the announcement would be made promptly thereafter. However, the day wore on through supper and lock-up time with no further word.

Warren, Lawrence, and I were together for a few minutes before being locked up, but were not very good company for each other because of our anxiety and frustration.

When the lock-up whistle sounded, I was completely exhausted and promptly went to bed while my cell-mates went to the first floor to watch television.

About eight o'clock, Pop came running back to the cell and gleefully announced, "They just said on television that Sanford is cutting you all out this week." I sat up so quickly that I banged my head against the bottom of the upper bunk and was stunned for a moment. Pop was jumping around in the corridor and yelling, "Sanford is cutting the Henderson boys out." Cheers of those who had stayed in their cells came from above and below. Pop reached through the bars a dozen times to shake hands or pound me on the back. (He could not enter the cell until the doors were opened by the guard, and the guard would not do this until all were ready to return from TV.)

I called to Lawrence who was in the cell directly below mine. One of his cell-mates had brought the news to him as soon as the announcement had been made. He was very happy, but anxious for details, as was I.

When the others returned from watching TV, several stopped by my cell to shake hands through the bars and express congratulations. It was then that I learned that the TV announcement was contained in a newscast from Washington and was based on reports from "reliable sources" rather than on any official statement from the Governor. This caused some misgivings, but I still gathered all of my belongings and placed them in a pillow case so that I would be ready to leave on a moment's notice. Lawrence called from below to say, "I have everything packed and I'm ready for a midnight ride. They can't come too soon to suit me."

As the "lights-out" signal came and the cell-block became quiet, I stretched out on my bunk and spent the night thinking of the things I would say to family and friends, and the things I most wanted to do when released.

The next morning (Independence Day) I raced to the "storebox" for a morning paper and frantically leafed through its pages. I couldn't believe it when no announcement from the Governor could be found.

Because it was a holiday for the supervisors, we had no work and no school. At nine o'clock, the loudspeaker announced that a movie was being shown in the auditorium. I went because it was a cool place to sit, but paid little attention to the movie as I was absorbed in my own thoughts. At lunchtime, a dozen inmates informed me of the details of the Governor's statement. They said that Lawrence, Charley and I were not to be released for another month, while the other four were to be released at once. I couldn't understand this, and I couldn't understand how these inmates could have gotten this information before any official statement had been issued. I kept hoping that they were mistaken. However, at 1:30, I was called to the warden's office and he handed me a copy of the Governor's statement, which went as follows:

July 4, 1961

STATEMENT BY GOVERNOR TERRY SANFORD
Raleigh, N. C.

The courts of our State and Nation exercise in the name of the people the powers of administration of justice. The Executive is charged with the exercise in the name of the people of an equally important attitude of a healthy society—that of mercy beyond the strict framework of the law.

The use of executive clemency is not a criticism of the courts, either expressed or implied. I have no criticism of any court or any judge. Executive clemency does not involve the changing of any judicial determination. It does not eliminate punishment; it does consider rehabilitation.

To decide when and where such mercy should be extended is a decision which must be made by the Executive. It cannot be delegated even in part to anyone else, and thus the decision is a lonely one.

It falls to the Governor to blend mercy with justice, as best he can, involving human as well as legal considerations, in the light of all circumstances after the passage of time, but before justice is allowed to overrun mercy in the name of the power of the State.

I fully realize that reasonable men hold strong feelings on both sides of every case where executive clemency is indicated. However, I accepted the responsibility of being Governor, and I will not shy away from the responsibility of exercising the power of executive clemency.

After careful consideration, I have today signed orders granting executive clemency of some degree to 29 prisoners.

These are all a matter of public record, but I would call your attention to seven of them because of widespread public interest.

I have reduced the sentences of seven of the men involved in the Henderson strike by three years each. Thus four are eligible for parole immediately and Auslander, Payton and Gore will be eligible for parole later this summer. (The eighth, Malcolm Jarrell, was released on parole in April.)

The prison record always has been one of the considerations, and outstanding work has been done by one of these men in teaching illiterates at Central Prison how to read and write.

The warden informed me that reporters were waiting to see if I would be allowed to issue a statement. He said, "You are free to do so if you want to. I'll have to check it, but I doubt that any changes will be made in it." I quickly wrote a brief statement and handed it to the warden. It appeared in *The News and Observer* of July 5th, 1961, as part of several stories. Clippings from that issue are reproduced below:

Boyd Payton May Go Free Next Month
By, ROY PARKER JR.

Gov. Sanford Tuesday reduced the prison sentences of textile union leader Boyd Payton and six other union members, making four immediately eligible for parole and paving the way to freedom for Payton and two others next month.

Sanford said he had decided to "blend mercy with justice" in the cases of the men convicted of conspiring to dynamite the Harriet-Henderson textile mill in Henderson during the bitter strike there in 1959.

Exercising executive clemency, the Governor cut three years from the sentences of each of the seven men.

Eligible For Parole.

By doing so, he made Johnnie Martin, Warren Walker, Edward Abbott and Calvin Pegram immediately eligible for parole by the State Paroles Board. They had originally been sentenced to five-to-seven year terms. They are all from Henderson.

Payton, Carolinas director of the Textile Workers Union of America; Charles Auslander, and Lawrence Gore will be eligible for parole in early August. They had originally been sentenced to six-to-10-year terms.

All entered prison November 3, 1960, after appeals to the State and U. S. Supreme Court had failed to overturn a Vance County jury verdict.

One Released Earlier.

Under State law, prisoners become eligible for parole after serving one-fourth of their sentences. One of the convicted union members, Malcolm Jarrell, has already been paroled. He was sentenced to a two-to-three-year prison term.

Sanford's action in moving to free the union members was not unexpected. Constant pressure has been on his office to make the move. The pressure has come from high places, including leaders of the national administration, churchmen, and union leaders. Week before last, The *News and Observer* revealed that Spencer Love, president of big Burlington Industries and a top spokesman for textile management, had recommended mercy for Payton.

The Governor announced that 22 other prisoners were being granted some form of executive clemency. He said he would reveal their names today.

Issues Statement.

He issued a statement about executive clemency.

He said: "Executive elemency does not involve changing any judicial determination. It does not eliminate punishment; it does consider rehabilitation. . . . "

In deciding on clemency for Payton and his colleagues, Sanford said: "The prison record always has been . . . a consideration, and outstanding work has been done by one of these men in teaching illiterates at Central Prison how to read and write."

He was referring to Payton, who has been conducting such classes for several months.

The Governor's move added another chapter to a story that started in late 1958 when TWUA members at Harriet-Henderson mill went on strike after contract negotiations broke down.

Hodges' Efforts Failed.

For month after bitter month, they stayed out, while President John D. Cooper brought in outside workers to fill their places. Gov. Luther Hodges, acting as mediator, sought to solve the strike after sending in Highway Patrol and National Guard forces to put down violence.

In April, 1959, Hodges' efforts appeared successful. But then Cooper revealed there were only a handful of jobs left open for the 1,000 strikers.

From then on, the broken strike dragged on until a few weeks ago, when the national headquarters of TWUA announced it was ending its involvement. It said the strike cost $1.5 million and had caused a bitter setback to its efforts throughout the South.

In the spring of 1959, the State Bureau of Investigation announced it had evidence that Payton and the seven others had conspired to dynamite the Henderson plant's power station.

In the trial, held at a special term of Vance County Superior Court, SBI testimony came mostly from Harold Aaron, a hired informer, who claimed he met with some of the men in a motel near Roanoke Rapids to plan violence which never came off.

Payton was linked to the motel room meeting by Aaron's

testimony about a telephone call between Payton and himself.

Sentenced By Mallard.

Judge Raymond Mallard handed down the sentences.

Appeals went to the State and U. S. Supreme Court. The State's high court upheld the convictions, although Justice William Bobbitt dissented in Payton's case, saying the evidence was insufficient. The U. S. court refused to hear the case.

Appeals for executive clemency were made to Gov. Hodges for months before the men went to prison. At one point, Arthur Goldberg, later Secretary of Labor in the Kennedy administration, made a personal visit to Hodges' office to discuss the cases.

Lie Test Given.

In December, Payton agreed to take a lie detector test in an attempt to prove his innocence. The official who gave the test said it revealed Payton was involved in the conspiracy for which he was convicted.

This, however, did not still a mounting pressure for his release. Sanford, during his political campaigns in 1960, had said, he would "give impartial study" to Payton's case, as he would to all appeals.

Adding to the impetus for Sanford to act was the news in April of this year that Aaron had received $1,100 for his work as SBI informer, and then that he had been arrested in Martinsville, Va., on charges of wounding a man who refused to leave a motel room occupied by Aaron and a 17-year-old girl.

Before leaving for the National Governors' Conference two and a half weeks ago, Sanford revealed he had asked the Paroles Board to again give him a report on Payton's case, along with reports in various other cases.

He conferred with Paroles Board Chairman Johnson Matthews the day before he left, and took a report on the case with him to the conference in Hawaii.

The paroles agency is used by the Governor as a consulting agency in his decisions on executive clemency.

—*The News and Observer* Raleigh, North Carolina, July 5, 1961

Joy, Sadness In Families Of Unionists

"I'm just overjoyed, we have been up in the air all day."

That was the reaction Tuesday from Mrs. Johnnie Martin, whose husband is one of four Henderson textile union members immediately eligible for paroles because of Gov. Sanford's action in cutting the terms of seven men serving time for conspiring to dynamite the Harriet-Henderson mill's power plant.

But union leader Boyd Payton and his wife were not so elated.

Mrs. Payton, whose husband will be eligible for parole in early

August, said she was "horribly disappointed."

"I had expected a pardon and no less because he is not guilty," she said in Charlotte.

Payton's Comment.

Payton, Carolinas director of the Textile Workers Union of America, told Central Prison Warden K. B. Baily he "was happy" Sanford acted, but "a little disappointed that he didn't get a pardon or a reduction in sentence to time served."

Some of those who had been most active in seeking Payton's release were not available for comment. Repeated efforts to get reaction from officials of the union in New York and Charlotte failed, although the news of Sanford's action came in mid-morning.

W. M. Nicholson, Charlotte lawyer who was Payton's counsel during his trial and who led attempts to get executive clemency, said he would consult with his associates today before making a statement.

Mrs. Martin said she was sure she spoke for the families of three other men who have now become eligible for parole. None of the other families were available yesterday, nor was Luther Jackson, head of the TWUA local in Henderson.

Apparently none of the families was told beforehand that Sanford would act so quickly after his return from the National Governors' Conference in Hawaii. Mrs. Martin said she heard on the radio that the Governor might act this week.

Mrs. Payton, however, said she had called a Fourth of July backyard dinner and had hoped to announce that her husband was being freed immediately.

"Ages" For Mrs. Payton.

Told that he could be out within a month, she said: "A little while is ages."

Payton, Lawrence Gore, and Warren Walker are in Central Prison. Walker is now eligible for immediate parole.

Martin is in a prison camp near Mocksville. Edward Abbott and Calvin Ray Pegram, also now eligible for parole, heard the news at a camp near Sanford.

Charles Auslander, who like Payton must wait several weeks, is in the Caledonia Prison Farm in Halifax County.

—*The News and Observer*, Raleigh, North Carolina,
July 5, 1961

* * * * *

I met Warren and Lawrence and we walked around the yard for an hour while we talked about the Governor's action. Lawrence and I kept telling Warren how happy we were that he and the others would be going home in a day or two, while he kept telling us how badly he felt because we all were not to be released at the same time.

Wednesday was a difficult day. Everyone wanted to talk about the matter and express their opinions or give their versions of the reasoning behind the kind of action which the Governor had taken. I would have preferred to give full time and attention to the school where I could temporarily forget my problems by being absorbed in the problems of others.

Special revival services were being held in the chapel each afternoon that week at 4:45 P.M. I had been attending and had found it to be very worthwhile. Captain Hipps of the Salvation Army in Goldsboro was in charge and was an excellent speaker. He was assisted by Major Mays of Atlanta, who used colored chalk to depict various Bible scenes. He would, without apparent purpose, make a lot of marks on the blackboard with different colored chalk. Then, with his gloved hands, he would spread it around. Suddenly a beautiful scene would appear while a "Tennessee Ernie" record played in the background. The entire service filled a great need during that particular time. On Wednesday, it was a special blessing.

That evening after I had retired, a guard came to say that I had a visitor and should go to the back hall. I found Bill Finlator waiting for me. He explained that he had been out of town, had just heard news about the Governor's action, and felt that he had to see me before sleeping. He expressed strong feelings to the effect that the Governor should have granted full pardon. When he was ready to leave and I was expecting him to give his usual brief prayer, he said, "Will you say a word of prayer and pray that I may understand the meaning of faith, and patience, and tolerance?" Imagine my feelings—to be asked to pray for this great and good man! This was his way of paying a great compliment to me, but I felt so undeserving and was ashamed of the weakness and lack of faith which had been my attitude throughout the day. I resolved that this attitude would change.

How thankful I was that Bill had made that visit on Wednesday, when I was called to the back-hall on Thursday and found my family waiting to see me. My thoughtful wife, knowing that our disappointment would be easier if we could share it together, had obtained special permission to visit me. Kitty and the kids looked like angels to me, and we were allowed to sit together in the large hallway for nearly an hour—the first time in almost nine months that we were not separated by bars and screens during our visits.

It was obvious to me that they had pledged themselves to express only happy thoughts and talk of the future. Thanks to Bill Finlator's visit, I was able to match their mood, and it was a wonderful hour.

* * * * *

On Saturday morning, July 8, Lawrence, Warren and I went to the movie. When it was about halfway through, a guard came in and called for Warren. He left with the guard, and later as we came from the auditorium a guard informed us that Pegram and Abbott had been brought by Central Prison to pick up Warren. All three were then on their way to Henderson where they would be released. Lawrence sang "Eight Little Indians" down to "And then there were three." It was good to see Lawrence returning, even slowly, to his usual happy disposition. He had been very ill, and most of his time in prison had been a real ordeal.

* * * * *

On July 10th, I was called before the parole board and questioned about whether or not I had a job, a place to live, sufficient finances. Mr. Hepler explained that this was the usual routine in preparing "release on parole" papers.

Mr. Cheatam, another member of the parole board, outlined the conditions of parole: "no staying out late; no association with persons of bad character; no drinking of alcoholic beverages; no leaving county without permission of parole officer; no leaving state without permission of the state parole board. If permission is granted to leave the state, you must report to the nearest police headquarters within 24 hours and explain your reasons for being in that state. Under no circumstances must you associate with ex-convicts."

* * * * *

A young inmate brought his "prison papers" to me on Sunday and said, "See if I ain't been here too long already."

This was a standing joke. Whenever anyone acted a little silly or did something strange, somebody would always say, "He's been here too long." However, this young fellow was very serious. The laughter which had started with his remark was quickly stifled, and several inmates crowded around as I began looking at his papers. The court record which he had received that day in the mail plainly stated that his sentences on two counts were to be served "concurrently," while his commitment papers stated that the two sentences were to be served "consecutively." He had already completed one sentence and had served two months of the second. Furthermore, he had not been considered for parole prior to completion of his first sentence because, apparently, the record on file in the prison was identical to the erroneous commitment paper.

I explained it to him, and he asked if anything could be done. I advised him to show the papers to the major and to say that he had discussed the matter with me. I said, "Tell the major that I have agreed to prepare a Writ for you if he doesn't object."

The boy raced to the major's office (in the middle of the prison yard) and came back shouting, "The major says you're right, and he will help to straighten it out if you'll do the writin'!"

I prepared the Writ on Monday morning and gave it to him at lunchtime. I believe he gave it to the major who then delivered it to the court. On Thursday morning, the major escorted the boy to court and Judge Carr issued an order for his release. Before leaving, he came back to thank me and ask how he could repay me. I said, "Just make sure they never have reason to bring you here again. That's all the pay I want."

He answered, "Don't worry about that—I've learned my lesson."

As we shook hands and he turned to leave, he said, "Boy, I

can't wait to see the look on Mom's face when I walk in. She'll be sure I escaped."

* * * * *

Sunday, July 16th, was visiting Sunday for white inmates. This would be the last time my family would have to make that trip. Mr. Powers had recommended that I be promoted to honor-grade, and I had been hoping it would be approved before Sunday. I had heard nothing further about it when my name was called on Sunday morning to meet my family in the usual place. It was wonderful to see them, but so frustrating to continue being treated like a desperate criminal when everyone knew that I was soon to be released. My family had great difficulty in understanding the necessity of drawing the "punishment" out to the final hour.

* * * * *

On Tuesday evening, just after we were locked up, a guard came to my cell and said, "Come on, Boyd, they want you up front. I think they are going to lock you up." I said, "What did I do?"

He laughed and said, "No, I think you've been promoted to honor-grade."

He led me to the front office where I was asked a few questions and signed some papers to qualify me for honor-grade. This meant that I could exchange my brown clothes for blue ones; would be allowed to transfer to the honor-grade dormitory where less restrictions were applied; could have visiting privileges on the front yard, and could be released on parole from Central Prison without being escorted by a guard to the prison camp nearest my home. The final point was about the only real benefit as far as I was concerned.

I wore white clothes in the school, so the blue ones would only be worn on weekends—and I would only be there for one more weekend. I did not want to move to the dormitory and leave Pop and Little Joe for these final days. I would have no more "visiting Sundays." Therefore, the "promotion" was, at this late date, somewhat empty of meaning. However, as I was reminded by Little Joe, "It would look good on my record."

* * * * *

As I came from the school on Wednesday afternoon, the major called me to his office, and asked, "Did you know that Walter Anderson, the SBI director, is to be the speaker for the Raleigh group at prayer meeting tonight?"

This was a real surprise to me and I so advised the major. He seemed to be debating whether he should say something else. I waited for further instructions and fully expected him to ask me to place someone else in charge of the service. After a moment, he said, "I just thought you should know about it before he arrives."

He turned and began shuffling papers on his desk. I assumed that I was dismissed.

Apparently, no one had told Mr. Anderson that I was the prayer leader. He seemed to be surprised as I took my place on the platform and announced the first hymn. Then, he appeared to me to be rather uncomfortable as I spoke for a few minutes about judging Christians by their works rather than by their words. My closing remarks were, "The church member who loudly proclaims that he is a Christian while harboring thoughts of malice, hatred, and prejudice is betraying the teachings of Jesus. The true Christian will make sure that his daily life is so lived that it will serve as a beacon to guide others to the Kingdom of God."

When I stepped down from the pulpit as Mr. Anderson was stepping up, he shook hands, and said, "Boyd, you should have been a preacher."

When he started speaking, he said, "Your chairman has laid down a great challenge for all of us. I endorse his remarks wholeheartedly."

* * * * *

On Thursday afternoon, I was called to the visiting room where I found Mr. Hugh Cannon, the Governor's director of administration. He said, "For several weeks, the Governor has wanted someone from his office to talk with you. We debated whether it should be before or after he had acted on your case. We decided that it should be after." He then explained the reasoning behind the Governor's actions and listed the reasons why the action could not have been taken earlier. He said, "The Governor is, of course, aware of the fact that parole is not what you wanted, but he felt that he could not go farther at this time. However, he wanted me to make it clear to you that he does not intend that parole restrictions should hamper your activities in any way. He wants you to be free to handle your job as you did before. If you have any trouble with the parole regulations, you should contact me."

I listened to him with mixed emotions. He was very kind and seemed to be completely sympathetic. For this, I was grateful. I was grateful, too, for the action which the Governor had taken and realized that another Governor might not have moved at all. However, under the mitigating circumstances existing in our case, I could not agree that his reasons for delay were valid. (Especially when I knew that the Governor was completely familiar with the "mitigations" and had expressed strong feelings against them on several occasions.) Furthermore, it seemed to me that special significance was attached to the fact that the Governor had felt that his action needed to be explained to me. I wondered if any other inmate had ever been given any explanation when a Governor had taken action in his behalf. I wondered, too, if this wasn't the final proof of what had been implied on several occasions during the previous eight and a half months—that my imprisonment was a source of embarrassment to the state and its officials.

Although many questions were racing through my mind, I refrained from speaking. Mr. Cannon spoke of the large volume of mail which the Governor had received in our behalf. He invited me to stop by his office to see it at my first opportunity. Finally, he informed me that Mr. Douglas Cater of the *Reporter* magazine had been asking for an interview with me and was then waiting in the warden's office to submit questions to me. He said, "The warden will not permit him to talk with you personally, but has agreed that he can submit questions to you through me if you are agreeable."

I indicated that I had no objections and, for the next hour, Mr. Cannon shuttled back and forth between the warden's office and the visiting room—bringing questions from Mr. Cater and taking my answers back to him. After I had answered what

I deemed to be the final question, Mr. Cannon said, "Mr. Cater says he has never written a story about a person that he hasn't seen. The warden has agreed that he may come by and observe you through the window unless you object. He has been given permission to inspect your cell, the dining hall, and the chapel."

Before I could reply, the warden and Mr. Cater appeared at the window. Mr. Cater waved and winked. Later, after I had returned to the prison yard, he passed me and looked as if he would speak, but was hurried away by the warden.

* * * * *

During those final days of July, rumors concerning our release were "a dime a dozen." Excepting Lawrence and me, it seemed that everyone had information concerning the "latest developments." However, the days dragged by without any official word. Our attorneys reported that on their last visit with parole board officials they had been assured that we would be released "on or about August 3." However, the only information as to how, when, and where, was given in terms of "the usual procedure is," or "regulations call for——."

It was not until late afternoon on August 2nd that we were called to the prison director's office and briefed as to the plans for our release. Mr. Randall informed me of a telephone conversation which he had with my wife, in which he had stressed the importance of giving no prior publicity concerning the release time and no one coming for me except my immediate family. He said, "I told her that I was sure you didn't want your grandson to see a newspaper picture of you coming out of prison." (Several months earlier, I had told Mr. Randall that we were expecting our first grandchild in late August.) His cruel remark brought an angry retort to my lips when I thought of how I had been paraded in desperado harness to the justice building for the lie detector test, but I controlled the impulse to speak and waited for further instructions.

Mr. Randal said, "Your wives will be at the main gate at six o'clock tomorrow morning. You should be ready to leave your cells at five. You will be brought to the warden's office where you can change to your street clothes and leave as soon as you are ready." After a moment he said, "That's it, unless you have a question." Neither of us did. He shook hands with us, and we returned to our cells to spend the longest night of our lives.

I was bathed, shaved, and dressed long before daylight and sat on my bunk between Pop and Little Joe for a long while. We talked in whispers in recalling some of the experiences which we had shared, and it was somewhat of a shock for me to realize how much I would miss them. When the guard came for me, Pop gave me a great bear hug, but Little Joe suddenly became intensely interested in straightening the articles in his wall cabinet and kept his back to me until I was led from the cell.

To our surprise, the warden was in his office when we arrived there at 5:30. He was very kind in his remarks about our conduct in prison and about his hopes for our future. He then brought our suitcases from a closet where they had been stored since being brought to the prison by our wives a week earlier. When we were dressed in our own clothes for the first time in nine months, we questioned what should be done with the prison clothes. The warden said, smiling, "Leave them on the chairs—I don't suppose you want them for souvenirs."

Chapter 3
PAROLE AND FREEDOM

Lawrence's wife, Hazel, and his son and daughter were waiting with my wife and daughters when we came to the big main gate. What a happy reunion as we stepped through that gate! What a great thrill to be *free!* What love and happiness and joy in the hugs and kisses being so generously distributed!

We arrived at our home shortly before eleven o'clock to find television cameras, a crowd of neighbors, and newsmen in our front yard. My cocker spaniel, "Snuffy," delighted the cameramen when he saw me step from the car and began racing around me with happy yelps, and jumping higher than my waist with his enthusiastic greeting. My marvelous neighbors, with their expressions of concern and their "welcome home," left me deeply touched and appreciative of their loyalty.

The day moved on amid happy confusion; interviews with newsmen, telephone calls, visits by friends and church people, and by our faithful ministers, the Reverend Garner and Reverend Ruff.

In the course of conversations with newsmen, I had expressed a desire to write a book concerning my experiences. One of the newspaper headlines read, "Paroled Boyd Payton Plans To Write Book on Jail Life."

I Meet My Parole Officer

On Friday, according to my "conditions of parole," I reported to the county parole office in Charlotte. I found my parole officer, Mr. George McConnell, with the newspaper stories and headlines spread out on his desk.

As soon as I had identified myself, and he had shaken my hand, he pointed to the newspapers and said, "I just had a call from Raleigh about this. Mr. Matthews (parole board chairman) is not happy about it. I don't want to say that you *can't*, or even that you *shouldn't*, write anything you want to, but—if you take my advice, you'll forget it, at least for the present."

I did not reply, and Mr. McConnell began to explain the "agreement" which I would be required to sign. It was a standard form, complicated by numerous conditions and restrictions, with the state seal at the top. The statement below the seal said, "Parole Agreement Between The North Carolina Board of Paroles and *Boyd E. Payton*, Parolee."

I felt stifled—as if I were entangled in a great web. I felt insulted and angry and nauseated. I quickly signed the document and almost ran from the building.

Nevertheless, during the months which followed, Mr. McConnell became a warm and trusted friend who did all in his power to ease the harshness of parole restrictions and help to overcome the obstacles which these restrictions caused. He was always a welcome visitor in our home and we had many splendid discussions (rarely about prisons or parole) while my daughters served refreshments of cokes and cookies or coffee and cake. On one occasion, he confided, "I'm embarrassed to come to your home as a your parole officer and be treated like an honored guest by your fine family. They've introduced me to your friends and neighbors as 'Daddy's parole officer' without any sign of shame or embarrassment."

My wife and I talked to him about how we had been concerned that the experience might warp the thinking of the girls in regard to equal justice, law and order, and our court system, and how pleased we were that all three seemed to have gained a greater sense of tolerance and understanding and were able to say: "What happened to Daddy was an exception. It doesn't mean that 'equal justice' is a farce, or that 'law and order' deserves any less respect, or that our 'court system' is a failure."

My "discharge from parole" was not granted until December 18, 1962 (a total of sixteen months). The constant concern about avoiding situations which might possibly result in parole violations; the perpetual problem of getting permission for travel and remembering to report continual changes in travel plans; and, the inconvenience (to say nothing of the stigma) of being recorded as a "convicted felon" in various cities, and having fingerprints made several times, was not a pleasant experience to say the least.

An amusing and somewhat ironic incident occurred during this period when I was invited to a cocktail party in Washington for freshman congressmen. After rejecting several offers to "have a drink on me," a friend who knew my story asked me to hold her drink while she lit a cigarette. Suddenly, she dropped her cigarette, lighter, and pocketbook, as she made a frantic grab to reclaim her drink while staring, with obvious distress, over my shoulder. I turned, and came face-to-face with former Governor Luther Hodges, who was then Secretary of Commerce.

I Lose My Job

As to my job—within two weeks after my release from prison, I was dismayed to learn that I would not be permitted to return to my former position as Carolina's director, but was to serve as an assistant to the national organizing director, Mr. John Chupka. In this position, I was to be stationed in New York City, but would be required to do extensive traveling whenever and wherever special problems required attention. Hence, although I had vowed over and over while in prison that I would never again be separated from my family for long periods of time, in less than two months of "freedom" I found myself sitting alone in a hotel room in San Francisco—after weeks of constant travel and many lonesome nights spent in hotel rooms.

Early in 1962, I accepted an assignment as the Union's upper South director, with headquarters in Washington, D. C., where it was possible to maintain an apartment and have Kitty with me at least part of the time.

My Impressions Of Prison Life

In August of 1962, I was invited by the *Greensboro Daily News* to write an article concerning my impressions of prison life. I did, and it was published on September 2nd under the headline, "Is Society In Debt To The Convict?" Portions of the article follow:

> When a convict is released from prison, it is said, "He has paid his debt to society." After serving nine months in prison, during which time I observed and studied my fellow inmates and the prison

system as objectively as possible, I am forced to ask, "When and how will society ever pay its debt to the convict?"

It would be the height of conceit for me to pose as an expert in this field and expect my opinion to be given equal weight with the opinions of those who have spent a lifetime with problems connected with crime and punishment, and I certainly do not expect this. However, I do believe that my imprisonment offered a rare opportunity to gain insight into prison operation and inmate behavior which would not be possible in any other way.

Therefore, I would hope that my observations may be accepted as a contribution to the wealth of material which has been gained through exhaustive research, in an effort to find a solution to a problem that often pricks the conscience of democratic and freedom-loving people who are concerned about men as human beings, and the question of moral values in the field of crime prevention and punishment.

The state legislature passes laws which determine the operation of the courts and the preservation of law and order; it amends, from time to time, the state criminal code which determines the severity of punishment for various crimes; it is responsible for providing ways and means of financing the state's crime prevention program and the operation of its penal system.

Let us assume that all of these legislators are outstanding citizens of the districts from which they have been selected and are honest and sincere people who want to perform their duties in an able and intelligent manner that will best promote the welfare and good name of the state as well as the best interests of the taxpayer who must foot the bill.

Yet, with little or no previous experience in law enforcement or crime prevention, with no knowledge of the operation of the state's prison system, with no information about prison conditions or inmate behavior except a report from a prison's director who seldom comes in personal contact with one of the human beings known as "convicts," whose lives he is supposed to direct while they are "wards of the state," how can a legislator make decisions on these matters which are even intelligent—to say nothing of moral or humanitarian considerations?

So laws are passed and the criminal code is established by legislators who must feel like the farmer who worked long and hard at keeping his gates in good repair but paid no attention to his fences and couldn't understand why his cattle kept getting out on the road.

Then the laws and criminal code are given to the police and the courts for enforcement. Here, we come to the judges. During my nine months in prison I was appalled by the intense hatred which I found among convicts toward judges, and I made a sincere effort to find the reason. From my conversations with inmates concerning judges, I secured two pictures. The first was of a pious individual who felt that he had been ordained by God to sit in judgment on all of God's children who came before him; that he was duty-bound and solemnly obligated to punish; and that his decisions were always right and proper and should not be subject to further question from any source.

The second picture was of a political henchman of political bosses whose only concern is to please the "powers-that-be" so that he can continue to ride the "gravy train" and who has little concern for matters of human rights, equal justice or punishment with mercy.

I, of course, cannot subscribe to either description as a blanket indictment of all judges. There may be some who would fit one of these descriptions or the other, but I believe that the great majority of judges are honest and sincere and would pride themselves on having real concern for the value of human beings.

However, like the legislator, do they have any real knowledge of the conditions to which they are sentencing those who stand before their "bar of justice?" Are they equipped and trained to recognize the "good" in each man? Do they consider it their duty to look for the "good" and seek to save it?

After all, a judge is a lawyer who may or may not have been a success in the practice of law. He is appointed or elected as a judge. If he knew anything about crime and punishment before assuming this powerful position, it was probably because he had been successful in "getting convictions" as a prosecutor.

In theory, every man is entitled to "his day in court." The theory is that he must be proved guilty of the crime with which he is charged. The theory is that the prosecutor, representing the "people," has the duty to bring out all of the facts—to get the truth.

However, anyone who has watched a prosecutor work will have to admit that his every word is designed to "put the prisoner behind bars" and that truth and the individual rights of the prisoner are secondary considerations to what he considers his prime objection of "getting a conviction."

After all, his reputation, his measure of success, his political future all depend on the number of convictions—the number of times he has been "on the winning side."

Is this the kind of training needed to make a humanitarian judge?

Has any judge ever spent time in prison except on a "guided tour" with three days prior notice so that everything could be made "ship-shape" for his visit?

Did any judge ever spend a night on a prison bunk which had most of the filling gone from the mattress and where the bed clothing was stiff with filth?

Did any judge ever eat a meal which was shoved to him under the door where roaches waited for what was scraped off or spilled?

Did he ever try eating a meal in his five-by-seven toilet while another person sat on the only available seat?

Did any judge ever see a mental case being "treated" in the prison "meditation" cell?

These are questions which are asked by inmates when they are asked to explain their hatred for law and order and their burning desire to strike back at some judge.

To say the least, this is a sad commentary on our society which requires sober thought and consideration by each of us if we are to be true to the principles upon which this nation was founded.

If, and I emphasize the "if," respect for law and order is lessening each year (even if this is only among the families and friends of those sent to prison), it is a serious matter. Democracy cannot survive without law and order. And if our present approach has become meaningless as a behavior guide and as a deterrent to those with criminal tendencies, then perhaps it is time that we began thinking of a system which is based on obedience to and respect for a Higher Law."

On a wall of one of the cells in which I spent dreary nights and days were written those words of Oscar Wilde:

> I know not whether laws be right;
> Or whether laws be wrong;
> All that we know who lie in jail
> Is that the wall is strong;
> And that each day is like a year,
> A year whose days are long —
> That every prison which men build
> Is built with bricks of shame,
> And bound with bars, lest Christ should see
> How men their brothers maim.

If a man could spend his time in prison learning something of himself, his purpose in being on earth—if he could learn to recognize the importance of moral values, he would be much more likely to adjust to living in and being a responsible and worthwhile part of the complex society in which we are all forced to live today.

Of course, there are some with whom this approach would have little, if any, chance for success. I have talked with men in prison to whom being a convict has become a profession because they don't know how to survive in competitive society. They are like those creatures who choose to drink until their senses are dulled in order to avoid facing their responsibilities and obligations. But there is something radically wrong with a man who considers prison as a haven, and there is something radically wrong with a society which forces this choice upon him.

Fortunately, the percentage of such people is small, and we should not use them as reasons for continuing a system which has outlived its usefulness—if, indeed, it ever was useful—in correcting human behavior or serving as a deterrent for crime. I spoke at one of the Sunday afternoon Brotherhood meetings in prison, and my theme was "Love, kindness, and understanding—the world's most powerful forces."

And I tried this approach with those who were considered the most hardened criminals. At first, they were suspicious and were looking for a trick, but when they were convinced that I was sincere and really concerned about them as human beings, not a single one failed to respond—and beneath each hardened crust, I found something good—something upon which a worthwhile life could have been built if love, kindness, and understanding had been applied at the right time.

There seems to be an unwritten law that no one in authority in the prison system should ever speak a kind word to a new inmate. My first impression of prison life was that everyone in authority seemed determined to make every new inmate look like, act like, and feel like a criminal at the earliest possible moment.

My second impression was that prison officials considered convicts only slightly better than animals and felt that they deserved only slightly better treatment.

Then as I saw young men 16, 17, and 18 years of age, thrown into association with those who were near to complete depravity, questions cried out for answers:

"If you wanted your child to learn good manners and have high moral standards, would you force him to associate with the town rowdies?

"If your child had been exposed to a dread disease, should he be confined with other children who were dying from effects of the dread disease?"

These questions, it seems to me, cry out to society for answers. They should prick the conscience of all of those who espouse the high sounding principles of our "free and democratic way of life." They are an indictment of our crime prevention methods.

Human values must be given first consideration; and, instead of a penal system which destroys human dignity and pride and which reduces morale to the lowest possible level, we must develop a system which promotes self-respect and the dignity of the individual.

I have talked with so many men who are now considered beyond redemption, but who I am convinced could have been rehabilitated at one time. Yet society was so determined to punish that no thought was given to any kind of rehabilitation for them.

How much better it would have been to have these men on probation, earning a living, and supporting their families, than to have them wasting away behind bars with their board and lodging being paid for by the taxpayers who must hire more and more guards to keep the ever-increasing number of inmates in confinement and must provide ever greater welfare monies to support the familes of these men.

Every man in prison is like a millstone around the neck of taxpayers.

If we are truly concerned about moral and human values; if we are truly concerned about the ever-increasing cost of our penal systems, then we must conclude that the present system is not the answer and that a new system must be found.

Petition For Pardon

On February 1, 1963, in behalf of the "Henderson Eight," Attorney Nicholson filed a new "Petition For Pardon" with Governor Sanford. An unusual feature of this document was the fact that it was supported by affidavits from seven of the jurymen who had rendered the "guilty" verdict in our trial. In addition, it carried six other affidavits to the effect that at least three of the jurymen had perjured themselves in order to sit in judgement on the "Henderson Eight." Furthermore, the new petition documented two cases in which the North Carolina Supreme Court had ruled in favor of defendants on points identical to those it had denied in our case. Finally, it called attention to the fact that the "special" court which tried our case had been constituted in violation of North Carolina law.

On August 3, 1963, Attorney Nicholson reported on a July 30th conference which he and union representative H. D. Lisk had attended with the Governor, for the purpose of discussing the petition. They were disappointed because, for the first time, the Governor seemed less cordial and somewhat irritated by their visit. Nicholson reported the conversation as follows:

Nicholson: When we presented the new petition it was indicated that you would probably want to discuss it with us after you had studied it. That was two months ago and we have heard nothing from you. We would like to discuss it now and see if you could give us some idea as to when we may expect favorable action.

Governor: You haven't given me the new evidence that I need.

Nicholson: No new evidence! [The new evidence was enumerated.] I don't know what more could be expected.

Governor: But that's all just legal—I need something dramatic that will sell it to the press.

Nicholson: Have you really read the petition? All you need to do is hand it to the press—it will sell itself in my opinion.

Governor: Oh yes, I've read it, and it's excellent both legally and technically, but the Parole Board says it doesn't justify pardon.

Nicholson: I just can't understand that. I think any fair appraisal of any one of the new points would be enough to justify pardon—to say nothing of the fact that seven of the jurymen are supporting the petition and recommending your favorable action. You said before that you felt these men were "framed" and that you considered the whole case a black mark on the good name of the State . . .

Governor: I still say that, and I'm not saying that I won't do something at the right time. This is not the opportune time. If you insist on an answer now, it will have to be "no."

H. D. Lisk: But Governor, the last time we were here you suggested that if we filed a new petition, without publicity, we could be assured of favorable action.

Governor: Well, I still haven't said I won't take favorable action—it's still open—it's still on my desk. I'm not closing the case—I just say don't press me at this time.

* * * * *

After waiting anxiously for months for some hopeful word from the Governor, during which time the title of "ex-con" continued to plague me whenever I made any statement or took any public action in connection with my work, I began to press our advisors for some plan of action designed to revive interest in the matter and promote favorable response (for pardon) from newspapers and the general public.

Once again, however, I had failed to reckon with political considerations. First, it was explained that the Governor had many problems in connection with the special session of the state legislature on re-districting, and he could not afford to take any action which would weaken his influence with the "powers that be." In addition, it was explained that a real fight was shaping up in the primary election in which Richardson Preyer, Governor Sanford's choice as his successor, was running for Governor.

After some particularly difficult experiences with the "ex-con" title during February of 1964, I was preparing to return to Washington from my home in Charlotte on February 28th when my wife suggested that she go with me as far as Raleigh, and that we should just drop by the Governor's office in an effort to talk with him or one of his administrative assistants.

We arrived in Raleigh about 10 A.M., and received a cordial reception from the Governor's director of administration, Hugh

Cannon. However, although he seemed to be much impressed with our recital of points which, in our opinion, would justify pardon, he gave us no hope for early action by the Governor.

As we were preparing to leave, I said, "Is it possible to arrange a conference with the Governor?" Mr. Cannon answered, "Oh, yes, that's no problem. Let me call Tom Lambeth." (Governor's administrative secretary). In a moment, Mr. Cannon turned from the phone and said, "He says he just talked to the Governor and he has agreed to see you, but can't do it today. He suggests that I get your phone number and he will call you tomorrow to confirm date and time."

Kitty flew back to Charlotte and I proceeded to Washington. We were quite pleased with our visit. It had given us both great satisfaction just to be able to present our case to someone close to the Governor.

On Tuesday, March 2nd, Mr. Lambeth informed me by phone that the Governor's schedule was full during the month of March, with only two possible open dates. He promised to call me again on Thursday, March 4th, to advise as to whether a conference would be possible during March. He did not call.

On March 10th, I tried to reach him, but was told that he had a breakfast appointment and would not be in until ten o'clock. I left word for him to call, but he did not. I tried to call again on March 12, 13th, 19th and 20th. In each case, I was told "Mr. Lambeth is not in, but he has your number and will call as soon as he can."

On March 21st, Kitty was returning to Washington with me. As we approached Raleigh, we decided to stop by the Governor's office—"just to see what might develop."

We arrived at the state capitol building at 1:30 P.M., and talked with a very friendly receptionist who informed us that Mr. Lambeth would not return from lunch until 2:30. We said we would wait. We sat on the only chairs in the large rotunda just outside the Governor's offices. At 2:45, the receptionist informed us that Mr. Lambeth had been told that we were waiting to see him. At 3:30, she told us that he would see us within a few minutes.

At 4 P.M., Graham Jones, the Governor's press agent, came through the rotunda and stopped for a friendly chat with us. (I had known him for a number of years and had always held him in high esteem.) As we were talking with him, Mr. Lambeth dashed up with flushed face and obvious irritation. Waving his hand toward the Governor's office, he said, "I just have a minute—I have to get back in there. The Governor will see you, but he won't talk about what you want to talk about until the fall. If you had let me know you were coming, I could have made an appointment."

I said, "We just came to make an appointment. We didn't expect to see the Governor today."

With obvious relief, he stammered, "Oh! wait 'till I get my book." We started to follow him toward his office but he hurried ahead and returned to us in the hallway, leafing through an appointment book. He said, "It looks like June 15th is the first available date—let's say at 2 P.M."

Kitty said, "But that will be after the Primary election."

I said, "That's right—and I had some things that I wanted to talk to him about before then."

Mr. Lambeth answered, "Write him a letter."

Kitty said, "We're afraid that he doesn't see our letters."

Mr. Lambeth became furious and said, "I saw the note on one of your letters, asking his secretary to deliver it to him personally. That isn't necessary. He sees everything. It's just not true that he doesn't get those letters."

Kitty said, "I was just going by a newspaper story which quoted him as saying, "I never see the letters that pour into the Governor's office requesting time cuts, pardons, or parole."

He said, "I don't believe that. I'd like to see the newspaper where you read that."

As I held my breath, not having discussed the matter with her, and doubting that she had saved the clipping, Kitty led Mr. Lambeth out of the dimly lit hallway and fished the well-worn clipping from numerous others she had in her purse. She told me later that she had carried it for nearly two years.

When he had finished reading it, Mr. Lambeth said, "It's a direct quote, so I suppose he said it, but he didn't mean it that way." Obviously ill at ease, he backed toward his office saying, "See you on June 15th."

* * * * *

We arrived at the state capitol building at 2 P.M. on June 15th and explained to the receptionist that we had an appointment with the Governor. In just a moment, a gentleman came from the Governor's office, introduced himself as "Joel Fleishman, legal assistant to the Governor," and invited us into the Governor's office.

Sitting in the Governor's chair behind the massive desk, Mr. Fleishman apologized for the Governor's absence and the fact that we had not been notified of his inability to meet with us.

Mr. Fleishman said, "The Secretary of Agriculture called the Governor yesterday and asked him to be in Washington this morning for an emergency conference on the tobacco problem. With Tom Lambeth at summer training camp, no one had thought to check the appointment schedule. I'm very sorry if you've been inconvenienced."

I said, "We've been waiting for nearly three years for ten minutes of the Governor's time, and I've driven 600 miles to be here today for the conference which Mr. Lambeth scheduled when we were here on March 21st. Would it be possible for us to see the Governor tomorrow if we waited over?"

He said, "No, I doubt that he could see you tomorrow. I'm not sure that he will even be here. In fact, I doubt that he can see you until sometime in July—I suppose you are aware of the political situation in the state." I assured him that I was.

Kitty spoke with some emotion about the blight on good families which had been caused by this injustice, and of the mental strain and "slow torture" caused by our inability to get honest answers, and by the ever-growing list of excuses for further delay.

Mr. Fleishman said, "Mrs. Payton, will you do me a favor—just stop worrying. Take my word, you have nothing to worry about. We have discussed this, and the Governor is going to take favorable action before he leaves office."

Kitty asked, "Does that mean around Christmas time?"

He answered, "No, it will be earlier—sometime in the fall. You could come back in September, but I don't believe that will be necessary. Just remember, you have nothing to worry about."

We were, of course, elated. I said, "If anyone had given us

that much assurance before, it would have saved a lot of worry and a lot of unnecessary letters and calls. You have just given all that we've been asking for these many months. I just couldn't understand why the Governor and Hugh Cannon have continued to insist that they needed more new evidence to justify pardon. Are you saying that the new petition is sufficient?"

Mr. Fleishman said, "I can say that I have discussed the new petition with the Governor, and he is definitely going to take favorable action before he leaves office."

He was very kind as we thanked him and prepared to leave. We were so relieved and happy that we almost skipped down the long walk from the State Capitol building to our car.

* * * * *

In August of 1964, I resigned my position with the union to become a team manager for the U. S. Labor Department's program of conducting tours for foreign trade-unionists to American trade-union centers. My first assignment was with a group from the Japanese Electrical Workers Union, known as Denki Roren. After ten days in Washington, we proceeded to New York City where we spent several days, visiting United Nations headquarters as well as numerous union offices and electricial plants.

The remainder of the 50-day tour schedule called for visits to Buffalo, Niagra Falls, Detroit, Chicago, New Oreleans, El Paso, Los Angeles, and San Francisco. The tour was going well, and I was thoroughly enjoying my new work. Within the first week, the members of my team and I had learned to communicate even without the interpreter and had become warm, personal friends. Therefore, it was a painful and unhappy parting when I received word in New Orleans that I was being replaced as team manager because Congressman Tuck of Virginia had protested the use of an "ex-con" in such a position of influence.

Back in Washington I learned, without anyone actually saying it, that political considerations had once again dictated a decision concerning my future. For the first time in my life, I was "terminated" and found myself eligible for unemployment compensation at age 56—after 39 years of steady employment.

Sympathetic friends talked of how the Walter Jenkins and Bobby Baker cases had caused embarrassment to the administration and how this had made everyone "touchy" about any situation which could possibly bring "further scandal" just before the presidential election. They also lamented the fact that pardon had not been granted before my employment by the government.

After a month of "vacation," during which President Johnson was safely re-elected and Mr. Dan Moore became the new Governor of North Carolina, I was fortunate in receiving a temporary assignment with the Industrial Union department of the AFL-CIO.

As November came to an end and Governor Sanford began his final month in office, without action on our petition for pardon, we began to have misgivings. However, whenever the matter was discussed with and by our friends, including the Reverend Billy Graham, the Reverend William Finlator, author Harry Golden, Charlotte attorney and state political leader David McConnell and columnist Kays Gary, we were told by several that they felt certain that the Governor was committed to taking favorable action on the petition.

On December 23rd, while in Charlotte for the holidays, I had lunch with Mr. Golden. He was irritated with the Governor for his delay in fulfilling what Mr. Golden had considered assurance that he would grant pardon. He repeated a previous statement to me in which he quoted the Governor as saying that he felt our conviction constituted a black mark on the good name of the state, which he wanted to erase before leaving office.

Mr. Golden was of the opinion that favorable action would come the next day (Christmas Eve) as part of the Governor's usual "Peace on Earth—Goodwill Toward Men" statement. "However," he said, "let's make sure that he has a reminder. Would your wife mind my sending a telegram to the Governor in her name?"

I assured him that she would not only not mind but would be most grateful for it.

He called his secretary and instructed her to send the following telegram:

    TELEGRAM — DO NOT PHONE — PLEASE DELIVER

Governor Terry Sanford　　　　　　　　December 23, 1964
Executive Mansion
Raleigh, N. C.

Dear Governor:
　I am Boyd Payton's wife. You have the mind and the heart to understand what it means to have your husband unable to pursue his life's work without the certificate of pardon from you.
　I could mention a hundred names at least, but the names that come to mind, the people who have authorized the use of their names at this moment include such Tar Heels as Kays Gary, W. W. Finlator, Harry Golden, Billy Graham, Mayor Brookshire, Rev. Frank Brown, who gladly join me in a personal appeal. My immediate neighbors have offered to run a bus to Raleigh to supplement this plea. I do not believe it is necessary. No one knows this case better than you do. Not only for Boyd's entire future, but for his wife of 32 years, and his children, we need this Christmas present to sustain us."
　　　　　　　　　　　　　　　　　　　　Katherine Payton

　Kitty was pleased about the telegram and very grateful to Mr. Golden. We were confident that it would bring the reply for which we had hoped and prayed so long—not only for ourselves, but for the other seven men and their families. We entered into the holiday preparations with renewed enthusiasm. However, when hour after hour of Christmas Eve and Christmas Day had been spent anxiously waiting for the next TV newscast, or jumping to answer each ring of the telephone, our spirits were less than lofty as we retired for the night after suffering through another hopeless (for us) "news-at-midnight," broadcast.
　Much time was spent during the next four days in contacting those who had spoken to the governor or one of his associates about the petition for pardon. In each case, a conversation was recalled which made it impossible for them to believe that pardon would not be granted.
　Therefore, when the mailman arrived at noon on December 30th with a letter addressed to "Mrs. Boyd Payton" and showing "Governor's Office" in the upper left-hand corner, we were positive that pardon had been granted. Amid cries of joy and happiness from our family, Kitty opened the letter and began reading aloud. Our joy and happiness were short-lived as we came to the realization that the governor was explaining the reasoning behind his decision not to grant pardon.

We sat in disbelief for several minutes, staring at each other without seeing. Kitty's face was drained of all color. Her eyes showed acute suffering. A pulse in her neck throbbed visibly with each heartbeat. The girls and I rushed to her side with alarm, but she brushed us away as she reached for the telephone. She said, "They can't get away with this. I'm calling Kays Gary and asking him to arrange for a press conference, and this time nobody can tell me what I can and can't say."

When Kays answered and she had read the letter to him, she turned to me and reported: "He says he can't believe it." After a few minutes, she handed the phone to me saying, "He wants to talk to you."

Kays related a conversation which he had held with Tom Lambeth in October in which Lambeth had assured him that the Governor would take favorable action before leaving office.

After exploring several plans of action, including Kitty's suggestion for a press conference, Kays suggested that I talk with Harry Golden and David McConnell while he talked with other friends. We agreed to keep in touch throughout the afternoon and evening.

I tried to call Mr. Golden, but learned that he was in New York City. Mr. McConnell agreed to keep trying to reach him for a discussion of the situation and his suggestion as to a plan of action. Mr. McConnell found the Governor's letter as hard to believe as had Kays Gary. He told of conversations with both Tom Lambeth and Joel Fleishman which had led him to believe that pardon was assured.

He called me later in the evening to report that he had talked with Mr. Golden and that he (Mr. Golden) was opposed to any publicity as long as any chance remained for the Governor to change his mind. He said, "Harry suggests that we alert everyone whom we feel has any influence with the Governor, but urge 'no publicity' until you and Mrs. Payton have talked with the Governor in person tomorrow."

Kitty and I arrived at the state capitol building at 11 A.M. on Governor Sanford's final day in office. We went directly to the office of Mr. Joel Fleishman who was obviously surprised to see us. We showed him the letter from the Governor, but he only glanced at it. We reminded him of his assurance of pardon when we had talked with him in the Governor's office on June 15th.

He said, "I told you that because I was positive then that the Governor would grant pardon. All I can say is that I did everything under the sun that I could do, but I was vetoed."

Kitty asked, "By whom?"

He said, "I can't talk about it. You'll have to talk to the Governor."

I said, "Can we see the Governor?"

He said, "He is not making appointments today, but he is in his office and I'm sure he'll see you if you wait your turn."

We thanked Mr. Fleishman and went to the Governor's outer office where ten other people were waiting to see him. The secretary entered our names on the bottom of the "visitors list."

When the last visitor had departed an hour and a half later, the Governor came to his door to greet us. As he shook my hand, he said, "This is the first opportunity I've had to talk with you, Boyd. Not that you weren't always available," he added with a laugh.

As he moved two chairs closer to the desk for us and took his place behind it, I said, "Governor, my wife received a letter from you yesterday which we just can't understand." He said, "That's what Jonathan Daniels, editor of the *Raleigh News and Observer*, told me when he called me about two o'clock this morning."

Kitty said, "We just can't believe that pardon is to be denied in view of the circumstances, and especially after Mr. Fleishman assured us on June 15th that we had nothing to worry about—that you would grant pardon before leaving office."

With a look of surprise, he left the room through a side door and was gone for several minutes. When he returned he said, "He says he did tell you that because he was sure that was what I would do."

Taking his place again behind the desk he said, "Well, the matter was closed when I signed that letter, but I am now reopening it. Suppose you tell me on what grounds I can grant pardon."

I began enumerating the points of the pardon petition, but he said, "My copy of that petition is in the archives. Do you have a copy with you?"

As I fished a copy from my briefcase, he laughed and said, "Oh, you just happen to have one with you."

I said, "I also have copies of the statements signed by seven of the jurymen which were attached to the original petition."

He said, "I'd like to see those."

After reading the jury statements, he asked, "May I keep these?" I assured him that he could.

He then began reading the petition page by page while making notes on a large pad. We waited, scarcely breathing.

After several minutes, while continuing to write, the Governor said, almost as if he were speaking to himself, "I need more clear-cut grounds."

Kitty said, "I remember that case a few weeks ago when you reduced a life sentence to five years, and the newspapers quoted you as saying you did it because it was the *just and right thing to do*. Wouldn't that apply to our case too?"

Without looking up from his writing, the Governor said, "But that wasn't pardon."

Kitty said, "No, but it was murder."

The Governor made no reply as he continued reading the petition and making notes. Some minutes later, he said, "Do you remember what Justice Bobbit (State Supreme Court) said when he dissented from the majority opinion in your case?"

Try as we might, we could not quote the full statement, although we had done so on several other occasions and had thought it was indelibly etched on our minds. He called Joel Fleishman and asked him to locate a copy of the dissenting opinion.

Finally the Governor asked, "Where are you going when you leave here?"

When I said that we would return to Charlotte, the Governor said, "Let's leave it like this: If you haven't heard to the contrary from this office by eight o'clock, you can go to bed tonight and rest easy—a pardon will be granted."

As we thanked the Governor and left his office, we were torn between a desire to shout for joy, and a gnawing fear that once again our high hopes would somehow be dashed to the ground.

Pardon At Last

We drove to Greensboro before trusting our emotional tension to allow eating, although we hadn't eaten since breakfast. We did not turn on the car radio but spent the time rehashing what had been said, and remembering the many other points which should have been mentioned. We continued with this during dinner and all the way to Charlotte.

Consequently, we were taken completely by surprise when we turned into our street and our headlights shone on a large crowd in front of our home.

Our faithful friend, Kays Gary, was there. He described it the next day as follows:

> Shouts Of 'We've Got It' Greet Payton On Return From Last Try In Raleigh
>
> There must have been 55 people in the street at 6:22 P.M. when the twin-beamed headlights swung off Montford and onto Wentworth Place.
>
> "It's them!" somebody said.
>
> "Oh, yes!" said another voice.
>
> And suddenly the laughter and back-slapping and jostling of the crowd dropped into silence. The little boys stopped shooting fireworks and the dogs stopped barking.
>
> Two girls, hand in hand, walked toward the headlights of the approaching car.
>
> "We got it! We got it!" they shouted. "We got the pardon, daddy! Oh, daddy!"
>
> The car braked to a stop.
>
> Daughters Sandy and Nancy had thrown themselves on the neck of mother and father, Kitty and Boyd Payton.
>
> "Are you sure?" came the muffled sobbing voice of Mrs. Payton. For almost a full minute they clung together crying.
>
> The crowd, all long-time neighbors of the Paytons, came up then. The women—all the women—kissed them both and there were tears. The men shook hands and said quiet things.
>
> "We didn't know ... we didn't know ... " Mrs. Payton kept saying.
>
> Boyd Payton, misty-eyed, smiled and looked almost stunned.
>
> Hours earlier he and Mrs. Payton had left the Capitol, where they had gone to make a last appeal to Governor Terry Sanford.
>
> They had left, after an hour with him, with no promises.
>
> While they were en route home the governor announced that he

was extending a full pardon, reversing his position of a few days ago.

"We didn't turn on the radio," Mrs. Payton said, tears streaming down her face. "We didn't know until now. Aren't these the greatest people in the world?"

They had left the governor's office in calm, Payton said, because Sanford had in their presence gone over every line of the petition for pardon, reviewed the appeal and every aspect of the case in meticulous detail.

"He did tell us that the case had been closed as far as he was concerned," Payton said, 'but as of that moment it was re-opened.'

"That was our only hope. . . . "

Wentworth Place, described by residents as "14 houses and 40 children," offered strong contrast to the scene more than four years ago when Boyd Payton went to prison convicted of a conspiracy he swore never took place.

The tears were different that day. The same people were there.

Now they swarmed around him, City Recorder William T. and Mrs. Grist, Ann Long, the Gordon Goldings, the Ward Hinkles, the Charlie Lees—a dozen families.

They were saying that Wentworth Place would have its biggest party in an hour or so.

Boyd Payton was saying that he had hopes now, for "a life of real service," either in the government's poverty program or as a member of the U.S. Mediation and Concilation Service.

Finally, chokingly, he said, "No man knows how precious his citizenship is until he loses it."

And finally in the darkened street he and his wife and daughters Nancy and Sandy, arms around each other, walked alone toward 4501 Wentworth, where Christmas lights still blinked around a Santa Claus.

Daughter Pat was rushing across town to join them.

The News and Observer carried the most complete story. It is reproduced below:

Sanford Pardons Boyd Payton
by ADRIAN KING

Boyd E. Payton, former textile union leader who served a prison sentence for conspiracy in a dynamiting plot connected with the 1959 mill strike at Henderson, was granted a pardon Thursday by Gov. Sanford. . . .

Payton, former Carolinas director of the Textile Workers Union of America, and seven other men were convicted of conspiring to dynamite a power plant at the Harriet-Henderson Cotton Mills during a long and bitter strike.

Payton received a 7-10 [sic] year sentence. He entered prison in late 1960, and in July of 1961 Gov. Sanford reduced the sentence to 3 to 7 years. Payton was paroled on Aug. 3, 1961, after serving nine months of his term.

He has contended all along that he was innocent of the conspiracy charge.

In his statement Thursday announcing the pardon for Payton, Gov. Sanford said:

"I, for one, do not believe a conviction should be allowed to dog the tracks of a man for all his life."

Sanford said he had talked with "a large number of people" about executive clemency for Payton, and "they are split 50-50 on whether I should grant a pardon."

"I have decided, out of a sense of compassion, to grant a pardon."

Payton, who lives in Charlotte, conferred with Sanford in the Governor's office earlier in the day. Sanford indicated to a reporter that he had not told Payton during their conference that he had decided to pardon him.

Lawrence Gore, a textile union aid to Payton, and Charles Auslander of Spray also were handed 7-10 [sic] sentences in the dynamiting conspiracy. Four Henderson men received 5 to 7 years and a fifth man got 2 to 3 years.

Gov. Sanford noted that in January 1963, seven of the jurors in the case petitioned for a full pardon for all eight of the defendants.

"I have decided not to take action on all of them," Sanford said. He cited reasons for pardoning Payton.

"The evidence against him was different," Sanford said. He noted that when Payton's conviction was upheld by the State Supreme Court, Justice William H. Bobbitt filed a dissenting opinion which stated, "In my view, the evidence, as to Payton, is insufficient to support the verdict."

Sandford said another reason for granting the pardon was that "Payton has been unable to earn a living, having cut his ties with the union, and having found that this conviction has been a bar to other employment."

Payton was dismissed last Oct. 26 as a guide for visiting Japanese electrical workers on a tour of the United States. He had been employed by St. John's College in Annapolis, Md., which administers such tours under a contract with the U.S. Labor and State departments.

Solons Complain

Payton told a reporter after his conference with Sanford that complaints from Rep. William Tuck of Virginia and Rep. William K. van Pelt of Wisconsin led to his dismissal.

He said his loss of the tour guide job resulted in a renewal of efforts by persons interested in getting him a full pardon.

Among those who urged a pardon for Payton were evangelist Billy Graham; Jonathan Daniels, editor of the *News and Observer*; Charlotte Mayor San Brookshire; Harry Golden, Charlotte author; Dave McConnel of Charlotte, former State Elections Board chairman; Payton's pastor, the Rev. Frank Brown of Charlotte; and the Rev. W. W. Finlator, pastor of Pullen Memorial Baptist church here. . . .

Payton's Comment

Payton, reached at his home in Charlotte, said "I am very happy and grateful to the governor. He is a man of great courage and integrity. My concern throughout the long ordeal has been my wife and family. They are the ones who have suffered."

Payton said he had two regrets: (1) "That the conviction was used to defeat the union's efforts to obtain a contract at the Harriet-Henderson Cotton Mills," and (2) "that the men involved with me did not get a pardon."

He added, "I'm not mad at anybody. I'm ready to let bygones be bygones. I could find a lot to be bitter about, but I'm looking to 1965 now with new hope."

—*The News and Observer*, Raleigh, North Carolina
January 1, 1965

On Sunday, January 3, 1965, *The Charlotte Observer* carried an editorial which is reproduced below:

A State Pardon For Boyd Payton

"It falls to the governor to blend mercy with justice, as best he can, involving human as well as legal considerations, in the light of all circumstances after the passage of time, but before justice is allowed to overrun mercy in the name of the power of the state."

This statement was made by Gov. Terry Sanford on July 6, 1961. The occasion was his reduction of prison terms for textile labor union leader Boyd Payton and six of Payton's associates in the strike at Henderson.

The governor's action made a parole possible for Payton after he had served nine months of a sentence received for conspiracy to dynamite a power substation at the struck plants. But the blot on Payton's record has dogged his footsteps since then.

Now Gov. Sanford has given the Charlottean a full pardon. The act is in keeping with what the governor had to say three years ago. It wipes the legal slate clean for a man highly thought of in his own community, and it restores his full citizenship rights. [sic]

This will possibly spare Payton the embarrassment he experienced last fall. He was dismissed from a job with the Labor Department after complaints were made about his record. The dismissal was attributed to a "lower echelon error" in hiring a man who had served a prison sentence.

Payton protested his innocence of conspiracy from the outset of the charge against him. He had support from Justice William H. Bobbitt of the State Supreme Court, who offered this dissent when the court upheld Payton's conviction:

"The crucial question is whether the circumstantial evidence is such that logical and legitimate inferences may be drawn therefrom to support the factual conclusion that Payton was a party to the alleged conspiracy. In my opinion, the correct answer is 'no.' However strong the suspicion, it seems to me that supposition and conjecture must be invoked to reach such factual conclusion."

Payton and his friends also cited the previous record and subsequent conduct of the state's prime witness against the defendants as evidence of the man's unreliability. Most appeals to the governor for clemency and pardon were based on this aspect of the trial.

Sanford said in 1961 that he would not grant full pardon "unless compelling new evidence is presented." He reconsidered the case only after a personal talk with Mr. and Mrs. Payton, a full review of the record and the reception of appeals from respected citizens of the city, state and nation.

The governor's decision was in order. Payton's experience can be put to good use in our society. He is concerned right now with earning a livelihood, but he might do the state a service by writing about his prison experience.

Upon leaving Central Prison in Raleigh, Payton stated that he was convinced the state's whole prison concept was wrong. He observed that while "kindness is the most powerful force" that can be applied in prison, an opposite approach is the general rule. He should elaborate.

If worthwhile changes in prison life and discipline resulted from such an effort, it would demonstrate again how the darkest of circumstances for the individual can be turned to brightening the lot of those who follow.

EPILOGUE

Restoration of Citizenship

Contrary to the statement made in the editorial on the preceding page, and contrary to general opinion of the public, granting of a pardon *does not automatically restore citizenship rights.*

North Carolina law provides that a "convicted felon" may have his rights of citizenship restored only by petitioning the Superior Court in his county of residence; having an "Order of Publication" concerning such petition posted on the courthouse wall for a period of ninety days; having at least five "respectable witnesses" testify as to his character and reputation; and having the presiding judge sign a "Decree" that citizenship is restored.

In my case, such a petition was filed by attorney Nicholson on March 11, 1965, and the Order of Publication was posted on the same day. This meant that the first opportunity for hearing would be during the term of Superior Court for Mecklenberg County which was due to open on June 14th.

On June 9th, attorney Nicholson informed me that the hearing had been set for June 22nd by the presiding judge, H. L. Riddle, Jr.

Kays Gary wrote the following story of the proceedings for the June 23rd issue of *The Charlotte Observer.*

Court Restores Citizenship To Boyd Payton

There were only a dozen people in Courtroom No. 4 of the Mecklenburg County Courthouse Tuesday.

They were there to help a man get back something he'd lost.

In a few minutes, smiling broadly, he had it and gripped it tightly in his left hand.

With his right he was shaking the hand of Superior Court Judge H. L. Riddle.

Boyd Payton after six years, had become a full citizen of the United States again.

The paper in his left hand said he now owned full citizenship just as though he'd never lost it.

"That's a little ironic, isn't it?" Payton said softly.

Wife Kitty and a daughter, Mrs. John P. Bell, had hugged him and there were tears of laughter and 4-year-old grandson, John, wanted to know "What is the citizenship grand-daddy got?"

"It means he's been a good boy," Mrs. Bell explained.

Payton was convicted of a conspiracy charge against Henderson Mills during a 1959 strike there. The regional director of the Textile Workers Union of America and seven other union members were sentenced to prison.

Insisting on his innocence from the beginning, Payton was paroled after 10 [sic] months in prison on Aug. 3, 1961, vowing to "spend my last breath proving my innocence and getting a full pardon."

He won the pardon from Gov. Sanford last Jan. 1.

From his parole to the pardon, his prison status has dogged his life.

After he ended his lifelong career as a labor leader in 1964 and accepted a part-time job as a Labor Department guide for touring foreign labor leaders, protests of his status forced his resignation from that job.

"I had hoped to serve the U.S. Mediation and Conciliation Service or some phase of the antipoverty program," Payton said.

The pardon made it possible. Full restoration of his citizenship cinches it because Payton is now a manpower specialist for the Neighborhood Youth Corps, a phase of the antipoverty program.

"There's responsibility for 6,000 kids in the District of Columbia and three counties in Maryland and Virginia," Payton said Tuesday.

"The objective is to find jobs for young people who must have jobs to stay in school. This counts for something and it's not just a job. Besides, a large part of it is contract negotiation—something I've been doing most of my life."

The Paytons, now living in a Washington apartment, are keeping their home here at 4501 Wentworth Place, hoping to return.

Among the dozen in the courtroom were Wentworth Place neighbors Gordon Golding, Mrs. William Foster and City Judge William T. Grist.

They, with Larry Cook and lawyer James Ledford, were there as character witnesses.

Nicholson asked Judge Riddle if he had any questions.

"I'm ready to sign the paper," the judge said.

Later, Payton shook his head thoughtfully.

"It's been a long time ... but just as no man knows what freedom is until he's lost it, no man can know what citizenship is until he doesn't have it ... to be without a country you love and serve ... not to vote ... to be able to get a passport ... to work for government. ..."

The Paytons had arrived at midnight Monday. They left

immediately after the hearing to return to Washington.

"Most people think that a pardon automatically restores your citizenship," Payton said. "It doesn't. Most who lose it don't ever bother to regain it the only way you can . . . this way. I meant to bother. I meant to spend my last breath. . . . "

He took a deep breath, figured he had a lot more left and that it was time to go back to work.

As Mr. Nicholson carried the "Decree" from the judge and made a little ceremony of presenting it to me, he said, "The judge has asked to meet you and your family."

Judge Riddle shook hands with us and said, "I'm happy to have had a small part in correcting what I've always thought was an injustice. I wish the best of everything for you in the future."

Confession of Harold Aaron

On Thursday, August 11, 1966, at about 9:30 P.M., my daughter, Nancy, answered the telephone in our Washington apartment. She called me and said, "It's long distance for you."

I took the phone from her, said "Hello," and a strange voice said, "Mr. Payton, could you come to Richmond tonight?"

I asked, "Who is this?"

He said, "You know me—can you come to Richmond?"

I answered, "Not unless I know who you are."

He said, "I used to be a member of the union in Leaksville."

I said, "I'm not with the union now, and I don't care to talk with you unless I know who you are."

I nearly dropped the phone when he said, "This is Harold Aaron. I guess you hate me so much you wouldn't speak to me anywhere."

I said, "No, I don't hate you—I feel sorry for you. I think you were used and didn't really know what you were doing."

He said, "You are so right—and now I can't sleep, can't eat, and can't work. My mother is a good Christian woman, and she says I won't have any peace until I talk with you and ask you to forgive me. I told her I'd have to do more than that. I said the only thing that will make it right is for me to tell my story to the newspapers and let them print it, and I'm ready to do just that."

I said, "Well, why don't you do it? You don't need me for that."

He said, "Yes I do, too. I want you to go with me to the newspapers, but I have to talk with you first."

I said, "Well, I wouldn't come alone."

He said, "That's all right, bring your lawyer with you or your wife—I don't care."

I turned to Kitty to explain. She and Nancy were breathless with suspence. Before I had finished explaining, Kitty was getting ready to go.

Turning back to the phone, I said, "All right, my wife and I will come. Where shall we meet you?"

He said, "I'm at the Downtowner Motel. Just ask for me at the desk."

With grave misgivings and thoughts of all kinds of possibilities for further difficulties, we began the 100-mile trip to Richmond.

We had thought of taking Nancy's tape recorder, but decided against it on the theory that he would not talk freely if he knew that it was being recorded, and we felt that the recording would be of little value unless he repeated his story to a reporter. Then, too, I was reluctant to use the same tactics that had been used by the state to send eight men to prison.

As we rode along, we rehashed the unbelievable experiences of the previous seven years.

We tried to predict what turn of events might be in store for us before this night was over. We thought it possible that Aaron could be playing a joke on us by sending us on a "wild-goose chase." We thought that he might not even be there (we had no way of knowing that the call had actually come from Richmond.) Kitty was concerned that he might be drinking, but I assured her that there had been no indication of this in the phone conversation. Then Kitty had a fearsome thought—"suppose he has his guns with him. . . ."

I decided that it would be wise to let someone, other than Nancy, know our destination and the reason for the trip. I stopped at a gas station and tried to call Kays Gary. He was on vacation, but I talked with Jack Claiborne, assistant editor of the *Charlotte Observer*, who was very interested in this latest development. He said, "I have a friend, ———, who is with the *Richmond Times-Dispatch*, and he knows your story. I'll call him and put him on the alert. You try to get Aaron to talk with him. This will be a big story for us, and I won't go home until you call me back."

We arrived at the Downtowner just at midnight. The desk clerk informed us that Mr. Aaron was in his room and was expecting us. He met us at the door with outstretched hand and a shy, self-conscious smile. He thanked us for coming. He said, "You'll never know what I've been through. I was afraid you'd think it was some kind of a trick or that I wanted something from you, and you wouldn't come. I don't want anything but to get this worry off my mind. You must know now that this was my only reason, else why would I say you could bring a witness?" (He pointed to my wife.)

A nearly full bottle of whiskey stood on his dresser, but he seemed to be completely sober. In fact, I was having some difficulty in reconciling this neatly dressed and well-groomed individual with the image of Aaron which I had carried in my mind for six years. The only time I had ever seen him in person was during his appearance as a witness for the state at our trial in Henderson. My memory of him on that occasion was of a rather unkempt and ill-dressed person who (at that time) typified my conception of what an "ex-convict, undercover spy" should look like. Naturally, the nightmare (for me) which resulted from his testimony did nothing to improve my image of him during the six years since I had seen him.

Aaron's room at the Downtowner had two double beds, with a telephone stand between them. Kitty sat in a large chair just inside the door. I sat on the edge of the bed farthest from her. Aaron stood for awhile beside the dresser. He seemed to be debating something in his mind. Finally, he picked up the bottle and asked if he could fix us a drink. When we declined, he put the bottle down, pulled a straight chair over and sat on it backwards.

He began talking. "Like I told you over the phone, I haven't been able to sleep, eat or work. I have a good upholstering business, but my wife has to run it now. I can't sit at a machine for five minutes any more. I'm too nervous to eat, and I just roll and toss when I go to bed. I can't stop thinking about what I did to you fellows. I've tried to talk to my wife about it, but she doesn't want to listen. She tells me to just forget about it. You see, she is concerned about the effect of more publicity on our son and on members of her family and mine who work at Fieldcrest Mills. She is a good woman. She tried to talk me out of working with the SBI, but I wouldn't listen. They made me think that I would be a big hero if I helped to put you fellows in prison. Boy, did they sell me a bill of goods. They treated me like a baby—nothing was too good for me. They even gave me three bodyguards. Now they wouldn't spit in my mouth if my stomach was on fire."

"My mother is the only one who understands what I've been going through. She is a good Christian woman, and she has told me a dozen times that I should talk with you and ask you to forgive me. I almost called you a few months ago when I read something by Billy Graham. I started to write and ask for his advice, but I never finished it. Then I thought of trying to talk to your friend, Kays Gary, but I never got up enough nerve even for that."

During this discourse, Aaron had changed positions several times, and had paced back and forth across the room two or three times. Finally, he asked, "Do you mind if I take a drink?" When we indicated that we had no objection, he quickly half filled a water glass and drank.

As he replaced the glass on the dresser, he said, "Do you realize that I may go to prison for what I am about to do?" He paused and seemed to be thinking. Then, as if talking to himself, he said, "Anyway, I sometimes think it would be a relief to go to prison if I could get this stuff off my mind."

After a moment, he said "Let me tell you one thing, though. As far as I am concerned Malcolm Seawell was the only straight-shooter of the bunch. He told me every time I talked to him to just tell the truth. Boy, if I had only listened to him, you fellows would never have gone to prison and I wouldn't be a nervous wreck. It was the SBI and others in State Government that wanted to get you. They didn't care about the others. They figured that your arrest would break the strike and kill the union."

"You know, the SBI fellows kept telling me I wouldn't have to testify, but when Jack Hooks came he said I would—'else we can't get Payton,' he said. You know, they tried every way possible right up to the first day of the trial to find some way to tie you in with something else, but they couldn't, so Jack Hooks said to me, 'The only thing we have on Payton is that phone call, and you're the only one who can testify about it.'

"I didn't want to do it, Mr. Payton, honest to God I didn't, but they said they could make me one of the conspirators if I didn't testify for the State."

"So, they took me to Jack Hooks' home in Kenley and played the tapes, and Jack Hooks coached me on what I was to say on the stand. By the way, would you like to see the original transcript which was made from those tapes?"

I asked, "Do you have it here?"

He said, "Sure, it's locked in the safe down in the office, but I can get it in a few minutes."

I said, "Yes, I'd like to see it."

He called the desk and told the clerk, "Look in the safe and get that large envelope with my name on it and have a boy bring it up."

While we were waiting, Aaron had another drink. He then explained that the official transcript had been given to him by mistake when he was supposed to have been given a copy. He said, "They've tried several times to get it back, but I've hung on to it." The reason the SBI is so anxious to get it back is because it has Jack Hooks' notes on the edges."

The transcript was delivered and he handed it to me. Sure enough, it was the official transcript, and was stamped "Confidential, Property of the State Bureau of Investigation." Sure enough, too, it showed numerous notations on the edges; and, in some cases, the typed words had been inked out and other words inked in.

I spent some time trying to read it, but found it so garbled and incomplete that it made little sense to me. Furthermore, it was then well after 2 A.M., and I was anxious to get Aaron in touch with the reporter, who, I assumed, was waiting at the *Times-Dispatch* office.

Aaron had been watching closely while I was examining the transcript. When I tossed it on the other bed, he asked, "What do you think of it?"

I said, "I believe Bunch Pegram said that it sounded like a bunch of drunks talking. I have to agree with him. I don't think it makes sense."

I asked, "What do you think about contacting someone from the *Richmond Times-Dispatch*? It's getting pretty late."

He said, "Yeah, that's right, but I still have more to tell you. I thought maybe you could write it up and I could sign it."

I said, "It would be much better if you told the whole story to a newspaperman. He could write it."

He said, "Well, let me finish about the coaching. They weren't satisfied with the way I was saying certain things when I was practicing what I was to say on the stand. They decided that I should hear the tapes again, and they took me to a motel in Goldsboro and played those dern tapes over and over. Then they made me practice giving answers to their questions."

At this point, the phone rang and Aaron answered. His end of the conversation went like this: "Yes, Mr. and Mrs. Payton are here now. No, I've just been talking to them. We haven't talked to the newspapers yet. Well, honey, you know I have to do it, else I can't live with myself. You know what I've been going through. Now, please stop crying—try to understand that it's for the best. Here, I'll let you talk to Mr. Payton."

He dropped the phone in my lap as if it were hot. I gingerly picked it up with the same feeling. I was totally unprepared for this development and didn't know what to say to his wife. I could hear her sobbing. When I said, "Hello," she cried, "Oh, Mr. Payton, what is my husband doing? He'll be the death of me yet. Please don't let him go to the newspapers. We have a 13-year-old son, and he just can't hold his head up with his friends if we have any more bad publicity."

I said, "I can sympathize with your concern about bad publicity. My wife and daughters have suffered through it for the past six years. As for going to the newspapers—that's your husband's decision to make." She asked to speak to him again. After listening for awhile, he said, "All right, I won't do anything tonight, and I'll call you tomorrow."

He was now extremely nervous and looked distressed. He picked up the bottle two or three times, but put it back each time without taking a drink. Finally he said, "See what I mean—she just doesn't understand, and I can't do it until she does."

He seemed to be in deep thought as he slowly poured another drink and gulped it down. After a moment, he said, "But I have to do it—I can't live like this. Tell you what—I'll talk to her in the morning and try to make her understand. Then I'll come to Washington and tell the whole story to anybody you name."

We were, naturally, disappointed, but felt that no purpose would be served by trying to get him to change his mind. We prepared to leave. It was then 3 A.M. However, he continued talking. "I'm traveling by bus. They took my license because I have eight marks against it—the last one was for driving 70 in a 60-mile zone, and it was a "bum rap." That old truck wouldn't do 70 if I drove it off Lover's Leap. They keep after me all the time, but that's nothing to what they'll do after I tell this story. The state won't let me live or work anywhere in North Carolina and I guess my name will really be 'mud' among my family and friends."

We were standing during this discourse, and kept edging toward the door. He seemed to be almost frantic to find something else to say which would hold our interest and prevent our leaving. Even as we were shaking hands with him, he was saying, "You know, those Henderson boys got a rough deal. I don't believe they ever intended to carry out any plans to damage company property. I wasn't even sure that they would show up at the truck-stop when I told the SBI they'd be there, and I was sure they wouldn't have any explosives with them. But, you see, I was caught between the 'devil and the deep blue sea.' The SBI was pushing me for action, and I had to put on a good act for them even though I was pretty sure the fellows hadn't bought what I was selling!"

As he shook hands for the third or fourth time and thanked us for coming, he said, "I should have done this long ago. I've been miserable ever since I did this thing to you, and every time your wife's nice card came at Christmas time or Easter, it just about tore my heart out."

As we were leaving Richmond, we stopped at the first phone booth and I called Jack Claiborne in Charlotte. When I had concluded the report, he said, "Okay, I'll call Jim Battan, our

Washington man, and ask him to keep in touch with you tomorrow in case Aaron keeps his promise.

We had mixed emotions as we made the return trip to Washington; but, rather strangely, the overriding feeling was one of great pity for Aaron and his family. We doubted that he would keep his promise to come to Washington and wondered what would have happened if we had taken a newsman with us or if we had taken the tape recorder.

Although exhausted, I went to work as usual on Friday, August 12th, and called Jim Battan a few minutes after nine o'clock. He said that he had just talked with Jack Claiborne. He gave me his schedule for the day, and listed several phone numbers where he might be reached.

About 12:30 P.M., Kitty called to inform me that Aaron had just called from Richmond to say that he had been delayed, but would be at the Ambassador Hotel in Washington at 4 P.M., and would call her from there. She quoted him as saying, "I've been trying to collect $112 that a woman here in Richmond owes me for upholstery work, but haven't been able to reach her. I wired my sister to send me some money. She called and said she would come to get me, but I told her not to do that because I had to come to Washington. I talked to my wife, too. She is still against me talking to the newspapers, but I told her it had to be done and she'd just have to try to understand."

Friday afternoon and evening passed without further word from Aaron. The same was true of Saturday. Jim Battan called several times to keep us informed of his whereabouts.

In the late afternoon of Saturday, Kitty called the Downtowner Motel and was told that Aaron was still registered. She did not ask to speak with him.

On Monday morning, August 15th, Kitty called the Downtowner again and was informed that Aaron was no longer registered there.

* * * * *

We have had no direct contact with Aaron since his call to Kitty on Friday, August 12th, 1966. However, while at our home in Charlotte on Saturday, September 24, 1966, I called Jack Claiborne and he invited us to his office to discuss the

Aaron meeting in greater detail.

Armed with copious notes which Kitty had religiously made on all incidents connected with the trial and its aftermath, she, Nancy, and I visited with Jack for nearly an hour during which time he suggested the possibility of his attempting to obtain the latest information about Aaron and exploring the likelihood of arranging for an interview with him.

On Wednesday, September 28th, Jack called Kitty and informed her that Aaron was a patient in the psychiatric ward of the Veteran's Hospital at Durham, North Carolina. He said that he and reporter Dwayne Wall were planning to go to the hospital the next day (with a tape recorder) and endeavor to talk with him.

On Saturday, October 1st, Jack reported to Kitty that they had talked with Aaron and that he had verified the fact that he had met with us in Richmond, but they could not pursue the details because of his condition.

Jack said that they were refused permission to see him, until they had talked with his doctors and related the story. He said the doctors knew nothing of Aaron's involvement in the Henderson situation, and "sat on the edges of their chairs" as they heard the story. They finally agreed that a discussion of the matter could possibly have therapeutic value in his treatment. However, when he was brought before them, it was obvious that a tape recorded interview was out of the question.

Jack reported that Aaron was highly nervous and had trouble controlling his emotions. When asked about the Richmond conference, he readily admitted that he had met with us; but when asked about the details of the conversation, he became almost frantic and begged not to be questioned further.

He expressed great fear of the SBI, and showed resentment against his wife. He spoke of his mother two or three times, and burst into tears each time.

We have heard nothing concerning Harold Aaron since this report of October, 1966.

In retrospect, it may be that his punishment is greater than that which he inflicted upon others.